Literary Reviews
in
British Periodicals
1798-1820

A Bibliography

Literary Reviews in British Periodicals
1798-1820
A Bibliography

With a Supplementary List of
General (Non-Review) Articles
on Literary Subjects

in two volumes
Vol. II

Compiled by
William S. Ward

Garland Publishing, Inc., New York & London

1972

Library of Congress Cataloging in Publication Data

Ward, William Smith, 1907-
   Literary reviews in British periodicals, 1798-1820.

   1. English literature--19th century--History and
criticism--Indexes. 2. English periodicals--Indexes.
I. Title.
Z2013.W36   016.809'034   72-2308
ISBN 0-8240-0512-0

Printed in the United States of America

Contents

Checklist of Reviews

(Continued)

Hodgson, John.
  Poems, Written at Lanchester. 1807. (P)
    Annual Review, 6 (1807), 563-64.
    Antijacobin Review, 28 (Dec. 1807), 404-07.
    British Critic, 30 (Oct. 1807), 441.
    Eclectic Review, 4 (Jan. 1808), 88-89.
    Literary Annual Register, 2 (Sept. 1808), 407-08.
    Monthly Review, 56 (July 1808), 285-90.
    Oxford Review, 3 (Mar. 1808), 274.
    Poetical Register, 6 (1807), 547.
    Satirist, 3 (Dec. 1808), 547-48. (Excerpts from other
      reviews.)

Hofland, Mrs. Barbara Hoole.
  See Barbara Hoole (afterwards Hofland).

Hogg, Cervantes.
  See Eaton Stannard Barrett.

Hogg, James.
  The Mountain Bard; Consisting of Ballads and Songs Founded
  on Facts and Legendary Tales. 1807. (P)
    Annual Review, 6 (1807), 554-57.
    Cabinet, 1 (July 1807), 332-33.
    Critical Review, s3,v12 (Nov. 1807), 237-44.
    Eclectic Review, 5 (Nov. 1809), 1062-63.
    Literary Annual Register, 1 (Aug. 1807), 370-73.
    Literary Panorama, 2 (Aug. 1807), 957-60.
    Oxford Review, 2 (Nov. 1807), 541-48.
    Poetical Register, 6 (1807), 548-49.
    Scots Magazine, 69 (Apr. 1807), 282-86.

  The Forest Minstrel; a Selection of Songs, Adapted to the
  Most Favourite Scottish Airs. Few of them Ever Published
  Before. 1810. (P)
    Critical Review, s3,v22 (Feb. 1811), 139-44.

  The Queen's Wake, a Legendary Poem. 1813. (P)
    La Belle Assemblée, ns,v12 (Oct. 1815), 176-78.
    British Critic, 41 (June 1813), 639-40.
    Country Magazine, 1 (July 1813), 259-67.
    Eclectic Review, 9 (June 1813), 647-53.
    Edinburgh Review, 24 (Nov. 1814), 157-74.
    Monthly Review, 75 (Dec. 1814), 435-37.
    New Universal Magazine, 2 (Apr. 1815), 282-88.
    Scots Magazine, 75 (Feb. 1813), 126-31.
    Theatrical Inquisitor, 2 (May 1813), 218-28.

  The Pilgrims of the Sun, a Poem. 1815. (P)
    Augustan Review, 1 (May 1815), 30-32.
    Champion, Feb. 12, 1815, pp. 54-55.
    Critical Review, s5,v1 (Apr. 1815), 399-409.
    Eclectic Review, s2,v3 (Mar. 1815), 280-91.

Hogg, James (continued)
New Annual Register, 36 (1815), [431].
New Monthly Magazine, 3 (Feb. 1815), 54.
New Universal Magazine, 2 (Feb. 1815), 116-21.
Salopian Magazine, 1 (May, July, 1815), 228-31, 273-74.
Scots Magazine, 76 (Dec. 1814), 930-32.
Theatrical Inquisitor, 6 (Feb. 1815), 130-38.

Mador of the Moor, a Poem. 1816. (P)
Antijacobin Review, 52 (June 1817), 328-35.
British Critic, ns,v7 (Jan. 1817), 97-100.
British Lady's Magazine, 4 (Oct. 1816), 251-55.
Champion, June 9, 1816, pp. 181-82.
Critical Review, s5,v4 (Aug. 1816), 130-43.
Eclectic Review, s2,v7 (Feb. 1817), 174-79.
Literary Panorama, ns,v4 (Aug. 1816), 731-40.
Monthly Review, 81 (Dec. 1816), 438-40.
New Monthly Magazine, 5 (June 1816), 444-45.
Scots Magazine, 78 (June 1816), 448-51.

The Poetic Mirror, or the Living Bards of Britain.   (Anon.)
1816. (P)
Augustan Review, 3 (Dec. 1816), 556-78.
British Lady's Magazine, 4 (Dec. 1816), 381-87.
Critical Review, s5,v4 (Nov. 1816), 456-71.
Eclectic Review, s2,v6 (Nov., Dec. 1816), 507-11, 585-89.
Monthly Magazine, 42 (Dec. 1816), 449.
Monthly Review, 84 (Dec. 1817), 356-65.
Portfolio, Political and Literary, 1 (Dec. 7, 1816), 121-
27.
Quarterly Review, 15 (July 1816), 468-75.
Scots Magazine, 79 (Feb. 1817), 46-51.

The Brownie of Bodsbeck; and Other Tales. 1818. (F)
British Critic, ns,v10 (Oct. 1818), 403-18.
British Lady's Magazine, s3,v1 (Aug.-Oct. 1818), 78-82,
124-27, 170-74.
Clydesdale Magazine, 1 (June, July 1818), 75-78, 121-25.
Literary Chronicle, 1 (June 15, 22, 1818), 177-79, 195-
98.
Literary Journal and General Miscellany, 1 (June 14, 21,
1818), 177-79, 195-98.

Dramatic Tales. (Anon.) (P)
Fireside Magazine (quoting Monthly Review), 1 (Apr. 1819),
151.
Monthly Review, 88 (Feb. 1819), 183-85.

The Jacobite Relics of Scotland; Being the Songs, Airs,
and Legends of the Adherents to the House of Stuart. 1819.
British Critic, ns,v13 (Jan. 1820), 76-85.
Caledonian, 1 (June 1820), 17-25.
Edinburgh Review, 34 (Aug. 1820), 148-60.

Hogg, James (concluded)
  Monthly Magazine, 49 (Apr. 1820), 49.

  Winter Evening Tales, Collected among the Cottagers in the
  South of Scotland. 1820. (F)
    Blackwood's Edinburgh Magazine, 7 (May 1820), 148-54.
    British Critic, ns,v13 (June 1820), 622-31.
    Caledonian, 1 (June 1820), 25-27.
    Gentleman's Magazine, 90² (Suppl. July-Dec. 1820), 611-13.
    Literary Chronicle, 2 (Apr. 29, May 13, 1820), 273-76,
      314-16.
    (Baldwin's) London Magazine, 1 (June 1820), 666-71.
    (Gold's) London Magazine, 1 (June 1820), 638-44.
    Lonsdale Magazine, 1 (July 1820), 307-12.
    Monthly Magazine, 49 (July 1820), 555-56.
    Monthly Review, ns,v93 (Nov. 1820), 263-67.
    New Hibernian Magazine, 1 (July 1820), 9-16.
    New Monthly Magazine, 14 (July 1820), 92.
    Spirit of the Magazines, no3 (1820), 138-39. (Quoting
      Blackwood's Edinburgh Magazine.)

Hogg, Thomas.
  St. Michael's Mount, in Cornwall; a Poem. 1811. (P)
    British Critic, 38 (Sept. 1811), 293-94.
    Poetical Register, 8 (1811), 627-28.

Holbrook, Mrs. Anne Catherine.
  Rebecca, or the Victim of Duplicity. (Anon.) 1808. (F)
    British Critic, 32 (Aug. 1808), 189.
    Critical Review, s3,v15 (Nov. 1808), 331-32.
    European Magazine, 53 (Mar. 1808), 198-202.
    Monthly Review, ns,v60 (Sept. 1809), 96.

Holcroft, Fanny.
  The Wife and Lover. 1815. (F)
    Critical Review, s5,v1 (Apr. 1815), 423.
    New Review, 2 (Dec. 1813), 628-29.
    Town Talk, 6 (Jan. 1814), 468-70.

  Fortitude and Frailty. 1817. (F)
    British Lady's Magazine, ns,v1 (Aug. 1817), 124.
    Critical Review, s5,v5 (Apr. 1817), 371-79.
    Monthly Review, ns,v84 (Nov. 1817), 334.

Holcroft, Thomas.
  The Inquisitor, a Play. (Anon.) 1798. (D)
    Critical Review, ns,v25 (Jan. 1799), 113-15.
    Monthly Mirror, 6 (Aug. 1798), 100.

  He's Much to Blame, a Comedy. (Anon.) 1798. (D)
    Critical Review, Appendix, v22 (1798), 541-46.
    Monthly Magazine, Suppl. v5 (July 15, 1798), 508.
    Monthly Mirror, 6 (July 1798), 38.

Holcroft, Thomas (continued)
    Monthly Review, ns,v26 (June 1798), 226.
    Monthly Visitor, 4 (May 1798), 95-102.

Knave or Not? A Comedy. 1798. (D)
    Antijacobin Review, 1 (July 1798), 51-54.
    British Critic, 12 (Aug. 1798), 183.
    Critical Review, ns,v22 (Feb. 1798), 232-34.
    Monthly Magazine, Suppl. v5 (July 15, 1798), 508.
    Monthly Mirror, 5 (May 1798), 293-94.
    Monthly Review, ns,v25 (Apr. 1798), 471-72.

A Tale of Mystery, a Melo-Drame. 1802. (D)
    Annual Review, 1 (1802), 692.
    British Critic, 23 (June 1804), 676.
    Critical Review, ns,v36 (Dec. 1802), 477.
    Monthly Magazine, Suppl. v15 (July 28, 1803), 632.
    Monthly Mirror, 14 (Nov. 1802), 338-42.
    Monthly Mirror, 15 (Jan. 1803), 41.
    Monthly Review, ns,v40 (Mar. 1803), 330.
    Poetical Register, 2 (1802), 455.

Hear Both Sides. A Comedy. 1803. (D)
    Annual Review, 2 (1803), 595.
    British Critic, 21 (May 1803), 554-55.
    Flowers of Literature, 2 (1803), 448.
    Monthly Magazine, Suppl. v15 (July 28, 1803), 631-32.
    Monthly Review, ns,v40 (Mar. 1803), 330-31.
    Poetical Register, 3 (1803), 463.

The Lady of the Rock. A Melo-Drame. 1805. (D)
    Annual Review, 4 (1805), 639-40.
    Antijacobin Review, 21 (May 1805), 70.
    British Critic, 25 (May 1805), 560.
    Critical Review, s3,v5 (May 1805), 106.
    Literary Journal, 5 (Feb. 1805), 206-07.

Memoirs of Bryan Perdue. A Novel. 1805. (F)
    Annual Review, 4 (1805), 644-49.
    British Critic, 27 (Jan. 1806), 80-82.
    Critical Review, s3,v7 (Jan. 1806), 14-24.
    Literary Journal, a Review..., 5 (Nov. 1805), 1136-44.
    Monthly Magazine, Suppl. v21 (July 25, 1806), 609.
    Monthly Review, ns,v52 (Feb. 1807), 215-16.
    New Annual Register, 26 (1805), [357].

Tales in Verse; Critical, Satirical, and Humorous. 1806.
(P)
    Annual Review, 5 (1806), 535-36.
    British Critic, 30 (Aug. 1807), 197-99.
    Critical Review, s3,v10 (Mar. 1807), 295-302.
    Cyclopaedian Magazine, 1 (Feb. 1807), 96.
    Eclectic Review, 2 (Oct. 1806), 833.

Holcroft, Thomas (concluded)
    Edinburgh Review, 9 (Oct. 1806), 101-11.
    Monthly Literary Recreations, 1 (Aug. 1806), 164-65.
    Monthly Mirror, ns,v1 (Feb. 1807), 122.
    New Annual Register, 27 (1806), [370].
    Poetical Register, 6 (1806), 501.

  The Vindictive Man. A Comedy. 1806. (D)
    Flowers of Literature, 5 (1806), 517.
    Monthly Mirror, ns,v1 (Feb. 1807), 126.
    Oxford Review, 1 (Jan. 1807), 70.
    Poetical Register, 6 (1806), 529.

  The Steward; or Fashion and Feeling. A Comedy. (Anon.) (D)
    Monthly Review, ns,v90 (Dec. 1819), 434.
    Theatre; or Dramatic and Literary Mirror, 2 (Oct. 2,
      1819), 98-99.

Holder, Rev. Mr. ____.
  The Secluded Man; or, the History of Mr. Oliver. 1798. (F)
    Critical Review, ns,v25 (Apr. 1799), 473.

Holford, George.
  True Patriotism; or Poverty Ennobled by Virtue. (Anon.) (D)
    Analytical Review, ns,v1 (May 1799), 535.
    British Critic, 14 (Nov. 1799), 549.
    Critical Review, ns,v29 (Aug. 1800), 471.
    Monthly Magazine, Suppl. v8 (Jan. 20, 1800), 1057.
    Monthly Review, ns,v30 (Oct. 1799), 210-11.

Holford, Mrs. M.
  Gresford Vale, and Other Poems. 1798. (P)
    Analytical Review, 27 (Apr. 1798), 423.
    Monthly Mirror, 5 (Feb. 1798), 96.
    Monthly Review, 25 (Apr. 1798), 476.

  Neither's the Man, a Comedy. 1799. (D)
    Analytical Review, ns,v1 (Feb. 1799), 147.
    British Critic, 14 (Oct. 1799), 428-29.
    Critical Review, ns,v27 (Oct. 1799), 236-38.
    Monthly Magazine, Suppl. v8 (Jan. 20, 1800), 1057.
    Monthly Mirror, 7 (May 1799), 293.
    New London Review, 1 (June 1799), 619.

  First Impressions, or the Portrait. A Novel. 1800. (F)
    Antijacobin Review, 7 (Dec. 1800), 416.
    Critical Review, ns,v32 (June 1801), 232-33.
    Monthly Mirror, 12 (July 1801), 42.

Holford, Margaret (later Mrs. Hodson).
  Wallace; or the Fight of Falkirk: A Metrical Romance.
  (Anon.) 1809. 2nd ed., 1810. (P)
    British Critic, 37 (Jan. 1811), 37-43.

Critical Review, s3,v19 (Feb. 1810), 130-49.
Eclectic Review, 6 (Dec. 1810), 1103-12.
European Magazine, 57 (June 1810), 444-50.
Gentleman's Magazine, 80¹ (Mar. 1810), 251.
Glasgow Magazine, 1 (Nov., Dec. 1810), 219-24, 293-303.
Literary Panorama, 8 (July 1810), 413-23.
Monthly Review, 62 (May 1810), 26-39.
Poetical Register, 8 (1810), 549.
Quarterly Review, 3 (Feb. 1810), 63-69.
Scots Magazine, 72 (Dec. 1810), 925-29.

Poems. 1811. (P)
Critical Review, s3,v22 (Mar. 1811), 286-87.
Eclectic Review, 7 (May 1811), 460-61.
Edinburgh Quarterly (Monthly) Magazine, 1 (June 1811), 293-96.
Monthly Review, 65 (July 1811), 244-47.
New Annual Register, 32 (1811), [365].
Poetical Register, 8 (1811), 604.
Scourge, 1 (Apr. 1811), 327-33.

Margaret of Anjou, a Poem. 1816. (P)
Augustan Review, 3 (Sept. 1816), 289-96.
British Critic, ns,v8 (July 1817), 82-89.
Eclectic Review, s2,v6 (July 1816), 73-78.
Literary Panorama, ns,v5 (Jan. 1817), 561-69.
Monthly Review, 81 (Dec. 1816), 354-62.
New Monthly Magazine, 5 (June 1816), 444.

Holland, Mrs. ____.
Tales of the Priory. 1820. (F)
(Gold's) London Magazine, 2 (July 1820), 52-58.

Holland, John.
Sheffield Park, a Descriptive Poem. 1820. (P)
Imperial Magazine, 2 (Oct. 1820), 854-57.
Lady's Monthly Museum, s3,v12 (Nov. 1820), 275.
Literary Chronicle, 2 (Oct. 14, 1820), 664-65.

Holliday, John.
The British Oak. A Poem. (Anon.) 1800. (P)
British Critic, 16 (Dec. 1800), 680-81.
Gentleman's Magazine, 71¹ (Jan. 1801), 45-46.
Monthly Review, 35 (June 1801), 211.

Holloway, William.
Poems on Various Occasions; Chiefly Descriptive, Elegiac, Didactic, and Pathetic. 1798. (P)
European Magazine, 34 (Aug. 1798), 111.

The Baron of Laudenbrooke. A Tale. (F)
European Magazine, 38 (Nov. 1800), 361.

The Peasant's Fate; a Rural Poem, with Miscellaneous
Pieces. 1802. 2nd ed., 1803. (P)
  Annual Review, 1 (1802), 652.
  Antijacobin Review, 11 (Apr. 1802), 397.
  British Critic, 19 (May 1802), 533-34.
  Critical Review, s2,v35 (June 1802), 232-34.
  European Magazine, 41 (Apr. 1802), 288.
  Flowers of Literature, 1 (1801-02), 456.
  Monthly Mirror, 13 (Feb. 1802), 97-99.
  Monthly Mirror, 15 (Feb. 1803), 113-14.
  Monthly Review, 40 (Jan. 1803), 97-98.
  Monthly Visitor, ns,v1 (July 1802), [316].
  New Annual Register, 23 (1802), [318].
  Poetical Register, 2 (1802), 431.

Scenes of Youth, or Rural Recollections; with Other Poems.
1803. (P)
  Annual Review, 2 (1803), 564-65.
  European Magazine, 44 (July 1803), 52.
  Lady's Monthly Museum, 14 (Jan. 1805), 63.
  Monthly Mirror, 16 (Sept. 1803), 172-75.
  Monthly Register, 3 (Aug. 1803), 139.
  Monthly Visitor, ns,v6 (Jan. 1804), 97-98.
  New Annual Register, 24 (1803), [328].
  Poetical Register, 3 (1803), 449.

The Minor Minstrel; or, Poetical Pieces, Chiefly Familiar
and Descriptive. 1808. (P)
  Le Beau Monde, 5 (Feb. 1809), 36-37.
  British Critic, 35 (June 1810), 632-33.
  Eclectic Review, 5 (May 1809), 489-90.
  Literary Panorama, 5 (Mar. 1809), 1117-20.
  Monthly Mirror, ns,v5 (Mar. 1809), 161.
  Poetical Register, 7 (1808), 559.

The Country Pastor, or Rural Philanthropist, a Poem.
1812. (P)
  Critical Review, s4,v2 (Sept. 1812), 330.
  Eclectic Review, 8 (Nov. 1812), 1183-84.
  Lady's Monthly Museum, s2,v14 (Jan. 1813), 51-53.
  Literary Panorama, 12 (July 1812), 48-51.
  Monthly Review, 68 (Aug. 1812), 433-34.
  New Annual Register, 33 (1812), [377].

Holman, J. G.
  The Red-Cross Knights, a Play. Founded on The Robbers of
  Schiller. 1799. (D)
    British Critic, 14 (Dec. 1799), 669.
    Monthly Mirror, 8 (Nov. 1799), 289.
    Monthly Review, ns,v32 (July 1800), 322-23.

  The Votary of Wealth. A Comedy. 1799. (D)
    Antijacobin Review, 3 (July 1799), 301-03.

British Critic, 14 (Sept. 1799), 312-13.
Critical Review, ns,v26 (July 1799), 351-52.
Monthly Magazine, v8 (Jan. 20, 1800), 1055.
Monthly Mirror, 7 (May 1799), 292-93.
Monthly Review, ns,v29 (Aug. 1799), 450.
New London Review, 2 (July 1799), 84-85.

The Gazette Extraordinary, a Comedy.. (D)
Poetical Register, 8 (1811), 639.

Holme, Rev. James.
Vulpina; or, the Crafty Sister, a Tale of the Nineteenth
Century. (P)
Monthly Magazine, 50 (Dec. 1820), 458.

Holstein, Anthony Frederick.
Sir Owen Glendower, and Other Tales. 1808. (F)
Critical Review, s3,v18 (Oct. 1809), 218-19.
Monthly Review, ns,v60 (Sept. 1809), 95-96.
Repository of Arts, 4 (July 1810), 39.
Satirist, 3 (Dec. 1808), 540-42.

The Assassin of St. Glenroy; or, the Axis of Life. 1810.
(F)
Antijacobin Review, 37 (Oct. 1810), 205.
British Critic, 34 (Nov. 1809), 524.
Critical Review, s3,v19 (Jan. 1810), 105-07.
Monthly Review, ns,v61 (Jan. 1810), 98-99.
Satirist, 7 (Aug. 1810), 179-80.
Satirist, 8 (May 1811), 453.

Love, Mystery, and Misery! 1810. (F)
Monthly Review, ns,v62 (Aug. 1810), 434-35.

The Miseries of an Heiress. 1810. (F)
Monthly Review, ns,v69 (Jan. 1811), 95.

L'Intriguante; or, the Woman (Women?) of the World. 1813.
(F)
Critical Review, s4,v4 (Nov. 1813), 556-57.
Monthly Review, ns,v73 (Mar. 1814), 319.

Bouverie, the Pupil of the World. 1814. (F)
Critical Review, s4,v6 (Dec. 1814), 548-56.
Monthly Review, ns,v76 (Jan. 1815), 101.

The Scotchwoman. 1814. (F)
Monthly Review, ns,v77 (July 1815), 321.

The Discontented Man; or, Love and Reason. 1815. (F)
Critical Review, s5,v2 (Oct. 1815), 430-31.
Monthly Review, ns,v79 (Jan. 1816), 101-02.

Holstein, Madame de Stael.
  See De Stael, Madame, Holstein.

Holsten, Esther.
  Ernestina. 1801. (F)
    British Critic, 17 (May 1801), 541.
    Critical Review, ns,v33 (Sept. 1801), 113.

Holt, Francis Ludlow.
  The Land We Live In. 1805. (D)
    British Critic, 25 (May 1805), 559-60.
    Critical Review, s3,v4 (Feb. 1805), 211.
    Literary Journal, a Review..., 5 (Jan. 1805), 96-97.
    Monthly Mirror, 19 (Feb. 1805), 113.

Homfray, Rev. Francis.
  Thoughts on Happiness, a Poem. 2nd ed. 1817. (P)
    Antijacobin Review, 57 (Nov. 1819), 209-16.
    Christian's Pocket Magazine, 2 (Jan. 1820), 42. (Digest-
      ed from Antijacobin Review.)
    Fireside Magazine (quoting Monthly Review), 1 (Jan.
      1819), 34-35.
    Monthly Review, 87 (Nov. 1818), 327.

Hone, William.
  Don Juan: with a Biographical Account of Lord Byron and
  His Family....Canto the Third. (Anon.) 1819. (P)
    Literary Chronicle, 1 (Oct. 16, 23, 1819), 338-39, 353-55.
    Literary Gazette, Nov. 6, 1819, pp. 707-08.

  The Dorchester Guide, or a House That Jack Built. (Anon.) (P)
    European Magazine, 76 (Dec. 1819), 529-34.

  The House That Jack Built. (Anon.) (P)
    Monthly Magazine, 48 (Dec. 1819), 453.

  The Financial House That Jack Built. (Anon.) (P)
    European Magazine, 76 (Dec. 1819), 529-34.

  The Political House That Jack Built. (Anon.) (P)
    European Magazine, 76 (Dec. 1819), 529-34.
    Lonsdale Magazine, 1 (June 1020), 269-72.
    Monthly Review, 90 (Nov. 1819), 330-31.

  The Constitutional House That Jack Built. (Anon.) (P)
    Lonsdale Magazine, 1 (June 1820), 269-72.

  Caroline, a Poem. (Anon.) (P)
    Monthly Magazine, 50 (Aug. 1820), 66.
    Monthly Review, 92 (July 1820), 333-34.

  The Man in the Moon. (Anon.) (P)
    Monthly Magazine, 49 (Feb. 1820), 72.

The Queen's Matrimonial Ladder, a National Toy. (Anon.) (P)
  Monthly Magazine, 50 (Sept. 1820), 169.

Hood, Catherine.
  Remonstrance, with Other Poems. 1801.
    British Critic, 18 (July 1801), 81-82.
    Critical Review, s2,v36 (Sept. 1802), 113-14.
    Monthly Review, 39 (Nov. 1802), 328.
    Poetical Register, 1 (1801), 439.

Hook, Sarah Ann.
  The Widowed Bride, or Celina. 1803. (F)
    Monthly Mirror, 15 (Feb. 1803), 115.

  Secret Machinations. (F)
    Literary Journal, a Review..., 5 (Jan. 1805), 95-96.

Hook, Theodore Edward.
  Catch Him Who Can! A Musical Farce. 1806. (D)
    British Critic, 29 (Feb. 1807), 201.
    Critical Review, s3,v8 (July 1806), 323.
    Literary Journal, ns,v2 (July 1806), 110.
    Monthly Magazine, Suppl. v22 (Jan. 25, 1807), 642.
    Monthly Mirror, 22 (Nov. 1806), 330.
    Monthly Review, ns,v51 (Oct. 1806), 212-13.
    Poetical Register, 6 (1806), 530-31.
    Universal Magazine, ns,v6 (July 1806), 53-54.

  The Invisible Girl. 1806. (D)
    Antijacobin Review, 25 (Dec. 1806), 425.
    British Critic, 28 (Aug. 1806), 198.
    Critical Review, s3,v8 (July 1806), 323.
    Literary Journal, a Review..., ns,v2 (July 1806), 109-10.
    Monthly Magazine, Suppl. v22 (Jan. 25, 1807), 642.
    Monthly Review, ns,v51 (Oct. 1806), 212-13.
    Poetical Register, 6 (1806), 531.

  Tekeli; or the Siege of Montgatz. A Melo-Drame. 1806. (D)
    Antijacobin Review, 25 (Dec. 1806), 425.
    Critical Review, s3,v10 (Jan. 1807), 101.
    Flowers of Literature, 5 (1806), 514.
    Literary Journal, a Review..., ns,v2 (Dec. 1806), 649.
    Monthly Review, ns,v51 (Dec. 1806), 441.
    Oxford Review, 1 (Jan. 1807), 71.
    Poetical Register, 6 (1806), 530.

  The Fortress; a Melo-Drama. From the French. 1807. (D)
    Poetical Register, 6 (1807), 565.

  Music Mad. A Dramatic Sketch. 1808. (D)
    British Critic, 34 (Aug. 1809), 186.
    Poetical Register, 7 (1808), 584.

The Man of Sorrow. By Alfred Allendale. 1808. (F)
   Le Beau Monde, 4 (Suppl. 1808), 358-64.
   British Critic, 31 (June 1808), 662.
   Critical Review, s3,v14 (July 1808), 330-31.
   Monthly Mirror, ns,v4 (July 1808), 34-38.
   Monthly Review, ns,v59 (July 1809), 320-21.

Killing No Murder, a Farce. (D)
   Critical Review, s3,v17 (Aug. 1809), 444-45.
   Dublin Satirist, 1 (Dec. 1809), 110-12.
   Monthly Mirror, ns,v6 (Aug. 1809), 101-04.
   Poetical Register, 7 (1809), 618-19.

Darkness Visible, a Farce. (D)
   Poetical Register, 8 (1811), 642.

The Trial by Jury; a Comic Piece. 1811. (D)
   British Critic, 41 (Mar. 1813), 303-04.
   Poetical Register, 8 (1811), 642.

Hoole, Barbara, later Mrs. Hofland.
   The History of an Officer's Widow, and Her Young Family.
   1809. (F)
   Critical Review, s3,v17 (Aug. 1809), 443.

La Fete de la Rose; or the Dramatic Flowers. 1809. (P)
   British Critic, 34 (July 1809), 69-70.
   Poetical Register, 8 (1810), 577-78.

A Season at Harrogate; in a Series of Poetical Epistles
from Benjamin Blunderhead Esq. to His Mother. (Anon.)
1812. (P)
   British Critic, 39 (June 1812), 631-32.

Iwanowna; or, the Maid of Moscow. (Anon.) (F)
   New Review, 2 (Sept. 1813), 240-41.

Ellen the Teacher. 1815. (F)
   Critical Review, s5,v1 (Apr. 1815), 423.
   Gentleman's Magazine, 85[1] (Mar. 1815), 252.

A Father as He Should Be. 1815. (F)
   Critical Review, s5,v2 (July 1815), 104-05.

Tales of the Priory. 1820. (F)
   Champion, July 15, 22, 1820, pp. 463, 479.
   Monthly Review, ns,v92 (July 1820), 321.

Hooper, Mrs. B.
   A Poem, Occasioned by the Cessation of Public Mourning for
   Her Royal Highness the Princess Charlotte, together with
   Sonnets and Other Productions. (P)
   British Lady's Magazine, s3,v1 (Oct. 1818), 177-78.

European Magazine, 74 (Nov. 1818), 434-35.
Gentleman's Magazine, 89[1] (Mar. 1819), 237.

Hope, Thomas.
  Anastasius; or Memoirs of a Greek. (Anon.) 1819. (F)
    Antijacobin Review, 57 (Jan. 1820), 442-50.
    (Baldwin's) London Magazine, 1 (Jan. 1820), 76-79.
    (Gold's) London Magazine, 1 (Jan., Mar., Apr. 1820), 57-
      67, 294-302, 410-14.
    New Monthly Magazine, 13 (Jan., Feb. 1820), 56-62, 192-98.

Hop(p)ner, J.
  Oriental Tales. 1805. (P)
    Literary Journal, 5 (Feb. 1805), 138-42.
    New Annual Register, 26 (1805), [355].

Horatius.
  See Horace Twiss.

Hornby, Mary.
  The Battle of Waterloo, a Tragedy. 1819. (D)
    British Stage and Literary Cabinet, 3 (May 1819), 131-33.

Horne, W. W.
  Hampstead Heath; a Poem, Sacred to Friendship. 1812. (P)
    New Review, 1 (Mar. 1813), 334-35.

  The Triumph. A Poem. 1815. (P)
    Literary Panorama, ns,v1 (Mar. 1815), 880.

Hornem, Horace.
  See Lord Byron.

Horner, W. G.
  The Mourner. (P)
    Fireside Magazine (quoting Monthly Magazine), 1 (Jan.
      1819), 37.
    Monthly Magazine, 46 (Dec. 1818), 445.

Hornet, Harry.
  No Popery! George Gordon's Ghost; Catholic Emancipation the
  Papists' Petition; the Prince Regent's Reply; the Middle
  Course; and Other Poems. (P)
    Monthly Review, 74 (June 1814), 215-16.

Horsley, T. I.
  The Watch Tower, an Historical Romance. (F)
    Literary Journal, a Review..., 3 (Mar. 1, 1804), 223-24.

Horwood, Miss _____.
  Instructive Amusement for Young Minds. 1815. (P)
    Lady's Monthly Museum, s3,v3 (Mar. 1816), 157.

Houghton, G.
  Eliza; an Elegy. (Anon.) 1800. (P)
    Critical Review, s2,v32 (June 1801), 228.

Houghton, Mary Arnold.
  The Mysteries of the Forest. (F)
    Repository of Arts, 4 (July 1810), 34.

  The Border Chieftains; or Love and Chivalry. 1813. (F)
    Monthly Review, ns,v73 (Jan. 1814), 105.
    New Review, 2 (Aug. 1813), 144-45.

  Emilia of Lindinau; or, the Field of Leipsic. 1815. (P)
    Augustan Review, 2 (June 1816), 613-15.
    Monthly Review, 79 (Feb. 1816), 211.

Howard, Frederick, Fifth Earl of Carlisle.
  The Step-Mother, a Tragedy. (Anon.) 1800. (D)
    Antijacobin Review, 7 (Oct. 1800), 205.
    European Magazine, 38 (July 1800), 42.
    London Review, 4 (Aug. 1800), 175-76.
    Monthly Review, ns,v35 (July 1801), 325-27.

  The Father's Revenge, a Tragedy; with Other Poems. 1800.
  (P-D)
    British Critic, 16 (Nov. 1800), 540-43.
    Monthly Magazine, Suppl. v10 (Jan. 20, 1801), 611.
    Monthly Mirror, 10 (Sept. 1800), 174-77.

  The Tragedies and Poems of Frederick, Earl of Carlisle.
  1801. (D-P)
    Critical Review, s2,v34 (Jan. 1802), 68-77.
    Monthly Mirror, 12 (Aug. 1801), 111.
    Monthly Review, 38 (June 1802), 205-06.
    Poetical Register, 1 (1801), 456.

  Verses on the Death of Lord Nelson. (Anon.) 1806. (P)
    British Critic, 27 (Feb. 1806), 185.
    British Critic, 28 (Aug. 1806), 195.
    Gentleman's Magazine, 76^2 (July 1806), 648.
    Literary Journal, a Review..., ns,v1 (Jan. 1806), 106-07.
    Monthly Review, 49 (Jan. 1806), 98.

Howard, John Owens.
  Clara; or, Fancy's Tale. (P)
    Critical Review, s5,v4 (Oct. 1816), 429.
    Monthly Review, 84 (Oct. 1817), 213-14.

Howard, Nathaniel.
  Bickleigh Vale, with Other Poems. 1804. (P)
    Annual Review, 3 (1804), 594.
    British Critic, 25 (May 1805), 556-57.
    European Magazine, 46 (Dec. 1804), 455,

Gentleman's Magazine, 78^1 (Feb. 1808), 144-45.
Imperial Review, 3 (Dec. 1804), 604.
Literary Journal, a Review..., 5 (Jan. 1805), 95.
Monthly Mirror, 18 (Dec. 1804), 385-88.
New Annual Register, 25 (1804), [353].
Poetical Register, 4 (1804), 494.

Howell, Mrs. _____.
  Anzoletta Zadoski. 1796. (F)
    British Critic, 11 (Feb. 1798), 197.

  The Spoiled Child. 1797. (F)
    Critical Review, ns,v25 (Feb. 1799), 233.

Hoyle, Rev. Charles.
  Moses Viewing the Promised Land, a Seatonian Prize Poem.
  1804. (P)
    Critical Review, s3,v4 (Mar. 1805), 326-28.
    Eclectic Review, 1 (May 1805), 340-42.

  Paul and Barnabas at Lystra, a Seatonian Prize Poem. 1806.
  (P)
    Critical Review, s3,v10 (Apr. 1807), 399-402.

  Exodus, an Epic Poem. 1807. (P)
    Annual Review, 6 (1807), 543-45.
    British Critic, 31 (May 1808), 496-502.
    Critical Review, s3,v13 (Apr. 1808), 428-34.
    Edinburgh Review, 11 (Jan. 1808), 362-70.
    Monthly Review, 58 (Apr. 1809), 364-73.
    New Annual Register, 28 (1807), [378].
    Oxford Review, 3 (Feb. 1808), 161-65.
    Poetical Register, 6 (1807), 536.
    Satirist, 1 (Jan. 1808), 409-13.
    Satirist, 5 (July 1809), 94-95. (Excerpts from other re-
      views.)

Hubbard, Rev. John Clarke.
  Jacobinism. A Poem. (Anon.) 1801. (P)
    British Critic, 18 (Oct. 1801), 385-89.
    Critical Review, s2,v35 (Aug. 1802), 474.
    European Magazine, 40 (Oct. 1801), 281-83.
    Monthly Mirror, 12 (Oct. 1801), 249-50.
    Monthly Review, 36 (Nov. 1801), 323.
    Poetical Register, 1 (1801), 445.

  The Triumphs of Poesy, a Poem. 1803. (P)
    Annual Review, 2 (1803), 585.
    Antijacobin Review, 14 (Mar. 1803), 321-22.
    British Critic, 21 (June 1803), 670-71.
    Critical Review, s2,v38 (May 1803), 113.
    European Magazine, 43 (Feb. 1803), 132.
    Monthly Review, 41 (Aug. 1803), 439-40.

Poetical Register, 3 (1803), 456.

Hucks, J.
  Poems. 1798. (P)
    Analytical Review, 27 (Mar. 1798), 292-94.
    British Critic, 11 (Mar. 1798), 312.
    Critical Review, s2,v23 (May 1798), 33-35.
    Monthly Magazine, Suppl. v5 (July 15, 1798), 507.
    Monthly Mirror, 6 (Aug. 1798), 94.
    Monthly Review, 26 (May 1798), 98-99.
    New Annual Register, 19 (1798), [308].

Huddesford, Rev. George.
  Bubble and Squeak, a Galli-Maufry of British Beef, with the
  Chopp'd Cabbage of Gallic Philosophy and Radical Reform.
  (Anon.) 1799. (P)
    Antijacobin Review, 3 (July 1799), 286-91.
    British Critic, 14 (Aug. 1799), 135-37.
    Critical Review, s2,v26 (July 1799), 351.
    European Magazine, 35 (June 1799), 400-01.
    Monthly Magazine, v8 (Jan. 20, 1800), 1050-51.
    Monthly Mirror, 8 (Sept. 1799), 158.
    New Annual Register, 20 (1799), [268].
    New London Review, 1 (June 1799), 618.

  Crambe Repetita; a Second Course of Bubble and Squeak, or
  British Beef Galli-Maufry'd; with a Devil'd Biscuit or Two
  to Help Digestion and Close the Orifice of the Stomach.
  (Anon.) 1799. (P)
    Antijacobin Review, 3 (July 1799), 292-94.
    British Critic, 14 (Aug. 1799), 138-40.
    Critical Review, s2,v26 (July 1799), 351.
    European Magazine, 36 (July 1799), 41-42.
    Monthly Magazine, Suppl. v8 (Jan. 20, 1800), 1050-51.
    Monthly Mirror, 8 (Sept. 1799), 158.
    Monthly Review, 30 (Sept. 1799), 104-05.
    New Annual Register, 20 (1799), [268].
    New London Review, 2 (Sept. 1799), 287-88.

  The Poems of George Huddesford. 1801. (P)
    Antijacobin Review, 9 (June 1801), 161-63.
    British Critic, 19 (Feb. 1802), 117-18.
    Monthly Review, 38 (July 1802), 272-76.
    New Annual Register, 22 (1801), [313].
    Poetical Register, 1 (1801), 428.

  The Scum Uppermost when the Middlesex Porridge-Pot Boils
  Over! An Heroic Election Ballad. (Anon.) 1802. (P)
    Antijacobin Review, 13 (Dec. 1802), 413-15.
    British Critic, 20 (Nov. 1802), 555-56.
    Critical Review, s2,v37 (Feb. 1803), 234.
    Monthly Review, 40 (Mar. 1803), 327-29.
    New Annual Register, 23 (1802), [318].

Poetical Register, 2 (1802), 443.

Bonaparte; an Heroic Ballad; with a Sermon in Its Belly.
(Anon.) 1803. (P)
   British Critic, 22 (1803), 311-12.
   Critical Review, s2,v39 (Sept. 1803), 102-05.
   Literary Journal, a Review..., 2 (Sept. 1, 1803), 216-18.
   Poetical Register, 3 (1803), 458.

The Wiccamical Chaplet, a Selection of Original Poetry, Com-
prising Smaller Poems, Serious and Comic; Classical Trifles;
Sonnets; Inscriptions and Epitaphs; Songs and Ballads; Mock-
Heroic Poems; Epigrams; Fragments; &c., &c. 1804. (P)
   Annual Review, 3 (1804), 575-77.
   British Critic, 23 (June 1804), 670-71.
   Imperial Review, 3 (Sept. 1804), 58-61.
   Lady's Monthly Museum, 16 (Apr. 1806), 274.
   Literary Journal, a Review..., 3 (Mar. 16, 1804), 290-91.
   Monthly Review, 49 (Feb. 1806), 201-06.
   New Annual Register, 25 (1804), [352-53].
   Poetical Register, 4 (1804), 484-85.

Les Champignons du Diable; or, Imperial Mushrooms: a Mock-
Heroic Poem; Including a Conference between the Pope and the
Devil, on His Holiness's Visit to Paris. (Anon.) 1805. (P)
   Antijacobin Review, 23 (Apr. 1806), 392-99.
   British Critic, 26 (Sept. 1805), 317-18.
   Critical Review, s3,v6 (Sept. 1805), 98-99.
   Monthly Review, 51 (Dec. 1806), 435-37.
   Poetical Register, 5 (1805), 496.

Hudson, Henry.
   The Hours, a Poem in Four Idylls. (P)
   Literary Gazette, July 25, 1818, p. 467.

Hughes, George.
   Emmanuel! A Poem. (Anon.) 1817. (P)
      Gentleman's Magazine, 87^2 (Dec. 1817), 533-34.
      Monthly Review, 86 (July 1818), 326-27.

Hughes, H.
   Retribution, and Other Poems. 1798. (P)
      Analytical Review, 28 (July 1798), 80.
      British Critic, 12 (July 1798), 72.
      Critical Review, s2,v25 (Jan. 1799), 112-13.
      Monthly Review, 27 (Oct. 1798), 231.
      Gentleman's Magazine, 82^2 (Aug. 1812), 151.

Hughes, Rev. T. S.
   Belshazzar's Feast. A Seatonian Prize Poem. 1818. (P)
      Monthly Repository, 13 (Apr. 1818), 276.
      Monthly Review, 86 (May 1818), 97-98.

Hugil, Mrs. ____.
  Isidora of Gallicia. 1798. (F)
    British Critic, 12 (July 1798), 74.
    Critical Review, ns,v22 (Apr. 1798), 478.
    Monthly Magazine, Suppl. v6 (1798), 517.

Huish, Robert.
  The Peruvians; a Poem. 1813.
    Critical Review, s4,v6 (July 1814), 66-71.

Hull, Thomas.
  Moral Tales, in Verse. 1797.
    Critical Review, s2,v22 (Mar. 1798), 293-97.
    Monthly Magazine, Suppl. v5 (July 15, 1798), 506.

Humdrum, Lady.
  Domestic Scenes. 1820. (F)
    La Belle Assemblée, ns,v21 (May 1820), 237-38.
    Monthly Review, ns,v91 (Apr. 1820), 441-42.

Humfrey, Nathaniel.
  A Poetical Sketch, with Other Poems. (P)
    Poetical Register, 3 (1803), 445.

Humphreys, John Doddridge, Jr.
  Prince Malcolm, with Other Poems. 1813. (P)
    Critical Review, s4,v5 (Jan. 1814), 77-82.
    European Magazine, 71 (Mar. 1817), 237-39.
    Gentleman's Magazine, 84^2 (Nov. 1814), 455.
    Monthly Review, 78 (Sept. 1815), 94-96.
    Tradesman, 12 (Mar. 1814), 239-41.

Hunt, Alicia.
  Caroline Lismore; or the Errors of Fashion. 1815. (F)
    British Critic, ns,v4 (Dec. 1815), 671-72.

Hunt, Leigh.
  Juvenilia; or, a Collection of Poems. 1801. (P)
    Antijacobin Review, 10 (Nov. 1801), 313-17.
    British Critic, 18 (Nov. 1801), 541.
    European Magazine, 40 (Aug. 1801), 114-15.
    Monthly Mirror, 11 (Apr. 1801), 254-56.
    Monthly Mirror, 12 (July 1801), 39.
    Monthly Review, 39 (Oct. 1802), 206-07.
    Poetical Register, 1 (1801), 430-31.
    Union Magazine and Imperial Register, 2 (Aug. 1801), 116-
      17.

  Critical Essays on the Performers of the London Theatres.
  1807. (Pr)
    Antijacobin Review, 33 (June 1809), 191.
    Cabinet, s2,v1 (Feb. 1809), 141-48.
    Critical Review, s3,v14 (Aug. 1808), 374-79.

Hunt, Leigh (continued)
    Lady's Monthly Museum, s2,v5 (July 1808), 42-43.
    London Review, 2 (Aug. 1809), 1-21.
    Monthly Mirror, s2,v3 (Feb. 1808), 105-09.
    Monthly Review, 57 (Dec. 1808), 423-29.
    Satirist, 2 (Mar. 1808), 75-84.

An Attempt to Shew the Folly and Danger of Methodism. 1811.
(Pr)
    Critical Review, s3,v19 (Jan. 1810), 86-88.
    Monthly Mirror, s2,v7 (Apr. 1810), 275-84.

The Feast of the Poets, and Other Pieces in Verse. By the
Editor of The Examiner. (Anon.) 1814. (P)
    Augustan Review, 2 (Mar. 1816), 287-91.
    British Critic, ns,v1 (May 1814), 549-51.
    Champion, Feb. 20, 1814, pp. 62-63.
    Critical Review, s4,v5 (Mar. 1814), 293-303.
    Eclectic Review, s2,v1 (June 1814), 628-29.
    Monthly Museum, 2 (June 1814), 21-24.
    Monthly Review, 75 (Sept. 1814), 100-03.
    New Monthly Magazine, 2 (Aug. 1814), 58.
    New Review, 3 (Apr. 1814), 337-39.
    New Universal Magazine, 1 (Oct. 1814), 297.
    Satirist, ns,v4 (Apr. 1814), 327-31.

The Descent of Liberty, a Mask. 1815. (P)
    Augustan Review, 2 (Mar. 1816), 287-91.
    British Critic, ns,v4 (Aug. 1815), 205-10.
    British Lady's Magazine, 1 (Apr. 1815), 277-81.
    Champion, Mar. 26, 1815, p. 102.
    Critical Review, s5,v1 (Mar. 1815), 284-88.
    Eclectic Review, s2,v3 (May 1815), 517-21.
    Monthly Review, 77 (Aug. 1815), 434.
    New Annual Register, 36 (1815), [431].
    Theatrical Inquisitor, 6 (Apr. 1815), 289-98.

The Story of Rimini; a Poem. 1816. (P)
    Augustan Review, 2 (May 1816), 474-79.
    Blackwood's Edinburgh Magazine, 2 (Nov. 1817), 194-201.
    British Lady's Magazine, 3 (Apr. 1816), 239-42.
    British Review, 7 (May 1816), 452-69.
    Dublin Examiner, 1 (June 1816), 129-43.
    Eclectic Review, s2,v5 (Apr. 1816), 380-85.
    Edinburgh Review, 26 (June 1816), 476-91.
    Literary Panorama, ns,v4 (Sept. 1816), 936-44.
    Monthly Review, 80 (June 1816), 138-47.
    New Monthly Magazine, 5 (Mar. 1816), 149.
    Quarterly Review, 14 (Jan. 1816), 473-81.

Foliage; or Poems Original and Translated. 1818. (P)
    British Critic, ns,v10 (July 1818), 90-96.
    Eclectic Review, s2,v10 (Nov. 1818), 484-93.

Hunt, Leigh (concluded)
Literary Gazette, Apr. 1818, pp. 210-12.
Monthly Magazine, 45 (May 1818), 346.
New Monthly Magazine, 10 (Sept. 1818), 162-65.
Quarterly Review, 18 (Jan. 1818), 324-35.

Hero and Leander, and Bacchus and Ariadne. 1819. (P)
(Baldwin's) London Magazine, 2 (July 1820), 45-55.

Amyntas, a Tale of the Woods; from the Italian of Torquato
Tasso. 1820. (P)
Edinburgh Magazine and Literary Miscellany (Scots Maga-
zine), s2,v7 (Sept. 1820), 215-18.
Literary Gazette, July 22, 1820, pp. 467-69.
Monthly Magazine, 50 (Aug. 1820), 64 65.
Monthly Review, 93 (Sept. 1820), 17-31.

Hunter, _____.
See Edward Quillinan.

Hunter, A.
Men and Manners; or, Concentrated Wisdom. 3rd ed. (F)
Annual Review, 7 (1808), 605.

Hunter, John.
A Tribute to the Manes of Unfortunate Poets. With Other
Poems on Various Subjects. 1798. (P)
Critical Review, s2,v23 (July 1798), 349-51.
Monthly Magazine, Suppl. v5 (July 15, 1798), 507.
Monthly Mirror, 6 (Aug. 1798), 94-95.
Monthly Review, 25 (Apr. 1798), 473-76.
Poetical Register, 2 (1802), 426.

Hunter, Mrs. John.
Letitia; or, the Castle without a Spectre. 1801. (F)
Antijacobin Review, 11 (Jan. 1802), 71-72.
British Critic, 18 (Dec. 1801), 667.
Critical Review, ns,v34 (Mar. 1802), 355-56.
Monthly Mirror, 13 (Jan. 1802), 29.
Monthly Mirror, ns,v39 (Dec. 1802), 427.
Union Magazine and Imperial Register, 3 (Feb. 1802), 110.

Poems. 1802. (P)
Annual Review, 1 (1802), 650.
British Critic, 20 (Nov. 1802), 409-13.
Edinburgh Review, 1 (Jan. 1803), 421-26.
Monthly Magazine, Suppl. v15 (July 28, 1803), 638.
Monthly Mirror, 19 (Jan. 1805), 43. (2nd ed.)
Monthly Review, 41 (Aug. 1803), 420-25.
New Annual Register, 23 (1802), [317].
Poetical Register, 2 (1802), 434.

Letters from Mrs. Palmerstone to Her Daughter, Inculcating

Morality, by Entertaining Narratives. 1803. (F)
  British Critic, 22 (Aug. 1803), 195.
  Critical Review, s3,v1 (Jan. 1804), 118.
  Monthly Magazine, Suppl. v16 (Jan. 25, 1804), 635.
  Monthly Review, ns,v44 (July 1804), 319.

The Unexpected Legacy. (F)
  Annual Review, 3 (1804), 544.
  Flowers of Literature, 3 (1804), 466.
  Imperial Review, 3 (Dec. 1804), 600.
  Literary Journal, a Review..., 3 (June 1, 1804), 609.
  Monthly Mirror, 20 (Aug. 1805), 114-15.
  Monthly Review, ns,v47 (June 1805), 206.

The Sports of the Genii. 1804. (P)
  Annual Review, 4 (1805), 623-24.
  British Critic, 25 (Jan. 1805), 34-35.
  Lady's Monthly Museum, 16 (Feb. 1806), 127.
  Monthly Magazine, Suppl. v20 (Jan. 31, 1806), 613-14.
  Monthly Mirror, 21 (Jan. 1806), 39.
  Monthly Review, 48 (Nov. 1805), 323.
  New Annual Register, 26 (1805), [356].
  Poetical Register, 5 (1805), 495.

Hunter, Maria.
  Ella; or, He's Always in the Way. 1798.
  Critical Review, ns,v24 (Dec. 1798), 470.

Huntly, Lydia.
  See Lydia Huntly Sigourney.

Hurdis, James.
  The Favourite Village; a Poem. 1800. (P)
  Antijacobin Review, 7 (Nov. 1800), 245-50.
  British Critic, 17 (Mar. 1801), 274-78.
  Critical Review, s2,v31 (Jan. 1801), 83-89.
  Monthly Magazine, Suppl. v10 (Jan. 20, 1801), 609.
  Monthly Mirror, 10 (Oct. 1800), 228-30.
  Monthly Review, 33 (Nov. 1800), 282-87.
  Monthly Visitor, 11 (Sept. 1800), 97-101.
  New Annual Register, 21 (1800), [328].

Poems. 1808. (P)
  Critical Review, s3,v14 (June 1808), 215-16.
  Gentleman's Magazine, 79[1] (Jan. 1809), 43-44.
  Retrospective Review, v1, pt.1 (1820), 57-69.
  Satirist, 4 (Feb. 1809), 189-90.

The Village Curate, and Other Poems. 1810. (P)
  Universal Magazine, ns,v12 (Dec. 1809), 481-86; ns,v13
    (Jan., Feb. 1810), 45-48, 123-26.

Hurry, Mrs. Ives.

Moral Tales for Young People. 1807. (F)
　　Eclectic Review, 3 (Dec. 1807), 1025.
　　Oxford Review, 2 (July 1807), 95-96.
　　Satirist, 4 (Feb. 1809), 207.

Artless Tales. 1808. (F)
　　Annual Review, 7 (1808), 618-19.
　　Gentleman's Magazine, 80[1] (Mar. 1810), 241-43.

Hurstone, J. P.
　Piccadilly Ambulator, or Old Q. (F)
　　Satirist, 2 (July 1808), 539-41.

Hutchinson, Miss A. A.
　Exhibitions of the Heart. 1799. (F)
　　British Critic, 15 (Apr. 1800), 432.
　　Critical Review, ns,v29 (Aug. 1800), 472.
　　Monthly Review, ns,v32 (Aug. 1800), 438.
　　New London Review, 3 (Jan. 1800), 84.

Friends Unmasked; or Scenes in Real Life. 1812. (F)
　　Monthly Review, ns,v69 (Dec. 1812), 435.

Hutton, Catherine.
　The Miser Married. 1813. (F)
　　Gentleman's Magazine, 83[2] (July 1813), 52.
　　Monthly Review, ns,v72 (Nov. 1813), 326.

The Welsh Mountaineer. 1817. (F)
　　Monthly Review, ns,v85 (Apr. 1818), 440-41.

Oakwood Hall. 1819. (F)
　　European Magazine, 75 (June 1810), 529-31.
　　Fireside Magazine (quoting Monthly Magazine), 1 (May
　　　1819), 197.
　　Gentleman's Magazine, 89[2] (Sept. 1819), 240-42.
　　Lady's Monthly Museum, s3,v9 (June 1819), 333-37.
　　Monthly Magazine, 47 (Apr. 1819), 255.
　　Monthly Review, ns,v90 (Oct. 1819), 214.

Hutton, W. H.
　Poems, Chiefly Tales. 1804.
　　British Critic, 25 (Mar. 1805), 320.
　　Gentleman's Magazine, 75[1] (Mar. 1805), 249.
　　Literary Journal, a Review..., 5 (Feb. 1805), 183-85.
　　Monthly Review, 47 (May 1805), 100-01.
　　Poetical Register, 4 (1804), 485-86.

Iliff, Mrs. Edward Henry.
　Poems upon Several Subjects. 1808. (P)
　　Annual Review, 7 (1808), 526-27.
　　European Magazine, 53 (Apr. 1808), 290-91.
　　Monthly Magazine, Suppl. v26 (Jan. 30, 1809), 632.

Poetical Register, 7 (1808), 563-64.

Impey, Elijah Barwell.
  Poems. 1811. (P)
    British Critic, 40 (Sept. 1812), 299-300.
    Eclectic Review, 7 (Dec. 1811), 1136-37.
    Monthly Review, 68 (July 1812), 320-23.
    New Annual Register, 32 (1811), [365].
    Poetical Register, 8 (1811), 616.

Inchbald, Elizabeth.
  To Marry or Not to Marry. 1805. (D)
    Annual Review, 4 (1805), 640.
    Antijacobin Review, 21 (June 1805), 208.
    British Critic, 25 (June 1805), 649-53.
    Critical Review, s3,v5 (July 1805), 333-34.
    Flowers of Literature, 4 (1805), 434.
    Monthly Magazine, Suppl. v20 (Jan. 31, 1806), 616.
    Monthly Review, ns,v49 (Feb. 1806), 216.
    New Annual Register, 26 (1805), [356].
    Poetical Register, 5 (1805), 503.

  The British Theatre: or, a Collection of Plays, Which Are
  Acted at the Theatre Royal, Drury Lane, Covent Garden, and
  Haymarket. Printed under Authority of the Managers, from
  the Prompt-Books; with Biographical and Critical Remarks.
  1808. (D)
    Annual Review, 7 (1808), 553-54.
    Monthly Magazine, Suppl. v27 (July 30, 1809), 663.

Ingersol, Charles Jared.
  Edwy and Elgiva; a Tragedy. 1801. (D)
    Antijacobin Review, 9 (Aug. 1801), 347-52.

Ingle, J.
  The Aerial Isles; or, the Visions of Malcolm. 1816. (P)
    British Stage and Literary Cabinet, 1(Dec. 1817), 272-73.
    Literary Panorama, ns,v5 (Mar. 1817), 940-42.
    Scots Magazine, 78 (Apr. 1816), 289-92.

Ingram, Henry.
  The Flower of the Wye. A Poem. 1815. (P)
    British Critic, ns,v6 (Sept. 1816), 315-17.
    Monthly Review, 79 (Jan. 1816), 98-99.

  Poems in the English and Scottish Dialects. 1812. (P)
    British Critic, 39 (June 1812), 634.
    Critical Review, s4,v1 (Feb. 1812), 218-19.
    Eclectic Review, 8 (Mar. 1812), 316.
    Gentleman's Magazine, 82¹ (Feb. 1812), 154-55.
    Literary Panorama, 11 (June 1812), 1018-20.
    Monthly Review, 67 (Mar. 1812), 326.

Ircastrensis.
  Love and Horror; an Imitation of the Present, and a Model
  for All Future Romances. 1815. (F)
    British Critic, ns,v5 (Jan. 1816), 104-05.

Ireland, William Henry.
  The Abbess, a Romance. 1799. (F)
    Critical Review, ns,v28 (Mar. 1800), 355-56.
    Gentleman's Magazine, 69² (July 1799), 601-02.
    Monthly Mirror, 9 (Jan. 1800), 38.
    New London Review, 2 (Aug. 1799), 180-81.

  Vortigern, an Historical Tragedy....And Henry the Second,
  an Historical Drama. Supposed to be Written by the Author
  of Vortigern. (Anon.) 1799. (D)
    British Critic, 15 (Feb. 1800), 191-92.
    European Magazine, 36 (Oct. 1799), 253.
    Monthly Review, ns,v29 (Aug. 1799), 445-46.

  Rimualdo, or the Castle of Badajos, a Romance. 1800. (F)
    British Critic, 16 (Nov. 1800), 555-56.
    Critical Review, ns,v31 (Apr. 1801), 474-75.
    European Magazine, 38 (Oct. 1800), 286.
    Monthly Magazine, Suppl. v10 (Jan. 20, 1801), 611.
    Monthly Mirror, 10 (Dec. 1800), 383-84.
    Monthly Review, ns,v34 (Feb. 1801), 203-04.

  Ballads in Imitation of the Antient. 1801. (P)
    Monthly Mirror, 11 (June 1801), 392-95.
    Poetical Register, 1 (1801), 434-35.

  Mutius Scaevola; or the Roman Patriot. An Historical
  Drama. 1801. (D)
    British Critic, 18 (Sept. 1801), 313-14.
    Critical Review, ns,v34 (Jan. 1802), 115-16.
    Monthly Mirror, 12 (Oct. 1801), 259.
    Monthly Review, ns,v37 (Apr. 1802), 435-36.
    Poetical Register, 1 (1801), 458.
    Union Magazine and Imperial Register, 2 (July 1801), 49.

  Rhapsodies. By W. H. Ireland, Author of the Shakespearian
  MSS. 1803. (P)
    Annual Review, 2 (1803), 568.
    British Critic, 23 (June 1804), 672.
    Literary Journal, a Review..., 2 (Aug. 16, 1803), 160-61.
    Monthly Register, 3 (Sept. 1803), 183.
    Monthly Review, 43 (Mar. 1804), 282-86.
    New Annual Register, 24 (1803), [327].
    Poetical Register, 3 (1803), 442-43.

  The Woman of Feeling. (Anon.) (F)
    Literary Journal, a Review..., 3 (June 1, 1804), 610.

Ireland, William Henry (continued)
The Angler, a Didactic Poem. By Charles Clifford. 1804.
(P)
British Critic, 28 (Dec. 1806), 676-77.
Monthly Mirror, 19 (May 1805), 323-24.
Monthly Review, 46 (Apr. 1805), 443-44.

Gondez, the Monk. A Romance of the Thirteenth Century.
1805. (F)
Flowers of Literature, 4 (1805), 423.

Effusions of Love, from Chatelar to Mary Queen of Scotland.
Translated from a Gallic Manuscript in the Scotch College
at Paris. Interspersed with Songs, Sonnets, and Notes. (P)
Monthly Review, 52 (Jan. 1807), 111.

All the Blocks! or, an Antidote to "All the Talents." A
Satirical Poem. By Flagellum. 1807. (P)
Antijacobin Review, 27 (July 1807), 294-300.
British Critic, 30 (Dec. 1807), 672.
Cabinet, 1 (June 1807), 259-60.
Critical Review, s3,v11 (July 1807), 316-19.
Cyclopaedian Magazine, 1 (Aug. 1807), 478.
Flower's Political Review, 1 (June 1807), 463-64.
Literary Annual Register, 1 (July 1807), 320.
Literary Panorama, 2 (July 1807), 746.
Monthly Mirror, ns,v2 (Oct. 1807), 253-54.
Monthly Review, 53 (June 1807), 221-22.
Poetical Register, 6 (1807), 554-55.
Satirist, 2 (Apr. 1808), 210.

Stultifera Navis; or the Modern Ship of Fools. 1807. (P)
Annual Review, 6 (1807), 586-87.
British Critic, 30 (July 1807), 83.
Cabinet, 1 (June 1807), 260.
Monthly Literary Recreations, 2 (May 1807), 392-93.
Oxford Review, 1 (June 1807), 680.
Poetical Register, 6 (1807), 552.

The Fisher Boy, a Poem, Comprising His Several Avocations
during the Four Seasons of the Year. By H. C. Esq. 1808. (P)
Annual Review, 7 (1808), 506-08.
Antijacobin Review, 31 (Oct. 1808), 181-83.
Le Beau Monde, 4 (Dec. 1808), 290.
British Critic, 33 (Feb. 1809), 185.
Critical Review, s3,v16 (Mar. 1809), 264-70.
Eclectic Review, 5 (Apr. 1809), 385-86.
European Magazine, 54 (July 1808), 37.
Gentleman's Magazine, 78[2] (Dec. 1808), 1100-01.
Monthly Review, 58 (Feb. 1809), 211-12.
Poetical Register, 7 (1808), 557-58.
Satirist, 6 (Apr. 1810), 411-13. (Excerpts from other
reviews.)

Ireland, William Henry (concluded)
    Universal Magazine, ns,v10 (July 1808), 54.

  The Sailor Boy; a Poem. By H. C. Esq. 1809. (P)
    Le Beau Monde, 1 (Oct. 1809), 39.
    British Critic, 35 (May 1810), 519-20.
    European Magazine, 56 (Sept. 1809), 209-10.
    Poetical Register, 7 (1809), 598.
    Satirist, 8 (Apr. 1811), 365-66.

  The Cottage Girl. A Poem. Comprising Her Several Avocations during the Four Seasons of the Year. By H. C. (P)
    Poetical Register, 8 (1810), 570.

  Neglected Genius, a Poem. Illustrating the Untimely and
  Unfortunate Fate of Many British Poets; from the Period of
  Henry the Eighth to the Era of the Unfortunate Chatterton.
  Containing Imitations of Their Different Styles. 1812. (P)
    Critical Review, s4,v2 (Nov. 1812), 554-56.
    Monthly Review, 70 (Feb. 1813), 203-05.

  Chalcographimania; or, the Portrait Collector and Print-
  seller's Chronicle.... By Satiricus Sculptor. 1814. (P)
    Critical Review, s4,v5 (Jan. 1814), 101-02.
    Meteor, or Monthly Censor, 1 (Jan. 1814), 213-15.
    New Annual Register, 35 (1814), [364].
    New Review, 3 (May 1814), 434-36.

  Scribbleomania; or the Printer's Devil's Polichronicon; a
  Sublime Poem. Edited by Anser Pen-drag-on, Esq. 1815. (P)
    New Monthly Magazine, 3 (May 1815), 356.
    New Universal Magazine, 2 (Mar. 1815), 199-203.
    Theatrical Inquisitor, 7 (Sept. 1815), 210.

Irenaeus.
  An Ode to His Grace the Duke of Wellington. 1814. (P)
    British Critic, ns,v2 (Aug. 1814), 216-17.
    Critical Review, s4,v5 (June 1814), 648.
    Monthly Review, 75 (Sept. 1814), 98-99.

Irishman, An.
  See Thomas Moore.

Irving, W. S.
  Fair Helen. A Tale of the Border. 1814. (P)
    Scots Magazine, 76 (May 1814), 355-60.

Irving, Washington.
  Salmagundi; or, the Whim-Whams and Opinions of Launcelot
  Langstaff, Esq. and Others. Reprinted from the American
  Edition, with an Introductory Essay and Explanatory Notes.
  By John Lambert. 1811. (Pr)
    Critical Review, s3,v23 (July 1811), 316-22.

Monthly Review, ns,v65 (Aug. 1811), 418-24.
Scourge, 3 (Mar. 1812), 205-14.

The Sketch Book of Geoffrey Crayon, Gent. 1819-20. (Pr)
   Arcadian, 1 (Mar. 1, 1820), 44-67.
   British Critic, 13 (June 1820), 645-54. (Vol. I.)
   British Critic, 14 (Nov. 1820), 514-25. (Vol. II.)
   Eclectic Review, s2,v13 (Jan. 1820), 38-44. (Vol. I.)
   Eclectic Review, s2,v14 (Oct. 1820), 290-96. (Vol. II.)
   Edinburgh Review, 34 (Aug. 1820), 160-76.
   Examiner, Apr. 16, 1820, pp. 252-53.
   Lady's Monthly Museum, s3,v12 (Oct. 1820), 217-18.
   Literary Chronicle, 2 (Mar. 18-Apr. 1, 1820), 177-80,
      195-97, 216-18. (Vol. I.)
   Literary Chronicle, 2 (Aug. 26-Sept. 2, 1820), 546-49,
      565-68. (Vol. II.)
   Literary Gazette, July 22, 1820, pp. 465-67.
   (Gold's) London Magazine, 2 (Sept., Oct. 1820), 281-84,
      391-97.
   Monthly Magazine, 50 (Nov. 1820), 362-63.
   Monthly Review, 93 (Oct. 1820), 198-207.
   New Annual Register, 41 (1820), [55].
   New Monthly Magazine, 13 (Mar. 1820), 303-05.

A History of New York. By Diedrick Knickerbocker. 1820.
(Pr)
   (Gold's) London Magazine, 2 (Dec. 1820), 577-88.

Irwin, Eyles.
   Nilus, a Poem; Occasioned by the Victory of Admiral Nelson
   over the French Fleet. (Anon.) 1798; 2nd ed. 1799. (P)
      British Critic, 14 (July 1799), 69-70.
      European Magazine, 34 (Dec. 1798), 399.
      Monthly Review, 27 (Dec. 1798), 456-57.

   Ode to Iberia. 1808. (P)
      Annual Review, 7 (1808), 533-34.
      Antijacobin Review, 31 (Dec. 1808), 417-18.
      Critical Review, s3,v15 (Nov. 1808), 329-30.
      Eclectic Review, 4 (Oct. 1808), 946.
      Gentleman's Magazine, 78^2 (Nov. 1808), 1013-14.
      Monthly Review, 57 (Oct. 1808), 209-10.

   The Fall of Saragossa; an Elegy. 1808. (P)
      European Magazine, 55 (May 1809), 396.

   Napoleon; or the Vanity of Human Wishes. 1814. (P)
      Critical Review, s4,v6 (Aug. 1814), 203.

Isaacs, Mrs. _____.
   Ariel; or the Invisible Monitor. (Anon.) 1801. (F)
      Critical Review, ns,v34 (Mar. 1802), 356.

342

Glenmore Abbey; or, the Lady of the Rock. (Anon.) 1805. (F)
   Literary Journal, a Review..., 5 (Aug. 1805), 887.
   Monthly Mirror, 20 (Oct. 1805), 256.

The Wood Nymph. (Anon.) 1806. (F)
   Literary Journal, a Review..., ns,v2 (Sept. 1806), 334-35.
   Monthly Mirror, 22 (Nov. 1806), 319.

Ella St. Laurence; or, the Village of Sellwood, and Its Inhabitants. 1809. (F)
   Le Beau Monde, 1 (May 1809), 134.

Tales of Today; Containing The Heiress of Riversdale, Juli-
et, and The Two Sisters. (F)
   Theatrical Inquisitor, 9 (Sept. 1816), 201-05.

Isdell, Sarah.
   The Irish Recluse; or, a Breakfast at the Rotunda. 1809.
   (F)
      British Critic, 35 (Jan. 1810), 72.
      British Critic, 35 (Mar. 1810), 300.
      Critical Review, s3,v18 (Nov. 1809), 329-30.
      Gentleman's Magazine, 79[2] (Nov. 1809), 1042.
      Monthly Review, ns,v61 (Jan. 1810), 99.

I-Spy-I.
   The Melviad; or the Birth, Parentage, Education, and
   Achievements of a Grete Mon. (P)
      Literary Journal, a Review..., 5 (May 1805), 547.
      Monthly Review, 47 (June 1805), 214.

J., E. S.
   Hildibrand and Una; or, the Knight and the Horse That Never
   Wearied. A Legendary Tale. 1799. (P)
      Monthly Mirror, 8 (Nov. 1799), 283-84.

   Poems. 1799. (P)
      British Critic, 17 (Mar. 1801), 313-14.
      Monthly Mirror, 8 (Dec. 1799), 348.
      Monthly Review, 31 (Jan. 1800), 99.

Jackson, John.
   Poems on Several Occasions. 1797. (P)
      Monthly Review, 25 (Feb. 1798), 237-38.

   An Address to Time, with Other Poems. 2nd ed., 1808. (P)
      Antijacobin Review, 32 (Jan. 1809), 80.
      British Critic, 34 (Oct, 1809), 405-06.
      Critical Review, s3,v14 (Aug. 1808), 444.
      Eclectic Review, 4 (Sept. 1808), 850.
      Gentleman's Magazine, 80[1] (Apr. 1810), 337-38.
      Monthly Repository, 3 (July 1808), 388-90.
      Monthly Review, 58 (Feb. 1809), 209-11.

Jackson, Joseph.
  The Reign of Liberty, a Poetical Sketch. 1797. (P)
    Gentleman's Magazine, 68¹ (June 1798), 509.

Jackson, S. R.
  The Lament of Napoleon, Misplaced Love, and Minor Poems. (P)
    British Lady's Magazine, s3,v3 (Dec. 1819), 281.
    Literary Chronicle, 2 (Apr. 29, 1820), 282.

Jaques.
  Satires. 1798. (P)
    Analytical Review, 27 (Apr. 1798), 423.
    British Critic, 11 (June 1798), 677.
    Critical Review, s2,v23 (June 1798), 230.
    Monthly Mirror, 5 (Mar. 1798), 158.
    Monthly Review, 25 (Mar. 1798), 328-29.

James, Charles.
  Suicide Rejected, an Elegy. 1797. (P)
    British Critic, 12 (Oct. 1798), 423-24.
    Monthly Mirror, 6 (Dec. 1798), 347-48.

  Poems. 1808. 3rd ed. (P)
    British Critic, 31 (June 1808), 659-60.
    Poetical Register, 7 (1808), 551.
    Universal Magazine, ns,v10 (July 1808), 44-46.

James, Isaac.
  Providence Displayed; or, the Remarkable Adventures of
  Alexander Selkirk. 1800. (F)
    Antijacobin Review, 8 (Mar. 1801), 319.

Jamesson, R. F.
  The Students of Salamanca. (D)
    New Annual Register, 35 (1814), [364-65].
    New Review, 3 (Jan. 1814), 43-44.

Jamieson, Alexander.
  A Grammar of Rhetoric and Polite Literature; Comprehending
  the Principles of Language of Style, the Elements of Taste
  and Criticism.... 1818. (Pr)
    Literary Panorama, ns,v8 (Jan. 1819), 1627-30.

Jamieson, John.
  Eternity, a Poem: Addressed to Freethinkers and Philosophical Christians. 1798. (P)
    Antijacobin Review, 2 (Apr. 1799), 394-95.
    Critical Review, s2,v26 (June 1799), 233-34.
    Lady's Monthly Museum, 2 (Apr. 1799), 324.
    New London Review, 1 (Feb. 1799), 201 [202].

Jamieson, Robert.
  Popular Ballads and Songs, from Tradition, Manuscripts, and

Scarce Editions, with Translations of Similar Pieces from
the Ancient Danish Language; and a Few Originals. 1806. (P)
    Critical Review, s3,v9 (Nov. 1806), 303-13.
    Literary Panorama, 1 (Dec. 1806), 472-81.
    Monthly Review, 52 (Jan. 1807), 19-31.

Jefferson, John.
    The Battle of Salamanca. A Poem. (Anon.) 1812. (P)
    British Critic, 40 (Oct. 1812), 408.
    Critical Review, s4,v2 (Nov. 1812), 553-54.
    Monthly Review, 69 (Nov. 1812), 328-29.
    Theatrical Inquisitor, 3 (Oct. 1813), 174-75.

Jefferson, Joseph.
    Horae Poeticae. Poems; Sacred, Moral, and Descriptive. To
    Which Are Added Four Essays. 1804. (P)
    Annual Review, 3 (1804), 586-87.
    Eclectic Review, 1 (June 1805), 417-19.
    Poetical Register, 4 (1804), 496.

Jefferys, John.
    The Pleasures of Retirement. With Other Poems. 1800. (P)
    British Critic, 17 (June 1801), 647-48.
    Critical Review, s2,v35 (June 1802), 231-32.
    Monthly Review, 38 (July 1802), 321-22.

Jeffrey, Francis, and John Gordon.
    The Craniad; or Spurzheim Illustrated. (Anon.) 1817. (P)
    Augustan Review, 2 (June 1816), 619-22.
    Blackwood's Edinburgh Magazine, 1 (June 1817), 288.
    Gentleman's Magazine, 87[2] (July 1817), 49-50.
    Literary Gazette, Apr. 26, 1817, pp. 212-13.

Jennings, Miss A.
    Retrospection, a Poem...and Other Small Pieces. 1808. (P)
    Satirist, 4 (Feb. 1809), 190-91.

Jennings, James.
    Poems; Consisting of the Mysteries of Mendip, the Magic
    Ball, Sonnets, Retrospective Wanderings, and Other Poems.
    1810. (P)
    Eclectic Review, 6 (Oct. 1810), 952-54.
    Monthly Review, 68 (Oct. 1810), 210.
    Poetical Register, 8 (1810), 571.

Jerningham, Edward.
    The Peckham Frolic; or Nell Gwyn. A Comedy. (Anon.)
    1799. (D)
    Analytical Review, ns,v1 (June 1799), 613-14.
    Antijacobin Review, 4 (Sept. 1799), 103-04.
    British Critic, 13 (Apr. 1799), 431.
    Critical Review, ns,v26 (July 1799), 354.
    Monthly Magazine, Suppl. v8 (Jan. 20, 1800), 1055-56.
    Monthly Mirror, 7 (May 1799), 293.

Monthly Review, ns,v29 (June 1799), 231-32.
New London Review, 1 (Mar. 1799), 303-04.

Poems and Plays. "New Edition." (P-D)
 Annual Review, 5 (1806), 529-30.
 Gentleman's Magazine, 76[1] (Mar. 1806), 244.
 Poetical Register, 6 (1806), 503.

The Old Bard's Farewell, a Poem. (Anon.) 1811. (P)
 British Critic, 39 (Jan. 1812), 77.
 Critical Review, s3,v23 (May 1811), 44-45.
 Gentleman's Magazine, 81[1] (Mar. 1811), 256.
 Monthly Mirror, ns,v9 (Feb. 1811), 137-38.
 Monthly Review, 64 (Mar. 1811), 321-22.
 Poetical Register, 8 (1811), 628-29.
 Satirist, 8 (Mar. 1811), 260-64.

Johnson, Rev. Benjamin.
 Original Poems. 1798. (P)
 Analytical Review, 28 (Dec. 1798), 587-90.
 Critical Review, s2,v27 (Sept. 1799), 109-10.
 Monthly Mirror, 7 (Mar. 1799), 168-69.

Johnson, C. H.
 John the Baptist; a Prize Poem. (Anon.) 1809. (P)
 Eclectic Review, 6 (Jan. 1810), 92.

Johnson, Mrs. D.
 The Brothers in High Life; or the North of Ireland. 1813.
 (F)
 British Critic, 42 (Aug. 1813), 196.
 Critical Review, s4,v4 (Aug. 1813), 218.
 Monthly Review, ns,v73 (Mar. 1814), 318.
 New Review, 2 (Aug. 1813), 184.

Johnson, Mary F.
 Original Sonnets and Other Poems. 1810. (P)
 Antijacobin Review, 39 (Aug. 1811), 429-31.
 British Critic, 38 (July 1811), 81-82.
 British Critic, 38 (Oct. 1811), 401-02.
 Critical Review, s3,v23 (Aug. 1811), 441-42.
 Monthly Review, 65 (July 1811), 329-32.
 Poetical Register, 8 (1810), 569-70.
 Universal Magazine, ns,v14 (Oct. 1810), 300-03.

Johnson, W. R.
 The History of England in Easy Verse, from the Invasion of
 Julius Caesar, to the Beginning of the Year 1806. (P)
 Monthly Mirror, 21 (June 1806), 394-95.

 The History of Greece, in Easy Verse; from the Earliest
 Period to the Conquest by the Romans. 1807. (P)
 Monthly Review, 55 (Apr. 1808), 437-38.

Johnstone, Mrs. Christian Isobel.
  The Saxon and the Gael; or the Northern Metropolis. (Anon.)
  1814. (F)
     British Critic, ns,v3 (June 1815), 659-61.
     Monthly Review, ns,v77 (July 1815), 320-21.
     Universal Magazine, s3,v3 (Aug. 1815), 117-18.

  Clan-Albin: A National Tale. (Anon.) 1815. (F)
     Literary and Statistical Magazine, 1 (Feb. 1817), 67-75.
     Monthly Review, ns,v80 (May 1816), 84-91.
     Scots Magazine, 77 (Nov. 1815), 849-54.

Jones, Harriet.
  The Family of Santraile; or, the Heir of Montault. A Romance. 1809. (F)
     Monthly Review, ns,v63 (Sept. 1810), 103.

Jones, J.
  Hawthorn Cottage; or the Two Cupids. 1815. (F)
     Antijacobin Review, 48 (Jan. 1815), 60-61.
     Critical Review, s5,v1 (Feb. 1815), 208.
     Monthly Review, ns,v79 (Feb. 1816), 214.

Jones, Jenkin.
  Hobby Horses, a Poetic Allegory. 1797. (P)
     Analytical Review, 27 (Mar. 1798), 286-89.
     British Critic, 11 (Apr. 1798), 435.
     Critical Review, s2,v22 (Mar. 1798), 354.
     Monthly Magazine, Suppl. v5 (July 15, 1798), 507.
     Monthly Review, 25 (Jan. 1798), 105-07.

  Pros and Cons for Cupid and Hymen; in a Series of Metrical
  Satiric Dialogues.... 1807. (P)
     Antijacobin Review, 28 (Nov. 1807), 328.
     Critical Review, s3,v12 (Sept. 1807), 102.
     Monthly Review, 55 (Feb. 1808), 222.
     Poetical Register, 6 (1807), 549-50.
     Satirist, 2 (Mar. 1808), 95.

Jones, John.
  Amatory Odes, Elegies, and Sonnets. (Anon.) 1798. (P)
     Lady's Monthly Museum, 2 (Apr. 1799), 324.
     Monthly Review, 28 (Mar. 1799), 352.
     Monthly Visitor, 6 (Apr. 1799), 424.
     New London Review, 1 (Mar. 1799), 302.

Jones, John Gale.
  Galerio and Nerissa, Including Original Correspondence...
  and a Few Domestic Anecdotes. (Anon.) 1814. (P-Pr)
     Monthly Mirror, 18 (Oct. 1804), 248-49.

Jones, Richard.
  Too Late for Dinner, a Farce. 1820. (D)

Monthly Review, ns,v92 (June 1820), 216-17.
Theatrical Inquisitor, 16 (Mar. 1820), 157-58.

Jones, T.
Confined in Vain; or a Double to Do. A Farce. 1805. (D)
Antijacobin Review, 20 (Apr. 1805), 419.
British Critic, 25 (June 1805), 684.
Critical Review, s3,v5 (May 1805), 105.
European Magazine, 47 (May 1805), 372.
Literary Journal, a Review..., 5 (Apr. 1805), 436.
Monthly Mirror, 21 (June 1806), 400.
Monthly Review, ns,v50 (May 1806), 102.

Jones, Thomas.
Poems; Consisting of Elegies, Sonnets, Songs, &c., and
Phantoms; or, the Irishman in England, a Farce. (P-D)
Annual Review, 2 (1803), 562.
European Magazine, 44 (Aug. 1803), 130.
Poetical Register, 3 (1803), 447.

Soldier's Fare; or Patriotism and Hospitality. (Anon.)
1805. (P)
Antijacobin Review, 22 (Sept. 1805), 78.
British Critic, 27 (Jan. 1806), 78-79.
European Magazine, 48 (Sept. 1805), 217-18.
Monthly Mirror, 20 (Oct. 1805), 258.

The Sons; or, Family Feuds. 1809. (D)
Antijacobin Review, 35 (Mar. 1810), 300-01.
Critical Review, s3,v18 (Sept. 1809), 107.
Gentleman's Magazine, 79² (Dec. 1809), 1137.
Monthly Review, ns,v61 (Jan. 1810), 105-06.
Satirist, 8 (Mar. 1811), 279-80.
Universal Magazine, ns,v12 (Oct. 1809), 299.

Miscellanies in Prose and Verse. 1820. (P-Pr)
Antijacobin Review, 59 (Oct. 1820), 140-41.
European Magazine, 78 (July 1820), 56.
Literary Chronicle, 2 (June 3, 1820), 360.

Joor, William.
The Battle of Eutaw Springs, and Evacuation of Charleston.
1807. (D)
Monthly Mirror, ns,v2 (Aug. 1807), 119-22.

Jordan, William.
The Jubilee. A Poem on the Fiftieth Anniversary of His
Majesty's Accession to the Throne. 1809. (P)
British Critic, 34 (Nov. 1809), 521.
Poetical Register, 8 (1810), 576.

Juvenal, Jeremiah.
See George Daniel.

348

Juvenis.
  Trafalgaris Pugna: The Battle of Trafalgar, a Latin Poem...
  with a Literal Translation in English Prose. 1807. (P)
    British Critic, 31 (Feb. 1809), 195.
    Critical Review, s3,v11 (Aug. 1807), 443-44.
    Critical Review, s3,v13 (Jan. 1808), 104-05.
    Monthly Review, 54 (Sept. 1807), 88.
    Satirist, 2 (Mar. 1808), 91. (Excerpts from other reviews.)
    Satirist, 3 (Oct. 1808), 336. (Excerpts from other re-
      views.)

Kames, Henry Home, Lord.
  Elements of Criticism. Ninth Edition. 1805. (Pr)
    Lady's Monthly Museum, 15 (Aug. 1805), 131-32.
    Monthly Mirror, 19 (June 1805), 295[389]-390.

Keats, John.
  Poems. 1817. (P)
    Champion, Mar. 9, 1817, p. 78.
    Eclectic Review, s2,v8 (Sept. 1817), 267-75.
    Edinburgh Magazine and Literary Miscellany (Scots Maga-
      zine), ns,v1 (Oct. 1817), 254-57.
    European Magazine, 71 (May 1817), 434-37.
    Examiner, June 1, July 6, 13, 1817, pp. 345, 428-29, 443-
      44.
    Monthly Magazine, 43 (Apr. 1817), 248.

  Endymion, a Poetic Romance. 1818. (P)
    British Critic, ns,v9 (June 1818), 649-54.
    Champion, June 7, 1818, pp. 362-64.
    Edinburgh Magazine and Literary Miscellany (Scots Maga-
      zine), ns,v7 (Aug., Oct. 1820), 107-10, 313-16.
    Edinburgh Review, 34 (Aug. 1820), 203-13.
    Examiner, Oct. 11, 1818, pp. 648-49.
    Literary Chronicle, 1 (May 18, 25, 1818), 114-15, 131.
    Literary Journal and General Miscellany, 1 (May 17, 24,
      1818), 114-15, 131.
    (Baldwin's) London Magazine, 1 (Apr. 1820), 380-89.
    Oxford Herald, June 6, 1818.
    Quarterly Review, 19 (Apr. 1818). 204-08.

  Lamia, Isabella, the Eve of St. Agnes, and Other Poems.
  1820. (P)
    British Critic, ns,v4 (Sept. 1820), 257-64.
    Eclectic Review, s2,v14 (Sept. 1820), 158-71.
    Edinburgh Magazine and Literary Miscellany (Scots Maga-
      zine), ns,v7 (Aug., Oct. 1820), 107-10, 313-16.
    Edinburgh Review, 34 (Aug. 1820), 203-13.
    Examiner, July 30, 1820, pp. 494-95.
    Guardian, Aug. 6, 1820.
    Indicator, 1 (Aug. 2, 9, 1820), 337-44, 345-52.
    Kaleidoscope, ns,v1 (Aug. 29, 1820), 69.
    Literary Chronicle, 2 (July 29, 1820), 484-85.

Literary Gazette, July 1, 1820, pp. 423-24.
(Baldwin's) London Magazine, 2 (Sept. 1820), 315-21.
(Gold's) London Magazine, 2 (Aug. 1820), 160-73.
Monthly Magazine, 50 (Sept. 1820), 166.
Monthly Review, 92 (July 1820), 305-10.
New Monthly Magazine, 14 (Sept. 1820), 245-48.
New Times, July 19, 1820.

Keep, W. A.
Incog; or Three Days at a Well Known Hotel. A Farce. (D)
   Theatrical Inquisitor, 11 (July 1817), 60.

Kelly, Mrs. Isabella.
Joscelina; or, the Rewards of Benevolence. 1797. (F)
   British Critic, 11 (Mar. 1798), 316-17.

Eva. (F)
   New London Review, 2 (Aug. 1799), 180.

The Baron's Daughter. A Gothic Romance. 1802. (F)
   Critical Review, ns,v36 (Sept. 1802), 117.
   New Annual Register, 23 (1802), [321-22].

The Secret. 1805. (F)
   British Critic, 26 (Oct. 1805), 442-43.
   Critical Review, s3,v6 (Dec. 1805), 437.
   Lady's Monthly Museum, 16 (Mar. 1806), 198-99.
   Literary Journal, a Review..., 5 (Oct. 1805), 1105.
   Monthly Review, ns,v51 (Oct. 1806), 207.

Jane de Dunstanville, or Characters as They Are. 1813. (F)
   Critical Review, s4,v5 (Jan. 1814), 97-99.
   New Review, 3 (Mar. 1814), 264-65.

Kelly, John.
Elements of Music, in Verse, Adapted to the Piano Forte,
and Calculated for Juvenile Study..... 1814. (P)
   British Critic, ns,v2 (Oct. 1814), 434-35.
   Monthly Review, 74 (May 1814), 103-05.

Kelsall, Charles.
A Letter from Athens, Addressed to a Friend in England.
(Anon.) 1812. (P)
   Critical Review, s4,v2 (Nov. 1812), 512-19.

Constantine and Eugene, or an Evening at Mount Vernon, a
Political Dialogue. By Junius Secundus. (F)
   Monthly Magazine, 45 (July 1818), 533.

Kemble, Mrs. C.
Smiles and Tears; or, the Widow's Stratagem. 1815. (D)
   British Lady's Magazine, 3 (Feb. 1816), 95-100.
   Theatrical Inquisitor, 8 (May 1816), 358-59.

Kemble, Charles.
  Plot and Counterplot, or the Portrait of Michael Cervantes.
  1808. (D)
    British Critic, 33 (June 1809), 634.
    Cabinet, 4 (Sept. 1808), 187.
    Poetical Register, 7 (1808), 583.

Kemble, Julia Anne.
  Secret Avengers; or the Rock of Slotzden. A Romance. (F)
    New Monthly Magazine, 2 (Dec. 1814), 444.

  Chronicles of an Illustrious House; or the Peer, the Lawyer,
  and the Hunch-back. By Anne of Swansea. 1816. (F)
    Monthly Review, ns,v79 (Apr. 1816), 438.

Kemble, S. and H.
  Flodden Field; a Dramatic Romance. (D)
    Literary Journal and General Miscellany, 2 (Mar. 6, 1819),
    145.

Kemble, Stephen George.
  Odes, Lyrical Ballads, and Poems on Various Occasions.
  1809. (P)
    Eclectic Review, 6 (Oct. 1810), 951.

Kemp, James.
  Northernhay, a Poem, Addressed to Solitude. 1808. (P)
    Antijacobin Review, 30 (Aug. 1808), 414-15.
    Critical Review, s3,v14 (July 1808), 328-29.
    Monthly Review, 58 (Feb. 1809), 212-13.
    Satirist, 6 (Apr. 1810), 416. (Excerpts from other re-
    views.)

Kemp, Joseph.
  The Siege of Isca; or the Battles of the West. (D)
    Poetical Register, 8 (1810), 598.

Kendal, Mrs. _____.
  Moreland Manor; or Who Is the Heir? 1806. (F)
    Literary Journal, a Review..., ns,v2 (Nov. 1806), 550-51.

Kendall, A.
  The Castle on the Rock, or Memoirs of the Elderland Family.
  (Anon.) 1798. (F)
    Analytical Review, 27 (Apr. 1798), 418-19.
    British Critic, 12 (July 1798), 74.
    European Magazine, 33 (Feb. 1798), 106.
    Monthly Magazine, Suppl. v6 (1798), 517.
    Monthly Mirror, 5 (May 1798), 290.
    Monthly Review, ns,v25 (Apr. 1798), 453.
    Monthly Visitor, 3 (Mar. 1798), 306-07.

  Derwent Priory; or Memoirs of an Orphan, in a Series of
  Letters. (Anon.) 1798. (F)

Analytical Review, 27 (June 1798), 643-44.
Antijacobin Review, 1 (Oct. 1798), 417-18.
British Critic, 12 (Sept. 1798), 305.
European Magazine, 33 (June 1798), 392.
Monthly Magazine, Suppl. v6 (1798), 517.
Monthly Mirror, 5 (May 1798), 290.
Monthly Review, ns,v26 (Aug. 1798), 457.

Tales of the Abbey. 1800. (F)
   Critical Review, ns,v31 (Feb. 1801), 235.
   Monthly Visitor, 11 (Oct. 1800), 193-96.

Tales and Poems. (P-F)
   Literary Journal, a Review, 3 (June 16, 1804), 681.
   Monthly Visitor, ns,v7 (May 1804), 204-05.

Kendall, Edward Augustus.
   Keeper's Travels in Search of His Master. (Anon.) 1798. (F)
   British Critic, 12 (Aug. 1798), 184.
   Monthly Mirror, 6 (Nov. 1798), 290.

The Sparrow. (Anon.) (F)
   Lady's Monthly Museum, 1 (Nov. 1798), 401-02.

The Crested Wren. 1799. (F)
   British Critic, 14 (Sept. 1799), 313.
   New London Review, 1 (June 1799), 616.

The Canary Bird, a Moral Fiction. (Anon.) (F-P)
   Monthly Mirror, 9 (Feb. 1800), 90.

The Stories of Senex; or, Little Histories of Little People.
(F)
   European Magazine, 38 (Nov. 1800), 363.

Kennedy, James.
   Glenochel: A Descriptive Poem. 1810. (P)
   British Critic, 39 (Jan. 1812), 77-78.
   Eclectic Review, 7 (Nov. 1811), 1029-30.
   New Annual Register, 32 (1811), [365].

Poems. (P)
   Kilmarnock Mirror, 1 (Dec. 1819), 241-51.
   Weaver's Magazine, 2 (Aug. 1819), 277-84.

Kennedy, Rev. R.
   A Poem on the Death of Her Royal Highness the Princess Char-
   lotte of Wales and Saxe-Cobourg. 1817. (P)
   Antijacobin Review, 53 (Feb. 1818), 530-34.
   British Critic, ns,v9 (Jan. 1818), 98-99.
   British Review, 11 (Feb. 1818), 1-37.
   Gentleman's Magazine, 88^1 (Jan. 1818), 50-51.
   Literary Gazette, Feb. 7, 1818, pp. 86-87.

Literary Panorama, ns,v7 (Mar. 1818), 772.
Monthly Review, 85 (Jan. 1818), 104-06.
New Monthly Magazine, 9 (Feb. 1818), 58.

Kenney, James.
  Society...with Other Poems. 1803. (P)
    Annual Review, 2 (1803), 569.
    Antijacobin Review, 16 (Dec. 1803), 421.
    British Critic, 22 (Nov. 1803), 554.
    European Magazine, 44 (Oct. 1803), 297.
    Flowers of Literature, 3 (1804), 462.
    Literary Journal, a Review..., 2 (Oct. 17, 1803), 408-10.
    Monthly Mirror, 16 (Nov. 1803), 321-23.
    Monthly Review, 44 (May 1804), 32-34.
    New Annual Register, 24 (1803), [320].
    Poetical Register, 3 (1803), 448.

  Raising the Wind, a Farce. (D)
    Annual Review, 2 (1803), 596.
    British Critic, 24 (Dec. 1804), 682.
    Poetical Register, 3 (1803), 467.

  Too Many Cooks, a Musical Farce. 1805. (D)
    Annual Review, 4 (1805), 641.
    British Critic, 26 (Sept. 1805), 320-21.
    Critical Review, s3,v4 (Mar. 1805), 325.
    Poetical Register, 5 (1805), 508.

  Ella Rosenberg, a Melo-Drama. (D)
    Annual Review, 7 (1808), 571.
    Monthly Review, ns,v57 (Sept. 1808), 99-100.
    Poetical Register, 7 (1808), 583.

  The World. A Comedy. 1808. (D)
    Annual Review, 7 (1808), 570.
    British Critic, 36 (Aug. 1810), 183.
    Monthly Magazine, Suppl. v25 (July 30, 1808), 597.
    Poetical Register, 7 (1808), 580.
    Satirist, 7 (1810), 596.

  Debtor and Creditor. A Comedy. 1814. (D)
    British Critic, ns,v1 (May 1814), 551.
    Monthly Review, ns,v74 (May 1814), 103.

  The Portfolio; or the Family of Anglade. 1816. (D)
    Monthly Review, ns,v79 (Feb. 1816), 213.
    Theatrical Inquisitor, 8 (June 1816), 447.

  A House Out at Windows. (D)
    Theatrical Inquisitor, 11 (July 1817), 58-59.

  The Touchstone; or, the World as It Goes. (D)
    Theatrical Inquisitor, 4 (July 1817), 56-58.

Valdi; or the Libertine's Son, a Poem. 1820. (P)
   Antijacobin Review, 58 (May 1820), 246-50.
   Literary Gazette, Mar. 11, 1820, pp. 163-64.
   New Monthly Magazine, 13 (May 1820), 521-23.

Kenney, John Henry.
   The Burniad: An Epistle to a Lady, in the Manner of Burns.
   With Poetic Miscellanies. 1808. (P)
      Annual Review, 7 (1808), 535.
      Antijacobin Review, 32 (Apr. 1809), 407-10.
      British Critic, 33 (Feb. 1809), 185.
      European Magazine, 53 (May 1808), 370.
      Monthly Review, 58 (Jan. 1809), 104-05.
      Poetical Register, 7 (1808), 560.

Kentish, Mrs. _____.
   Poems on Various Subjects. 1819. (P)
      Monthly Review, 91 (Feb. 1820), 214.

Ker, Mrs. Anne.
   The Heiress de Montalde; or, the Castle of Bezanto. 1799.
   (F)
      New London Review, 2 (Oct. 1799), 388-89.

   Adeline St. Julian; or, the Midnight Hour. 1800. (F)
      Antijacobin Review, 7 (Oct. 1800), 201-02.
      Critical Review, ns,v29 (May 1800), 116.
      Monthly Review, ns,33 (Sept. 1800), 103.
      New London Review, 3 (Apr. 1800), 375.

   Modern Faults. 1804. (F)
      Critical Review, s3,v3 (Sept. 1804), 116.
      Literary Journal, a Review..., 3 (June 16, 1804), 682.

   Edric the Forester; or, the Mysteries of the Haunted Chambers. 1817. (F)
      Gentleman's Magazine, 88[2] (Suppl. July-Dec. 1818), 617.
      Monthly Review, ns,v86 (June 1818), 213-14.

Kerr, Symon.
   Scottish Poems, Songs, &c. 1802. (P)
      Critical Review, s2,v38 (July 1803), 357-58.
      Imperial Review, 4 (May 1805), 587-93.
      Monthly Mirror, 19 (June 1805), 396.
      Monthly Visitor, ns,v4 (May 1803), 96-97.
      New Annual Register, 23 (1802), [318].
      Poetical Register, 3 (1803), 451.

Kett, Rev. Henry.
   Emily, a Moral Tale. 1809. (F)
      British Critic, 35 (Jan. 1810), 63-68.
      British Critic, 40 (Dec. 1812), 640-41.
      Critical Review, s3,v17 (June 1809), 220.

Monthly Review, ns,v62 (May 1810), 110-11.
Quarterly Review, 2 (Nov. 1809), 314-19.

King, Charlotte, and Sophia King.
  Trifles of Helicon. 1798. (P)
    Analytical Review, 27 (Feb. 1798), 133.
    British Critic, 12 (July 1798), 72.
    Critical Review, s2,v22 (Mar. 1798), 353-54.
    Monthly Review, 26 (May 1798), 101.

King, Miss E.
  Poems and Reflections. By a Young Lady. 1815. (P)
    Critical Review, s5,v2 (Oct. 1815), 426-28.

King, Edward.
  Hymns to the Supreme Being, in Imitation of the Eastern
  Songs. 1798. (P)
    British Critic, 13 (Feb. 1799), 189.

King, Sophia (see also Charlotte King and Sophia King).
  Waldorf; or, the Dangers of Philosophy. 1798. (F)
    Critical Review, ns,v24 (Sept. 1798), 112-14.
    Monthly Magazine, Suppl. v6 (1798), 517.
    Monthly Mirror, 6 (Aug. 1798), 98.
    Monthly Review, ns,v26 (June 1798), 221-22.

  Cordelia; or a Romance of Real Life. 1799. (F)
    Critical Review, ns,v28 (Feb. 1800), 235-36.
    New London Review, 2 (Aug. 1799), 183.

  The Victim of Friendship; a German Romance. 1800. (F)
    Antijacobin Review, 7 (Dec. 1800), 416.
    Critical Review, ns,v32 (June 1801), 232.

King, William.
  Britannia Triumphant over the French Fleet, by Admiral Nelson, off the Mouth of the Nile. 1799. (P)
    Analytical Review, ns,v1 (May 1799), 527.
    Antijacobin Review, 3 (Aug. 1799), 437.
    British Critic, 14 (Oct. 1799), 428.
    Critical Review, s2,v26 (May 1799), 112.
    New London Review, 1 (May 1799), 510.

Kinnaird, Douglas.
  The Merchant of Bruges; or Beggar's Bush. 1815. (D)
    Theatrical Inquisitor, 8 (Mar. 1816), 211-13.

Knight, Ann Cuthbert.
  A Year in Canada; with Other Poems. 1816. (P)
    British Critic, ns,v6 (July 1816), 92-94.
    British Lady's Magazine, 3 (May 1816), 323-26.
    Eclectic Review, s2,v6 (Oct. 1816), 404.
    Literary Panorama, ns,v5 (Oct. 1816), 56-61.

<u>Monthly</u> <u>Review</u>, 79 (Apr. 1816), 433.

Knight, Charles.
  <u>Arminius</u>; <u>or</u>, <u>the</u> <u>Deliverance</u> <u>of</u> <u>Germany</u>. 1814.   (D)
    <u>British</u> <u>Critic</u>, ns,v2 (July 1814), 102-03.
    <u>European</u> <u>Magazine</u>, 66 (Sept. 1814), 236.
    <u>Monthly</u> <u>Review</u>, ns,v75 (Oct. 1814), 213-14.

  <u>The</u> <u>Bridal</u> <u>of</u> <u>the</u> <u>Isles</u>: <u>A</u> <u>Mask</u>. 1817. (P)
    <u>Gentleman's</u> <u>Magazine</u>, 88[1] (Apr. 1818), 342.
    <u>Literary</u> <u>Gazette</u>, Jan. 10, 1818, p. 21.
    <u>Monthly</u> <u>Review</u>, 86 (June 1818), 211.

Knight, E. P.
  <u>A</u> <u>Chip</u> <u>off</u> <u>the</u> <u>Old</u> <u>Block</u>; <u>or</u>, <u>the</u> <u>Village</u> <u>Festival</u>. 1815.
  (D)
    <u>Theatrical</u> <u>Inquisitor</u>, 7 (Sept. 1815), 211.

Knight, Henry Gally.
  <u>Iberia's</u> <u>Crisis</u>; <u>a</u> <u>Fragment</u> <u>of</u> <u>an</u> <u>Epic</u> <u>Poem</u>. (Anon.)
  1809. (P)
    <u>British</u> <u>Critic</u>, 35 (Feb. 1810), 185.
    <u>Critical</u> <u>Review</u>, s3,v18 (Dec. 1809), 441-42.
    <u>Monthly</u> <u>Review</u>, 61 (Apr. 1810), 446-47.
    <u>Poetical</u> <u>Register</u>, 7 (1809), 604-05.

  <u>Ilderim</u>; <u>a</u> <u>Syrian</u> <u>Tale</u>. (Anon.) 1816. (P)
    <u>Augustan</u> <u>Review</u>, 3 (Oct. 1816), 396-98.
    <u>British</u> <u>Critic</u>, ns,v7 (Feb. 1817), 181-86.
    <u>British</u> <u>Lady's</u> <u>Magazine</u>, 4 (Nov. 1816), 312-15.
    <u>Eclectic</u> <u>Review</u>, s2,v6 (Nov. 1816), 489-99.
    <u>Monthly</u> <u>Review</u>, 83 (Aug. 1817), 370-81.
    <u>Scourge</u> <u>and</u> <u>Satirist</u>, 12 (Aug. 1816), 142-49.

  <u>Phrosyne</u>, <u>a</u> <u>Grecian</u> <u>Tale</u>. <u>Alashtar</u>, <u>an</u> <u>Arabian</u> <u>Tale</u>. 1817.
  (P)
    <u>British</u> <u>Critic</u>, ns,v8 (Aug. 1817), 151-64.
    <u>Literary</u> <u>Gazette</u>, June 21, 1817, p. 338.
    <u>Monthly</u> <u>Review</u>, 83 (Aug. 1817), 370-81.

  <u>Eastern</u> <u>Sketches</u>, <u>in</u> <u>Verse</u>. 1819. (P)
    <u>Quarterly</u> <u>Review</u>, 22 (July 1819), 149-58.

Knight, J.
  <u>The</u> <u>Honest</u> <u>Thieves</u>, <u>a</u> <u>Farce</u>. (D)
    <u>British</u> <u>Critic</u>, 11 (Jan. 1798), 76.

Knight, J. A.
  <u>Poems</u> <u>on</u> <u>Religious</u> <u>Subjects</u>. 1800. (P)
    <u>British</u> <u>Critic</u>, 16 (Sept. 1800), 319.

Knight, Richard Payne.
  <u>The</u> <u>Progress</u> <u>of</u> <u>Civil</u> <u>Society</u>. <u>A</u> <u>Didactic</u> <u>Poem</u>. (P)

Antijacobin Review, 5 (Apr. 1800), 454-57.

An Analytical Inquiry into the Principles of Taste. 1805.
(Pr)
British Critic, 29 (Jan., Feb. 1807), 1-21, 168-90.
Critical Review, s3,v6 (Nov. 1805), 225-37.
Edinburgh Review, 7 (Jan. 1806), 295-328.
Literary Journal, a Review..., ns,vl (Feb. 1806), 113-28.
Monthly Mirror, 20 (July 1805), 25-30.
Monthly Review, 21 (June 1806), 141-57.

A Monody on the Death of the Right Honourable Charles James
Fox. 1807. (P)
Annual Review, 6 (1807), 574.
Monthly Mirror, ns,v2 (Aug. 1807), 108-09.
Monthly Review, 53 (July 1807), 318-20.
Poetical Register, 6 (1807), 551.
Satirist, 1 (Jan. 1808), 431. (Excerpts from other re-
views.)

Knight, Thomas.
The Turnpike Gate, a Musical Entertainment. 1799. (D)
British Critic, 15 (Mar. 1800), 318.
Monthly Mirror, 8 (Dec. 1799), 350-51.
Monthly Review, ns,v31 (Jan. 1800), 90-92.
New London Review, 2 (Dec. 1799), 606-07.

Knight, William.
The First Day in Heaven. A Fragment. (Anon.) 1820.
Literary Gazette, July 22, 1820, p. 471.

Knowles, James Sheridan.
Virginius, a Tragedy. 1820. (D)
Glasgow Magazine, 1 (Oct. 1820), 39-51.
Lonsdale Magazine, 1 (Aug. 1820), 362-64.
Monthly Review, ns,v93 (Sept. 1820), 53-58.
Theatrical Inquisitor, ns,vl (Oct. 1820), 299-303.

Knox, William.
The Lonely Hearth, and Other Poems. 1818. (P)
Edinburgh Magazine and Literary Miscellany (Scots Maga-
zine), ns,v4 (Mar. 1819), 252-54.

La Fontaine, Augustus.
Baron de Fleming; or, the Rage of Nobility. (F)
Literary Journal, a Review..., 3 (June 16, 1804), 682.

Henrietta Bellman; or, the New Family Picture. 1804. (F)
Critical Review, s3,v6 (Oct. 1805), 215-16.
Lady's Monthly Museum, 13 (Oct. 1804), 270.
Monthly Mirror, 17 (June 1804), 400.

Eliza, or Family-Papers. 1810. (F)
Monthly Review, ns,v64 (Feb. 1811), 216.

The New Arcadia, or the Interior of Two Families. 1810. (F)
    Monthly Review, ns,v64 (Feb. 1811), 215-16.

Lace, T. G.
   Ode on the Present State of Europe. 1811. (P)
      Antijacobin Review, 40 (Sept. 1811), 91-93.
      Critical Review, s3,v23 (July 1811), 330-31.
      Eclectic Review, 7 (Aug. 1811), 740-41.
      Monthly Review, 66 (Nov. 1811), 325-26.

Lacey, James Murray.
   The Farm House; a Tale, with Amatory, Pastoral, Elegiac,
   and Miscellaneous Poems, Sonnets, &c. 1809. (P)
      Antijacobin Review, 33 (Aug. 1809), 412-13.
      British Critic, 34 (Sept. 1809), 299.
      Cabinet, ns,v1 (Aug. 1809), 152.
      Literary Panorama, 6 (July 1809), 687-88.
      Monthly Review, 60 (Dec. 1809), 433.
      Poetical Register, 7 (1809), 596.

Lady, A.
   See Mrs. Elizabeth Bonhote.
   See Mrs. Frances Maria Cowper.
   See Mrs. Catherine Ann Dorset.
   See Mrs. Anne Ritson.
   See Mrs. Melesina Chevenix Trench.
   See Anna Jane Vardill.
   See Elizabeth Zornlin.

Lady and Her Brother, A.
   See Elizabeth Sophia Tomlins.

Lake, John.
   The Golden Glove, or the Farmer's Son, a Comedy. 1815. (D)
      Critical Review, s5,v2 (July 1815), 101-02.
      Monthly Review, ns,v80 (May 1816), 98-100.
      Theatrical Inquisitor, 7 (Aug. 1815), 132-33.

Lamb, Lady Caroline.
   Glenarvon. (Anon.) 1816. (F)
      Augustan Review, 3 (Oct. 1816), 350-54.
      British Critic, ns,v5 (June 1816), 627-33.
      British Lady's Magazine, 4 (Aug. 1816), 101-03.
      Monthly Review, 80 (June 1816), 217-18.
      New Monthly Magazine, 5 (June 1816), 443-44.
      Scourge and Satirist, 12 (Sept. 1816), 228-35.
      Theatrical Inquisitor, 9 (Aug. 1816), 122-25.

Lamb, Charles.
   Poems, by S. T. Coleridge, Second Edition. To Which Are
   Now Added Poems by Charles Lamb and Charles Lloyd. 1797.
   (P)
      Critical Review, s2,v23 (July 1798), 266-68.

Lamb, Charles (continued)
    Freemason's Magazine, 1 (Aug. 1798), 128.

    Blank Verse, by Charles Lloyd and Charles Lamb.   1798. (P)
    Analytical Review, 27 (May 1798), 522-23.
    British Critic, 11 (June 1798), 678.
    Critical Review, s2,v24 (Oct. 1798), 232-34.
    European Magazine, 33 (May 1798), 329.
    Monthly Magazine, Suppl. v5 (July 15, 1798), 507.
    Monthly Mirror, 6 (Aug. 1798), 97.
    Monthly Review, 27 (Sept. 1798), 104-05.
    New Annual Register, 19 (1798), [309].

    A Tale of Rosamund Gray and Old Blind Margaret.   1798. (F)
    Analytical Review, ns,v1 (Feb. 1799), 208-09.
    Critical Review, ns,v25 (Apr. 1799), 472-73.
    Monthly Magazine, Suppl. v7 (July 20, 1799), 541.
    Monthly Review, ns,v32 (Aug. 1800), 447.

    John Woodvil; a Tragedy.   1802.   (D)
    Annual Review, 1 (1802), 688-92.
    British Critic, 19 (June 1802), 646-47.
    Edinburgh Review, 2 (Apr. 1803), 90-96.
    Monthly Magazine, Suppl. v14 (Jan. 25, 1803), 600.
    Monthly Mirror, 13 (Apr. 1802), 254-56.
    Monthly Review, ns,v40 (Apr. 1803), 442-43.
    Poetical Register, 2 (1802), 451-52.

    Tales from Shakespear; Designed for the Use of Young Per-
    sons.   1807.   (Pr)
    Antijacobin Review, 26 (Mar. 1807), 298.
    British Critic, 33 (May 1809), 525.
    Critical Review, s3,v11 (May 1807), 97-99.
    Gentleman's Magazine, 78^2 (Nov. 1808), 1001.
    Literary Panorama, 3 (Nov. 1807), 294-95.
    Monthly Mirror, ns,v2 (July 1807), 39.
    Satirist, 4 (July 1809), 93.   (Excerpts from other re-
        views.)

    Mrs. Leicester's School; or, the History of Several Young
    Ladies, Related by Themselves. (Anon.)   1807.   (Pr)
    British Critic, 33 (Jan. 1809), 77.
    Critical Review, s3,v15 (Dec. 1808), 444.
    Eclectic Review, 5 (Jan. 1809), 95.
    Literary Panorama, 5 (Feb. 1809), 876.

    The Adventures of Ulysses.   1808.   (Pr)
    Antijacobin Review, 32 (Jan. 1809), 80-81.
    British Critic, 32 (Dec. 1808), 648-49.
    Critical Review, s3,v15 (Dec. 1808), 443.
    Eclectic Review, 5 (Oct. 1809), 973.
    European Magazine, 54 (Nov. 1808), 384.
    Monthly Review, ns,v59 (May 1809), 105-06.

Lamb, Charles (concluded)
Satirist, 7 (Aug. 1810), 198-99. (Excerpts from other reviews.)

Specimens of English Dramatic Poets, Who Lived about the
Time of Shakespear. 1808. (Pr)
Annual Review, 7 (1808), 562-70.
British Critic, 34 (July 1809), 73.
Critical Review, s3,v20 (May 1810), 80-82.
Monthly Review, ns,v58 (Apr. 1809), 349-56.
Poetical Register, 7 (1809), 572.

Stories of Old Daniel; or Tales of Wonder and Delight.
(Anon.) 1808. (F)
British Critic, 33 (Jan. 1809), 78.
European Magazine, 53 (Apr. 1808), 289.
Literary Panorama, 5 (Nov. 1808), 272.
Monthly Magazine, Suppl. v25 (July 30, 1808), 598.

Poetry for Children. (Anon.) 1809. (P)
Critical Review, s3,v18 (Oct. 1809), 223.
European Magazine, 56 (Nov. 1809), 378.
Monthly Review, 64 (Jan. 1811), 102.

The Beauty and the Beast, or a Rough Outside with a Gentle
Heart; a Poetical Version of an Ancient Tale. 1811. (P)
Universal Magazine, ns,v16 (July 1811), 47.

The Works of Charles Lamb. 1818. (P-Pr-F)
Blackwood's Edinburgh Magazine, 3 (Aug. 1818), 599-610.
British Lady's Magazine, s3,v2 (June 1819), 262-64.
British Critic, ns,v11 (Feb. 1819), 139-47.
Champion, May 16, 23, 1819, pp. 313-14, 328-30.
European Magazine, 75 (Apr. 1819), 346-47.
Examiner, Mar. 21, 28, 1819, pp. 187-89, 204-06.
Fireside Magazine (quoting British Critic and Gentleman's
Magazine), 1 (Apr., Sept. 1818), pp. 153, 358.
Gentleman's Magazine, 89^2 (July, Aug. 1819), 48-51, 138-
40.
Indicator, Jan. 31, Feb. 7, 1821, pp. 129-36, 137-39.
(Quoting from The Examiner.)
Literary Chronicle, 1 (July 6, 1818), 223-25.
Literary Gazette, Aug. 16, 1819, pp. 516-17.
Literary Journal and General Miscellany, 1 (July 4, 25,
1818), 223-25, 275-76.
Literary Panorama, ns,v8 (Jan. 1819), 1646-53.
Monthly Magazine, 46 (Sept. 1818), 158.
Monthly Review, 90 (Nov. 1819), 253-59.
New Monthly Magazine, 14 (Aug. 1820), 129-33.

Lamb, Mary.
Mary Lamb contributed to Mrs. Leicester's School, Tales
from Shakespear, and Poetry for Children. See Charles Lamb.

Lambert, C. D. L.
  The Adventures of Cooroo, a Native of the Pellew Islands.
  1805. (F)
    Annual Review, 4 (1805), 655-56.
    British Critic, 25 (May 1805), 561.
    Critical Review, s3,v5 (July 1805), 330-31.
    Literary Journal, a Review..., 5 (Apr. 1805), 436.

Lamont, Mrs. Aeneas.
  Poems, and Tales in Verse. 1818. (P)
    Fireside Magazine (quoting Monthly Review), 1 (May 1819),
    187.
    Literary Panorama, ns,v8 (Jan. 1819), 1641.
    Monthly Review, 88 (Mar. 1819), 324-25.

Lancaster, Agnes.
  The Abbess of Valtiera; or, the Sorrows of a Falsehood. (F)
    Lady's Monthly Museum, s3,v3 (Jan. 1816), 40-42.

Lancet, Lemuel.
  A Medico-Metrical Address to the Students at the University
  of Edinburgh.... 1801. (P)
    Critical Review, s2,v37 (Mar. 1803), 355.
    Monthly Review, 37 (Apr. 1802), 438-39.

Landor, Walter Savage.
  Gebir, a Poem. (Anon.) 1798. (P)
    Antijacobin Review, 17 (Feb. 1804), 182-84. (2nd ed.)
    British Critic, 15 (Feb. 1800), 190.
    Critical Review, s2,v27 (Sept. 1799), 29-39.
    Gentleman's Magazine, 69[2] (Suppl. 1799), 1144.
    Monthly Magazine, Suppl. v8 (Jan. 20, 1800), 1051-52.
    Monthly Review, 31 (Feb. 1800), 206-08.
    Poetical Register, 3 (1803), 452.

  Poems, from the Arabic and Persian, with Notes, by the
  Author of "Gebir." (Anon.) 1800. (P)
    Gentleman's Magazine, 71[1] (Jan. 1801), 59.
    Monthly Mirror, 18 (Aug. 1804), 113.
    Monthly Review, 44 (July 1804), 331-33.

  Poetry, by the Author of "Gebir." 1802. (P)
    Annual Review, 1 (1802), 663-66.
    Antijacobin Review, 13 (Nov. 1802), 307.
    British Critic, 20 (Oct. 1802), 432-33.
    Critical Review, s2,v38 (June 1803), 235-36.
    New Annual Register, 23 (1802), [318].
    Poetical Register, 2 (1802), 437.

  Gebirus, Poema. 1803. (P)
    Antijacobin Review, 17 (Feb. 1804), 179-82.
    Literary Journal, a Review..., 2 (Dec. 31, 1803), 727.

Simonidea. (Anon.) 1806. (P)
  Antijacobin Review, 26 (Apr. 1807), 354-58.
  British Critic, 28 (Nov. 1806), 560-61.
  Critical Review, s3,v11 (May 1807), 100.
  Gentleman's Magazine, 78¹ (May 1808), 430-31.
  Literary Journal, a Review..., ns,v1 (Apr. 1806), 443-44.
  Monthly Magazine, Suppl. v23 (July 30, 1807), 643.
  Monthly Mirror, 21 (June 1806), 391.
  Monthly Review, 50 (June 1806), 211.
  Oxford Review, 1 (Feb. 1807), 225-31.
  Poetical Register, 6 (1806), 512.

Count Julian, a Tragedy. (Anon.) 1812. (D)
  New Annual Register, 34 (1813), [409].
  New Review, 1 (Feb. 1813), 173-75.
  Quarterly Review, 8 (Sept. 1812), 86-92.

Lane, William.
  Poems. 1806. (P)
  Eclectic Review, 3 (June 1807), 546.

Lantier, E. F.
  Adolphe and Blanche; or, Travellers in Switzerland.
  Translated from the French by Frederic Schoberl. (F)
    Annual Review, 3 (1804), 544-48.
    British Critic, 24 (Oct. 1804), 439.
    Literary Journal, a Review..., 2 (Dec. 31, 1803), 730.

Late Resident in the East, A.
  See John Hobart Caunter.

Late Teacher, A.
  See William Singleton.

Lathom, Francis.
  The Midnight Bell. 1798. (F)
    Monthly Magazine, Suppl. v5 (July 15, 1798), 509.

  Men and Manners. 1799. (F)
    British Critic, 13 (June 1799), 665-66.
    Critical Review, ns,v27 (Sept. 1799), 114-15.
    Monthly Magazine, Suppl. v8 (Jan. 20, 1800), 1053.
    Monthly Review, ns,v31 (Feb. 1800), 136-41.
    New London Review, 1 (May 1799), 508.

  Mystery. 1800. (F)
    British Critic, 15 (May 1800), 552.
    Critical Review, ns,v30 (Sept. 1800), 116.
    Monthly Magazine, Suppl. v9 (July 20, 1800), 640.
    Monthly Mirror, 9 (May 1800), 286.
    Monthly Review, ns,v33 (Oct. 1800), 207.
    New London Review, 3 (Apr. 1800), 373.

Lathom, Francis (continued)
The Dash of the Day, a Comedy. 1800. (D)
Antijacobin Review, 7 (Oct. 1800), 205-06.
British Critic, 18 (Aug. 1801), 196.
Critical Review, ns,v32 (Aug. 1801), 468-69.
Monthly Mirror, 12 (Sept. 1801), 186.
Monthly Review, ns,v34 (Apr. 1801), 441.

Holiday Time; or, the School-Boy's Frolic. 1800. (D)
Critical Review, ns,v34 (Mar. 1802), 355.
Monthly Mirror, 12 (Dec. 1801), 407.

Astonishment!!! A Romance of a Century Ago. 1802. (F)
Antijacobin Review, 16 (Sept. 1803), 94-96.
Critical Review, ns,v37 (Jan. 1803), 116-17.
Flowers of Literature, 2 (1803), 442.
Monthly Magazine, Suppl. v15 (July 28, 1803), 639.
Monthly Review, ns,v43 (Apr. 1804), 441.
New Annual Register, 23 (1802), [321].

The Wife of a Million, a Comedy. 1802. (D)
Annual Review, 1 (1802), 693.
British Critic, 21 (Feb. 1803), 192.
Critical Review, ns,v37 (Mar. 1803), 356.
Monthly Magazine, Suppl. v15 (July 28, 1803), 631.
Monthly Mirror, 15 (Apr. 1803), 255.
Poetical Register, 2 (1802), 454-55.

Very Strange but Very True! or the History of an Old Man's
Young Wife. 1803. (F)
Annual Review, 2 (1803), 605.
Antijacobin Review, 16 (Sept. 1803), 93-94.
Flowers of Literature, 2 (1803), 464.
Monthly Register, 3 (Sept. 1803), 183.

The Impenetrable Secret: Find It Out! 1805. (F)
British Critic, 26 (Dec. 1805), 671-72.
Cabinet, 2 (Oct. 1807), 179.
Critical Review, s3,v6 (Dec. 1805), 438.
Lady's Monthly Museum, 16 (Mar. 1806), 196-97.
Monthly Mirror, 20 (Dec. 1805), 383-84.
Monthly Review, ns,v53 (Aug. 1807), 437.

The Mysterious Freebooter, or the Days of Queen Bess; a
Romance. 1806. (F)
Annual Review, 4 (1805), 654-55.
British Critic, 27 (June 1806), 671-72.
Critical Review, s3,v8 (July 1806), 327.
Literary Journal, a Review..., ns,v1 (Mar. 1806), 332.
Monthly Mirror, 21 (May 1806), 328-29.

Human Beings. 1807. (F)
Annual Review, 5 (1806), 543.

Lathom, Francis (concluded)
    British Critic, 29 (Jan. 1807), 77.
    Critical Review, s3,v10 (Jan. 1807), 101-02.
    Flowers of Literature, 5 (1806), 503.
    Monthly Literary Recreations, 1 (Dec. 1806), 485.
    Monthly Magazine, Suppl. v22 (Jan. 25, 1807), 643.
    Monthly Mirror, ns,v1 (Jan. 1807), 50.
    New Annual Register, 27 (1806), [372].
    Oxford Review, 1 (Mar. 1807), 315-16.

    The Fatal Vow, or St. Michael's Monastery, a Romance. 1807.
    (F)
    Annual Review, 6 (1807), 666.
    Critical Review, s3,v13 (Jan. 1808), 105.
    Cyclopaedian Magazine, 1 (Dec. 1807), 735-36.
    Monthly Literary Recreations, 3 (Nov. 1807), 389-95.
    Monthly Review, ns,v58 (Feb. 1809), 216-17.
    New Annual Register, 28 (1807), [379].
    Oxford Review, 3 (Feb. 1808), 170.

    The Unknown; or the Northern Gallery, a Romance. 1808. (F)
    Cabinet, 3 (Mar. 1808), 189-90.

    London; or, Truth without Treason. 1809. (F)
    Critical Review, s3,v17 (June 1809), 179-82.
    Lady's Monthly Museum, ns,v6 (June 1809), 318.

Lathy, Thomas Pike.
    Usurpation; or the Inflexible Uncle. 1805. (F)
    Literary Journal, a Review..., 5 (Mar. 1805), 321.

    The Paraclete. 1805. (F)
    Literary Journal, a Review..., 5 (Aug. 1805), 887.
    Monthly Mirror, 20 (Nov. 1805), 325.

    The Invisible Enemy; or, the Mines of Wielitska. A Polish
    Romance. 1806. (F)
    Critical Review, s3,v9 (Nov. 1806), 328.
    Literary Journal, ns,v2 (Sept. 1806), 334-35.
    Monthly Literary Recreations, 1 (Sept. 1806), 240.
    Monthly Mirror, ns,v1 (Jan. 1807), 47.

    Gabriel Forrester; or, the Deserted Son. 1807. (F)
    Critical Review, s3,v12 (Nov. 1807), 331-34.
    Monthly Magazine, Suppl. v24 (Jan. 30, 1808), 630.
    Monthly Review, ns,v62 (June 1810), 213.
    Oxford Review, 2 (Oct. 1807), 433-34.

    The Angler, a Poem, in Ten Books. With Proper Instructions
    in the Art, Rules to Choosing Fishing Rods, Lines, Hooks,
    &c. 1819. (P)
    Fireside Magazine (quoting New Monthly Magazine), 1 (May
        1819), 199.

Literary Gazette, Jan. 2, 1818, p. 6.
New Monthly Magazine, 11 (Mar. 1819), 161.

Lawler, Dennis.
  Sharp and Flat, a Musical Farce. 1813. (D)
    New Review, 2 (Sept. 1813), 306-07.

Lawrence, James Henry.
  Love; an Allegory. To Which Are Added Several Poems and
  Translations. 1802. (P)
    Annual Review, 1 (1802), 662.
    Antijacobin Review, 14 (Jan. 1803), 80.
    British Critic, 20 (Dec. 1802), 676.
    British Critic, 21 (Mar. 1803), 312-13.
    Critical Review, s2,v37 (Apr. 1803), 476.
    Poetical Register, 2 (1802), 442.

  The Empire of the Nairs; or, the Rights of Women, an Utop-
  ian Romance. 1811. (F)
    British Critic, 38 (Sept. 1811), 297-98.
    Critical Review, s3,v23 (Aug. 1811), 399-403.
    Monthly Review, ns,v69 (Oct. 1812), 214-15.

  The Englishman at Verdun; or the Prisoner of Peace. 1813.
  (D)
    Antijacobin Review, 45 (Oct. 1813), 316-17.
    British Critic, 42 (July 1813), 80.
    Monthly Review, ns,v77 (July 1815), 321-22.
    New Review, 2 (Oct. 1813), 373-77.

Lawrence, Thomas Dawson.
  The Miscellaneous Productions of Thomas Dawson Lawrence.
  1806. (P)
    New Annual Register, 28 (1807), [378-79].
    Oxford Review, 1 (Mar. 1807), 328-32.

Lawson, John.
  The Maniac, with Other Poems. 1810. (P)
    Baptist Magazine, 3 (Jan. 1811), 34.
    Eclectic Review, 6 (Dec. 1810), 1137.
    Monthly Review, 64 (Feb. 1811), 214.
    Poetical Register, 8 (1810), 571.

  Orient Harping; a Desultory Poem. 1820. (P)
    Christian's Pocket Magazine, 3 (Nov. 1820), 247. (Digest-
      ed from Monthly Review.)
    Monthly Review, 93 (Sept. 1820), 97-100.

Lawton, Hugh.
  Poems. 1814. (P)
    Monthly Review, 80 (May 1816), 100-02.

Layman, A.

See Sharon Turner.

Leadbeater, Mary.
  Poems. 1808. (P)
    Annual Review, 7 (1808), 540-41.
    Antijacobin Review, 33 (May 1809), 89-90.
    Belfast Monthly Magazine, 1 (Oct. 1808), 137-40.
    British Critic, 32 (Oct. 1808), 408.
    Critical Review, s3,v15 (Oct. 1808), 217-18.
    Cyclopaedian Magazine, 2 (June 1808), 346-48.
    Eclectic Review, 4 (Sept. 1808), 815-20.
    Monthly Review, 57 (Dec. 1808), 372-74.

  Cottage Dialogues among the Irish Peasantry. With Notes
  and a Preface, by Maria Edgeworth. 1813. (Pr)
    British Review, 1 (June 1811), 399-418.
    Literary Panorama, 13 (July 1813), 927-32.

  Tales for Cottagers, Accommodated to the Present Condition
  of the Irish Peasantry. By Mary Leadbeater and Elizabeth
  Shakleton. 1814. (F)
    Monthly Review, ns,v76 (Jan. 1815), 110.
    New Monthly Magazine, 2 (Sept. 1814), 156.

Le Brun, Pigault.
  History of a Dog, Written by Himself, and Published by a
  Gentleman of His Acquaintance. Translated. 1804. (F)
    Flowers of Literature, 3 (1804), 455.

  Monsieur Botte; a Romance. 1804. (F)
    Critical Review, s3,v3 (Oct. 1804), 237.
    Literary Journal, a Review..., 2 (Sept. 1, 1803), 218.

  My Uncle Thomas. A Romance. (F)
    Critical Review, s3,v3 (Oct. 1804), 237.

Lee, Harriet. (See also Harriet and Sophia Lee.)
  Clara Lennox; or, the Distressed Widow. 1797. (F)
    Critical Review, ns,v23 (May 1798), 114-15.
    Monthly Mirror, 6 (Aug. 1798), 93.

  The Mysterious Marriage; or, the Heirship of Roselva.
  1798. (D)
    British Critic, 12 (July 1798), 73.
    Critical Review, ns,v22 (Apr. 1798), 475-76.
    Monthly Mirror, 5 (Mar. 1788), 166-69.
    Monthly Review, ns,v26 (May 1798), 96.

Lee, Harriet, and Sophia Lee.
  Canterbury Tales for the Year 1797. By Harriet Lee. 1798.
  (F)
    British Critic, 12 (Sept. 1798), 306.
    Critical Review, ns,22 (Feb. 1798), 170-73.

366

Dublin Magazine, 1 (Aug. 1798), 141.
Monthly Review, ns,v25 (Apr. 1798), 469-70.

Canterbury Tales. Volume II. By Sophia Lee. 1798. (F)
Critical Review, ns,v23 (June 1798), 204-09.
Monthly Magazine, Suppl. v5 (July 15, 1798), 509.
Monthly Review, ns,v27 (Dec. 1798), 416-19.

Canterbury Tales. Volume III. By Sophia and Harriet Lee.
1799. (F)
British Critic, 14 (Oct. 1799), 431.
Critical Review, ns,v26 (June 1799), 186-93.
Monthly Magazine, Suppl. v7 (July 20, 1799), 542.
Monthly Magazine, Suppl. v8 (Jan. 20, 1800), 1053-54.
New London Review, 2 (Aug. 1799), 181-82.

Canterbury Tales. Volume IV. By Harriet Lee. 1801. (F)
British Critic, 21 (Jan. 1803), 82.
Critical Review, ns,v33 (Oct. 1801), 207-15.
European Magazine, 41 (Mar. 1802), 201.
Monthly Review, ns,v38 (July 1802), 331-32.

Canterbury Tales. Volume V. By Harriet Lee. 1805. (F)
Annual Review, 4 (1805), 655.
Cabinet, 3 (May 1808), 335.
Literary Journal, a Review..., ns,v1 (Feb. 1806), 221.
Monthly Review, ns,v55 (Mar. 1808), 332.
New Annual Register, 26 (1805), [357].

Lee, Henry.
Dash, a Tale. 1817. 3rd ed. (P)
Antijacobin Review, 52 (May 1817), 237-38.
Gentleman's Magazine, 87[1] (June 1817), 533-34.
Literary Gazette, Aug. 30, 1817, p. 133.
Monthly Review, 84 (Oct. 1817), 210-11.

Poetic Impressions....Including the Washing-day, Brewing-
day, Quarter-day, and Saturday. 1817. (P)
Antijacobin Review, 52 (May 1817), 238-43.
La Belle Assemblée, ns,v18 (Nov. 1818), 224-26.
Critical Review, s5,v5 (May 1817), pp. 544-45.
European Magazine, 71 (May 1817), 437.
Literary Gazette, Aug. 30, 1817, pp. 133-34.
Monthly Review, 84 (Oct. 1817), 211.

Lee, Sophia. (See also Harriet Lee and Sophia Lee, above.)
The Life of a Lover, in a Series of Letters. 1804. (F)
Annual Review, 4 (1805), 653-54.
Antijacobin Review, 24 (June 1806), 136-39.
British Critic, 24 (Sept. 1804), 317-18.
Critical Review, s3,v2 (July 1804), 324-30.
Imperial Review, 2 (July 1804), 363-70.
Lady's Monthly Museum, 13 (Nov. 1804), 343.

Literary Journal, a Review..., 4 (Aug. 1804), 187-92.
Monthly Magazine, Suppl. v18 (Jan. 28, 1805), 595.
Monthly Review, ns,v45 (Dec. 1804), 359-66.
New Annual Register, 26 (1805), [357].

Lefanu, Alicia.
The Flowers; or, the Sylphid Queen. (P)
Gentleman's Magazine, 80¹ (Mar. 1810), 246.

Rosara's Chain; or the Choice of Life, a Poem. 1812. (P)
Critical Review, s4,v1 (Jan. 1812), 101-03.
Monthly Review, 68 (May 1812), 107.

Strathallan. (F)
Antijacobin Review, 52 (Apr. 1817), 126-27.
British Lady's Magazine, 4 (Dec. 1816), 387-91.

Leolin Abbey. 1819. (F)
European Magazine, 76 (Oct. 1819), 340-43.
Gentleman's Magazine, 90¹ (Mar. 1820), 247.
Monthly Review, ns,v90 (Oct. 1819), 214-15.

Lefanu, Mrs. H.
The Indian Voyage. 1804. (F)
British Critic, 24 (Nov. 1804), 560.
Imperial Review, 3 (Dec. 1804), 600.
Literary Journal, a Review..., 4 (Oct. 1804), 435.

Leftley, Charles. (See also Charles Leftley and Wm. Linley.)
An Epistle in Verse; Written from America. 1819. (P)
Monthly Review, 91 (Apr. 1820), 436-37.

Leftly, Charles, and William Linley.
Sonnets, Odes, and Other Poems, by the Late Mr. Charles
Leftley; together with a Short Account of His Life and
Writings. To Which Is Added a Poetical Collection, Consist-
ing of Elegies, Ballads, and Sketches, on Various Subjects,
Chiefly Descriptive. 1814. (P)
British Critic, ns,v6 (July 1816), 85-90.
Champion, Aug. 28, 1814, pp. 279-80.
Eclectic Review, s2,v3 (June 1815), 623-28.
Gentleman's Magazine, 85¹ (June 1815), 536-37.
Lady's Monthly Museum, s3,v11 (Jan. 1820), 42.
Literary Chronicle, 1 (Nov. 20, 1819), 421.
Monthly Review, 79 (Feb. 1816), 139-44.
New Universal Magazine, 3 (July 1815), 35-36.

Leigh, Chandos.
Juvenile Poems, and Other Pieces. 1817. (P)
Champion, Sept. 28, 1817, p. 309.
Monthly Magazine, 45 (Apr. 1818), 249.
Theatrical Inquisitor, 11 (Oct., Nov. 1817), 287-89, 353-
61.

Poesy; a Satire, with Other Poems. (Anon.) 1818. (P)
  Literary Gazette, Oct. 10, 1818, p. 643.

Leigh, Richard.
  Grieving's a Folly, a Comedy. 1809. (D)
    Le Beau Monde, 2 (Nov. 1809), 100.
    British Critic, 35 (Jan. 1810), 70-71.
    Monthly Panorama, 1 (Feb. 1810), 125.
    Poetical Register, 7 (1809), 616.
    Satirist, 9 (July 1811), 76.

  Where To Find a Friend. 1815. (D)
    Augustan Review, 2 (Jan. 1816), 55-59.
    British Lady's Magazine, 3 (Jan. 1816), 28-33.
    Critical Review, s5,v2 (Dec. 1815), 629-35.
    Monthly Review, ns,v79 (Jan. 1816), 96.
    Theatrical Inquisitor, 7 (Dec. 1815), 461.

Leigh, Sir Samuel Egerton.
  Munster Abbey, a Romance; Interspersed with Reflections on
  Virtue and Morality. 1797. (F)
    Critical Review, ns,v22 (Feb. 1798), 237-38.

Le Maistre, J. G.
  Frederic Latimer; or, the History of a Young Man of Fashion.
  (Anon.) 1799. (F)
    Critical Review, ns,v29 (Aug. 1800), 471.
    Monthly Mirror, 9 (Jan. 1800), 36.
    Monthly Review, ns,v32 (Aug. 1800), 438.

Le Mesurier, Thomas.
  Poems, Chiefly Sonnets. (Anon.) 1799. (P)
    British Critic, 18 (Dec. 1801), 661-62.
    Critical Review, s2,v34 (Apr. 1802), 473.
    Monthly Review, 36 (Oct. 1801), 145-48.

Lennox, Charlotte.
  The History of Sir George Warrington; or, the Political
  Quixote. (Anon.) 1797. (F)
    Antijacobin Review, 2 (Feb. 1799), 133-36.
    Critical Review, ns,v23 (May 1798), 112-14.
    Monthly Magazine, Suppl. v5 (July 15, 1798), 509.
    Monthly Mirror, 6 (Aug. 1798), 94.

Le Noir, Mrs. Elizabeth Anne.
  Village Anecdotes, or the Journal of a Year. 1804. (F)
    British Critic, 23 (Feb. 1804), 199-200.
    European Magazine, 45 (Mar. 1804), 190-95.
    Flowers of Literature, 3 (1804), 466-67.
    Lady's Monthly Museum, 13 (Sept. 1804), 200-01.
    Monthly Magazine, Suppl. v18 (Jan. 28, 1805), 595.
    Monthly Mirror, 17 (Mar. 1804), 175.
    Monthly Review, ns,v47 (June 1805), 207.

Monthly Visitor, ns,v6 (Mar. 1804), 316.

Clara de Montfier, a Moral Tale. 1809. (F)
  Critical Review, s3,v20 (Aug. 1810), 442.

Leonard, Eliza Lucy.
  The Ruby Ring; or the Transformations. 1816. (P)
    Gentleman's Magazine, 86^2 (Nov. 1816), 442.
    Monthly Review, 83 (May 1817), 97.
    New Monthly Magazine, 5 (July 1816), 537-38.

Lester, Elizabeth B.
  The Quakers. A Tale. 1817. (F)
    Monthly Review, ns,v85 (Mar. 1818), 329.

Lettice, John.
  Fables for the Fire-Side. 1812. (P)
    Augustan Review, 1 (Sept. 1815), 520-22.
    British Critic, 41 (May 1813), 419-20.
    European Magazine, 66 (July 1814), 40-42.

Letts, Charles, Jr.
  Emma, or the Dying Penitent. 1799. (P)
    British Critic, 15 (Apr. 1800), 430.
    Critical Review, s2,v28 (Feb. 1800), 232-33.
    Monthly Review, 31 (Mar. 1800), 320.

Lewes, John Lee.
  Poems. (P)
    Gentleman's Magazine, 82^1 (May 1812), 454-57.

  National Melodies, and Other Poems. (P)
    New Monthly Magazine, 7 (Apr. 1817), 250.

Lewis, Matthew Gregory.
  Ambrosio; or the Monk, a Romance. 1798. 4th ed. (F)
    Monthly Mirror, 5 (Mar. 1798), 157-58.

  The Castle Spectre, a Drama. 1798. (D)
    Analytical Review, 28 (Aug. 1798), 179-91.
    British Critic, 11 (Apr. 1798), 436-37.
    Critical Review, ns,v22 (Apr. 1798), 476-78.
    Monthly Magazine, Suppl. v5 (July 15, 1798), 508.
    Monthly Magazine, Suppl. v6 (1798), 515.
    Monthly Mirror, 5 (Feb. 1798), 106-09.
    Monthly Review, ns,v26 (May 1798), 96.
    Monthly Visitor, 3 (Jan. 1798), 105-08.

  The Love of Gain: A Poem. 1799. (P)
    Analytical Review, ns,v1 (May 1799), 522-24.
    British Critic, 13 (May 1799), 547-49.
    Critical Review, s2,v27 (Oct. 1799), 231.
    Monthly Magazine, Suppl. v7 (July 20, 1799), 536.

Lewis, Matthew Gregory (continued)
    Monthly Mirror, 7 (Mar. 1799), 165.
    Monthly Review, 30 (Sept. 1799), 22-25.
    New Annual Register, 20 (1799), [263].
    New London Review, 1 (Mar. 1799), 299-300.

    Rolla; or the Peruvian Hero, a Tragedy. 1799. (D)
    Monthly Mirror, 11 (Feb. 1801), 111-12.

    The East Indian, a Comedy. 1800. (D)
        British Critic, 15 (Mar. 1800), 317-18.
        Monthly Magazine, Suppl. v9 (July 20, 1800), 641.
        Monthly Review, ns,v32 (July 1800), 255-58.
        New London Review, 3 (Feb. 1800), 183.

    Tales of Wonder. 1800. (P)
        Antijacobin Review, 8 (Mar. 1801), 322-27.
        British Critic, 16 (Dec. 1800), 681.
        Critical Review, s2,v34 (Jan. 1802), 111-12.
        Monthly Magazine, Suppl. v11 (July 20, 1801), 605-06.
        Poetical Register, 1 (1801), 436.

    Adelmorn, the Outlaw. A Romantic Drama. 1801. (D)
        British Critic, 18 (Nov. 1801), 545.
        Critical Review, ns,v34 (Feb. 1802), 231-32.
        Poetical Register, 1 (1801), 462-63.

    Tales of Terror. (Anon.) 1801. (P)
        British Critic, 17 (June 1801), 649.
        Critical Review, s2,v34 (Jan. 1802), 112-14.
        Poetical Register, 1 (1801), 437.

    Alfonso, King of Castile, a Tragedy. 1801. (D)
        Annual Review, 1 (1802), 685-88.
        British Critic, 20 (Nov. 1802), 558-59.
        Critical Review, ns,v34 (Mar. 1802), 355.
        Edinburgh Review, 1 (Jan. 1803), 314-17.
        Monthly Mirror, 13 (June 1802), 410-11.
        Poetical Register, 1 (1801), 461.

    The Bravo of Venice. A Romance, Translated from the Ger-
    man. 1805. (F)
        Flowers of Literature, 5 (1806), 498.
        Monthly Magazine, Suppl. v20 (Jan. 31, 1806), 616.

    Rugatino, or the Brave of Venice. 1805. (D)
        Critical Review, s3,v8 (May 1806), 99.
        Monthly Magazine, Suppl. v21 (July 25, 1806), 609.
        Poetical Register, 5 (1805), 508.

    Adelgitha; or, the Fruits of a Single Error, a Tragedy.
    1806. (D)
        La Belle Assemblée, Suppl. v2 (1807), 34-37.

Lewis, Matthew Gregory (concluded)
   British Critic, 31 (June 1808), 661-62.
   Critical Review, s3,v11 (May 1807), 108-09.
   Monthly Review, ns,v50 (July 1806), 329.
   Poetical Register, 6 (1806), 527.

   Feudal Tyrants; or, the Counts of Carlsheim and Sargans.
   A Romance. Taken from the German. 1807. (F)
   Flowers of Literature, 5 (1806), 501-02.
   Literary Journal, a Review..., ns,v2 (Nov. 1806), 480-85.
   Monthly Literary Recreations, 1 (Nov. 1806), 405.
   Oxford Review, 1 (Jan. 1807), 71-72.

   Romantic Tales. 1808. (F)
   Annual Review, 7 (1808), 616-18.
   British Critic, 33 (Mar. 1809), 247-54.
   Cabinet, ns,v1 (Mar., Apr. 1809), 246-49, 338-43.
   Critical Review, s3,v15 (Dec. 1808), 355-66.
   Gentleman's Magazine, 79¹ (Feb. 1809), 141-44.
   Satirist, 3 (Nov. 1808), 409-15.

   Venoni, or the Novice of St. Mark's: A Drama. 1809. (D)
   Le Beau Monde, 2 (Nov. 1808), 100-01.
   British Critic, 36 (Aug. 1810), 183-84.
   Monthly Panorama, 1 (Feb. 1810), 125-27.
   Poetical Register, 7 (1809), 617.

   Monody on the Death of Sir John Moore. (P)
   Monthly Review, 61 (Feb. 1810), 207-08.
   Poetical Register, 7 (1809), 600-01.

   One O'Clock! or, the Knight and the Wood Daemon. A Grand
   Musical Romance. 1811. (D)
   British Critic, 40 (Dec. 1812), 639-40.
   Poetical Register, 8 (1811), 640-41.

Lewis, William.
   The Bard's Lament, a Vision, and Other Poems, Sacred to the
   Memory of the Princess Charlotte. 1818. (P)
   La Belle Assemblée, ns,v17 (Jan. 1818), 33-34.
   British Lady's Magazine, ns,v2 (Apr. 1818), 170-71.
   European Magazine, 73 (Jan. 1818), 52-53.
   Literary Panorama, ns,v7 (Mar. 1818), 940-41.
   Monthly Review, 85 (Jan. 1818), 103.
   New Monthly Magazine, 9 (Mar. 1818), 153.

Leyburn, T.
   Occasional Address...on the Opening of the Odechorologeum,
   at the Argyle Rooms. (P)
   Literary Panorama, 7 (Mar. 1810), 1191-93.

Leyden, John.
   Scenes of Infancy, Descriptive of Teviotdale. 1803. (P)

Annual Review, 2 (1803), 563.
British Critic, 23 (May 1804), 483-88.
Imperial Review, 2 (Aug. 1804), 515-21.
Lady's Monthly Museum, 13 (July 1804), 57-58.
Literary Journal, 2 (Dec. 16, 1803), 652-53.
Monthly Review, 45 (Sept. 1804), 62-65.
New Annual Register, 24 (1803), [328].
North British Magazine, 1 (Feb., Mar. 1804), 121-24, 169-74.
Poetical Register, 3 (1803), 446.

The Poetical Remains of the Late Dr. John Leyden, with Memoirs of His Life. By the Rev. James Morton. 1819. (P)
Antijacobin Review, 58 (Aug. 1820), 540-48.
Blackwood's Edinburgh Magazine, 5 (Apr. 1819), 3-8.
Eclectic Review, s2,v12 (Sept. 1819), 275-86.
Edinburgh Monthly Review, 2 (July 1819), 48-57.
Fireside Magazine (quoting Edinburgh Monthly Review), 1 (Aug. 1819), 317.
Monthly Review, 91 (Jan. 1820), 61-68.

Liardet, Wilbraham.
The Case of the Hypochondriac Explained, and the Cure Made Known.... 1806. (P)
Critical Review, s3,v9 (Oct. 1806), 217.
Monthly Mirror, 22 (Dec. 1806), 398-99.
Monthly Review, 53 (Aug. 1807), 438.

Fifty of Aesop's Fables Rendered into Verse. (P)
Monthly Review, 54 (Oct. 1807), 211.

Lickbarrow, Isabella.
Poetical Effusions. 1814. (P)
Monthly Review, 76 (Feb. 1815), 211.

Liddiard, Mrs. J. S. Anna.
Poems. 1810. (P)
Hibernia Magazine, 2 (July 1810), 59.
Political Guardian, 1 (July, Aug. 1810), 25-27, 54-56.

The Sgelaighe; or, a Tale of Old, with a Second Edition of "Poems," Published in Dublin, and Additions. 1811. (P)
Critical Review, s4,v1 (Jan. 1812), 108.
Monthly Review, 67 (Mar. 1812), 323.
Poetical Register, 8 (1811), 620.

Kenilworth, a Mask. 1815. (P)
Monthly Review, 78 (Dec. 1815), 431-32.

Theodore and Laura, a Tale. 1816. (P)
Monthly Review, 80 (June 1816), 207-08.

Mount Leinster; or, the Prospect: A Poem Descriptive of

Irish Scenery. (Anon.) (P)
  Dublin Magazine, 1 (Apr. 1820), 316-17.
  Gentleman's Magazine, 90[1] (Suppl. Jan.-June 1820), 616.
  Monthly Review, 92 (June 1820), 209-10.
  New Monthly Magazine, 12 (Nov. 1819), 454-55.

Liddiard, Rev. William.
  The Life-Boat; or, Dillon O'Dwire, a Poem. 1815. (P)
    Monthly Review, 79 (Feb. 1816), 208-10.

  Mont St. Jean, a Poem. (P)
    Monthly Review, 80 (June 1816), 207-08.

Linley, William. (See also Charles Leftley and Wm. Linley.)
  Forbidden Apartments. A Tale. 1800. (F)
    Critical Review, ns,v32 (June 1801), 231.

Linn, John Blair.
  The Power of Genius, a Poem. 1804. (P)
    Annual Review, 3 (1804), 571.
    Antijacobin Review, 18 (July 1804), 306-07.
    British Critic, 25 (Mar. 1805), 316-17.
    Critical Review, s3,v5 (May 1805), 29-36.
    Eclectic Review, 1 (Jan. 1805), 54-59.
    Evangelical Magazine, 12 (Aug. 1804), 373-74.
    Monthly Magazine, Suppl. v19 (July 28, 1805), 658.
    Monthly Review, 45 (Nov. 1804), 319-20.
    Monthly Visitor, ns,v7 (May-Aug. 1804), 13-15, 113-15,
      221-27, 333-36.
    Poetical Register, 4 (1804), 490-91.
    Universal Magazine, ns,v1 (June 1804), 608-10.

Linwood, Mary.
  Leicestershire Tales. 1808. (F)
    Monthly Magazine, Suppl. v26 (Jan. 30, 1809), 636.
    Monthly Review, ns,v60 (Sept. 1809), 96.
    Satirist, 4 (Jan. 1809), 85-87.

  The Anglo-Cambrian, a Poem. 1818. (P)
    La Belle Assemblée, 18 (Suppl. 1818), 342-44.
    Fireside Magazine (quoting Monthly Magazine), 1 (Jan.
      1819), 37.
    Literary Gazette, Nov. 21, 1818, pp. 739-40.
    Monthly Magazine, 46 (Dec. 1818), 444.
    Monthly Review, 90 (Dec. 1819), 433-34.

Lister.
  Veronica; or, the Mysterious Stranger. (F)
    New London Review, 1 (Apr. 1799), 405.

Little, Thomas.
  See Thomas Moore.

Littlejohn, P.
  The Mistake; or, Something beyond a Joke. 1800. (F)
    Critical Review, ns,v31 (Mar. 1801), 355.
    Monthly Mirror, 11 (Apr. 1801), 256.
    Monthly Review, ns,v35 (July 1801), 331-32.

Littleton, Mr. _____.
  The German Sorceress; a Romance. (F)
    Monthly Register, 3 (Sept. 1803), 182.

Llewellen, Mrs. S.
  Read, and Give It a Name. 1814. (F)
    Critical Review, s5,v1 (Mar. 1815), 313.
    Monthly Review, ns,v75 (Dec. 1814), 434-35.

Lloyd, Charles. (Also see Charles Lloyd and Charles Lamb.)
  Edmund Oliver. 1798. (F)
    Analytical Review, 27 (June 1798), 638-43.
    Antijacobin Review, 1 (Aug. 1798), 176-80.
    British Critic, 15 (June 1800), 675-76.
    Critical Review, ns,v23 (July 1798), 302-06.
    Monthly Magazine, Suppl. v6 (1798), 517.
    Scientific Magazine (Freemason's Magazine), 11 (Aug.
      1798), 128.

  Lines Suggested by the Fast, Appointed on Wednesday, Febru-
  ary 27, 1799. 1799. (P)
    Analytical Review, ns,v1 (Mar. 1799), 316-17.
    Antijacobin Review, 2 (Apr. 1799), 428-33.
    British Critic, 14 (Aug. 1799), 186.
    Critical Review, s3,v26 (May 1799), 111.
    Monthly Magazine, Suppl. v7 (July 20, 1799), 536.
    Monthly Review, 29 (May 1799), 98-99.

  Nugae Canorae. Poems by Charles Lloyd. 1819. (P)
    Blackwood's Edinburgh Magazine, 6 (Nov. 1819), 154-62.
    Champion, Oct. 17, 1819, pp. 665-66.
    Examiner, Oct. 24, 1819, pp. 685-86.
    Monthly Review, 92 (July 1820), 284-94.

  Isabel, a Tale. (F)
    Champion, Jan. 2, 1820, p. 12.
    Examiner, Mar. 19, 1820, p. 190.
    Monthly Review, ns,v92 (July 1820), 284-94.

  Desultory Thoughts in London, Titus and Gisippus, with
  Other Poems. 1821. (P)
    Literary Gazette, Dec. 30, 1820, pp. 835-36.

Lloyd, Charles, and Charles Lamb.
  Poems, by S. T. Coleridge, Second Edition. To Which Are
  Now Added Poems by Charles Lamb and Charles Lloyd. 1797.
  (P)

375

Critical Review, s2,v23 (July 1798), 266-68.
Freemason's Magazine, 1 (Aug. 1798), 128.

Blank Verse. By Charles Lloyd and Charles Lamb. 1798. (P)
Analytical Review, 27 (May 1798), 522-23.
British Critic, 11 (June 1798), 678.
Critical Review, s2,v24 (Oct. 1798), 232-34.
European Magazine, 33 (May 1798), 329.
Monthly Magazine, Suppl. v5 (July 15, 1798), 507.
Monthly Mirror, 6 (Aug. 1798), 97.
Monthly Review, 27 (Sept. 1798), 104-05.
New Annual Register, 19 (1798), [309].

Lloyd, Rev. David.
Characteristics of Men, Manners, and Sentiments; or the
Voyage of Life. The Second Edition Revised, and Other
Poems. (P)
British Critic, 41 (Feb. 1813), 188-89.
Eclectic Review, 10 (Dec. 1813), 601-10.

Lloyd, Mary.
Brighton, a Poem, Descriptive of the Place and Parts Adja-
cent; and Other Poems. 1809. (P)
British Critic, 36 (Oct. 1810), 406-07.
Critical Review, s3,v18 (Sept. 1809), 106-07.
Monthly Review, 60 (Sept. 1809), 101-03.
Poetical Register, 7 (1809), 599.

Llwyd, Richard.
Beaumaris Bay, a Poem; with Notes Descriptive and Explana-
tory, Particulars of the Druids.... 1800. (P)
Annals of Philosophy, 1 (1801), 292.
Antijacobin Review, 6 (May 1800), 82.
British Critic, 15 (June 1800), 672.
Critical Review, s2,v29 (June 1800), 235-36.
Gentleman's Magazine, 71^1 (Jan. 1801), 63.
Monthly Magazine, Suppl. v10 (Jan. 20, 1801), 610.
Monthly Review, 32 (July 1800), 318-19.

Gayton Wake; or, Mary Dod, and Her List of Merits. 1804.
(P)
Antijacobin Review, 19 (Nov. 1804), 300.
Critical Review, s3,v4 (Mar. 1805), 326.
Monthly Review, 50 (Aug. 1806), 432.

Poems, Tales, Odes, Sonnets, Translations from the British
&c., &c. 1804. (P)
Annual Review, 3 (1804), 598.
Critical Review, s3,v5 (May 1805), 103-04.
Gentleman's Magazine, 75^2 (Oct. 1805), 941-42.
Monthly Review, 50 (Aug. 1806), 432-34.
Poetical Register, 4 (1804), 491.

Lobb, Richard.
  The Contemplative Philosopher; or, Short Essays on the Various Objects of Nature.... (Anon.) (P)
    Universal Theological Magazine, 3 (Jan. 1805), 47-53.

Lockhart, John Gibson, and John Wilson (Christopher North).
  Peter's Letters to His Kinsfolk. (Anon.) 1819. (F)
    British Lady's Magazine, s3,v3 (Nov. 1819), 228-30.
    Literary Chronicle, 1 (Aug. 7-21, 1819), 179-81, 197-99, 215-18.
    Literary Gazette, July 31, 1819, pp. 481-84.

Lofft, Capel.
  Laura; or, an Anthology of Sonnets (on the Petrarcan Model) and Elegiac Quatuorzains, English, Italian, Spanish..... 1814. (P)
    Augustan Review, 3 (Nov. 1816), 524-26.
    Critical Review, s4,v6 (Aug. 1814), 204-05.
    Eclectic Review, s2,v2 (Nov. 1814), 502-13.
    Gentleman's Magazine, 84^2 (Nov. 1814), 452-54.
    Literary Panorama, ns,v1 (Oct. 1814), 64-71.
    Monthly Review, 78 (Oct. 1815), 186-96.

Longshanks, Henry.
  Harry Dee; or, the Scotchman Detected. 1805. (P)
    British Critic, 26 (Dec. 1805), 666-67.
    Monthly Mirror, 20 (Aug. 1805), 114.
    Monthly Review, 47 (July 1805), 331.

Louis.
  Sonnets and Other Metrical Pieces. (P)
    Critical Review, s3,v19 (Mar. 1810), 334.

Lowe, John, Jr.
  Poems. 1803. (P)
    British Critic, 21 (Apr. 1803), 433.
    Critical Review, s2,v38 (June 1803), 197-201.
    Monthly Magazine, Suppl. v15 (July 28, 1803), 637.
    Monthly Review, 41 (May 1803), 100-01.

Lowe, Richard.
  Verses on the Death of the Late Right Honourable Horatio Nelson.... 1806. (P)
    Critical Review, s3,v7 (Mar. 1806), 333-35.
    Lady's Monthly Museum, 16 (May 1806), 347.
    Poetical Register, 6 (1806), 518.

Lowth, Robert.
  Billesdon Coplow. (Anon.) 1804. (P)
    Critical Review, s3,v4 (Mar. 1805), 326.
    Literary Journal, a Review..., 4 (Nov. 1804), 536.

Lucas, Rev. Charles.

The Castle of St. Donats; or, the History of Jack Smith.
1798. (F)
  Analytical Review, ns,v1 (Jan. 1799), 100.
  Critical Review, ns,v26 (July 1799), 357.
  Monthly Magazine, Suppl. v7 (July 20, 1799), 541.
  Monthly Review, ns,v29 (May 1799), 89-90.

The Infernal Quixote; a Tale of the Day. 1800. (F)
  Antijacobin Review, 7 (Dec. 1800), 416.
  Critical Review, ns,v37 (Sept. 1801), 113.

The Abyssinian Reformer, or the Bible and the Sabre. 1808.
(F)
  Critical Review, s3,v14 (June 1808), 186-90.
  Monthly Review, ns,v62 (June 1810), 212-13.

Poems on Various Subjects. 1810. (P)
  British Critic, 38 (Oct. 1811), 408.
  Monthly Review, 65 (July 1811), 332-34.
  Poetical Register, 8 (1810), 554-55.

Joseph, a Religious Poem. Historical, Patriarchal, and
Typical. 1811. (P)
  British Critic, 39 (Feb. 1812), 189-90.
  Eclectic Review, 10 (Dec. 1813), 601-10.
  Monthly Review, 72 (Dec. 1813), 411-20.

Gwelygordd; or the Child of Sin. 1820. By the Author of
The Infernal Quixote, The Abyssinian Reformer, &c. (F)
  Antijacobin Review, 59 (Nov. 1820), 237-45.

Lucas, William.
  The Fate of Bertha. A Poem. 1800. (P)
    Antijacobin Review, 8 (Jan. 1801), 64.
    British Critic, 18 (Aug. 1801), 196.
    Critical Review, s2,v32 (June 1801), 227.
    Gentleman's Magazine, 71² (Oct. 1801), 920.
    Monthly Mirror, 12 (Sept. 1801), 180.
    Monthly Review, 35 (July 1801), 327.

  The Duellists; or, Men of Honour. A Story, Calculated to
  Shew the Folly, Extravagance, and Sin of Duelling. 1805.
  (F)
    Annual Review, 4 (1805), 655.
    Antijacobin Review, 22 (Sept. 1805), 86.
    Antijacobin Review, 22 (Dec. 1805), 422.
    British Critic, 26 (Oct. 1805), 441-42.
    Critical Review, s3,v6 (Oct. 1805), 218.
    Eclectic Review, 2 (Feb. 1806), 153-55.
    Flowers of Literature, 4 (1805), 420.
    Lady's Monthly Museum, 16 (Jan. 1806), 54.
    Literary Journal, a Review..., 5 (Aug. 1805), 886-87.
    Monthly Mirror, 20 (Oct. 1805), 258.

Monthly Review, ns,v51 (Nov. 1806), 335-36.

The Travels of Humanius in Search of the Temple of Happiness, an Allegory. 1809. (F?)
   Critical Review, s3,v17 (Aug. 1809), 439-40.
   Literary Panorama, 6 (July 1809), 689.

Lucian, Lory, and Jerry Juvenal.
  British Purity; or the World We Live In. 1804. (P)
   Annual Review, 3 (1804), 575.
   Critical Review, s3,v3 (Nov. 1804), 357-58.
   Imperial Review, 3 (Dec. 1804), 603.
   Monthly Mirror, 18 (Dec. 1804), 390-92.
   New Annual Register, 25 (1804), ⌊354⌋.
   Poetical Register, 4 (1804), 502.

Lumpwitz, Professor.
  See Henry William Bunbury.

Luttrell, Henry.
  Lines Written at Ampthill Park. (Anon.) 1819. (P)
   Literary Gazette, Mar. 27, 1819, p. 193.
   Monthly Review, 88 (Apr. 1819), 433-36.

  Advice to Julia. A Letter in Rhyme. (Anon.) 1820. (P)
   Blackwood's Edinburgh Magazine, 7 (Aug. 1820), 520-27.
   Edinburgh Monthly Review, 4 (Dec. 1820), 665-73.
   European Magazine, 78 (Nov. 1820), 440-41.
   Literary Chronicle, 2 (Sept. 2, 1820), 561-63.
   Literary Gazette, July 8, 1820, pp. 435-37.
   (Gold's) London Magazine, 2 (Sept. 1820), 285-91.
   New Hibernian Magazine, 1 (Aug. 1820), 108-11.
   New Monthly Magazine, 14 (Aug. 1820), 151-53.
   Quarterly Review, 23 (July 1820), 505-10.

Lyon, Emma.
  Miscellaneous Poems. 1812. (P)
   Critical Review, s4,v2 (Aug. 1812), 216.
   Monthly Review, 70 (Feb. 1813), 213-14.

Lysaght, Mr. _____.
  Mr. Lysaght's Poems. (P)
   Hibernia Magazine, 3 (June 1811), 372.

Lyttleton, Mr. _____.
  Fiesco, Count of Lavagne. An Historical Novel. (F)
   Literary Journal, a Review..., 5 (Mar. 1805), 321.

  The Lottery of Life, or the Romance of a Summer. 1802. (F)
   Critical Review, ns,v38 (May 1803), 115.
   Monthly Magazine, Suppl. v15 (July 28, 1803), 639.
   New Annual Register, 23 (1802), ⌊322⌋.

M., E.
See Edward Mangin.

M_____, J_____.
Atys, or Human Weakness. A Poetical Essay. (P)
British Critic, 17 (Jan. 1801), 80-81.
Monthly Mirror, 11 (Jan. 1801), 38.
Monthly Review, 33 (Dec. 1800), 428-29.

M____d, J.
The Life of Napoleon, as It Should Be Handed Down to Pos-
terity. 1804. (F)
Antijacobin Review, 18 (Aug. 1814), 397-98.
British Critic, 24 (Aug. 1804), 198-99.

M_____, Lady.
See Catherine Rebecca, Lady Manners.

M., P. S.
Parental Duplicity; or the Power of Artifice. 1797. (F)
Analytical Review, 27 (Jan. 1798), 83-84.
British Critic, 11 (June 1798), 681.
Monthly Mirror, 5 (June 1799), 351.
Monthly Review, ns,v26 (May 1798), 106.

Mac, Theophilus.
Edward the Second, a Tragedy, and Other Poems. 1809. (D-P)
British Critic, 36 (Nov. 1810), 522-23.
Poetical Register, 8 (1810), 592-93.

McCarthy, Eugene.
The Battle of Waterloo; or, Buonaparte Defeated, a Dramatic
Sketch. (D)
Theatrical Inquisitor, 8 (June 1816), 451-52.

MacCarthy, George, Jr.
The Rise and Progress of Sunday Schools....Together with
a General View of the Benefits Resulting from Their Influence on the Habits of the Poor.... 1816. (P)
Monthly Review, 83 (May 1817), 61-63.

MacCarthy, Thomas.
Montalto; or, the Heart Unveiled. 1819. (P)
Literary Journal and General Miscellany, 2 (Feb. 27,
1819), 134-35.
Monthly Review, 90 (Oct. 1819), 213-14.

Maccauley, Miss E.
Effusions of Fancy; Consisting of the Birth of Friendship,
the Birth of Affection, and the Birth of Sensibility.
1812. (P)
British Critic, 41 (May 1813), 421-22.
Gentleman's Magazine, 82^2 (Nov. 1812), 455-56.

Monthly Review, 69 (Dec. 1812), 432.

Theatric Revolution; or, Plain Truth, Addressed to Common
Sense. 1819. (P)
    British Stage and Literary Cabinet, 3 (June 1819), 169-70.

McCreery, John.
    The Press: A Poem. Published as a Specimen of Topography.
    1803. (P)
        Annual Review, 2 (1803), 591.
        British Critic, 23 (Apr. 1804), 432-33.
        Flowers of Literature, 3 (1804), 461.
        Literary Journal, a Review..., 2 (Dec. 31, 1803), 725-26.
        Monthly Magazine, Suppl. v17 (July 28, 1804), 666.
        Monthly Review, 43 (Apr. 1804), 403-07.
        Poetical Register, 3 (1803), 439-40.

Macdonald, W. P.
    The Moneiad; or, the Power of Money. 1818. (P)
        Literary Journal, and General Miscellany, 1 (Apr. 19,
        1818), 53-54.

    The Influence of Wealth on Human Happiness. 1819. (P)
        Literary Chronicle, 1 (Aug. 7, 1819), 181-82.

Macdonald, William Russell.
    A Paraphrase on the Economy of Human Life. (P)
        Literary Gazette, Mar. 21, 1818, pp. 182-83.

M'Henry, James.
    The Bard of Erin, and Other Poems, Mostly National. (P)
        Belfast Monthly Magazine, 2 (Feb. 1809), 136-38.

M'Kenzie, Andrew.
    Poems and Songs on Different Subjects. 1810. (P)
        Belfast Monthly Magazine, 5 (Nov. 1810), 373-75.

Mackenzie, Anna Maria.
    Dusseldorf; or, the Fraticide. A Romance. 1798. (F)
        Critical Review, ns,v24 (Oct. 1798), 236.
        Monthly Magazine, Suppl. v6 (1798), 517.
        Monthly Mirror, 6 (Nov. 1798), 293.
        Scientific Magazine (Freemason's Magazine), 11 (Dec.
        1798), 466.

    Martin and Mansfeldt; or, the Romance of Franconia. (F)
        Annual Review, 1 (1802), 726.

Mackenzie, Sir George Stewart.
    An Essay on Some Subjects Connected with Taste. 1817. (Pr)
        British Critic, ns,v1 (Feb. 1818), 143-57.
        Literary and Statistical Magazine, 2 (Nov. 1818), 419-28.

Mackenzie, Mary Jane.
  Geraldine; or, Modes of Faith and Practice. (Anon.) 1820.
  (F)
    Lady's Monthly Museum, s3,v12 (July 1820), 33-35.
    Monthly Magazine, 49 (Apr. 1820), 262.
    Monthly Review, ns,v92 (Aug. 1820), 412-18.

Mackenzie, William.
  The Sorrows of Seduction; with Other Poems. (Anon.) 1805.
  (P)
    British Critic, 25 (Apr. 1805), 439-40.
    British Critic, 27 (Feb. 1806), 186. (2nd ed.)
    Critical Review, s3,v5 (May 1805), 104.
    Eclectic Review, 1 (May 1805), 355-57.
    European Magazine, 47 (Apr. 1805), 288.
    Gentleman's Magazine, 76[1] (Feb. 1806), 144-45.
    Lady's Monthly Museum, 14 (June 1805), 419.
    Monthly Mirror, 19 (Apr. 1805), 256-57.
    Monthly Mirror, 21 (Jan. 1806), 41. (2nd ed.)
    Monthly Review, 50 (June 1806), 208.
    Poetical Register, 6 (1806), 505-06.
    Repository of Arts, 3 (May 1810), 316.
    Universal Magazine, ns,v4 (July 1805), 50-52.
    Universal Magazine, ns,v13 (Apr. 1810), 307-09.

Mackey, Mrs. Mary.
  The Scraps of Nature. A Poem. 1810. (P)
    British Stage and Literary Cabinet, 1 (Sept. 1817), 210-
    12.

Macklin, Andrew.
  The Counterfeit, a Farce. (D)
    Annual Review, 3 (1804), 605.

MacLaurin, John.
  The Works of the Late John MacLaurin. 1798. (P)
    Critical Review, s2,v25 (Apr. 1799), 435-42.

M'Mullan, Mrs. _____.
  The Naiad's Wreath. 1816. (P)
    British Lady's Magazine, 5 (Feb. 1817), 89-94.
    Monthly Review, 82 (Feb. 1817), 212-13.

  The Crescent; a National Poem, to Commemorate the Glorious
  Victory at Algiers. (P)
    British Lady's Magazine, 5 (Feb. 1817), 89-94.
    Literary Gazette, May 10, 1817, p. 244.
    Monthly Review, 86 (May 1818), 100.

  Britain; or, Fragments of Poetical Aberration. (P)
    La Belle Assemblée, ns,v17 (May 1818), 226-27.
    Literary Gazette, June 6, 1818, p. 357.
    Monthly Review, 89 (Aug. 1819), 434-35.

Monody on the Lamented Demise of His Late Majesty, and His
Royal Highness the Duke of Kent. 1820. (P)
  Literary Gazette, Feb. 12, 1820, p. 103.

Macneill, Hector.
  The Links o' Forth; or, a Parting Peep at the Carse o'
  Stirling; a Plaint. 1799. (P)
    British Critic, 15 (Apr. 1800), 430.
    Critical Review, s2,v27 (Dec. 1799), 470-71.
    European Magazine, 36 (Oct. 1799), 254.
    Lady's Monthly Museum, 3 (Nov. 1799), 403.
    Monthly Magazine, Suppl. v9 (July 20, 1800), 640.
    Monthly Review, 31 (Mar. 1800), 324.

  The Poetical Works of Hector Macneill. 1001. (P)
    Critical Review, s2,v34 (Mar. 1802), 289-96.
    Eclectic Review, 3 (Feb. 1807), 170-72.
    Monthly Magazine, Suppl. v13 (July 20, 1802), 658.
    Monthly Visitor, 14 (Sept. 1801), 99.
    Poetical Register, 1 (1801), 426-27.
    Union Magazine and Imperial Register, 3 (May 1802), 327-
    29.

  Memoirs of the Life and Character of Gilbert Purring, the
  Younger, of Caernarvon; with Important Observations on Modern Fashionable Education. (Anon.) (F)
    Literary Journal, a Review..., 5 (May 1805), 548.

  The Pastoral; or, Lyric Muse of Scotland. 1808. (P)
    British Critic, 34 (Dec. 1809), 586-96.
    Critical Review, s3,v17 (May 1809), 67-73.
    Poetical Register, 7 (1808), 549.
    Scots Magazine, 71 (Jan. 1809), 38-42.

  Town Fashions, or Modern Manners Delineated; a Satirical
  Dialogue; with James and Mary, a Rural Tale. (Anon.) (P)
    Poetical Register, 8 (1810), 586.
    Scots Magazine, 72 (Mar. 1810), 201-05.

  Bygane Times, and the Late Come Changes; or, a Bridge
  Street Dialogue, in Scottish Verse. (Anon.) (P)
    Poetical Register, 8 (1811), 634-35.
    Scots Magazine, 73 (Jan. 1811), 42-46.

  The Scottish Adventures, or the Way to Rise; an Historical
  Tale. 1812. (F)
    Monthly Review, ns,v68 (May 1812), 108-09.
    Scots Magazine, 74 (Feb. 1812), 127-31.

Macquin, Abbe Ange-Denis.
  Tabella Cibaria; or the Bill of Fare...Relating to the
  Pleasures of Gastronomy, and the Mysterious Art of Cook-
  ery. (Anon.) 1820. (P)

Blackwood's Edinburgh Magazine, 7 (Sept. 1820), 667-74.
British Critic, ns,v14 (Aug. 1820), 185-89.
New Monthly Magazine, 14 (Sept. 1820), 336.

Macro.
The Scotiad, or Wise Men of the North!!! A Serio-Comic and
Satiric Poem. 1809. (P)
    British Critic, 34 (Nov. 1809), 520.
    Poetical Register, 7 (1809), 609.

Maddocks, Rodrigo.
The Damnation of Ruvomisha. 1811. (P)
    Scourge, 1 (May 1811), 367-71.

Major, Henry.
Egbert and Birtha, a Tale. (P)
    Ireland's Mirror, 2 (June 1805), 309-11.

Malcolm, David.
The Sorrows of Love, a Poem. (Anon.) 1802. (P)
    Annual Review, 1 (1802), 659.
    British Critic, 20 (Sept. 1802), 318-19.
    Critical Review, s2,v34 (Mar. 1802), 354.
    Monthly Magazine, Suppl. v14 (Jan. 25, 1803), 597.
    Monthly Mirror, 13 (Jan. 1802), 28.
    Poetical Register, 1 (1801), 426.

Malcolm, Sir John.
Persia, a Poem. (Anon.) (P)
    New Monthly Magazine, 2 (Sept. 1814), 156.

Malden, Miriam.
Jessica Mandeville; or, the Woman of Fortitude. 1804. (F)
    Imperial Review, 3 (Dec. 1804), 601.
    Literary Journal, a Review..., 4 (Oct. 1804), 434.
    Monthly Review, ns,v47 (June 1805), 207.

Malek, Merwan Edn Abdallah.
An Elegy Supposed To Be Written in the Gardens of Ispahan.
1800. (P)
    Antijacobin Review, 7 (Nov. 1800), 318.
    British Critic, 17 (Feb. 1801), 191.
    Critical Review, s2,v31 (Feb. 1801), 228-29.
    Gentleman's Magazine, 71[1] (Jan. 1801), 59.
    Monthly Mirror, 11 (Mar. 1801), 177.
    Monthly Review, 34 (Jan. 1801), 95.

Malkin, Benjamin Heath.
Almahide and Hamet, a Tragedy. 1804. (D)
    Annual Review, 3 (1804), 605.
    British Critic, 25 (June 1805), 683-84.
    Imperial Review, 1 (Mar. 1804), 433-36.
    Monthly Magazine, Suppl. v19 (July 28, 1805), 660.

Monthly Mirror, 22 (July 1806), 42.
Monthly Review, ns,v46 (Feb. 1805), 188-92.
Poetical Register, 4 (1804), 507.

Mallet, David.
Mustapha, a Tragedy. (Anon.) 1814. 1st ed., 1739?. (D)
Antijacobin Review, 49 (Oct. 1815), 329-34.
British Critic, ns,vl (Feb. 1814), 216.
Critical Review, s4,v5 (Apr. 1814), 443-46.
Eclectic Review, ns,vl (June 1814), 631-44.
Literary Panorama, 15 (Apr. 1814), 353-54.

Mallet, Peter Paul.
See Rev. Richard Warner.

Man, Henry.
The Miscellaneous Works, in Verse and Prose, of the Late
Henry Man. (P-Pr)
Poetical Register, 2 (1802), 430.

Mandanis.
Patronage, a Poem: An Imitation of the Seventh Satire of
Juvenal. 1820. (P)
Gentleman's Magazine, 90[1] (May 1820), 440-41.
Literary Chronicle, 2 (Apr. 22, 1820), 265-66.
(Baldwin's) London Magazine, 2 (Dec. 1820), 627-28.
(Gold's) London Magazine, 1 (May 1820), 528.
Monthly Magazine, 49 (May 1820), 355-56.
Monthly Review, 93 (Oct. 1820), 213.

Mangin, Edward.
Oddities and Outlines. 1806. By E. M. (F)
Literary Journal, a Review..., ns,v2 (July 1806), 111-12.

George the Third. (Anon.) 1807. (F)
Monthly Magazine, Suppl. v24 (Jan. 30, 1808), 630.
Monthly Mirror, ns,v2 (July 1807), 35-37.
Monthly Review, ns,v56 (June 1808), 206.
Oxford Review, 2 (Aug. 1807), 190-91.
Satirist, 3 (Oct. 1808), 334.

An Essay on Light Reading, as It May Be Supposed to Influ-
ence Moral Conduct and Literary Taste. 1808. (Pr)
British Critic, 32 (Sept. 1808), 312.
Eclectic Review, 4 (Sept. 1808), 841-42.
Gentleman's Magazine, 78[2] (Oct. 1808), 914-16.
Satirist, 4 (Feb. 1809), 179-84.

Mangnall, Richmal.
Half an Hour's Lounge; or Poems. 1805. (P)
Annual Review, 4 (1805), 566.
British Critic, 27 (Jan. 1806), 79.
Literary Journal, a Review..., 5 (Dec. 1805), 1325-26.

Monthly Review, 51 (Sept. 1806), 103.
Poetical Register, 6 (1806), 512-13.

Mann, James.
  Macbeth, a Poem. (Anon.) 1817. (P)
  Monthly Review, 83 (Aug. 1817), 431-32.
  New Monthly Magazine, 7 (June 1817), 445.

Manners, Catherine Rebecca, Lady.
  Reviews of Poetry, Ancient and Modern. By Lady M******.
  1799. (P)
    Analytical Review, ns,v1 (June 1799), 623-24.
    Antijacobin Review, 3 (Aug. 1799), 435-36.
    British Critic, 15 (Apr. 1800), 428-30.
    Critical Review, s2,v26 (Aug. 1799), 476.
    Gentleman's Magazine, 69^2 (Aug. 1799), 689.
    Monthly Magazine, Suppl. v8 (Jan. 20, 1800), 1050.
    Monthly Mirror, 8 (July 1799), 28.
    Monthly Review, 30 (Dec. 1799), 390-93.
    Monthly Visitor, 9 (Feb., Mar. 1800), 215-16, 313-19.
    New Annual Register, 20 (1799), [265].
    New London Review, 3 (Apr. 1800), 375-77.

Manners, Catherine, née Pollok, later Lady Stepney.
  Castle Nuovier, or Henry and Adelina. 1806. (P)
    Literary Journal, a Review..., ns,v1 (June 1806), 671-72.
    Monthly Literary Recreations, 1 (Aug. 1806), 155.

Manners, George.
  Edgar; or Caledonian Feuds. A Tragedy. 1806. (D)
    Antijacobin Review, 25 (Dec. 1806), 425.
    Cabinet, 2 (Nov. 1807), 252.
    Critical Review, s3,v9 (Sept. 1806), 100.
    Flowers of Literature, 5 (1806), 501.
    Literary Journal, a Review..., ns,v2 (July 1806), 109.
    Monthly Magazine, Suppl. v22 (Jan. 25, 1807), 642.
    Monthly Mirror, 22 (Oct. 1808), 263.
    Monthly Review, ns,v52 (Jan. 1807), 95.
    Poetical Register, 6 (1806), 527-28.

Mannings, John Spelman.
  Cromer, a Descriptive Poem. (Anon.) 1806. (P)
    Literary Journal, a Review..., ns,v2 (Aug. 1806), 217-18.
    Monthly Mirror, 22 (Sept. 1806), 187-213 [187-89].
    Monthly Review, 51 (Nov. 1806), 332-33.
    Poetical Register, 6 (1806), 512.

Mant, Alicia Catherine.
  Ellen; or the Young Godmother, a Tale for Youth. 1814. (F)
    British Critic, ns,v3 (Mar. 1815), 313.
    Lady's Monthly Museum, s3,v3 (Apr. 1816), 222.

  Caroline Lismore; or, the Errors of Fashion. A Tale.

1815. (F)
  Critical Review, s5,v2 (Oct. 1815), 429-30.
  Lady's Monthly Museum, s3,v3 (Mar. 1816), 156.
  Literary Panorama, ns,v3 (Nov. 1815), 245-46.
  Monthly Review, ns,v79 (Jan. 1816), 102.

  Montague Newburgh, or the Mother and Son. 1817. (F)
  Critical Review, s5,v5 (Apr. 1817), 431-32.
  Gentleman's Magazine, 87[1] (Suppl., Jan.-June 1817), 612.
  Literary Panorama, ns,v6 (June 1817), 418-19.
  Monthly Review, ns,v83 (July 1817), 324.
  New Monthly Magazine, 7 (May 1817), 349.

Mant, Richard.
  Verses to the Memory of Joseph Warton. 1800. (P)
  Critical Review, s2,v31 (Feb. 1801), 230.
  Gentleman's Magazine, 71[1] (June 1801), 543.
  Monthly Magazine, Suppl. v11 (July 20, 1801), 605.
  Monthly Review, 36 (Nov. 1801), 323-24.

  Poems. 1806. (P)
  British Critic, 28 (Nov. 1806), 559-60.
  Critical Review, s3,v10 (Mar. 1807), 282-95.
  Edinburgh Review, 11 (Oct. 1807), 167-71.
  Poetical Register, 6 (1806), 507.
  Satirist, 1 (Jan. 1808), 428-29.

  The Slave, and Other Poetical Pieces; Being an Appendix to
  Poems by the Rev. Richard Mant. 1807. (P)
  Christian Observer, 6 (Feb. 1807), 124-26.
  Literary Annual Register, 2 (Feb. 1808), 77.
  New Annual Register, 28 (1807), [378].
  Oxford Review, 1 (Mar. 1807), 326-28.
  Poetical Register, 6 (1807), 548.

Marriot, John.
  A Short Account of John Marriot, Including Extracts from
  Some of His Letters, to Which Are Added Some of His Poet-
  ical Productions. 1803. (P)
  Annual Review, 2 (1803), 562.
  British Critic, 22 (Oct. 1803), 429-30.
  Critical Review, s3,v2 (June 1804), 230-33.
  Poetical Register, 3 (1803), 453.

Marshall, Thomas.
  A Poem on the Death of Admiral Lord Nelson, with Hints for
  Erecting a National Monument. 1806. (P)
  Monthly Mirror, 21 (Mar. 1806), 176-77.
  Monthly Mirror, 40 (Jan. 1806), 97-98.

Martin, George.
  Night, a Poem. (Anon.) 1811. (P)
  British Critic, 39 (Mar. 1812), 306.

Eclectic Review, 8 (Apr. 1812), 434.
Evangelical Magazine, 20 (May 1812), 188-89.
Monthly Review, 68 (Aug. 1812), 432.

Martin, H.
Helen of Glenross. By the Author of Historic Tales.
1801. (F)
    Critical Review, ns,v34 (Mar. 1802), 356.
    Monthly Review, ns,v41 (May 1803), 103.

Martin, James.
Translations from Ancient Irish MSS., and Other Poems.
1811. (P)
    Monthly Review, 67 (Feb. 1812), 219-20.

Mason, James.
The Natural Son. A Tragedy. (D)
    Literary Journal, a Review..., 5 (Mar. 1805), 321-22.

Mason, William.
The Poetical Works of the Author of the "Heroic Epistle to
Sir William Chambers." 1805. (P)
    Annual Review, 4 (1805), 573.
    Flowers of Literature, 4 (1805), 431.
    Lady's Monthly Museum, 15 (Sept. 1805), 201.
    Monthly Mirror, 20 (July 1805), 31-32.
    Monthly Review, 48 (Sept. 1805), 105.

Masters, Martin Kedgwin.
The Progress of Love. A Poem. 1807. (P)
    Annual Review, 6 (1807), 572-73.
    British Critic, 30 (July 1807), 80-81.
    Cabinet, 1 (May 1807), 188-91.
    Critical Review, s3,v12 (Nov. 1807), 292-96.
    Cyclopaedian Magazine, 1 (July 1807), 413-14.
    Literary Annual Register, 1 (May 1807), 220-21.
    Oxford Review, 2 (Aug. 1807), 195-97.
    Poetical Register, 6 (1807), 545.

Lost and Found, a Comedy. (D)
    Poetical Register, 8 (1811), 637-38.

Masterton, Charles.
The Seducer, a Tragedy. 1811. (D)
    Critical Review, s4,v1 (Apr. 1812), 445.
    Monthly Review, ns,v68 (June 1812), 208-09.
    Poetical Register, 8 (1811), 636-37.

Amyntor and Adelaide; or, a Tale of Life. 1816. (P)
    Critical Review, s5,v4 (Oct. 1816), 429-30.
    Monthly Review, 84 (Dec. 1817), 433-34.
    New Monthly Magazine, 6 (Dec. 1816), 441.
    Theatrical Inquisitor, 9 (Oct. 1816), 288-90.

Mathews, Mrs. Charles.
  Poems by the Late Mrs. Charles Mathews. 1802. (P)
    Critical Review, s2,v37 (Apr. 1803), 474.
    Monthly Mirror, 15 (Apr. 1803), 252-53.
    Monthly Review, 43 (Jan. 1804), 95.

Mathias, Thomas James.
  The Grove. A Satire. By the Author of The Pursuits of
  Literature. 1798. (P)
    Critical Review, s2,v22 (Feb. 1798), 230-31.
    Gentleman's Magazine, 68[1] (Mar. 1798), 240.
    Monthly Magazine, Suppl. v5 (July 15, 1798), 507.
    Monthly Mirror, 5 (Jan. 1798), 33-34.
    Monthly Review, 25 (Apr. 1798), 472.

  The Pursuits of Literature. A Satirical Poem in Four Dialogues. (Anon.) 1798. 4th ed. (P)
    Analytical Review, 27 (June 1798), 607-10.
    Critical Review, s2,v24 (Dec. 1798), 418-23.
    Dublin Magazine and Irish Monthly Register, 1 (Dec.
      1798), 385-87.
    Edinburgh Magazine or Literary Miscellany, ns,v13 (Apr.
      1799), 249-57.
    Monthly Visitor, 3 (Mar. 1798), 299-306.
    New Review, 1 (Mar. 1813), 332-34. (16th ed.)

  The Shade of Alexander Pope on the Banks of the Thames.
  1799. By the Author of The Pursuits of Literature. (P)
    Analytical Review, ns,v1 (Mar. 1799), 314-15.
    Antijacobin Review, 2 (Mar. 1799), 280-85.
    British Critic, 13 (May 1799), 463-67.
    Critical Review, s2,v26 (July 1799), 289-92.
    Gentleman's Magazine, 69[2] (Aug. 1799), 682-84.
    Monthly Magazine, Suppl. v7 (July 20, 1799), 535-36.
    Monthly Mirror, 7 (Mar. 1799), 163-64.
    Monthly Review, 31 (Jan. 1800), 100-03.
    New Annual Register, 20 (1799), [269].
    New London Review, 1 (Feb. 1799), 183-85.

  Pandolfo Attonito! or, Lord Galloway's Poetical Lamentation
  on the Removal of the Arm-Chairs from the Pit at the Opera-
  House! (Anon.) 1800. (P)
    Monthly Review, 32 (July 1800), 317-18.

  Canzoni e Prose Toscane. 1808. (P)
    British Critic, 29 (Mar. 1807), 315-16.

Matter-of-Fact, Martin.
  The Present Times; or the First Three Months of 1812.
  1812. (P)
    Antijacobin Review, 42 (Aug. 1812), 428-30.
    Antijacobin Review, 44 (Feb. 1813), 192-93.
    Critical Review, s4,v3 (Jan. 1813), 105.

Matthews, W. D.
  Naval Triumph; or Nelson's Last Wreath. 1809. (P)
    Monthly Review, 60 (Oct. 1809), 214-15.

Maturin, Charles Robert.
  The Wild Irish Boy. 1808. By the Author of Montorio. (F)
    Annual Review, 7 (1808), 594-603.
    Oxford Review, 3 (Mar. 1808), 298-99.
    Satirist, 2 (July 1808), 529-38.

  The Milesian Chief; a Romance. 1811. By the Author of
  Montorio and The Wild Irish Boy. (F)
    British Critic, 39 (Feb. 1812), 197.
    Critical Review, s4,v1 (Apr. 1812), 388-97.
    Monthly Review, ns,v67 (Mar. 1812), 322-23.

  Bertram; or, the Castle of Aldobrand, a Tragedy. 1816. (D)
    Antijacobin Review, 50 (June 1816), 537-44.
    Augustan Review, 3 (Aug. 1816), 178-85.
    British Critic, ns,v5 (May 1816), 502-09.
    British Lady's Magazine, 3 (June 1816), 402-06.
    British Review, 8 (Aug. 1816), 64-81.
    Critical Review, s5,v3 (May 1816), 537-39.
    Dublin Examiner, 1 (Sept. 1816), 383-91.
    Eclectic Review, ns,v6 (Oct. 1816), 379-86.
    Literary and Statistical Magazine, 1 (May 1817), 188-93.
    Monthly Review, ns,v80 (June 1816), 179-89.
    Theatrical Inquisitor, 8 (June 1816), 438-40.

  Manuel, a Tragedy. 1817. By the Author of Bertram. (D)
    Black Dwarf, 1 (Mar. 12, 1817), 109-10.
    British Lady's Magazine, 5 (Apr. 1817), 228-40.
    European Magazine, 71 (Apr. 1817), 336-39.
    Literary Gazette, Mar. 29, 1817, p. 148.
    Monthly Review, ns,v83 (Aug. 1817), 391-95.
    Theatrical Inquisitor, 10 (Mar. 1817), 201-07.

  Women; or, Pour et Contre. A Tale. By the Author of Bertram, etc. 1818. (F)
    British Critic, ns,v9 (June 1818), 627-32.
    British Lady's Magazine, s3,v2 (Feb., Mar. 1819), 76-77,
      126-27.
    Dublin Magazine, 1 (Jan. 1820), 59-60.
    Fireside Magazine (quoting Quarterly Review), 1 (Mar.
      1819), 111.
    Literary and Statistical Magazine, 2 (Aug. 1818), 296-
      305.
    Literary Gazette, July 11, 1818, pp. 437-39.
    Monthly Review, ns,v86 (Aug. 1818), 403-15.
    New Monthly Magazine, 10 (Sept. 1818), 169.
    Quarterly Review, 19 (July 1818), 321-28.
    Scots Magazine (Edinburgh Magazine and Literary Miscel-
      lany), ns,v2 (Apr. 1818), 337-42.

Fredolfo, a Tragedy. 1819. (D)
  Fireside Magazine (quoting Monthly Magazine), 1 (Sept.
  1819), 354.
  Monthly Magazine, 48 (Aug. 1819), 57-58.
  Theatrical Inquisitor, 15 (Sept., Oct. 1819), 142-46.
  200-04.

Melmoth, the Wanderer. A Tale. By the Author of Bertram.
1820. (F)
  Blackwood's Edinburgh Magazine, 8 (Nov. 1820), 161-68.
  Dublin Magazine, 2 (Dec. 1820), 487-90.
  Eclectic Review, ns,v14 (Dec. 1820), 553-58.
  Literary Gazette, Nov. 18, 1820, pp. 737-39.
  (Gold's) London Magazine, 2 (Dec. 1820), 588-601.
  Monthly Magazine, 50 (Dec. 1820), 455.
  New Monthly Magazine, 14 (Dec. 1820), 662-68.

Maurice, Thomas.
  The Crisis, or the British Muse to the British Minister and
  Nation. By the Author of Indian Antiquities. 1798. (P)
    Analytical Review, 28 (Oct. 1798), 403-07.
    Antijacobin Review, 1 (July 1798), 34-37.
    British Critic, 12 (July 1798), 65-67.
    British Critic, 22 (Aug. 1803), 190-91. (2nd ed.)
    Critical Review, s2,v25 (Jan. 1799), 110-11.
    Critical Review, s2,v38 (Aug. 1803), 467. (2nd ed.)
    Monthly Magazine, Suppl. v6 (1798), 514.
    Monthly Mirror, 6 (Aug. 1798), 98.
    Monthly Review, 27 (Oct. 1798), 231-32.
    Monthly Visitor, 5 (Dec. 1798), 420-21.
    New Annual Register, 19 (1798), [310].
    New London Review, 1 (Feb. 1799), 203.

  Grove Hill, a Descriptive Poem; with an Ode to Nature. By
  the Author of Indian Antiquities. 1799. (P)
    Antijacobin Review, 5 (Feb. 1800), 204-06.
    British Critic, 13 (June 1799), 588-92.
    Critical Review, s2,v26 (Aug. 1799), 399-404.
    Lady's Monthly Museum, 3 (Sept. 1799), 236-39.
    Monthly Magazine, Suppl. v8 (Jan. 20, 1800), 1051.
    Monthly Mirror, 8 (Sept. 1799), 154-55.
    Monthly Review, 29 (Aug. 1799), 419-22.
    Monthly Visitor, 9 (Feb. 1800), 171.
    New Annual Register, 20 (1799), [266-67].
    New London Review, 2 (Sept. 1, 1799), 269-70.

  Poems, Epistolary, Lyric, and Elegiacal. 1800. (P)
    Antijacobin Review, 7 (Sept. 1800), 32-34.
    British Critic, 15 (May 1800), 481-86.
    Critical Review, s2,v31 (Mar. 1801), 300-03.
    European Magazine, 37 (June 1800), 460.
    Monthly Magazine, Suppl. v9 (July 20, 1800), 639.
    Monthly Mirror, 10 (Dec. 1800), 375-77.

Monthly Review, 38 (May 1802), 77-82.
New *Annual* *Register*, 21 (1800), [325-26].
New *London* Review, 3 (May 1800), 452-55.

Select Poems. By the Author of *Indian* *Antiquities*. 1803.
(P)
  Annual Review, 2 (1803), 554-56.
  Monthly *Magazine*, Suppl. v17 (July 28, 1804), 666.
  Monthly *Mirror*, 16 (Aug., Oct. 1803), 101-06, 242-46.
  New *Annual* *Register*, 24 (1803), [327].

The *Fall* *of* *the* *Mogul,* *a* *Tragedy*. *With* *Other* *Occasional*
Poems. By the Author of *Indian* *Antiquities*. 1806. (D)
  Annual Review, 5 (1806), 537.
  British *Critic*, 28 (1806), 289-94.
  Literary *Journal,* *a* *Review*..., 5 (Mar. 1805), 322.
  Literary *Journal,* *a* *Review*..., ns,v2 (Sept. 1806), 333-34.
  Monthly *Mirror*, 22 (Oct. 1806), 258-63.
  Monthly Review, ns,v53 (Aug. 1807), 438.
  New *Annual* *Register*, 27 (1806), [370].
  Poetical *Register*, 6 (1806), 525.

Richmond *Hill*: *A* *Descriptive* *and* *Historical* *Poem*. By the
Author of *Indian* *Antiquities*. 1807. (P)
  Antijacobin *Review*, 30 (June 1808), 156-67.
  British *Critic*, 31 (Feb. 1808), 119-24.
  Critical *Review*, s3,v14 (July 1808), 328.
  European *Magazine*, 53 (Apr., May 1808), 279-82, 366-68.
  Literary *Annual* *Register*, 2 (Apr. 1808), 170-73.
  Monthly *Magazine*, Suppl. v24 (Jan. 30, 1808), 628-29.
  Monthly *Mirror*, ns,v3 (Feb. 1808), 101-03.
  Monthly *Review*, 55 (Feb. 1808), 132-38.
  Poetical *Register*, 6 (1807), 536-37.

Elegiac *Lines,* *Sacred* *to* *the* *Memory* *of* *Henry* *Hope*. 1811.
(P)
  General *Chronicle*, 2 (July 1811), 298-99.

Westminster *Abbey,* *with* *Other* *Occasional* *Poems*. By the
Author of *Indian* *Antiquities*. 1813. (P)
  British *Critic*, 42 (Dec. 1813), 547-51.
  Champion, Feb. 27, 1814, p. 71.

Mavor, William Fordyce.
  Youth's *Miscellany;* *or,* *Father's* *Gift* *to* *His* *Children*.
  (Anon.) 1797.
    Monthly *Visitor*, 4 (June 1798), 215.

Maxey, Samuel.
  The *Victory* *of* *Trafalgar*: *a* *Naval* *Ode*. 1806. (P)
    Antijacobin *Review*, 23 (Feb. 1806), 211-12.
    Critical *Review*, s3,v7 (Mar. 1806), 331-32.
    General *Review*, 1 (Jan. 1806), 91.

Literary Journal, a Review..., ns,vl (Feb. 1806), 220-21.
Monthly Mirror, 21 (May 1806), 333.
Monthly Review, 49 (Mar. 1806), 316.

Mayne, John.
  Glasgow, a Poem. 1803. (P)
    Annual Review, 2 (1803), 567-68.
    Antijacobin Review, 15 (July 1803), 307-10.
    British Critic, 21 (June 1803), 673.
    Critical Review, s3,vl (Apr. 1804), 475.
    European Magazine, 43 (June 1803), 457-58.
    Gentleman's Magazine, 73² (Dec. 1803), 1157.
    Monthly Magazine, Suppl. vl7 (July 28, 1804), 666.
    Monthly Mirror, 16 (July 1803), 40.
    Monthly Register, 3 (Aug. 1803), 140.
    Monthly Review, 42 (Nov. 1803), 326-28.
    Poetical Register, 3 (1803), 449.

  English, Scots, and Irishmen. A Patriotic Address to the
  Inhabitants of the United Kingdom. 1803. (P)
    Critical Review, s2,v39 (Sept. 1803), 105-06.

  The Siller Gun. 1808. (P)
    Annual Review, 7 (1808), 534-35.
    Antijacobin Review, 31 (Nov. 1808), 304-07.
    Le Beau Monde, 4 (Sept. 1808), 121-22.
    British Critic, 32 (Dec. 1808), 634-35.
    Cabinet, 4 (Sept. 1808), 183-87.
    Critical Review, s3,vl4 (Aug. 1808), 444-45.
    Eclectic Review, 5 (May 1809), 488-89.
    European Magazine, 54 (Sept. 1808), 211.
    Gentleman's Magazine, 78² (Dec. 1808), 1103-04.
    Lady's Monthly Museum, s2,v5 (Oct. 1808), 194-96.
    Literary Panorama, 4 (Sept. 1808), 1093-94.
    Monthly Magazine, Suppl. v26 (Jan. 30, 1809), 633.
    Monthly Review, 59 (May 1809), 29-34.
    Poetical Register, 7 (1808), 560.
    Satirist, 6 (May 1810), 518. (Excerpts from other re-
      views.)

Mayo, Rev. Robert W.
  The Abdication of Ferdinand; or, Napoleon at Bayonne; an
  Historical Play. 1809. (D)
    Le Beau Monde, 2 (Nov. 1809), 101.
    British Critic, 35 (Jan. 1810), 71-72.
    Poetical Register, 7 (1809), 615.

Medley, Sarah.
  Original Poems, Sacred and Miscellaneous. 1807. (P)
    Eclectic Review, 4 (Dec. 1808), 1134.

Meeke, Mrs. Mary.
  The Mysterious Wife. By Gabrielli. 1797. (F)

Critical Review, ns,v23 (June 1798), 232-33.
Monthly Mirror, 6 (July 1798), 34.

Palmira and Ermance. 1797. (F)
    Critical Review, ns,v24 (Oct. 1798), 236-37.

Which Is the Man? 1801.
    Critical Review, ns,v32 (Aug. 1801), 469.

The Mysterious Husband. By Gabrielli. 1801. (F)
    Critical Review, ns,v33 (Nov. 1801), 353.

Independence. By Gabrielli. 1802.
    Critical Review, ns,v37 (Feb. 1803), 237.
    New Annual Register, 23 (1802), [322].

Amazement. (F)
    Literary Journal, a Review..., 3 (May 1, 1804), 491.

The Old Wife and Young Husband. (F)
    Literary Journal, a Review..., 3 (May 16, 1804), 550.

The Nine Day's Wonder. (F)
    Literary Journal, a Review, 4 (Oct. 1804), 435.

Something Odd. (Anon.) 1804. (F)
    Critical Review, s3,v3 (Oct. 1804), 238.
    Literary Journal, a Review..., 3 (May 1, 1804), 491.
    Monthly Mirror, 18 (Nov. 1804), 320.

Something Strange. By Gabrielli. 1806. (F)
    Literary Journal, a Review..., ns,v2 (Aug. 1806), 218.

Melmoth, Henry.
  Sorrows of Memory, and Other Poems. (P)
    Poetical Register, 7 (1808), 564-65.

Melville, Theodore.
  The White Knight; or, the Monastery of Morne. A Romance.
  1802. (F)
    British Critic, 20 (Sept. 1802), 322.
    Critical Review, ns,v35 (Aug. 1802), 476-77.
    Monthly Magazine, Suppl. v14 (Jan. 25, 1803), 599.
    Monthly Mirror, 14 (Oct. 1802), 257.
    Monthly Review, ns,v39 (Dec. 1802), 427.
    New Annual Register, 23 (1802), [322].
    Union Magazine and Imperial Register, 4 (Sept. 1802),
      191-92.

  The Benevolent Monk; or, the Castle of Olalla, a Romance.
  1807. (F)
    British Critic, 30 (Aug. 1807), 199.
    Critical Review, s3,v12 (Sept. 1807), 104.

<u>Monthly</u> <u>Literary</u> <u>Recreations</u>, 2 (Apr. 1807), 309-10.
<u>Monthly</u> <u>Review</u>, ns,v62 (June 1810), 213.

Member of the Honourable Society of Lincoln's Inn, A.
See Daniel Cabanel.

Mendham, James, Jr.
  <u>The</u> <u>Adventures</u> <u>of</u> <u>Ulysses</u>; <u>or</u> <u>the</u> <u>Return</u> <u>to</u> <u>Ithaca</u>, <u>a</u> <u>Clas</u>-
  <u>sical</u> <u>Drama</u> <u>from</u> <u>Homer</u>. 1810. (D)
    <u>Antijacobin</u> <u>Review</u>, 39 (May 1811), 94.
    <u>British</u> <u>Critic</u>, 37 (June 1811), 625.
    <u>Critical</u> <u>Review</u>, s3,v23 (May 1811), 108-09.
    <u>Poetical</u> <u>Register</u>, 8 (1810), 594.

Mercer, James.
  <u>Lyric</u> <u>Poems</u>. 1804. 2nd ed. (P)
    <u>Annual</u> <u>Review</u>, 3 (1804), 563-64.
    <u>British</u> <u>Critic</u>, 23 (Jan. 1804), 81-82.
    <u>Edinburgh</u> <u>Review</u>, 7 (Jan. 1806), 471-78.
    <u>Monthly</u> <u>Magazine</u>, Suppl. v19 (July 28, 1805), 658.
    <u>Poetical</u> <u>Register</u>, 4 (1804), 493.

Merivale, John Herman. (See also Robert Bland and John
      Herman Merivale.)
  <u>The</u> <u>Minstrel</u>; <u>or</u> <u>the</u> <u>Progress</u> <u>of</u> <u>Genius</u>. <u>In</u> <u>Continuation</u>
  <u>of</u> <u>the</u> <u>Poem</u> <u>Left</u> <u>Unfinished</u> <u>by</u> <u>Dr</u>. <u>Beattie</u>. 1808. (P)
    <u>Annual</u> <u>Review</u>, 7 (1808), 483-87.
    <u>Le</u> <u>Beau</u> <u>Monde</u>, 4 (Suppl. 1808), 352-58.
    <u>British</u> <u>Critic</u>, 36 (Sept. 1810), 302-03.
    <u>Critical</u> <u>Review</u>, s3,v13 (Mar. 1808), 265-74.
    <u>Eclectic</u> <u>Review</u>, 4 (July 1808), 611-15.
    <u>Monthly</u> <u>Review</u>, 59 (June 1809), 214-16.
    <u>New</u> <u>Annual</u> <u>Register</u>, 29 (1808), [406].
    <u>Poetical</u> <u>Register</u>, 7 (1808), 550.
    <u>Satirist</u>, 5 (Sept. 1809), 310-11. (Excerpts from other
      reviews.)

  <u>Ode</u> <u>on</u> <u>the</u> <u>Deliverance</u> <u>of</u> <u>Europe</u>. 1814. (P)
    <u>Antijacobin</u> <u>Review</u>, 46 (May 1814), 441-47.
    <u>British</u> <u>Critic</u>, ns,v2 (July 1814), 98.
    <u>Eclectic</u> <u>Review</u>, s2,v1 (June 1814), 622-27.
    <u>Gentleman</u>'<u>s</u> <u>Magazine</u>, 84[1] (May 1812), 478.
    <u>Literary</u> <u>Panorama</u>, 15 (June 1814), 735-38.
    <u>New</u> <u>Review</u>, 3 (June 1814), 531-32.
    <u>Universal</u> <u>Magazine</u>, ns,v21 (June 1814), 483.

  <u>Orlando</u> <u>in</u> <u>Roncesvalles</u>. 1814. (P)
    <u>British</u> <u>Critic</u>, ns,v2 (Sept. 1814), 256-65.
    <u>Eclectic</u> <u>Review</u>, s2,v2 (Sept. 1814), 227-37.
    <u>Monthly</u> <u>Review</u>, 75 (Nov. 1814), 301-07.

Merry, Andrew.
  <u>The</u> <u>Last</u> <u>Dying</u> <u>Words</u> <u>of</u> <u>the</u> <u>Eighteenth</u> <u>Century</u>, <u>a</u> <u>Pindaric</u>

Ode. 1800. (P)
British Critic, 16 (Oct. 1800), 437.
Critical Review, s2,v28 (Mar. 1800), 354.
Gentleman's Magazine, 70[2] (Oct. 1800), 972.
Monthly Magazine, Suppl. v9 (July 20, 1800), 639.
Monthly Review, 31 (Feb. 1800), 208-09.
New London Review, 3 (Jan. 1800), 86.

Messieurs Tag, Rag, and Bobtail.
See Isaac D'Israeli.

Methone, R.
The Pride of Birth, a Satire; in Imitation of the Eighth
Satire of Juvenal. (Anon.) 1801. (P)
British Critic, 17 (Apr. 1801), 431-32.
Monthly Magazine, Suppl. v11 (July 20, 1801), 605.
Monthly Review, 35 (May 1801), 45-46.
Poetical Register, 1 (1801), 449.

Meyler, William.
Poetical Amusement on the Journey of Life. 1806. (P)
Antijacobin Review, 23 (Jan. 1806), 102-03.
British Critic, 27 (Mar. 1806), 316.
Critical Review, s3,v7 (Mar. 1806), 329-31.
Gentleman's Magazine, 76[1] (May 1806), 451.
Literary Journal, a Review..., ns,v2 (Aug. 1806), 174-76.
Monthly Magazine, Suppl. v22 (Jan. 25, 1807), 641.
Monthly Review, 52 (Jan. 1807), 91-92.
Poetical Register, 6 (1806), 501-02.

Military Amateur, A.
See Morgan Odoherty.

Millikin, Anna.
Plantagenet; or, Secrets of the House of Anjou: A Tale of
the Twelfth Century. 1802. (F)
Annual Review, 1 (1802), 727.
Critical Review, ns,v37 (Jan. 1803), 117.
Monthly Magazine, Suppl. v15 (July 28, 1803), 639.
New Annual Register, 23 (1802), [321].

The Rival Chiefs; or the Battle of Mere. A Tale of Ancient
Times. (F)
Literary Journal, 5 (Mar. 1805), 321.

Millingen, J. G.
The Bee Hive; a Musical Farce. (D)
Poetical Register, 8 (1811), 642.

Mills, J. H.
Poetical Trifles. (P)
Monthly Literary Recreations, 1 (Dec. 1806), 492.

Milman, Henry Hart.
  Judicium Regale. 1814. (P)
    Quarterly Review, 15 (Apr. 1816), 69-85.

  Ode on the Arrival of the Potentates in Oxford; and Judicium Regale, an Ode. (P)
    Monthly Review, 74 (July 1814), 315-17.

  Fazio, a Tragedy. 1815. (D)
    Augustan Review, 2 (Mar. 1816), 239-44.
    British Critic, ns,v4 (Oct. 1815), 418-25.
    British Lady's Magazine, 2 (Dec. 1815), 394-97.
    Champion, Sept. 10, 17, 1815, pp. 294-95, 303.
    Critical Review, s5,v3 (June 1816), 627-32.
    European Magazine, 68 (Oct. 1815), 342-44.
    Monthly Review, ns,v84 (Oct. 1817), 199-209.
    Quarterly Review, 15 (Apr. 1816), 69-85.
    Theatrical Inquisitor, 7 (July 1815), 43-48.

  Samor, Lord of the Bright City. 1818. (P)
    British Critic, ns,v10 (July 1818), 52-59.
    British Lady's Magazine, s3,v1 (July-Sept. 1818), 30-34,
      123.
    Fireside Magazine (quoting Monthly Review), 1 (Feb.
      1819), 69.
    Fireside Magazine (quoting Quarterly Review), 1 (Mar.
      1819), 111.
    Fireside Magazine (quoting Monthly Magazine, 1 (Sept.
      1819), 355.
    Literary Chronicle, 1 (June 8, 15, 1818), 161-63, 179-81.
    Literary Gazette, Apr. 25, 1818, pp. 260-61.
    Literary Journal and General Miscellany, 1 (June 7, 14,
      1818), 161-63, 179-81.
    Miniature Magazine, 2 (Dec. 1818), 40-41.
    Monthly Magazine, 45 (July 1818), 534.
    Monthly Magazine, 48 (Aug. 1819), 60.
    Monthly Review, 87 (Dec. 1818), 337-56.
    New Annual Register, 39 (1818), [185-92].
    New Monthly Magazine, 10 (Oct. 1818), 247-49.
    Quarterly Review, 19 (July 1818), 328-47.
    Theatrical Inquisitor, 13 (July, Aug. 1818), 41-51, 118-
      22.

  The Fall of Jerusalem, a Dramatic Poem. 1820. (P)
    Blackwood's Edinburgh Magazine, 7 (May 1820), 121-31.
    British Critic, ns,v14 (July 1820), 32-40.
    British Review, 15 (June 1820), 365-77.
    Caledonian, 1 (Sept. 1820), 168-82.
    Christian's Pocket Magazine, 3 (Oct. 1820), 199. (Di-
      gested from Monthly Review.)
    Dublin Magazine, 2 (July 1820), 49-60.
    Eclectic Review, s2,v14 (July 1820), 87-98.
    Edinburgh Magazine and Literary Miscellany (Scots Maga-
      zine), ns,v7 (Dec. 1820), 528-36.

Imperial Magazine, 2 (June, July 1820), 458-64, 539-46.
Literary Chronicle, 2 (Apr. 22, 1820), 257-59.
Literary Gazette, Apr. 15, 1820, 241-44.
(Baldwin's) London Magazine, 1 (June 1820), 679-86.
(Gold's) London Magazine, 1 (May 1820), 514-24.
Monthly Magazine, 49 (July 1820), 557-58.
Monthly Review, 92 (Aug. 1820), 422-31.
New Monthly Magazine, 13 (June 1820), 684-87.
Quarterly Review, 23 (May 1820), 198-225.

Milne, Christian.
  Simple Poems on Simple Subjects. (P)
    Annual Review, 4 (1805), 591.
    British Critic, 27 (May 1806), 550-51.
    Literary Journal, a Review..., 5 (Sept. 1805), 999.
    Monthly Magazine, Suppl. v20 (Jan. 31, 1806), 614.
    Monthly Review, 50 (May 1806), 96-98.

Milon, M.
  The Fan, a Poem. (P)
    La Belle Assemblée, ns,v12 (Sept. 1815), 127-28.

Milton, John.
  L'Allegro, a Poem. (P)
    Satirist, 1 (Dec. 1807), 314-16.

Minifie, Miss _____.
  The Union. 1803. (F)
    Critical Review, s3,v1 (Feb. 1804), 238.
    Monthly Review, ns,v45 (Nov. 1804), 313-14.

Minimus, Pindar.
  See Pindar Minimus.

Mitford, John.
  Poems of a British Sailor. (P)
    New Bon Ton Magazine, 1 (June 1818), 118.

  The Adventures of Johnny Newcome in the Navy. By Alfred
  Burton (pseud.). (P)
    Fireside Magazine, 1 (Feb. 1819), 64-66.
    New Monthly Magazine, 10 (Oct. 1818), 254.

Mitford, Rev. John.
  Agnes, the Indian Captive. With Other Poems. 1811. (P)
    British Critic, 40 (Sept. 1812), 301-02.
    Eclectic Review, 8 (Aug. 1812), 855.
    Monthly Review, 67 (Mar. 1812), 324.
    Poetical Register, 8 (1811), 613-14.

Mitford, Mary Russell.
  Poems. 1810. (P)
    British Critic, 35 (May 1810), 515-16.

Critical Review, s3,v20 (July 1810), 327-29.
Eclectic Review, 6 (Apr. 1810), 374-76.
Literary Panorama, 10 (Nov. 1810), 844.
Monthly Review, 63 (Sept. 1810), 97-98.
New Annual Register, 31 (1810), [368].
Quarterly Review, 4 (Nov. 1810), 514-18.

Christina, the Maid of the South Seas. 1811. (P)
Antijacobin Review, 39 (July 1811), 260-68.
British Critic, 38 (Nov. 1811), 474-81.
Critical Review, s3,v23 (July 1811), 264-74.
Eclectic Review, 7 (June 1811), 548-56.
Edinburgh Monthly Magazine and Review (Scotish Review),
  1 (Sept. 1812), 31-41.
Glasgow Magazine, 2 (June 1811), 142.
Literary Panorama, 10 (Aug. 1811), 215-19.
Monthly Review, 65 (July 1811), 249-56.
New Annual Register, 32 (1811), [365].
Poetical Register, 8 (1810), 548-49.

Poems: Second Edition, with Considerable Additions.
1811. (P)
Antijacobin Review, 40 (Sept. 1811), 47-52.
British Critic, 38 (Aug. 1811), 187-89.
Eclectic Review, 9 (Apr. 1813), 396-406.
European Magazine, 60 (Aug. 1811), 124.
Literary Panorama, 11 (May 1812), 833-34.
Monthly Review, 68 (July 1812), 318-19.
Poetical Register, 8 (1811), 605.

Watlington Hill, a Poem. 1812. (P)
British Critic, 40 (Aug. 1812), 175-77.
General Chronicle, 6 (Sept. 1812), 23-30.

Narrative Poems on the Female Character. Vol. I. 1813.
(P)
Augustan Review, 1 (Dec. 1815), 854-56.
British Critic, 42 (Sept. 1813), 230-37.
Critical Review, s4,v3 (June 1813), 638-46.
Eclectic Review, 9 (Apr. 1813), 396-406.
New Review, 1 (Jan. 1813), 124-29.

Mitford, William.
An Inquiry into the Principles of Harmony in Language, and
of the Mechanics of Verse, Modern and Antient. 2nd ed.
(Pr)
British Critic, 30 (Oct. 1807), 359-67.

Molleson, Alexander.
The Sweets of Society, a Poem; and a Few Miscellaneous
Poems. By the Author of Melody the Soul of Music, an Es-
say. 1801. (Pr)
British Critic, 18 (July 1801), 83.

European Magazine, 39 (Feb. 1801), 118.
Poetical Register, 1 (1801), 438.

Miscellanies in Prose and Verse. 1806. (P)
Antijacobin Review, 25 (Sept. 1806), 89-90.
Critical Review, s3,v10 (Jan. 1807), 97-98.
Eclectic Review, 3 (Mar. 1807), 253-54.
European Magazine, 50 (Aug. 1806), 128-29.
Literary Annual Register, 1 (Oct. 1807), 456-57.
Literary Journal, a Review..., ns,v2 (Sept. 1806), 335-36.
Monthly Mirror, 22 (Nov. 1806), 318.
Monthly Review, 53 (Aug. 1807), 446-47.

Adam and Margaret; or, the Cruel Father Punished for His
Unnatural Conduct to His Innocent Daughter: a Narrative of
Real Incidents. 1809. (F?)
European Magazine, 56 (Dec. 1809), 446-47.
Monthly Review, ns,v61 (Jan. 1810), 109-10.

Monck, John Berkeley.
Some Occasional Verses, on the Opening of the Reading Lit-
erary Institution. 1808. (P)
British Critic, 31 (Feb. 1808), 196.
Literary Annual Register, 2 (May 1808), 218.

Moncrieff, William Thomas.
The Diamond Arrow; or, the Postmaster's Wife and the May-
or's Daughter. 1816. (D)
Theatrical Inquisitor, 8 (May 1816), 357.

All at Coventry; or, Love and Laugh. 1816. (D)
Theatrical Inquisitor, 8 (May 1816), 357.

Wanted a Wife; or, a Cheque on My Banker. 1819. (D)
Fireside Magazine (quoting Monthly Review), 1 (July
1819), 266.
Monthly Review, ns,v89 (May 1819), 101.

Ivanhoe; or the Jewess. A Chivalric Play. 1820. (D)
Literary Chronicle, 2 (May 20, 1820), 326.
Theatrical Inquisitor, 16 (Mar. 1820), 135-38.

Monney, William.
Caractacus, a New Tragedy, with Remarks on English Dramatic
Tragedy; and Structures on Theatrical Committees, Managers,
and Players. 1816. (D)
Critical Review, s5,v4 (Oct. 1816), 404-12.
Periodical Devil upon Two Sticks, 1 (June 15, 1816), 41-
42.

Montague, Edward.
The Citizen, a Hudibrastic Poem; to Which Is Added Nelson's
Ghost, a Poem. 1806. (P)

British Critic, 28 (Dec. 1806), 676.
Monthly Mirror, 22 (July 1806), 39.
Monthly Review, 50 (May 1806), 103.
Poetical Register, 6 (1806), 506-07.

The Castle of Berry Pomeroy. 1806. (F)
Literary Journal, a Review..., ns,v2 (Oct. 1806), 445.
Monthly Literary Recreations, 1 (Oct. 1806), 323.

Montgomery, James.
The Wanderer of Switzerland, and Other Poems. 1806. (P)
Annual Review, 4 (1805), 555-58.
British Critic, 28 (July 1806), 80-81.
Critical Review, s3,v8 (Aug. 1806), 363-72.
Cyclopaedian Magazine, 1 (Apr. 1807), 217-18.
Eclectic Review, 2 (May 1806), 378-83.
Edinburgh Review, 9 (Oct. 1806), 347-54.
General Review, 1 (Mar. 1806), 266-70.
Literary Journal, a Review..., ns,v1 (Apr. 1806), 433-35.
Monthly Literary Recreations, 1 (Dec. 1806), 491-92.
Monthly Magazine, Suppl. v21 (1806), 607-08.
Monthly Mirror, 21 (Apr. 1806), 252-53.
Monthly Repository, 1 (July 1806), 377-80.
Monthly Review, 50 (Aug. 1806), 436-38.
New Annual Register, 26 (1805), [355].
Northern Star, 1 (Dec. 1817), 533-36.
Poetical Register, 5 (1805), 485-86.
Quarterly Review, 6 (Dec. 1811), 405-19.
Theological and Biblical Magazine, 6 (Dec. 1806), 532-33.

Poems. (P)
Antijacobin Review, 24 (May 1806), 102-03.
Universal Magazine, ns,v5 (June 1806), 327-33 [504-21].

Poems on the Abolition of the Slave Trade.
See James Montgomery, James Grahame, and E. Benger, below.

The West Indies, and Other Poems. 1810. (P)
Antijacobin Review, 38 (Mar. 1811), 320-22.
British Critic, 36 (Sept. 1810), 277-83.
Critical Review, s3,v21 (Nov. 1810), 249-59.
Eclectic Review, 6 (Sept. 1810), 644-51.
Glasgow Magazine, 2 (Sept. 1811), 369-74.
Monthly Review, 64 (Feb. 1811), 144-52.
New Monthly Magazine, 2 (Oct. 1814), 229-30.
The Philanthropist, 1 (1811), 93-100, 196-200.
Poetical Register, 8 (1810), 559-60.
Quarterly Review, 6 (Dec. 1811), 405-19.
Satirist, 10 (Feb. 1812), 144-46.

The World before the Flood. With Other Occasional Pieces.
1813. (P)
Baptist Magazine, 6 (July 1814), 290-92.

British Critic, 42 (Nov. 1813), 518-20.
British Critic, ns,v2 (July 1814), 34-45.
British Review, s5,v5 (Oct. 1813), 111-23.
Christian Observer, 13 (Oct. 1814), 657-66.
Critical Review, s4,v3 (June 1813), 618-24.
Eclectic Review, s2,v1 (May 1814), 441-56.
European Magazine, 64 (Sept. 1813), 235-36.
Meteor, or General Censor, 1 (Nov. 1813), 41-56.
Monthly Review, 73 (Feb. 1814), 144-53.
New Review, 2 (Dec. 1813), 573-77.
Quarterly Review, 11 (Apr. 1814), 78-87.
Scots Magazine, 75 (June 1813), 438-43.
Theatrical Inquisitor, 3 (Aug. 1813), 38-43.
Tradesman, 11 (July, Aug. 1813), 46-49, 136-40.

Verses to the Memory of the Late Richard Reynolds of Bris-
tol. 1816. (P)
    Critical Review, s5,v5 (Jan. 1817), 36-42.
    Eclectic Review, s2,v7 (Jan. 1817), 77-79.
    Literary Panorama, ns,v5 (Dec. 1816), 414-16.
    Monthly Review, 82 (Feb. 1817), 211-12.

Thoughts on Wheels. 1817. (P)
    Gentleman's Magazine, 87[1] (May 1817), 438-39.
    Literary Panorama, ns,v6 (May 1817), 245-49.
    Monthly Review, 85 (Feb. 1818), 220.

Greenland, and Other Poems. 1819. (P)
    British Critic, ns,v12 (Aug. 1812), 211-18.
    British Lady's Magazine, s3,v3 (Oct. 1819), 180-82.
    Christian's Pocket Magazine, 1 (June 1819), 96-103.
    Christian's Pocket Magazine, 1 (Oct. 1819), 363-64. (Di-
       gested from Edinburgh Monthly Review and Eclectic Re-
       view.)
    Christian's Pocket Magazine, 2 (Mar. 1820), 155. (Di-
       gested from Monthly Review.)
    Eclectic Review, s2,v12 (Sept. 1819), 210-28.
    Fireside Magazine, 1 (July 1819), 254-55.
    Fireside Magazine (quoting Monthly Magazine), 1 (July
       1819), 277.
    Gentleman's Magazine, 89[2] (Aug. 1819), 145-46.
    Literary and Statistical Magazine, 3 (Nov. 1819), 379-80.
    Literary Gazette, Apr. 24, 1819, pp. 257-58.
    Monthly Magazine, 47 (June 1819), 445.
    Monthly Review, 91 (Jan. 1820), 56-61.

Montgomery, James, James Grahame, and E. Benger.
    Poems on the Abolition of the Slave Trade. 1809. (P)
       Christian Observer, 9 (Feb. 1810), 103-17.
       Critical Review, s3,v22 (Jan. 1811), 38-47.
       Eclectic Review, 6 (Apr., May 1810), 289-306, 440-50.
       Monthly Review, 64 (Feb. 1811), 144-52.
       Scots Magazine, 72 (June 1810), 439-44.

Montolieu, Mrs. _____.
  The Enchanted Plants. Fables in Verse. (Anon.) 1800. (P)
    British Critic, 15 (May 1800), 512-16.
    Critical Review, s2,v29 (June 1800), 232-35.
    Monthly Magazine, 9 (July 1820), 638.
    Monthly Review, 33 (Nov. 1800), 311-12.
    New London Review, 3 (May 1800), 471-73.
    Poetical Register, 1 (1801), 439.

  The Festival of the Rose, with Other Poems. 1802. (P)
    Antijacobin Review, 18 (May 1804), 44-46.
    Lady's Monthly Museum, 13 (July 1804), 61.
    Poetical Register, 2 (1802), 432.

Moody, Elizabeth.
  Poetic Trifles. 1799. (P)
    British Critic, 14 (July 1799), 72.
    Critical Review, s2,v25 (Feb. 1799), 229-30.
    Monthly Magazine, Suppl. v7 (July 20, 1799), 537.
    Monthly Review, 27 (Dec. 1798), 442-47.
    Monthly Visitor, 6 (Apr. 1799), 411-13.
    Monthly Visitor, 8 (Sept. 1799), 37.
    New Annual Register, 19 (1798), [310].

Moonshine, Mauritius.
  The Battle of the Bards, an Heroic Poem. 1800. (P)
    Antijacobin Review, 7 (Sept. 1800), 58-59.
    Critical Review, s2,v30 (Dec. 1800), 475.
    Monthly Mirror, 10 (Sept. 1800), 172-73.

  More Wonders! an Heroic Epistle to M. G. Lewis, Esq. With
  a Praescript Extraordinary, and an Ode on the Union. 1801.
  (P)
    Antijacobin Review, 8 (Apr. 1801), 416-19.
    Critical Review, s2,v34 (Apr. 1802), 469-70.
    Monthly Mirror, 11 (Feb. 1801), 108-10.
    Poetical Register, 1 (1801), 448-49.
    Union Magazine and Imperial Register, 1 (Mar. 1801), 197.

Moore, Frances.
  Manners. (Anon.) 1817. (F)
    Monthly Review, ns,v85 (Mar. 1818), 327-28.

  A Year and a Day. By Madame Panache, Author of Manners.
  1818. (F)
    Fireside Magazine (quoting Monthly Review), 1 (June
      1819), 226.
    Literary Panorama, ns,v9 (July 1819), 887.
    Monthly Review, ns,v88 (Apr. 1819), 446.

Moore, Francis.
  The Age of Intellect, or Clerical Showfolk, and Wonderful
  Layfolk. (P)

Monthly Magazine, 47 (July 1819), 539.
Theatre, or Dramatic and Literary Mirror, 2 (Aug. 7,
1819), pp. 35-37.

Moore, George.
Theodosius de Zulvin, the Monk of Madrid. (F)
Monthly Magazine, Suppl. v17 (July 28, 1804), 667.
Monthly Review, ns,v43 (Apr. 1804), 440-41.

Tales of the Passions, in Which Is Attempted an Illustra-
tion of Their Effects on the Human Mind. 1808. (F)
Annual Review, 7 (1808), 619-21.
Le Beau Monde, 5 (Feb. 1809), 35-36.
British Critic, 32 (Oct. 1808), 414-16.
Oxford Review, 3 (Mar. 1808), 299-304.

Moore, Rev. Henry.
Poems, Lyrical and Miscellaneous. 1803. (P)
Annual Review, 2 (1803), 588-91.
Critical Review, s2,v38 (June 1803), 210-16.
Gentleman's Magazine, 73^1 (Feb. 1803), 155.
Literary Annual Register, 1 (Feb. 1807), 78-79.
Literary Journal, a Review..., ns,v1 (Apr. 1806), 383-89.
Literary Panorama, 1 (Jan. 1807), 727-28.
Monthly Magazine, Suppl. v15 (July 28, 1803), 636-37.
Monthly Mirror, 21 (June 1806), 393.
Monthly Register, 3 (May 1803), 14-15.
New Annual Register, 24 (1803), [326-27].
Poetical Register, 3 (1803), 438.
Universal Magazine, ns,v2 (Sept.-Dec., 1804), 255-60.
447-51, 541-46.

Moore, Rev. James L.
The Columbiad: An Epic Poem, on the Discovery of America
and the West Indies by Columbus. 1798. (P)
Critical Review, s2,v23 (May 1798), 66-68.
Monthly Magazine, Suppl. v5 (July 15, 1798), 506.
Monthly Mirror, 6 (Aug. 1798), 99.

Moore, John.
Mordaunt; Sketches of Life, Characters, and Manners, in
Various Countries. (Anon.) 1800. (F)
British Critic, 15 (Mar. 1800), 318-19.
Monthly Magazine, Suppl. v9 (July 20, 1800), 640.
Monthly Review, ns,v32 (June 1800), 149-52.

The Post Captain, or the Wooden Walls Well Manned; Compre-
hending a View of Naval Society and Manners. (Anon.)
1806. (F)
British Critic, 27 (May 1806), 551-52.
Critical Review, s3,v10 (Mar. 1807), 325-26.
Monthly Magazine, Suppl. v21 (July 25, 1806), 609.

Moore, Marian.
  Ariana and Maud. 1803. (F)
    Critical Review, ns,v37 (Mar. 1803), 356.
    Monthly Magazine, Suppl. v15 (July 28, 1803), 639.

Moore, Mrs. Robert.
  Eveleen Mountjoy; or, Views of Life. 1819. (F)
    Gentleman's Magazine, 90[1] (Jan. 1820), 53-54.
    Monthly Review, ns,v91 (Feb. 1820), 215.

Moore, Thomas.
  The Poetical Works of the Late Thomas Little. 1801. (P)
    British Critic, 18 (1801), 540-41.
    Critical Review, s2,v34 (Feb. 1802), 200-05.
    Monthly Magazine, Suppl. v13 (July 20, 1802), 658.
    Monthly Mirror, 12 (Nov. 1801), 316-17.
    Monthly Review, 39 (Oct. 1802), 174-79.
    New Annual Register, 23 (1802), [314].
    Poetical Register, 1 (1801), 431.
    Union Magazine and Imperial Register, 1 (June 1801), 442-
    43.

  Epistles, Odes, and Other Poems. 1806. (P)
    Annual Review, 5 (1806), 498-99.
    Antijacobin Review, 24 (July 1806), 263-71.
    Le Beau Monde, 1 (Nov.-Dec. 1806), 37-41, 97-101.
    Critical Review, s3,v9 (Oct. 1806), 113-28.
    Eclectic Review, 2 (Oct. 1806), 811-15.
    Edinburgh Review, 8 (July 1806), 456-65.
    Flowers of Literature, 5 (1806), 500-01.
    Literary Journal, a Review..., ns,v1 (June 1806), 646-57.
    Monthly Literary Recreations, 1 (July 1806), 84-85.
    Monthly Mirror, 22 (Sept. 1806), 182-83.
    Monthly Review, 51 (Sept. 1806), 59-70.
    Poetical Register, 6 (1806-07), 499.
    Universal Magazine, ns,v5 (May 1806), 428-33.

  Corruption and Intolerance; Two Poems. Addressed to an
  Englishman by an Irishman. (Anon.) 1808. (P)
    Antijacobin Review, 31 (Nov. 1808), 308-09.
    Le Beau Monde, 4 (Sept. 1808), 119-21.
    British Critic, 32 (Nov. 1808), 517-18.
    Cyclopaedian Magazine, 2 (Oct. 1808), 567-69.
    Monthly Mirror, ns,v4 (Sept. 1808), 173-76.
    Monthly Review, 58 (Apr. 1809), 418-22.
    Poetical Register, 7 (1808-09), 569.
    Satirist, 6 (May 1810), 517. (Excerpts from other Re-
    views.)
    Satirist, 7 (July 1810), 80-89.

  The Sceptic: A Philosophical Satire. By the Author of
  Corruption and Intolerance. 1809. (P)
    Monthly Review, 60 (Sept. 1809), 103-04.

Moore, Thomas (continued)
    Poetical Register, 8 (1810), 581.

  Irish Melodies. 1812-24. (P)
    La Belle Assemblée, 30 (Dec. 1824), 260.
    Blackwood's Edinburgh Magazine, 11 (Jan. 1822), 62-67.
    British Stage and Literary Cabinet, 2 (Dec. 1818), 268-71.
    British Stage and Literary Cabinet, 5 (June 1821), 165-68.
    Edinburgh Reflector, 1 (Dec. 23, 1818), 223.
    Examiner, Jan. 3, 10, 1819, pp. 11, 43-44.
    Fireside Magazine (quoting Monthly Review), 1 (Feb. 1819),
        71.
    Lady's Monthly Museum, s3,v20 (Dec. 1824), 336.
    Literary Chronicle, Nov. 1821, pp. 705-07.
    Literary Gazette, May 12, 1821, pp. 290-91.
    Literary Gazette, Nov. 6, 1824, p. 705.
    Literary Journal, 1 (Oct. 10, 1818), 448-49.
    (Baldwin's) London Magazine, 3 (June 1821), 659-63.
    Monthly Review, 71 (June 1813), 113-26.
    Monthly Review, 74 (June 1814), 183-87.
    Monthly Review, 87 (Dec. 1818), 419-33.
    New Monthly Magazine, s2,v12 (1824), 555.
    Quarterly Review, 7 (June 1812), 374-82.
    Quarterly Review, 28 (Oct. 1822), 138-44.
    Theatrical Inquisitor, 7 (Aug. 1815), 128-31.

  Intercepted Letters; or the Two-penny Post Bag. By Thomas
  Brown, the Younger. 1813. (P)
    Antijacobin Review, 46 (Mar. 1814), 266-68. (11th ed.)
    Critical Review, s4,v3 (Apr. 1813), 421-26.
    Drakard's Paper, Apr. 4, 1813, p. 101.
    Monthly Review, 70 (Apr. 1813), 436-38. (3rd ed.)
    New Annual Register, 34 (1813), [409].
    New Review, 2 (July 1813), 83-86.
    Satirist, 13 (Dec. 1813), 553-57.
    Scourge, 5 (May 1813), 390-400.

  A Series of Sacred Songs, Duets, and Trios. 1816. (P)
    Blackwood's Edinburgh Magazine, 1 (Sept. 1817), 630-31.
    British Review, 8 (Aug. 1816), 164-69.
    Critical Review, s5,v3 (June 1816), 607-16.
    Christian's Pocket Magazine, 2 (Feb. 1820), 89-91. (Di-
        gested from Monthly Review.)
    Edinburgh Monthly Review, 1 (Jan. 1819), 41-47.
    Fireside Magazine (quoting Monthly Review), 1 (Feb. 1819),
        76.
    Monthly Review, 90 (Dec. 1819), 413-20.

  Lalla Rookh, an Oriental Romance. 1817. (P)
    Asiatic Journal, 4 (Nov. 1817), 457-67.
    La Belle Assemblée, Suppl. ns,v16 (1817), 344-46.
    Blackwood's Edinburgh Magazine, 1 (June, Aug. 1817),
        279-85, 503-10.

Moore, Thomas (continued)
    British Critic, ns,v7 (June 1817), 604-16.
    British Lady's Magazine, ns,vl (Sept. 1817), 180-81.
    British Review, 10 (Aug. 1817), 30-54.
    Champion, May 25, 1817, 165.
    Critical Review, s5,v5 (June 1817), 560-81.
    Eclectic Review, s2,v8 (Oct. 1817), 340-53.
    Edinburgh Review, 29 (Nov. 1817), 1-35.
    European Magazine, 72 (July 1817), 55-58.
    Gentleman's Magazine, 87[1] (June 1817), 535-37.
    Knight Errant, 1 (July 5, 1817), 5-9.
    Literary and Political Examiner, 1 (Mar. 1818), 113-15.
    Literary and Statistical Magazine, 1 (Aug. 1817), 297-307.
    Literary Gazette, May 31, 1817, pp. 292-95.
    Literary Panorama, ns,v6 (Sept. 1817), 897-913.
    Monthly Magazine, 43 (June 1817), 450-51.
    Monthly Review, 83 (June-July 1817), 177-201, 285-99.
    New Monthly Magazine, 8 (Aug. 1817), 52.
    Newry Magazine, 4 (Mar.-Apr. 1818), 1-5.
    Sale-Room, 1 (May 31, 1817), 173-75.
    Scots Magazine, 79 (July 1817), 528-31.

The Fudge Family in Paris. Edited by Thomas Brown, the
Younger. 1818. (P)
    Blackwood's Edinburgh Magazine, 3 (May 1818), 129-36.
    British Critic, ns,v9 (May 1818), 496-501.
    British Lady's Magazine, ns,v2 (June 1818), 273-74.
    Champion, (Apr. 26, 1818), 267-68.
    Champion, Mar. 21, Apr. 4-11, 1819, 190, 220-21, 236-37.
    Edinburgh Magazine and Literary Miscellany (Scots Maga-
        zine), ns,v2 (June 1818), 553-58.
    European Magazine, 73 (May 1818), 517-19.
    Gentleman's Magazine, 88[1] (June 1818), 527-28.
    Literary and Political Examiner, 1 (May 1818), 195-203.
    Literary Chronicle, 1 (May 4, 1818), 87-89.
    Literary Gazette, Apr. 25, 1818, pp. 265-67.
    Literary Journal and General Miscellany, 1 (Apr. 26-May 3,
        1818), 71-72, 87-89.
    Monthly Magazine, 45 (May 1818), 342-44.
    Monthly Review, 85 (Apr. 1818), 426-32.
    New Bon Ton Magazine, 1 (May 1818), 49-52.
    Yellow Dwarf, 1 (Apr. 25, 1818), 132-35.

Replies to the Letters of the Fudge Family. Edited by
Thomas Brown [Thomas Moore?]. 1818. (P)
    La Belle Assemblée, ns,v18 (Dec. 1818), 272-74.
    British Lady's Magazine, s3,v2 (Jan. 1819), 37.
    Literary Gazette, Dec. 5, 1818, pp. 771-73.
    Monthly Magazine, 46 (Jan. 1819), 531.
    Monthly Review, 88 (Jan. 1819), 111.

Tom Crib's Memorial to Congress. By One of the Fancy.
1819. (P)

Moore, Thomas (concluded)
  La Belle Assemblée, ns,v19 (Apr. 1819), 179-80.
  Edinburgh Magazine and Literary Miscellany (Scots Maga-
    zine), s2,v4 (Apr. 1819), 300-04.
  Fireside Magazine (quoting Monthly Review and Monthly
    Magazine), 1 (May, June 1819), 196, 225.
  Fireside Magazine, 1 (July 1819), 257-58.
  Literary Gazette, Mar. 13, 1819, pp. 163-65.
  Literary Panorama, s2,v9 (June 1819), 685-88.
  Miniature Magazine, 1 (Sept. 1820), 165-67.
  Monthly Magazine, 47 (Apr. 1819), 254.
  Monthly Review, 88 (Apr. 1819), 436-40.

  National Airs. 1818-27. (P)
  Examiner, Feb. 13, 1820, p. 105.
  Examiner, Dec. 1, 1822, p. 774.
  Literary Gazette, Dec. 14, 1822, p. 785.
  Monthly Magazine, 53 (June 1822), 448.

Moore, Thomas George.
  The Bachelor. 1809. (F)
  Le Beau Monde, 1 (Apr. 1809), 36.
  Critical Review, s3,v16 (Apr. 1809), 430-31.
  Monthly Magazine, Suppl. v27 (July 30, 1809), 667.
  Satirist, 4 (Feb. 1809), 185-88.
  Satirist, 7 (Sept. 1810), 304.

More, Hannah.
  Coelebs in Search of a Wife. Comprehending Observations on
  Domestic Habits and Manners, Religion and Morals. 1809. (F)
  British Critic, 33 (May 1809), 481-94.
  Cabinet, ns,v1 (Apr. 1809), 347-55.
  Critical Review, s3,v16 (Mar. 1809), 252-64.
  Edinburgh Review, v14 (Apr. 1809), 145-51.
  European Magazine, 56 (Sept.-Nov. 1809), 196-201, 283-87,
    373-78.
  Evangelical Magazine, 17 (July 1809), 289.
  Literary and Statistical Magazine, 3 (May 1819), 183.
  Literary Panorama, 6 (May 1809), 259-68.
  Monthly Magazine, Suppl. v27 (July 30, 1809), 663-67.
  Monthly Mirror, ns,v5 (Apr. 1809), 223-36.
  Monthly Review, ns,v58 (Feb. 1809), 128-36.
  Satirist, 4 (Apr. 1809), 384-90.
  Satirist, 7 (Nov. 1810), 511-12.
  Scots Magazine, 71 (June-July 1809), 435-41, 516-24.
  Universal Magazine, ns,v11 (Apr., June 1809), 327-36,
    515-24.

  Christian Morals. 1813.
  Antijacobin Review, 45 (Sept.-Oct., Dec., Suppl. 1813),
    251-63, 321-37, 521-33, 643-58.

  Sacred Dramas; Chiefly Intended for Young Persons. 1815.

19th ed. (D)
  Critical Review, s5,v2 (Aug. 1815), 204-05.
  Eclectic Review, ns,v3 (Apr. 1815), 404.

Moral Sketches of Prevailing Opinions and Manners, Foreign
and Domestic. 1819. (Pr)
  British Review, 14 (Nov. 1819), 458-74.

Morehead, Robert.
  Poetical Epistles, and Specimens of Translation. (Anon.)
  1813. (P)
  Blackwood's Edinburgh Magazine, 1 (Sept. 1817), 626-30.
  Monthly Review, 79 (Apr. 1816), 392-99.

Morell, Rev. Thomas.
  The Christian Pastor, a Poem. (Anon.) 1809. (P)
  Baptist Magazine, 1 (Nov. 1809), 463.
  Eclectic Review, 5 (Oct. 1809), 964-65.
  Literary Panorama, 8 (Nov. 1810), 1257-61.

Morgan, Mr. _____.
  Knyghte of the Golden Locks. (P)
  Monthly Magazine, Suppl. v7 (July 20, 1799), 536.

Morgan, Lady (née Sydney Owenson).
  See Sydney Owenson, afterwards Lady Morgan.

Morgan, T.
  Poetry. 1797. (P)
  Critical Review, s2,v24 (Nov. 1798), 351.

Morgan, William.
  Long Ashton, a Poem; Descriptive of the Local Scenery of
  That Village and Its Environs. 1814. (P)
  British Critic, ns,v2 (Aug. 1814), 216.
  Monthly Review, 75 (Oct. 1814), 214-15.

Moriarty, Mrs. Henrietta Maria.
  Crim. Con. 1812. (F)
  Critical Review, s4,v2 (Sept. 1812), 331-32.

  A Hero of Salamanca; or, the Novice Isabel. 1813. (F)
  Critical Review, s4,v3 (Mar. 1813), 332-33.
  Monthly Review, ns,v71 (June 1813), 212-13.

Morley, G. T.
  Deeds of Darkness; or the Unnatural Uncle, a Tale of the
  Sixteenth Century. 1805. (F)
  Critical Review, s3,v7 (Jan. 1806), 107-08.
  Literary Journal, a Review..., 5 (Apr. 1805), 436.
  Monthly Magazine, Suppl. v21 (July 25, 1806), 609.

Morley, Thomas.
  The Mechanic, a Poem. 1801. (P)
    British Critic, 19 (Jan. 1802), 83.
    Critical Review, s2,v35 (June 1802), 235.
    Monthly Review, 37 (Feb. 1802), 212.

Morris, Lord Rokeby.
  The Fall of Mortimer, a Tragedy. (D)
    Monthly Mirror, ns,v2 (Nov. 1807), 332.
    Monthly Review, ns,v54 (Oct. 1807), 211.
    Poetical Register, 6 (1807), 562.

Morris, Edward.
  The Secret, a Comedy. 1799. (D)
    Critical Review, ns,v26 (June 1799), 234-36.
    Monthly Mirror, 7 (June 1799), 356.
    Monthly Review, ns,v28 (Apr. 1799), 469-70.
    New London Review, 2 (Aug. 1799), 191.

Morritt, J. B. S.
  Miscellaneous Translations and Imitations of the Minor
  Greek Poets. 1802. (P)
    British Critic, 22 (Aug. 1803), 190.
    Monthly Review, 39 (Oct. 1802), 202-04.

Mortimer, Edward.
  Montoni; or, the Confessions of the Monk of St. Benedict.
  (F)
    English Censor, 1 (Feb. 1809), 151-54.

Morton, Mrs. _____.
  Beacon Hill, a Local Poem, Historic and Descriptive.   1797.
  (P)
    Analytical Review, ns,v1 (Mar. 1799), 311-13.

Morton, Thomas.
  Secrets Worth Knowing. 1798. (D)
    British Critic, 12 (July 1798), 73.
    Critical Review, ns,v23 (May 1798), 110-11.
    Monthly Magazine, Suppl. v6 (1798), 516.
    Monthly Mirror, 6 (July 1798), 38.
    Monthly Review, ns,v26 (June 1798), 226-27.
    Monthly Visitor, 3 (Apr. 1798), 413.

  Speed the Plow, a Comedy. 1800. (D)
    British Critic, 16 (Nov. 1800), 555.
    Critical Review, ns,v30 (Nov. 1800), 349-51.
    Monthly Mirror, 9 (Feb. 1800), 108-11.
    Monthly Mirror, 10 (July 1800), 38.
    Monthly Review, ns,v33 (Dec. 1800), 426-28.
    Monthly Visitor, 9 (Apr. 1800), 422-28.

  Speed the Plough. 1800. 4th ed. (D)

New London Review, 3 (Apr. 1800), 379-80.

The School of Reform; or How to Rule a Husband. 1805. (D)
   Annual Review, 4 (1805), 642-43.
   Antijacobin Review, 21 (May 1805), 69-70.
   British Critic, 26 (Oct. 1805), 440-41.
   Flowers of Literature, 4 (1805), 433.
   Literary Journal, a Review..., 5 (June 1805), 642-43.
   Monthly Mirror, 21 (May 1806), 333.
   Monthly Mirror, 19 (Feb. 1805), 117-21.
   Monthly Review, ns,v47 (May 1805), 99.
   Poetical Register, 5 (1805), 505.

Town and Country, a Comedy. 1807. (D)
   Annual Review, 6 (1807), 599.
   Flowers of Literature, 5 (1806), 515.
   Monthly Magazine, Suppl. v23 (July 30, 1807), 644.
   New Annual Register, 28 (1807), [379].
   Oxford Review, 2 (July 1807), 91-92.
   Poetical Register, 6 (1807), 564.

The Knight at Snowdoun, a Musical Drama. 1811. (D)
   Poetical Register, 8 (1811), 641.

Education, a Comedy. 1813. (D)
   British Critic, 41 (June 1813), 641-42.
   Monthly Review, ns,v73 (Jan. 1814), 100.
   New Review, 2 (July 1813), 89-92.
   Scourge, 5 (June 1813), 469-78.

The Slave, a Musical Drama. 1816. (D)
   British Stage and Literary Cabinet, 1 (Jan. 1817), 12-14.
   Theatrical Inquisitor, 9 (Dec. 1816), 414-17.

A Roland for an Oliver, a Farce. 1819. (D)
   British Stage and Literary Cabinet, 3 (June 1819), 166-67.
   Fireside Magazine (quoting Monthly Review), 1 (July 1819),
      266.
   Monthly Review, ns,v89 (May 1819), 101.

Henri Quatre; or Paris in the Olden Time, a Musical Romance.
1820. (D)
   Monthly Review, ns,v92 (June 1820), 217.
   Theatrical Inquisitor, 16 (June 1820), 385-86.

Moser, Joseph.
   Moral Tales; Consisting of the Reconciliation, a Sketch of
   the Belvoir Family; a Fairy Tale in the Modern Style; Cle-
   mentia and Malitia.... 1797. (F)
      Analytical Review, 27 (Feb. 1798), 201-03.
      British Critic, 11 (May 1798), 562.
      Critical Review, ns,v23 (May 1798), 115.
      European Magazine, 34 (July 1798), 40.

411

Monthly Magazine, Suppl. v5 (July 15, 1798), 508.
Monthly Mirror, 5 (Apr. 1798), 222.
Monthly Review, ns,v25 (Mar. 1798), 346-47.

The Hermit of Caucasus, an Oriental Romance. 1797. (F)
  Critical Review, ns,v25 (Feb. 1799), 233.
  Monthly Magazine, Suppl. v7 (July 20, 1799), 542.

Tales and Romances, of Ancient and Modern Times. 1800. (F)
  British Critic, 17 (Jan. 1801), 81.

British Loyalty, or Long Live the King! A Dramatic Effu-
sion, with Songs and Dances. 1809. (D)
  British Critic, 34 (Nov. 1809), 520-21.
  European Magazine, 56 (Nov. 1809), 379-81.
  Gentleman's Magazine, 79² (Nov. 1809), 1041-42.
  Monthly Magazine, Suppl. v28 (Jan. 31, 1810), 665.
  Monthly Review, ns,v60 (Nov. 1809), 324-25.

Mosse, Mrs. Henrietta Rouvierre.
  Arrivals from India; or Time's Great Master. 1812. (F)
  Critical Review, s4,v2 (Sept. 1812), 332.

  Bride and No Wife. (F)
  New Monthly Magazine, 9 (Mar. 1818), 153.

Mott, Thomas.
  The Stranger's Visit, with Other Minor Poems. 1813. (P)
  Monthly Review, 72 (Nov. 1813), 324-25.

Moultrie, Rev. George.
  False and True, a Play. (Anon.) 1798. (D)
  Analytical Review, 28 (Sept. 1798), 297.
  British Critic, 13 (June 1799), 664.
  Monthly Magazine, Suppl. v7 (July 20, 1799), 538.
  Monthly Mirror, 6 (Sept. 1798), 164.
  Monthly Review, ns,v28 (Jan. 1799), 106-07.

Mower, Arthur.
  The Welsh Mountaineer. 1811. (F)
  Antijacobin Review, 42 (July 1812), 299-300.
  Monthly Review, ns,v67 (Mar. 1812), 322.

  The White Cottage, a Tale. (Anon.) 1817. (F)
  Monthly Review, ns,v83 (May 1817), 99.

Mudford, William.
  Augustus and Mary, or the Maid of Buttermere, a Domestic
  Tale. 1804. (F)
  Antijacobin Review, 18 (Aug. 1804), 398.
  British Critic, 21 (June 1803), 674.
  Critical Review, ns,v38 (July 1803), 358.
  Flowers of Literature, 3 (1804), 449.

Monthly Mirror, 16 (July 1803), 40.
Monthly Review, ns,v43 (Apr. 1804), 441-42.

Nubilia in Search of a Husband; Including Sketches of Modern Society, and Interspersed with Moral and Literary Disquisitions. (Anon.) 1809. (F)
Antijacobin Review, 33 (June 1809), 183-87.
British Critic, 34 (Aug. 1809), 187.
British Critic, 35 (Feb. 1810), 187-88.
Critical Review, s3,v17 (Aug. 1809), 439.
European Magazine, 56 (Oct. 1809), 287-90.
Literary Panorama, 6 (Sept. 1809), 1105-06.
Monthly Review, ns,v59 (July 1809), 299-304.
Satirist, 5 (Aug. 1809), 174-82.
Satirist, 7 (Dec. 1810), 595-96. (Excerpts from other reviews.)
Scots Magazine, 71 (Aug. 1809), 585-98.
Universal Magazine, ns,v12 (July-Aug. 1809), 34-38, 120-27.

The Life and Adventures of Paul Plaintive, Esq.... By Martin Gribaldus Swammerdam, His Nephew and Executor. 1811. (F)
British Critic, 39 (Jan. 1812), 81-82.
Universal Magazine, ns,v16 (Nov. 1811), 391-99.

Mudie, Robert.
Glenfergus. (Anon.) 1820. (F)
Dublin Magazine, General Repository, 1 (Mar. 1820), 232-37.
Kaleidoscope, 2 (Mar. 21, 1820), 141-42. (From The Scotsman.)
Literary Chronicle, 2 (Mar. 25, 1820), 193-95.
Monthly Review, ns,v91 (Apr. 1820), 440-41.

Munnings, J. S.
A Dramatic Dialogue between an English Sailor and a Frenchman. 1802. (D)
Monthly Review, 41 (June 1803), 218-20.

Murmur, Sir Fretful.
More Miseries!! Addressed to the Morbid, the Melancholy, and the Irritable. 1806. (Pr)
Le Beau Monde, 1 (Mar. 1807), 275-77.
European Magazine, 51 (Apr. 1807), 290.
Flowers of Literature, 5 (1806), 507.
Literary Journal, a Review..., ns,v2 (Nov. 1806), 504-06.
Monthly Review, 52 (Jan. 1807), 110-11.

Murphy, Arthur.
Arminius, a Tragedy. 1790. (D)
Analytical Review, 28 (July 1798), 80-93.
Antijacobin Review, 1 (Aug. 1798), 191-93.
British Critic, 12 (Oct. 1798), 415-19.
Critical Review, ns,v24 (Nov. 1798), 353-56.

Monthly Mirror, 6 (Sept. 1798), 163-64.
Monthly Review, ns,v27 (Dec. 1798), 394-99.

The Bees. A Poem from the Fourteenth Book of Vaniere's
Praedium Rusticum. 1799. (P)
   Analytical Review, ns,vl (May 1799), 514-17.
   British Critic, 14 (Sept. 1799), 309.
   Monthly Magazine, Suppl. v7 (July 20, 1799), 536.
   Monthly Mirror, 7 (June 1799), 349.

The Force of Conscience. A Poem, in Imitation of the Thir-
teenth Satire of Juvenal. 1799. (P)
   British Critic, 14 (Sept. 1799), 308-09.
   Monthly Magazine, Suppl. v8 (Jan. 20, 1800), 1052.

Murphy, Dennis Jasper.
   Fatal Revenge; or, the Family of Montorio, a Romance.
   1807. (F)
   Annual Review, 6 (1807), 668-69.
   Monthly Literary Recreations, 3 (Oct. 1807), 310-13.
   Quarterly Review, 3 (May 1810), 339-47.

Murray, Mrs. _____.
   Henry Count de Kolinski; a Polish Tale. 1810.   (F)
   Critical Review, s3,v20 (June 1810), 218-19.
   Gentleman's Magazine, 80[1] (Apr. 1810), 355.
   Monthly Review, ns,v62 (Aug. 1810), 435.
   Repository of Arts, 4 (July 1810), 34.

Murray, Hugh.
   The Swiss Emigrants, a Tale. (Anon.) 1804.   (F)
   Antijacobin Review, 17 (Feb. 1804), 189-90.
   British Critic, 23 (Apr. 1804), 434.
   Critical Review, s3,vl (Mar. 1804), 357-58.
   Lady's Monthly Museum, 13 (Oct. 1804), 273-74.
   Literary Journal, a Review..., 3 (Mar. 1, 1804), 227-28.
   Monthly Magazine, Suppl. vl8 (Jan. 28, 1805), 595.
   Monthly Visitor, ns,v6 (Feb. 1804), 207-08.
   North British Magazine, 2 (Aug. 1804), 117-18.

   Corasmin; or, the Minister, a Romance. By the Author of
   The Swiss Emigrants. 1814. (F)
   Critical Review, s5,vl (Mar. 1815), 313.
   Gentleman's Magazine, 85[1] (Suppl. Jan.-June 1815), 612-
   13.
   Monthly Review, ns,v75 (Dec. 1814), 433-34.

Murray, Lindley.
   Sequel to the English Reader; or, Elegant Selections in
   Prose and Poetry: Designed to Improve the Highest Class of
   Learners, in Reading; to Establish a Taste for Just and Ac-
   curate Composition.... 1805. (Pr)
   Eclectic Review, 1 (June 1805), 425-26.

Musgrave, Agnes.
  The Confession. 1801. (F)
    Critical Review, ns,v33 (Oct. 1801), 237.

  William de Montfort, or the Sicilian Heiresses. 1808. (F)
    Critical Review, s3,v14 (June 1808), 218-20.
    Monthly Review, ns,v58 (Jan. 1809), 101.

Mussenden, Edward.
  An Ode. The Glorious Defeat of the French Fleet, near the
  Nile, by Admiral Sir Horatio Nelson. 1798. (P)
    British Critic, 15 (June 1800), 674.

Myers, T.
  Nelson, Triumphant, a Poem. 1806. (P)
    Antijacobin Review, 23 (Feb. 1806), 209-10.
    British Critic, 29 (Apr. 1807), 427-28.
    Monthly Review, 49 (Mar. 1806), 317.

Myrtle, Marmaduke.
  See Thomas Dermody.

Nares, Edward.
  Thinks-I-To-Myself. A Serio-Ludicro, Tragico-Comico Tale.
  Written by Thinks-I-To-Myself Who? (Anon.) 1811. (F)
    British Critic, 38 (Aug. 1811), 170-76.
    British Critic, 42 (Aug. 1813), 193-95.
    Critical Review, s3,v24 (Dec. 1811), 382-92.
    Gentleman's Magazine, 81^2 (Oct. 1811), 355-57.
    Monthly Review, ns,v66 (Oct. 1811), 207-08.
    New Annual Register, 32 (1811), [366].
    Universal Magazine, ns,v16 (Oct. 1811), 308-13.

  I Says, Says I. By Thinks-I-To-Myself. (Anon.) 1812. (F)
    British Critic, 39 (Apr. 1812), 418.
    Universal Magazine, ns,v17 (May 1812), 398.

Nason, George.
  The Science of Ethics, a Poem. 1799. (P)
    Critical Review, s2,v25 (Apr. 1799), 468-69.

  Aphono and Ethina, Including the Science of Ethics, Founded
  on the Principles of Universal Science. (P)
    British Critic, 15 (June 1800), 673-74.
    Critical Review, s2,v31 (Jan. 1801), 111-12.
    Monthly Review, 32 (Aug. 1800), 437-38.

Nathan, Mrs. _____.
  Elvington. 1819. (F)
    Antijacobin Review, 56 (May 1819), 229-34.
    Fireside Magazine (quoting Antijacobin Review), 1 (July
      1819), 273.

Neale, Cornelius.
  Lyrical Dramas; with Domestic Hours, a Miscellany of Odes
  and Songs. 1819. (P)
    Eclectic Review, s2,v12 (Oct. 1819), 346-53.
    Literary Gazette, Sept. 25, 1819, pp. 609-11.
    Monthly Review, 92 (Aug. 1820), 402-07.
    New Monthly Magazine, 12 (Nov. 1819), 457.

Neele, Henry.
  Odes, and Other Poems. 1816. (P)
    British Lady's Magazine, 5 (Mar. 1817), 161-65.
    British Lady's Magazine, ns,v2 (June 1818), 271-73.
    Champion, Dec. 30, 1820, pp. 852-53.
    Critical Review, s5,v5 (Feb. 1817), 207-09.
    Eclectic Review, s2,v8 (Dec. 1817), 601-03.
    Gentleman's Magazine, 90^1 (Jan. 1820), 55.
    Literary Gazette, Oct. 18, 1817, p. 245.
    Literary Journal and General Miscellany, 1 (Apr. 26,
    1818), 70-71.
    Literary Panorama, ns,v5 (Feb. 1817), 765-68.
    Monthly Magazine, 43 (Feb. 1817), 64.
    Monthly Review, 84 (Oct. 1817), 209-10.

Neri, Mary Ann.
  The Hour of Trial, a Tale. (F)
    Annual Review, 7 (1808), 604-05.
    Antijacobin Review, 31 (Oct. 1808), 192-95.

Neville, O.
  The Lay of the Last Minstrel Travesty. (Anon.) 1811. (P)
    Monthly Review, 64 (Mar. 1811), 315.
    Poetical Register, 8 (1811), 610-11.

Newenham, Francis.
  The Pleasures of Anarchy; a Dramatic Sermon. (Anon.)
  1809. (P)
    Antijacobin Review, 34 (Nov. 1809), 314-15.
    British Critic, 35 (Mar. 1810), 297-98.
    Monthly Review, 66 (Sept. 1811), 110-11.
    Poetical Register, 8 (1810), 594.

Newenham, Thomas.
  The Warning Drum, a Call to the People of England to Resist
  Invaders. 1803. (P)
    Critical Review, s2,v39 (Sept. 1803), 106-07.

Newman, John Henry, and John William Bowden.
  St. Bartholomew's Eve, a Tale of the Sixteenth Century.
  (Anon.) 1818. (P)
    Antijacobin Review, 56 (Aug. 1819), 525-27.
    Literary Gazette, Oct. 30, 1819, pp. 690-92.
    New Monthly Magazine, 13 (Jan. 1820), 91.

Newman, Sarah.
  Poems on Subjects Connected with Scripture. 1811. (P)
    British Critic, 38 (Sept. 1811), 295.
    Christian Observer, 10 (Oct. 1811), 644-49.
    Evangelical Magazine, 20 (May 1812), 188.

Newport, Matthew.
  Don Emanuel, a Poem. 1813. (P)
    British Critic, 42 (Sept. 1813), 293-94.
    Eclectic Review, 10 (Dec. 1813), 601-10.
    Monthly Review, 76 (Feb. 1815), 209-11.

Newton, Charles.
  Poems. (P)
    British Critic, 15 (Feb. 1800), 191.

Nicholson, John.
  Paetus and Arria, a Tragedy. 1809. (D)
    British Critic, 34 (Sept. 1809), 300-01.
    Critical Review, s3,v17 (May 1809), 108.
    New Annual Register, 30 (1809), [372].
    Poetical Register, 8 (1810), 593.

Nicol, Rev. James.
  Poems Chiefly in the Scottish Dialect. 1805. (P)
    Critical Review, s3,v8 (June 1806), 216-17.
    Literary Journal, a Review..., ns,v1 (Mar. 1806), 330-31.
    Monthly Mirror, 22 (Aug. 1806), 112.
    Monthly Review, 51 (Dec. 1806), 432-34.
    Poetical Register, 5 (1805), 489.

Noble, Thomas.
  The Dawn of Peace, an Ode; and Amphion, or the Force of Con-
  cord, Regulation, and Peace, an Ode. 1801. (P)
    British Critic, 19 (Jan. 1802), 82.
    Critical Review, s2,v34 (Apr. 1802), 470-71.
    Monthly Mirror, 13 (May 1802), 332-33.
    Poetical Register, 1 (1801), 446.

  Blackheath, a Poem; Lumena, or the Ancient British Battle;
  and Various Other Poems. 1808. (P)
    Le Beau Monde, 4 (Aug. 1808), 75-78.
    British Critic, 32 (Sept. 1808), 293-96.
    Critical Review, s3,v15 (Oct. 1808), 170-79.
    Literary Annual Register, 2 (Nov. 1808), 498-99.
    Monthly Mirror, ns,v4 (Oct. 1808), 223-29.
    Monthly Review, 60 (Sept. 1809), 34-42.
    Poetical Register, 7 (1808), 549-50.

Nooth, Charlotte.
  Original Poems, and a Play. 1815. (P-D)
    Augustan Review, 1 (Aug. 1815), 376-80.

Eglantine; or, the Family of Fortesque. 1816. (F)
  Augustan Review, 3 (Oct. 1816), 362-66.
  Critical Review, s5,v4 (Sept. 1816), 318.
  Monthly Review, ns,v83 (May 1817), 99.

Norcott, William.
  The Metropolis, a Poem. (Anon.) (P)
    Ireland's Mirror, 2 (June 1805), 313-17.
    Ireland's Mirror, 3 (Feb. 1806), 97-99.

  The Seven Thieves. By the Author of The Metropolis. (P)
    Cyclopaedian Magazine, 1 (July 1807), 419-21.

  The Law Scrutiny, or Attornies' Guide. (Anon.) (P)
    Cyclopaedian Magazine, 1 (Feb. 1807), 98.

Norris, Mrs. _____.
  Second Love; or, the Way to Be Happy. 1805. (F)
    Flowers of Literature, 4 (1805), 433.
    Literary Journal, a Review..., 5 (July 1805), 772.

  The Strangers. 1806. (F)
    Critical Review, s3,v8 (Aug. 1806), 443.

  Olivia and Marcella; or, the Strangers. (2nd ed. of The
  Strangers.) 1806. (F)
    Flowers of Literature, 5 (1806), 509.
    Monthly Literary Recreations, 2 (Feb. 1807), 151.

  Julia of England. 1808. (F)
    Antijacobin Review, 30 (July 1808), 302-04.
    British Critic, 32 (Aug. 1808), 190.
    Monthly Review, ns,v59 (July 1809), 319-20.

  Euphronia, or the Captive, a Romance. 1810. (F)
    Monthly Mirror, ns,v7 (Apr. 1810), 292.

Northmore, Thomas.
  Washington, or Liberty Restored: A Poem. 1809. (P)
    British Critic, 40 (Sept. 1812), 298-99.
    Critical Review, s3,v19 (Jan. 1810), 88-96.
    Poetical Register, 7 (1809), 587.
    Quarterly Review, 2 (Nov. 1809), 365-75.
    Satirist, 6 (Jan., Mar. 1810), 87-98, 282-91.

Nott, John.
  Sappho; after a Greek Romance. (Anon.) (F)
    Annual Review, 2 (1803), 603-04.
    Monthly Magazine, Suppl. v17 (July 28, 1804), 666-67.
    Monthly Register, 3 (Sept. 1803), 184.

Noyes, Robert.
  Distress: A Pathetic Poem. 2nd ed. 1808. (P)

British Critic, 36 (Nov. 1810), 517-19.
Critical Review, s3,v17 (June 1809), 217-18.
Eclectic Review, 5 (Apr. 1809), 384.
Monthly Review, 68 (Nov. 1810), 315-18.

Nunnez, Fabricia.
  See Peter Coxe.

Nutt, T.
  The Writings of a Person in Obscurity, and Native of the
  Isle of Wight. 1806. (P)
    British Critic, 29 (Mar. 1807), 312-13.

O., D., Radical Laureate.
  Ginger Bread; a Grand Pindaric, in Honour of the Radicals
  and Whigs. 1819. (P)
    Antijacobin Review, 58 (Mar. 1820), 79-83.

O., S.
  See Sydney Owenson.

Observer, An.
  See John Corry.

O'Caustic, Carol.
  The Laughable Lover. A Comedy. 1806. (D)
    Antijacobin Review, 25 (Dec. 1806), 424-25.
    British Critic, 27 (June 1806), 669-70.
    Critical Review, s3,v8 (June 1806), 212.
    Literary Journal, a Review..., ns,v1 (June 1806), 671.
    Monthly Review, ns,v51 (Oct. 1806), 213.
    Poetical Register, 6 (1806), 5 (1806), 526-27.

Odoherty, Mr. _____.
  The Feast of Bellona, and Other Poems. By a Military Amateur. 1819. (P)
    Blackwood's Edinburgh Magazine, 5 (May 1819), 206-10.

Oedipus, Andrew.
  The Sphinx's Head Broken; or, a Poetical Epistle to Thomas
  James M*th**s. 1798. (P)
    British Critic, 11 (June 1798), 677.
    Critical Review, s2,v22 (Feb. 1798), 229-30.
    Gentleman's Magazine, 68^2 (Aug. 1798), 694.
    Monthly Mirror, 5 (Feb. 1798), 101-02.
    Monthly Review, 25 (Apr. 1798), 473.

Officer in the Indian Army, An.
  See Capt. _____ French.

Officer's Wife, An.
  See Mrs. Susan Fraser.

Ogg, George.
  Admonition, a Poem on the Fashionable Modes of Female
  Dress; with Miscellaneous Pieces in Verse. 1806. (P)
    British Critic, 30 (Oct. 1807), 439-40.
    Critical Review, s3,v10 (Feb. 1807), 217-18.
    European Magazine, 50 (Nov. 1806), 386.
    Monthly Mirror, ns,v1 (Mar. 1807), 191.
    Monthly Review, 54 (Oct. 1807), 211.

Ogilvie, John.
  Britannia: A National Epic Poem. To Which Is Prefixed a
  Critical Dissertation on Epic Machinery. 1801. (P)
    Antijacobin Review, 11 (Mar. 1802), 272-80.
    British Critic, 18 (Dec. 1801), 640-51.
    Critical Review, s2,v32 (Aug. 1801), 392-404.
    Monthly Magazine, Suppl. v13 (July 20, 1802), 657.
    Monthly Review, 37 (Apr. 1802), 359-64.
    Monthly Visitor, 14 (Oct. 1801), 206-09.
    New Annual Register, 22 (1801), [310-11].
    Poetical Register, 1 (1801), 424.
    Scots Magazine, 63 (July 1801), 485.

O'Keefe, Miss _____.
  Patriarchal Times, or the Land of Canaan. (F)
    Eclectic Review, 7 (Nov. 1811), 1029.

  Dudley, 1819. (F)
    La Belle Assemblée, ns,v20 (Oct. 1819), 184-85.
    European Magazine, 76 (Nov. 1819), 440-42.
    Miniature Magazine, ns,v1 (July 1820), 54-58.
    Monthly Review, ns,v90 (Sept. 1819), 105.

O'Keefe, John.
  The Farmer. 1800. (D)
    British Critic, 16 (Oct. 1800), 438.
    New London Review, 3 (Apr. 1800), 377.

  The Positive Man. 1800. (D)
    New London Review, 3 (Apr. 1800), 377.

  Love in a Camp; or, Patrick in Russia. 1800. (D)
    New London Review, 3 (June 1800), 567.

  The Highland Reel. 1800. (D)
    New London Review, 3 (June 1800), 567.

O'Kelly, Mr. _____.
  The Giant's Causeway and the Lake of Killarney. (P)
    Walker's Hibernian Magazine, 23 (Aug. 1808), 499-500.

Old Ben.
  Brazena; or, the Enchanted Island. An Epic Poem. (P)
    Loyalist; or Anti-Radical, 1 (1820), 49-52, 73-75.

Old Oxonian, An.
  See Rev. Samuel Partridge.

Ollier, Charles.
  Altham and His Wife. A Domestic Tale. (Anon.) 1818. (F)
    Blackwood's Edinburgh Magazine, 3 (Aug. 1818), 542-45.
    Eclectic Review, ns,v10 (Oct. 1818), 389-97.
    Fireside Magazine (quoting Monthly Review), 1 (June
      1819), 226.
    Literary Chronicle, 1 (July 6, 1818), 225-28.
    Literary Gazette, Mar. 20, 1819, pp. 180-81.
    Literary Journal and General Miscellany, 1 (July 4, 1818),
      225-28.
    Monthly Review, ns,v88 (Apr. 1819), 446.

One of the Fancy.
  See Thomas Moore.

Opie, Amelia.
  The Father and Daughter. 1801. 2nd ed. 1801. (F)
    Critical Review, ns,v35 (May 1802), 114-17.
    European Magazine, 40 (Sept. 1801), 194.
    Flowers of Literature, 1 (1801-02), 451.
    Monthly Magazine, Suppl. v11 (July 20, 1801), 606.
    Monthly Mirror, 11 (May 1801), 327.
    Monthly Review, 35 (June 1801), 163-66.

  Elegy to the Memory of the Late Duke of Bedford. 1802. (P)
    Critical Review, s2,v36 (Dec. 1802), 475-76.
    Monthly Review, 38 (May 1802), 99.
    New Annual Register, 23 (1802), [317].
    Poetical Register, 2 (1802), 440-41.

  Poems. 1802. (P)
    Annual Review, 1 (1802), 669-70.
    British Critic, 20 (Nov. 1802), 553-55.
    Critical Review, s2,v36 (Dec. 1802), 413-18.
    Edinburgh Review, 1 (Oct. 1802), 113-21.
    European Magazine, 42 (July 1802), 43-44.
    Monthly Magazine, Suppl. v14 (Jan. 25, 1803), 598.
    Monthly Mirror, 14 (July 1802), 39-41.
    Monthly Review, 39 (Dec. 1802), 434-35.
    New Annual Register, 23 (1802), [317].
    Poetical Register, 2 (1802), 430.

  Adeline Mowbray; or the Mother and Daughter. 1805. (F)
    Annual Review, 4 (1805), 653.
    Critical Review, s3,v4 (Feb. 1805), 219-21.
    Flowers of Literature, 4 (1805), 416.
    General Review, 1 (Jan. 1806), 22-27.
    Lady's Monthly Museum, 14 (May 1805), 343.
    Lady's Monthly Museum, 15 (Sept. 1805), 198-99.
    Literary Journal, a Review..., 5 (Feb. 1805), 171-75.

Opie, Mrs. Amelia (continued)
 Monthly Magazine, Suppl. v19 (July 28, 1805), 660.
 Monthly Mirror, 19 (Mar. 1805), 180.
 Monthly Review, ns,v51 (Nov. 1808), 320-21.
 New Annual Register, 26 (1805), [357].

 Simple Tales. 1806. (F)
  La Belle Assemblée, Suppl. v1 (1806), 40-41.
  British Critic, 31 (May 1808), 566-67.
  Critical Review, s3,v8 (Aug. 1806), 443-46.
  Edinburgh Review, 8 (July 1806), 465-71.
  Literary Journal, a Review..., ns,v2 (Aug. 1806), 159-67.
  Monthly Review, ns,v53 (Aug. 1807), 438.

 The Warrior's Return, and Other Poems. 1808. (P)
  Annual Review, 7 (1808), 522-24.
  Le Beau Monde, 4 (Suppl. 1808), 364-75.
  British Critic, 34 (Aug. 1809), 183-84.
  Eclectic Review, 5 (Mar. 1809), 274-77.
  Gentleman's Magazine, 78^2 (July 1808), 612-13.
  Monthly Pantheon, 2 (Jan. 1809), 6-17.
  Monthly Review, 57 (Dec. 1808), 436-38.
  Poetical Register, 6 (1807), 541.
  Universal Magazine, ns,v9 (Apr. 1808), 306-07.

 Temper, or Domestic Scenes: A Tale. 1812. (F)
  British Critic, 39 (May 1812), 526.
  Country Magazine, 1 (Jan. 1813), 23-31.
  Critical Review, s4,v1 (June 1812), 621-26.
  Gentleman's Magazine, 82^2 (Nov. 1812), 463-64.
  Monthly Review, ns,v68 (June 1812), 217.
  The Scotish Review (Edinburgh Monthly Review), 1 (Sept. 1812), 197-216.

 Tales of Real Life. 1813. (F)
  British Critic, ns,v2 (Dec. 1814), 653-54.
  Critical Review, s4,v4 (Aug. 1813), 190-200.
  Gentleman's Magazine, 85^1 (May 1815), 433-34.
  Monthly Review, ns,v72 (Nov. 1813), 326-27.

 Valentine's Eve. 1816. (F)
  Augustan Review, 2 (June 1816), 583-85.
  British Lady's Magazine, 4 (Sept. 1816), 180-81.
  Monthly Review, ns,v79 (Apr. 1816), 438-39.

 New Tales. 1818. (F)
  British Critic, ns,v10 (Sept. 1818), 287-98.
  British Lady's Magazine, s3,v2 (Feb. 1819), 78-80.
  Edinburgh Monthly Review, 1 (Mar. 1819), 276-95.
  European Magazine, 74 (Aug. 1818), 153.
  Fireside Magazine (quoting Edinburgh Monthly Magazine and Monthly Review), 1 (Apr., May 1819), 156, 188.
  Literary Gazette, Aug. 15, 1818, pp. 517-18.

Opie, Mrs. Amelia (concluded)
  Monthly Magazine, 46 (Sept. 1818), 158.
  Monthly Review, ns,v88 (Mar. 1819), 327-28.
  Scots Magazine, ns,v3 (Sept. 1818), 260-62.

  Tales of the Heart. 1820. (F)
  La Belle Assemblée, ns,v22 (Nov. 1820), 236-37.
  Lady's Monthly Museum, s3,v12 (Aug. 1820), 95-98.
  Literary Chronicle, 2 (July 22, 1820), 466-67.
  (Gold's) London Magazine, 2 (Aug. 1820), 178-80.
  Monthly Magazine, 50 (Sept. 1820), 168.
  Monthly Review, ns,v92 (Aug. 1820), 375-87.

Orchestikos, G.
  Convivialia et Saltatoria; or, a Few Thoughts upon Poetry
  and Dancing. To Which Is Annexed a Poetical Epistle in
  Praise of Tobacco. 1800. (P)
  Antijacobin Review, 7 (Dec. 1800), 416-17.
  British Critic, 17 (Feb. 1801), 190.
  Critical Review, s2,v32 (June 1801), 227.
  Monthly Review, 35 (June 1801), 210-11.

Orme, J. B.
  The Pursuit of Happiness. (Anon.) 1799. (P)
  British Critic, 15 (Feb. 1800), 190.
  Critical Review, s2,v26 (Aug. 1799), 475-76.
  Monthly Magazine, Suppl. v8 (Jan. 20, 1800), 1051.
  Monthly Review, 30 (Nov. 1799), 347.
  New London Review, 2 (July 1799), 81-82.

  Poems. 1805. (P)
  British Critic, 29 (Mar. 1807), 311-12.
  Literary Journal, a Review..., 5 (Sept. 1805), 999-1000.

  The Muses' Tribute, a Monody to the Memory of That Most Il-
  lustrious Statesman, the Right Honourable William Pitt.
  By J. B. Orme, Author of The Pursuit of Happiness. (P)
  Gentleman's Magazine, 76[1] (May 1806), 449.
  Poetical Register, 6 (1806), 513.

Ormsby, Anne.
  Memoirs of a Family in Switzerland, Founded on Facts.
  (Anon.) 1802. (F)
  Annual Review, 1 (1802), 720.
  Critical Review, ns,v36 (Oct. 1802), 236.
  Monthly Magazine, Suppl. v15 (July 28, 1803), 639.
  New Annual Register, 23 (1802), [321].

  The Soldier's Family; or Guardian Genii, a Romance. 1807.
  (F)
  British Critic, 30 (Aug. 1807), 199.
  Critical Review, s3,v12 (Sept. 1807), 104.
  Monthly Literary Recreations, 2 (June 1807), 471-72.

Monthly Review, ns,v62 (June 1810), 212.

Oscar.
   See Mrs. Leman Grimstone.

Osn, Ebn.
   See Benjamin Stephenson.

O'Sullivan, Michael John.
   See Michael John Sullivan.

Oulton, Walley Chamberlain.
   Botheration, or a Ten Years' Blunder. 1798. (D)
      British Critic, 13 (Mar. 1799), 311.
      Critical Review, ns,v25 (Jan. 1799), 118.

   The Sixty-Third Letter: A Musical Farce. 1802. (D)
      Critical Review, ns,v37 (Jan. 1803), 115-16.
      Monthly Mirror, 14 (Aug. 1802), 116.
      Poetical Register, 2 (1802), 455.

   _Poems, Chiefly Comic and Hudibrastic; Containing Burlesque
   Translations, Dramatic Pieces, and Miscellanies_. (P)
      Poetical Register, 8 (1810), 558.

   My Landlady's Gown, a Farce. (D)
      Theatrical Inquisitor, 9 (Sept. 1816), 208.

   Frightened to Death! a Musical Farce. (D)
      Monthly Review, ns,v82 (Apr. 1817), 431-32.
      Theatrical Inquisitor, 10 (Mar. 1817), 207-08.

Outline, Oliver.
   New Canterbury Tales, or the Glories of the Garrison.
   1811. (P)
      British Critic, 40 (Nov. 1812), 541-42.
      Monthly Review, 68 (July 1812), 335.

Owen, John.
   The Fashionable World Displayed. By Theophilus Christian.
   1804. (P?)
      Antijacobin Review, 18 (June 1804), 205-12.
      Lady's Monthly Museum, 14 (Feb. 1805), 128.
      Monthly Review, 45 (Nov. 1804), 332-33.

Owenson, Sydney, afterwards Lady Morgan.
   St. Clair, or the Heiress of Desmond. 1803. (F)
      Antijacobin Review, 40 (Dec. 1811), 404-14.
      British Critic, 38 (Nov. 1811), 522-23. (3rd ed.)
      European Magazine, 45 (Jan. 1804), 57.
      Flowers of Literature, 3 (1804), 463.
      Literary Journal, a Review..., 2 (Nov. 16, 1803), 537-38.
      Monthly Magazine, Suppl. v17 (July 28, 1804), 667.

Owenson, Sydney (continued)
    Monthly Mirror, 17 (Jan. 1804), 33.
    Monthly Review, ns,v43 (Mar. 1804), 266-68.

  The Novice of St. Dominick. 1806. (F)
    Antijacobin Review, 30 (June 1808), 187-90.
    Flowers of Literature, 5 (1806), 508.
    Monthly Magazine, Suppl. v20 (Jan. 31, 1806), 616.
    Monthly Review, ns,v52 (Jan. 1807), 99.

  The Wild Irish Girl. 1806. (F)
    Anonymous, 1 (Oct. 20, 1807), 207-30.
    Critical Review, s3,v9 (Nov. 1806), 327-28.
    Flowers of Literature, 5 (1806), 518.
    Literary Journal, a Review..., ns,v2 (Dec. 1806), 582-86.
    Monthly Literary Recreations, 1 (Aug. 1806), 155.
    Monthly Magazine, Suppl. v22 (Jan. 25, 1807), 643.
    Monthly Mirror, ns,v1 (Jan. 1807), 49-50.
    Monthly Review, ns,v57 (Dec. 1808), 378-81.

  The Lay of an Irish Harp, or Metrical Fragments. 1807. (P)
    Annual Review, 6 (1807), 547.
    La Belle Assemblée, Suppl. v2 (1807), 43.
    British Critic, 33 (Jan. 1809), 75-77.
    Monthly Review, 57 (Dec. 1808), 374-78.
    Oxford Review, 2 (Nov. 1807), 550-52.
    Poetical Register, 6 (1807), 539.
    Satirist, 3 (Nov. 1808), 447. (Excerpts from other re-
    views.)

  Woman; or, Ida of Athens. 1809. (F)
    Annual Review, 7 (1808), 588-94.
    Antijacobin Review, 32 (Apr. 1809), 364-76.
    Le Beau Monde, 1 (Apr. 1809), 35-36.
    Belfast Monthly Magazine, 2 (Feb. 1809), 140-43.
    British Critic, 33 (May 1809), 525.
    Critical Review, s3,v16 (Mar. 1809), 282-88.
    Dublin Satirist, 1 (Nov. 1809), 53-56.
    Lady's Monthly Museum, ns,v7 (Aug. 1809), 97.
    Monthly Magazine, Suppl. v27 (July 30, 1809), 667.
    Monthly Review, ns,v58 (Feb. 1808), 196-200.
    Quarterly Review, 1 (Feb. 1809), 50-52.
    Satirist, 4 (Feb. 1809), 192-94.
    Walker's Hibernian Magazine, Aug. 1809, p. 433.

  Patriotic Sketches of Ireland. 1807. (Pr)
    Satirist, 4 (May 1809), 517.
    Universal Magazine, ns,v8 (Nov. 1807), 417-20.

  The Missionary; an Indian Tale. 1811. (F)
    Antijacobin Review, 38 (Apr. 1811), 377-85.
    British Critic, 37 (June 1811), 631.
    Critical Review, s3,v23 (June 1811), 182-95.

Owenson, Sydney (concluded)
   Glasgow Magazine, 2 (May 1811), 65.

  O'Donnell: A National Tale. 1814. (F)
   Augustan Review, 2 (May 1816), 518-21.
   Critical Review, s4,v6 (Sept. 1814), 277-88.
   Monthly Museum, 1 (Apr. 1814), 430-34.
   Monthly Review, ns,v74 (May 1814), 110-11.

  France. 1817. (Pr)
   Antijacobin Review, 53 (Oct. 1817), 109-27.
   British Critic, ns,v8 (Sept. 1817), 259-79.
   Monthly Magazine, 44 (Sept. 1817), 155.
   Scots Magazine, ns,v1 (Sept. 1817), 141-46.

  Florence Macarthy: An Irish Tale. 1818. (F)
   Antijacobin Review, 55 (Feb. 1819), 509-21.
   British Lady's Magazine, s3,v2 (Jan. 1819), 31-35.
   British Review, 13 (May 1819), 482-94.
   Champion, Dec. 20, 1815, pp. 808-10.
   Edinburgh Monthly Review, 1 (June 1819), 655-62.
   Fireside Magazine, 1 (Jan. 1816), 30-31.
   Fireside Magazine (quoting New Monthly Magazine and Anti-
     jacobin Review), 1 (Feb., Apr. 1819), 78, 79, 157.
   Fireside Magazine (quoting Edinburgh Monthly Review and
     British Review), 1 (July, Aug. 1819), 271, 308-09.
   Literary Gazette, Dec. 5, 1818, pp. 769-71.
   Monthly Magazine, 46 (Jan. 1819), 531.
   New Monthly Magazine, 10 (Jan. 1819), 529-33.
   Newry Magazine, 4 (Nov.-Dec. 1818), 375-81.
   Scots Magazine, ns,v3 (Dec. 1818), 551-56.

P., F. H.
  The Castle of Caithness; a Romance of the Thirteenth Cen-
  tury. 1802. (F)
   Critical Review, ns,v36 (Dec. 1802), 478.

P., P.
  A True Account of the Deplorable Malady of H***y W****y, a
  Wiltshire Clothier: Shewing How He Mistook a Barber for a
  Clergyman in a Red Coat; and a Lancer...for a Scimitar....
  1798. (P)
   Antijacobin Review, 1 (Nov. 1798), 544-46.

P____, P____., Poet Laureate.
  See George Daniel.

Palin, Ralph.
  Iphotelle; or the Longing Fit. A Poem. 1810. (P)
   Antijacobin Review, 39 (May 1811), 94-95.
   British Critic, 37 (Apr. 1811), 407-08.
   Critical Review, s3,v23 (June 1811), 213-14.
   Monthly Review, 66 (Sept. 1811), 109.

Poetical Register, 8 (1810), 558-59.

Pallet, Peter Paul.
  See Rev. Richard Warner.

Palmer, Alicia Tyndal.
  The Husband and the Lover, an Historical and Moral Romance.
  (Anon.) 1809. (F)
    British Critic, 34 (July 1809), 74.
    Critical Review, s3,v19 (Feb. 1810), 161-68.
    European Magazine, 56 (July, Sept.-Oct. 1809), 39-43,
      201-05, 279-83.
    Gentleman's Magazine, 81 (Mar. 1811), 260.
    Monthly Mirror, ns,v6 (Aug. 1809), 99.
    Monthly Review, ns,v60 (Sept. 1809), 95.
    Satirist, 8 (Jan. 1811), 100-01.

  The Daughters of Isenberg, a Bavarian Romance. 1810. (F)
    British Critic, 36 (Sept. 1810), 303-04.
    Critical Review, s3,v21 (Oct. 1810), 153-60.
    Monthly Mirror, ns,v8 (Oct. 1810), 285-86.
    Monthly Review, ns,v63 (Sept. 1810), 102-03.
    Quarterly Review, 4 (Aug. 1810), 61-67.

  The Sons of Altringham. 1811. (F)
    Critical Review, s4,v1 (May 1812), 537-44.

  The Creation and Fall of Man. A Poem. (P)
    Monthly Review, 40 (Jan. 1803), 102.

Palmer, Joseph Budworth (originally Joseph Budworth).
  Windermere: a Poem. 1798. (P)
    Analytical Review, 28 (July 1798), 79.
    Antijacobin Review, 1 (Oct. 1798), 464-65.
    British Critic, 12 (Aug. 1798), 182.
    European Magazine, 33 (June 1798), 393.
    Gentleman's Magazine, 68^2 (Nov. 1798), 974-75.
    Monthly Magazine, Suppl. v6 (1798), 514.
    Monthly Mirror, 5 (June 1798), 350-51.
    Monthly Mirror, 6 (July 1798), 32-33.
    Monthly Review, 27 (Sept. 1798), 105-06.
    Scientific Magazine (Freemason's Magazine), 1 (Oct. 1798),
      274.

  A Fortnight's Ramble to the Lakes in Westmoreland, Lanca-
  shire, and Cumberland. 3rd ed. 1810. (P)
    Gentleman's Magazine, 80^2 (July-Aug. 1810), 41-43, 141-46.

Palmer, Shirley.
  The Swiss Exile, a Poem. 1804. (P)
    British Critic, 25 (Jan. 1805), 85-86.
    Critical Review, s3,v9 (Nov. 1806), 330-31.
    Eclectic Review, 2 (Dec. 1806), 1046.

Monthly Review, 54 (Sept. 1807), 89.

Palmerston, Viscount.
See Henry John Temple, Viscount Palmerston.

Pangloss, Peter.
The Young Rosciad, an Admonitory Poem, Well-seasoned with
Attic Salt. 1805. (P)
   Antijacobin Review, 21 (Aug. 1805), 432.
   British Critic, 26 (Dec. 1805), 667-68.
   Critical Review, s3,v6 (Oct. 1805), 213-14.
   European Magazine, 48 (July 1805), 44.
   Monthly Mirror, 20 (Aug. 1805), 112-13.
   Monthly Review, 48 (Nov. 1805), 320-22.

Memoirs of Sylvester Daggerwood, Comedian, Deceased, Includ-
ing Many Years of Provincial Vicissitudes.... 1807. (P)
   Critical Review, s3,v10 (Apr. 1807), 437.
   Monthly Review, ns,v54 (Oct. 1807), 212.

Panton, Mary.
Eloise and Other Poems. By a Young Lady. 1815. (P)
   British Critic, ns,v3 (June 1815), 654-55.

Papworth, J. B., Francis Wrangham, and W. Combe.
Poetical Sketches of Scarborough. 1813. (P)
   Monthly Review, 72 (Sept. 1813), 72-79.

Paradise, Marat.
The Luniad, an Epic Poem. (P)
   Satirist, 7 (Sept.-Nov. 1810), 226-30, 366-71, 444-51.

Park, Gratiano.
Affectation; or, the Close of the Eighteenth Century: A
Satire. 1799. (P)
   Antijacobin Review, 5 (Feb. 1800), 206-08.
   Critical Review, s2,v28 (Mar. 1800), 353-54.
   Monthly Review, 31 (Jan. 1800), 95.
   New London Review, 2 (Dec. 1799), 603.

Park, Thomas.
Cupid Turned Volunteer. 1804. (P)
   Annual Review, 3 (1804), 568-70.
   Lady's Monthly Museum, 14 (Feb. 1805), 131.
   Poetical Register, 4 (1804), 484.

Nugae Modernae. Morning Thoughts and Midnight Musings: Consisting of Casual Reflections, Egotisms in Prose and Verse.
1818. (P-Pr)
   Eclectic Review, s2,v11 (Jan. 1819), 84-87.

Parker, Emma.
Elfrida, Heiress of Belgrove. 1811. (F)

British Critic, 42 (Aug. 1813), 195-96.
Critical Review, s4,v1 (Feb. 1812), 219-20.
Monthly Review, ns,v67 (Mar. 1812), 321.

Virginia; or, the Peace of Amiens. 1811. (F)
British Critic, 42 (Sept. 1813), 297-98.
Critical Review, s4,v1 (Jan. 1812), 109-10.
Monthly Review, ns,v67 (Mar. 1812), 321.

Aretas. 1813. (F)
Critical Review, s4,v4 (July 1813), 107-09.
Monthly Review, ns,v72 (Nov. 1813), 325-26.
New Review, 2 (Aug. 1813), 209-11.

The Guerilla Chief. 1815. (F)
Monthly Review, ns,v78 (Dec. 1815), 436.

Self-Deception; in a Series of Letters. 1816. (F)
Critical Review, s5,v4 (Nov. 1816), 511-16.
Monthly Review, ns,v83 (May 1817), 97.

Parker, John.
Miscellaneous Poems, in Prose and Verse. 1804. (P)
British Critic, 23 (Apr. 1804), 434.
Monthly Mirror, 17 (Apr. 1804), 261.

Parkinson, James.
Dangerous Sports, a Tale, Addressed to Children. (F)
European Magazine, 37 (June 1800), 461.
New London Review, 3 (June 1800), 566.

Parlante, Priscilla.
See the Hon. Mary Ann Cavendish Bradshaw.

Parlby, Major Brook Bridges.
Revenge; or, the Novice of San Martino, a Tragedy. (D)
Gentleman's Magazine, 89[1] (Jan. 1819), 58.
Literary Gazette, June 27, 1818, pp. 410-11.
Monthly Review, ns,v90 (Dec. 1819), 434-35.
Theatre, or Dramatic and Literary Mirror, 1 (Feb. 6,
Mar. 20, 1819), 36, 87-89.
Theatrical Inquisitor, 15 (Nov. 1819), 253-59.
Ulster Register, 4 (July 10, 1818), 38-41.

Parnell, William, later Parnell-Hayes, M.P.
Maurice and Berghetta; or, the Priest of Rahery. 1819. (F)
La Belle Assemblée, ns,v20 (Nov. 1819), 231-33.
Christian's Pocket Magazine, 1 (Oct. 1819), 364. (Digest-
ed from Eclectic Review.)
Eclectic Review, ns,v12 (Sept. 1819), 245-67.
Gentleman's Magazine, 90[1] (Mar. 1820), 247-48.
Literary Gazette, July 24, 1819, pp. 468-70.
Monthly Magazine, 48 (Sept. 1819), 156.

New Monthly Magazine, 12 (Oct. 1819), 331-32.
Quarterly Review, 21 (Apr. 1819), 471-86.

Parry, John.
Helpless Animals! or, Bachelor's Fare: A Musical Interlude.
(D)
British Stage and Literary Cabinet, 4 (Nov. 1818), 77.
Theatrical Inquisitor, 15 (Dec. 1819), 321-22.

High Notions; or, a Trip to Exmouth. A Musical Entertain-
ment. (D)
Monthly Review, ns,v88 (Mar. 1819), 323.
Theatre, or Dramatic Literary Mirror, Feb. 1819.

Parsey, Arthur.
The Deserted Village Restored. The Blind Beggar of Bethnal
Green. Pastorals. 1815. (P)
Eclectic Review, s2,v5 (Apr. 1816), 398-99.
Monthly Review, 79 (Feb. 1816), 211.

Parsons, Mrs. Eliza.
Women As They Are. 1796.
Monthly Mirror, 5 (Jan. 1798), 31.

An Old Friend with a New Face. 1797. (F)
British Critic, 11 (May 1798), 562.
Scientific Magazine (Freemason's Magazine), 11 (July
1798), 49.

Anecdotes of Two Well-Known Families. 1798. (F)
Analytical Review, 27 (June 1798), 644-45.
British Critic, 12 (Aug. 1798), 184.
Critical Review, ns,v23 (July 1798), 353.
Monthly Magazine, Suppl. v6 (1798), 517.
Monthly Review, ns,v27 (Nov. 1798), 332-33.

The Valley of St. Gothard. 1799. (F)
Critical Review, ns,v26 (July 1799), 358.
Monthly Mirror, 8 (Aug. 1798), 96.
New London Review, 1 (June 1799), 615.

The Miser and His Family. 1800. (F)
Critical Review, ns,v32 (May 1801), 105-06.
Monthly Magazine, Suppl. v11 (July 20, 1801), 606.

The Peasant of Ardenne Forest. 1801. (F)
British Critic, 21 (Jan. 1803), 83.

The Mysterious Visit! 1803. (F)
Flowers of Literature, 2 (1803), 457.

Murray House. 1805. (F)
Flowers of Literature, 4 (1805), 429.

<u>Literary</u> <u>Journal</u>, 3 (June 1, 1804), 609-10.

The <u>Convict</u>; <u>or</u>, <u>Navy</u> <u>Lieutenant</u>. 1807. (F)
  <u>British</u> <u>Critic</u>, 30 (July 1807), 84.
  <u>Flowers</u> <u>of</u> <u>Literature</u>, 5 (1806), 500.
  <u>Lady</u>'s <u>Monthly</u> <u>Museum</u>, ns,v6 (Feb. 1809), 98.

Parsons, William.
  <u>Travelling</u> <u>Recreations</u>. 1807. (P)
    <u>Annual</u> <u>Review</u>, 6 (1807), 588.
    <u>British</u> <u>Critic</u>, 31 (May 1808), 548.
    <u>Cabinet</u>, 4 (Aug. 1808), 111-12.
    <u>Monthly</u> <u>Review</u>, 56 (June 1808), 211-12.
    ·<u>Poetical</u> <u>Register</u>, 6 (1807), 542-53.
    <u>Satirist</u>, 4 (Mar. 1809), 311-12. (Excerpts from other re-
    views.)
    <u>Universal</u> <u>Magazine</u>, ns,v9 (Jan. 1808), 40-42.

Partridge, Rev. Samuel.
  <u>Rhyming</u> <u>Riddles</u>, <u>&c</u>. <u>For</u> <u>the</u> <u>Amusement</u> <u>of</u> <u>Young</u> <u>Oxonians</u>.
  By an Old Oxonian. 1813.
    <u>Antijacobin</u> <u>Review</u>, 44 (June 1813), 617-19.

Pastor, Paul.
  <u>Something</u> <u>New</u> <u>for</u> <u>Charity</u>; <u>a</u> <u>Sermon</u> <u>in</u> <u>Verse</u>. 1812. (P)
    <u>British</u> <u>Critic</u>, 40 (Dec. 1812), 635-36.

Pasty, Carolina Petty.
  See Elizabeth Cobbold.

Paterson, Walter.
  <u>The</u> <u>Legend</u> <u>of</u> <u>Iona</u>, <u>with</u> <u>Other</u> <u>Poems</u>. 1812. (P)
    <u>British</u> <u>Critic</u>, ns,v4 (July 1815), 94-95.
    <u>Monthly</u> <u>Review</u>, 77 (June 1815), 149-53.
    <u>Scots</u> <u>Magazine</u>, 76 (Mar. 1814), 204-09.

Patrick, Mrs. F. C.
  <u>More</u> <u>Ghosts</u>! By the Wife of an Officer, Author of <u>The</u>
  <u>Irish</u> <u>Heiress</u>. 1798. (F)
    <u>Critical</u> <u>Review</u>, ns,v24 (Oct. 1798), 236.
    <u>Monthly</u> <u>Magazine</u>, Suppl. v6 (1798), 517.

  The <u>Jesuit</u>; <u>or</u>, <u>the</u> <u>History</u> <u>of</u> <u>Anthony</u> <u>Babington</u>, <u>Esq</u>.
  By the Authoress of <u>More</u> <u>Ghosts</u>, <u>The</u> <u>Irish</u> <u>Heiress</u>, etc.
  1799. (F)
    <u>British</u> <u>Critic</u>, 14 (Aug. 1799), 190.
    <u>Critical</u> <u>Review</u>, ns,v27 (Sept. 1799), 115.
    <u>Monthly</u> <u>Magazine</u>, Suppl. v8 (Jan. 20, 1800), 1053.
    <u>Monthly</u> <u>Review</u>, ns,v30 (Sept. 1799), 95-97.

Patrick, Rev. Richard.
  <u>The</u> <u>Death</u> <u>of</u> <u>Prince</u> <u>Bagration</u>, <u>or</u> <u>the</u> <u>French</u> <u>Defeated</u> <u>in</u>
  <u>Russia</u> <u>and</u> <u>Poland</u>. 1813. (P)

British Critic, 42 (Oct. 1813), 411.
Critical Review, s4,v4 (Aug. 1813), 217-18.
Eclectic Review, 10 (Dec. 1813), 601-10.
Literary Panorama, 14 (Nov. 1813), 602-05.
Monthly Review, 72 (Oct. 1813), 214-15.
New Review, 2 (Oct. 1813), 353-54.

Paul, Rev. Hamilton.
Paul's First and Second Epistles to the Dearly Beloved the
Female Disciples or Female Students of Natural Philosophy
in Anderson's Institution, Glasgow. (P)
Monthly Review, 32 (July 1800), 321-22.

Paulding, James Kirke.
The Lay of the Scottish Fiddle, a Poem. From the Fourth
Edinburgh Edition. (Anon.) 1814. (P)
British Critic, ns,vl (Apr. 1814), 440-42.
Monthly Review, 77 (June 1815), 143-48.
New Annual Register, 35 (1814), [364].
New Monthly Magazine, 2 (Aug. 1814), 58.
New Review, 3 (May 1814), 439-40.
Quarterly Review, 10 (Jan. 1814), 463-67.

The Backwoodsman. A Poem. 1818. (P)
Eclectic Review, s2,v12 (Oct. 1819), 394-400.

Payne, John Howard.
Lispings of the Muse: A Selection from Juvenile Poems. (P)
British Stage, 1 (Apr. 1817), 74-76.

Accusation; or, the Family of D'Anglade. (D)
Theatrical Inquisitor, 11 (Oct. 1817), 289-96.

Brutus; or, the Fall of Tarquin, an Historical Tragedy.
1818. (D)
British Critic, ns,vll (Jan. 1819), 75-82.
Fireside Magazine (quoting Monthly Review and British
Critic), 1 (Mar. 1818), 115, 117.
Literary Journal and General Miscellany, 1 (Dec. 1818),
621-25.
Monthly Review, ns,v88 (Jan. 1819), 90-96.
Quarterly Review, 22 (Jan. 1820), 402-15.

Virginia, or Patrician Perfidy, an Historical Tragedy. (D)
(Gold's) London Magazine, 2 (Dec. 1820), 601-13.

Paynter, D. W.
The Muse in Idleness. 1819. (P)
Monthly Magazine, 48 (Jan. 1820), 541.
Monthly Review, 92 (June 1820), 209.

Peacock, Miss _____.
The Little Emigrant, a Tale. Interspersed with Moral

432

Anecdotes and Instructive Conversations. (F)
  Monthly Review, ns,v29 (Aug. 1799), 464.

Peacock, Thomas Love.
  Palmyra, and Other Poems. 1806. (P)
    British Critic, 27 (Feb. 1806), 186-87.
    British Critic, 31 (Jan. 1808), 82.
    Critical Review, s3,v7 (Feb. 1806), 210-11.
    Lady's Monthly Museum, 16 (June 1806), 414-15.
    Literary Annual Register, 2 (Mar. 1808), 118.
    Literary Journal, 5 (Dec. 1805), 1326-27.
    Monthly Magazine, Suppl. v20 (Jan. 31, 1806), 614.
    Monthly Review, 49 (Mar. 1806), 323-25.
    Poetical Register, 6 (1806), 504.

  The Genius of the Thames; a Lyrical Poem. 1810. (P)
    Antijacobin Review, 37 (Sept. 1810), 82-84.
    British Critic, 36 (Aug. 1810), 177-80.
    Critical Review, s3,v21 (Dec. 1810), 439-40.
    Eclectic Review, 7 (Feb. 1811), 165-68.
    Gentleman's Magazine, 80[2] (Oct. 1810), 354-57.
    Monthly Magazine, Suppl. v30 (Jan. 31, 1811), 672-77 [73].
    Monthly Review, 65 (June 1811), 210-11.
    Monthly Review, 70 (Mar. 1813), 321-22.
    Poetical Register, 8 (1810), 561.
    Satirist, 7 (Aug. 1810), 180-86.
    Satirist, 9 (Dec. 1811), 493-94. (Excerpts from other
      reviews.)

  The Philosophy of Melancholy...with a Mythological Ode.
  1812. (P)
    Antijacobin Review, 41 (Apr. 1812), 337-43.
    Critical Review, s4,v1 (Mar. 1812), 327-30.
    Eclectic Review, 8 (Oct. 1812), 1030-35.
    New Annual Register, 33 (1812), 377.
    New Review, 1 (Feb. 1813), 147-49.

  Sir Hornbook; or Childe Launcelot's Expedition. A Grammat-
  ico-Allegorical Ballad. (Anon.) 1814. (P)
    British Critic, ns,v1 (May 1814), 543-45.
    European Magazine, 65 (Jan. 1814), 45.
    Literary Panorama, 15 (May 1814), 546-47.
    Monthly Review, 74 (June 1814), 214.

  Headlong Hall. 1816. (F)
    British Lady's Magazine, 4 (Sept. 1816), 176-77.
    Critical Review, s5,v3 (Jan. 1816), 69-72.
    Eclectic Review, ns,v5 (Apr. 1816), 372-80.
    Literary Panorama, ns,v4 (Apr. 1816), 29-33.
    Monthly Review, ns,v82 (Mar. 1817), 330.
    New Monthly Magazine, 5 (Feb. 1816), 66.

Melincourt. By the Author of <u>Headlong Hall</u>. 1817. (F)
  British <u>Critic</u>, ns,v8 (Oct. 1817), 430-42.
  Critical <u>Review</u>, s5,v5 (May 1817), 494-502.
  <u>Literary</u> <u>Gazette</u>, Mar. 22, 1817, p. 132.
  Monthly <u>Magazine</u>, 43 (June 1817), 453.
  Monthly <u>Review</u>, ns,v83 (July 1817), 322-23.
  New <u>Monthly</u> <u>Magazine</u>, 7 (May 1817), 349.

Rhododaphne; <u>or, the</u> <u>Thessalian</u> <u>Spell, a</u> <u>Poem</u>. (Anon.)
1818. (P)
  La <u>Belle</u> <u>Assemblée</u>, ns,v17 (Mar. 1818), 128-31.
  Fireside <u>Magazine</u> (quoting <u>Monthly</u> <u>Review</u>), 1 (Apr.
    1819), 151.
  <u>Literary</u> <u>Gazette</u>, Feb. 21, 1818, pp. 114-15.
  <u>Literary</u> <u>Panorama</u>, ns,v8 (May 1818), 212-16.
  Monthly <u>Magazine</u>, 45 (Apr. 1818), 250.
  Monthly <u>Review</u>, 88 (Feb. 1819), 178-82.

Nightmare <u>Abbey</u>. By the Author of <u>Headlong Hall</u>. 1818.
(F)
  European <u>Magazine</u>, 75 (Mar. 1819), 254-55.
  <u>Literary</u> <u>Gazette</u>, Dec. 12, 1818, pp. 787-88.
  <u>Literary</u> <u>Journal</u> <u>and</u> <u>General</u> <u>Miscellany</u>, 1 (Dec. 5, 1818),
    573-74.
  Monthly <u>Review</u>, ns,v90 (Nov. 1819), 327-29.
  <u>Tickler</u>, 1 (Dec. 1, 1818), 8-9.

Peake, R. B.
  Walk <u>for a</u> <u>Wager</u>; <u>or, a</u> <u>Bailiff's</u> <u>Bet</u>. A <u>Musical</u> <u>Farce</u>.
  (D)
    Theatre; <u>or</u> <u>Dramatic</u> <u>and</u> <u>Literary</u> <u>Mirror</u>, 2 (Sept. 4,
      1819), 71-72.
    Theatrical <u>Inquisitor</u>, 15 (Sept. 1819), 146-48.

Pearce, William.
  Netley <u>Abbey, an</u> <u>Operatic</u> <u>Farce</u>. (D)
    Poetical <u>Register</u>, 1 (1801), 463.

Pearson, Miss _____.
  The <u>Illustrious</u> <u>Exile</u> <u>of</u> <u>Albion</u>; <u>with</u> <u>Poems</u> <u>on</u> <u>Several</u> Occasions. 1815. (P)
    Theatrical <u>Inquisitor</u>, 7 (Aug. 1815), 121-28.

Pearson, Richard, Jr.
  The <u>Battles</u> <u>of</u> <u>Talavera</u>, <u>Salamanca</u>, <u>Vittoria</u>, <u>and the</u> <u>Pyre</u>-
  nees. <u>With</u> <u>Other</u> <u>Poems</u>. 1813. (P)
    Antijacobin <u>Review</u>, 45 (Nov. 1813), 459.
    British <u>Critic</u>, 42 (Dec. 1813), 614-15.
    Critical <u>Review</u>, s4,v4 (Oct. 1813), 442-43.
    Monthly <u>Review</u>, 72 (Nov. 1813), 323-24.
    New <u>Review</u>, 2 (Nov. 1813), 514.

Pearson, S.

Poems on Various Subjects. 1800. (P)
   British Critic, 16 (Aug. 1800), 201.
   Monthly Mirror, 9 (Apr. 1800), 224-25.

Peck, Mrs. _____.
   The Young Rosiniere, or Sketches of the World. (F)
      Hibernia Magazine, 1 (Mar. 1810), 181-83.
      Lady's Monthly Museum, ns,v7 (Sept. 1809), 154-59.
      Walker's Hibernian Magazine, Sept. 1809, pp. 527-28.

   Vaga; or a View of Nature. 1813. (F)
      Dublin Magazine, 1 (Apr. 1813), 364-65.
      Monthly Review, ns,v71 (June 1813), 213.

Peebles, William.
   The Crisis; or, the Progress of Revolutionary Principles,
   a Poem. 1804. (P)
      British Critic, 25 (June 1805), 680-81.
      Eclectic Review, 1 (July 1805), 524-27.
      Imperial Review, 3 (Dec. 1804), 523-28.
      Lady's Monthly Museum, 15 (Sept. 1805), 199.
      North British Magazine and Review, 3 (Jan. 1805), 38.
      Poetical Register, 5 (1805), 486.

Peers, Charles.
   Christ's Lamentation over Jerusalem. A Seatonian Prize
   Poem. 1805. (P)
      British Critic, 27 (June 1806), 668-69.
      Critical Review, s3,v7 (Feb. 1808), 213-14.
      Eclectic Review, 2 (June 1806), 461-62.
      Lady's Monthly Museum, 16 (Apr. 1806), 275.
      Poetical Register, 5 (1805), 494.

Pelham, M.
   The Rational Brutes; or Talking Animals. 1799. (F?)
      Monthly Mirror, 9 (Feb. 1800), 90.

   First Going to School; or, the Story of Tom Brown and His
   Sisters. (F)
      Imperial Review, 3 (Dec. 1804), 605.

Pen-Drag-On, Anser.
   See William Henry Ireland.

Penley, S.
   The Sleeping Draught, a Farce. 1818. (D)
      Monthly Review, ns,v85 (Apr. 1818), 439.

Penn, Granville.
   Original Lines and Translations. (Anon.) 1815. (P)
      Antijacobin Review, 48 (Feb. 1815), 127-29.
      British Critic, ns,v4 (Sept. 1815), 325-27.
      Eclectic Review, s2,v3 (June 1815), 619-21.

435

Literary *Panorama*, ns,v1 (Mar. 1815), 883-85.

Penn, John.
Critical, *Poetical,* *and* *Dramatic* *Works.* 1798. (P-D)
Analytical *Review,* 28 (Dec. 1798), 606-08.
Critical *Review,* s2,v23 (May 1798), 118.
Critical *Review,* s2,v24 (Dec. 1798), 475-76.
Monthly *Magazine,* Suppl. v5 (July 15, 1798), 506.
Monthly *Review,* 26 (May 1798), 68-71.

Poems. *Consisting* *of* *Original* *Works,* *Imitations,* *and*
Translations. 1801. (P)
Antijacobin *Review,* 10 (Oct. 1801), 189-92.
British *Critic,* 18 (Jan. 1802), 15-18.
Monthly *Magazine,* Suppl. v13 (July 20, 1802), 659.
Monthly *Review,* 40 (Apr. 1803), 367-72.
New *Annual* *Register,* 22 (1801), [313].
Poetical *Register,* 1 (1801), 427.

Pennie, J. F.
The *Royal* *Minstrel;* *or,* *the* *Witcheries* *of* *Endor.* *An* *Epic*
Poem. (P)
Gentleman's *Magazine,* 88[1] (June 1818), 524-26.
Literary *Gazette,* Apr. 10, May 15, 1819, pp. 225-26, 306-
07.
Monthly *Magazine,* 44 (Dec. 1817), 454-55.

Pentycross, Rev. T.
Witenham *Hill,* *a* *Descriptive* *Poem.* 1812. 3rd ed. (P)
Eclectic *Review,* 8 (Sept. 1812), 967-68.

Penwarne, John.
Contemplation, *a* *Poem;* *with* *Tales* *and* *Other* *Poetical* *Com-*
positions. 1807. (P)
Annual *Review,* 6 (1807), 567-69.
Le *Beau* *Monde,* 4 (Dec. 1808), 288-89.
Critical *Review,* s3,v12 (Nov. 1807), 330-31.
Monthly *Magazine,* Suppl. v24 (Jan. 30, 1808), 629.
Monthly *Review,* 57 (Sept. 1808), 89-92.
Poetical *Register,* 6 (1807), 544.
Satirist, 1 (Dec. 1807), 297-99.
Satirist, 4 (Mar. 1809), 311. (Excerpts from other re-
views.)

Pepperpod, Peter.
The *Literary* *Bazaar;* *or,* *Poets'* *Council.* *A* *Grand* *Historic,*
Heroic, *Serio-Comic,* *Hudibrastic* *Poem.* 1816. (P)
Critical *Review,* s5,v4 (Sept. 1816), 319.
Gentleman's *Magazine,* 87[1] (Apr. 1817), 344-45.

Peregrine, Peter.
Matilda *Montford.* *A* *Romantic* *Novel.* 1809. (F)
Monthly *Review,* ns,v60 (Sept. 1809), 97-98.

Perry, William.
  Trafalgar, the Sailor's Play. 1807. (D)
    Cabinet, 2 (Sept. 1807), 110-11.
    Gentleman's Magazine, 77[1] (May 1807), 444-46.
    Monthly Review, ns,v53 (July 1807), 315-17.

Peterkin, A.
  Britannia's Tears, a Vision. 1800. (P)
    British Critic, 16 (Oct. 1800), 436-37.
    Critical Review, s2,v29 (Aug. 1800), 467-68.
    Monthly Magazine, Suppl. v10 (Jan. 20, 1801), 610.
    Monthly Mirror, 10 (Nov. 1800), 301.
    Monthly Review, 31 (Mar. 1800), 320-21.
    Monthly Visitor, 11 (Nov. 1800), 318.

Pfeil, J. W.
  A Miscellany of Poetry. 1818. (P)
    Literary Panorama, ns,v8 (Jan. 1819), 1643-46.

Philagricola, Terrae Filius.
  See Rev. Stephen Weston.

Philippart, Mrs. John.
  Victoria. (P)
    Gentleman's Magazine, 83[2] (Aug. 1813), 150.

  Muscovy, a Poem. 1813. (P)
    New Review, 2 (Oct. 1813), 410.

Philips, Mrs. Lucius.
  Heaven's Best Gift. 1798. (F)
    Critical Review, ns,v24 (Sept. 1798), 114.
    Monthly Mirror, 6 (Oct. 1798), 228.

Phillips, Charles.
  The Loves of Celestine and St. Aubert; a Romantic Tale.
  1811. (F)
    Antijacobin Review, 39 (Aug. 1811), 414-19.
    British Critic, 37 (June 1811), 631-32.

  The Consolation of Erin; an Eulogy. 1811. (P)
    Antijacobin Review, 39 (Aug. 1811), 431-33.
    British Critic, 39 (Mar. 1812), 309.

  The Emerald Isle, a Poem. 1812. (P)
    Antijacobin Review, 42 (June 1812), 152-60.
    Literary Panorama, 11 (June 1812), 1039-42.
    Quarterly Review, 16 (Oct. 1816), 27-30.

  A Garland for the Grave of Richard Brinsley Sheridan.
  1816. (P)
    Augustan Review, 3 (Nov. 1816), 474-82.
    British Lady's Magazine, 4 (Nov. 1816), 315-18.

Critical Review, s5,v4 (Nov. 1816), 480-87.
Dublin Examiner, 1 (Oct. 1816), 401-14.
Eclectic Review, s2,v6 (Nov. 1816), 502-06.
Theatrical Inquisitor, 11 (Nov.-Dec. 1817), 362-67, 445-50.

The Lament of the Emerald Isle. 1817. (P)
   Black Dwarf, 1 (Dec. 17, 1817), 779-80.
   Literary and Political Examiner, 1 (Mar. 1818), 70-72.
   Monthly Magazine, 44 (Jan. 1818), 541.
   Monthly Review, 84 (Dec. 1817), 431-32.
   Theatrical Inquisitor, 11 (Dec. 1817), 450-55.

The Ocean Cavern: A Tale of the Tonga Isles. 1819. (P)
   Fireside Magazine (quoting Monthly Magazine), 1 (Sept.
   1819), 355.
   Literary Chronicle, 1 (Sept. 4, 1819), 244-45.
   Monthly Magazine, 48 (Aug. 1819), 59.

The Arab. (P)
   Fireside Magazine (quoting Monthly Magazine), 1 (Sept.
   1819), 355.
   Monthly Magazine, 48 (Aug. 1819), 49.

Philokosmos.
   The Fashionable World Reformed. (P)
   European Magazine, 53 (Feb. 1808), 126.

Philo-Nauticus.
   See Lawrence Hynes Halloran.

Philopatria, Jr.
   Lines Addressed to His Royal Highness the Prince of Wales
   on His Being Appointed Regent. 1811. (P)
      Antijacobin Review, 38 (Apr. 1811), 425.
      British Critic, 37 (Mar. 1811), 295.
      Monthly Review, 64 (Mar. 1811), 322-23.
      Poetical Register, 8 (1811), 627.

Pickar, Mary.
   The Castle of Roviego; or, Retribution. A Romance. (F)
      Monthly Review, ns,v58 (Jan. 1809), 101.

Pickersgill, Joshua.
   The Three Brothers: A Romance. 1803. (F)
      Critical Review, ns,v39 (Oct. 1803), 168-72.
      Gentleman's Magazine, 74^2 (Nov. 1804), 1047.
      Monthly Magazine, Suppl. v16 (Jan. 25, 1804), 634.

Pierpont, John.
   Airs of Palestine, a Poem. (P)
      Fireside Magazine (quoting Monthly Review), 1 (Apr.
      1819), 152.
      Monthly Review, 88 (Feb. 1819), 206-08.

Pilkington, Mrs. Mary.

Obedience Rewarded, and Prejudice Conquered; or the History
of Mortimer Lascelles. 1798. (F)
  British Critic, 12 (July 1798), 75.
  Critical Review, ns,v22 (Mar. 1798), 349.

Amusing Recreations; or a Collection of Charades and Riddles
on Political Characters, and Various Subjects. 1798. (P)
  Analytical Review, 27 (Apr. 1798), 423-24.
  Monthly Review, 25 (Apr. 1798), 477.

Edward Barnard, or Merit Exalted. 1798. (F)
  Lady's Monthly Museum, 1 (Oct. 1798), 320-21.

Tales of the Hermitage, Written for the Instruction and
Amusement of the Rising Generation. (Anon.) 1798. (F)
  Critical Review, ns,v25 (Jan. 1799), 110.
  Lady's Monthly Museum, 1 (Sept. 1798), 239-40.

Henry, or the Foundling; to Which Are Added, The Prejudiced
Parent; or, the Virtuous Daughter. 1799. (F)
  Analytical Review, ns,v1 (Apr. 1799), 421-22.
  Critical Review, ns,v31 (Feb. 1801), 227.
  Lady's Monthly Museum, 2 (Feb. 1799), 145-46.
  Monthly Mirror, 7 (Jan. 1799), 35.
  New London Review, 1 (Mar. 1799), 297.

Miscellaneous Poems. (P)
  Lady's Monthly Museum, 2 (May 1799), 402-03.

Marmontel's Tales. Selected and Abridged for the Instruc-
tion and Amusement of Youth. 1799. (F)
  Critical Review, ns,v26 (Aug. 1799), 478.
  New London Review, 1 (Apr. 1799), 408.

The Spoiled Child; or, Indulgence Counteracted. 1799. (F)
  European Magazine, 36 (Nov. 1799), 327.
  Monthly Review, ns,v31 (Apr. 1800), 428.
  New London Review, 2 (Sept. 1799), 286.

The Asiatic Princess. 1800. (F)
  European Magazine, 38 (Oct. 1800), 286.
  Monthly Mirror, 10 (Dec. 1800), 375.

Edward, a Tale, for Young Persons. 1800. (F)
  Antijacobin Review, 10 (Nov. 1801), 312-13.
  Monthly Visitor, 13 (May 1801), 91-92.

New Tales of the Castle; or the Noble Emigrants. 1800. (F)
  Antijacobin Review, 6 (May 1800), 56.
  Critical Review, ns,v28 (Apr. 1800), 469.
  Monthly Mirror, 9 (Jan. 1800), 33-34.
  Monthly Review, ns,v34 (Feb. 1801), 201-02.

New London Review, 3 (Feb. 1800), 176.

Memorial Tales for the Instruction of Young Ladies Just Leaving School and Entering upon the Theatre of Life. 1802. (F)
British Critic, 21 (Mar. 1803), 315.

Crimes and Characters; or, the New Foundling. 1805. (F)
Flowers of Literature, 4 (1805), 419.

Violet Vale; or Saturday Night. 1806. (F)
Monthly Mirror, 22 (Dec. 1806), 400.

The Calendar; or Monthly Recreations; Chiefly Consisting of Dialogues between an Aunt and Her Nieces.... 1807. (F)
Critical Review, s3,v11 (July 1807), 327.
Satirist, 1 (Nov. 1807), 209.

Ellen, Heiress of the Castle. (F)
Critical Review, s3,v12 (Sept. 1807), 102-03.
Monthly Literary Recreations, 3 (July 1807), 72.
Monthly Review, ns,v62 (June 1810), 212.

Pinchard, Mrs. _____.
The Ward of Delamere; a Tale. 1815. (F)
Monthly Review, ns,v78 (Nov. 1815), 324-25.
New Monthly Magazine, 3 (May 1815), 355.

Pindar, Minimus.
Little Odes to Great Folks. 1808. (P)
Antijacobin Review, 31 (Dec. 1808), 351-58.
British Critic, 34 (July 1809), 72.
Critical Review, s3,v15 (Sept. 1808), 103.
Monthly Review, 59 (May 1809), 99.
Poetical Register, 7 (1808), 570-71.

Pindar, Peter.
See John Wolcot.

Pindar, Peter, Jr.
The Hop-Boy; or, Idalia's Grove. 1804. (F)
British Critic, 26 (Oct. 1805), 443.
Literary Journal, a Review..., 4 (July 1804), 92.
Monthly Mirror, 18 (Sept. 1804), 182.
Monthly Mirror, 20 (Dec. 1805), 395.

The Royal Bloods. (P)
Satirist, 10 (Feb. 1812), 120-22.
Theatrical Inquisitor, 2 (Apr. 1813), 154-58.

Pinn, William.
Poems on Various Occasions. 1800. (P)
Antijacobin Review, 8 (Jan. 1801), 62.
Critical Review, s2,v32 (June 1801), 227.

Monthly Mirror, 12 (July 1801), 39.

Piscator.
  See Thomas P. Lathy.

Pitt, William.
  The Bullion Debate: A Serio-Comic Satiric Poem. 1811. (P)
    British Critic, 39 (Jan. 1812), 80.
    Critical Review, s3,v23 (Aug. 1811), 443.
    Monthly Review, 65 (Aug. 1811), 446-47.

Plastic, Sir Peter.
  The Absent Man, a Narrative. 1817. (F)
    Critical Review, s5,v5 (May 1817), 542.
    Monthly Review, ns,v83 (May 1817), 98.

Planché, James Robinson (see also George Daniel and James
      Robinson Planché).
  The Vampire; or, the Bride of the Isles. A Romantic Melo-
  drama. (D)
    Theatrical Inquisitor, ns,v1 (Aug. 1820), 138-39.

Plumptre, Annabella. (See also Anne and Annabella Plumptre.)
  The Western Mail; Being a Selection of Letters Made from
  the Bag Taken from the Western Mail.... 1801. (F?)
    Critical Review, ns,v32 (July 1801), 352.

Plumptre, Anne.
  The Rector's Son. 1798. (F)
    British Critic, 11 (May 1798), 562.
    Critical Review, ns,v23 (May 1798), 114.
    Monthly Magazine, Suppl. v5 (July 15, 1798), 509.
    Monthly Mirror, 5 (June 1798), 349.
    Monthly Review, ns,v26 (May 1798), 107-08.
    Scientific Magazine (Freemason's Magazine), 11 (July
      1798), 50.

  Something New; or, Adventures at Campbell House. 1801. (F)
    Critical Review, ns,v34 (Apr. 1802), 475-76.
    Monthly Magazine, Suppl. v13 (July 20, 1802), 659.
    Monthly Mirror, 15 (June 1803), 404.
    Monthly Review, ns,v41 (May 1803), 103.

  The History of Myself and My Friend. 1813. (F)
    La Belle Assemblée, Suppl. ns, v6 (1812), 354-60.
    British Critic, 41 (Mar. 1813), 304.
    Critical Review, s4,v2 (Dec. 1812), 636-43.
    Monthly Review, ns,v69 (Nov. 1812), 332-33.
    New Review, 1 (June 1813), 627-32.

Plumptre, Anne, and Annabella Plumptre.
  Tales of Wonder, of Humour, and of Sentiment. (F)
    Literary Gazette, Jan. 10, 1818, pp. 20-21.

Plumptre, James.
  Four Discourses on Subjects Relating to the Amusement of
  the Stage. 1809. (D)
    British Critic, 37 (Apr. 1811), 356-62.

  Original Dramas: Containing Royal Beneficence, or the
  Emperor; Winter; Kendrew, of the Coal Mine; &c. 1818. (D)
    Christian Observer, 19 (Feb. 1820), 121-32.
    Fireside Magazine (quoting Gentleman's Magazine), 1 (July
      1819), 274.
    Gentleman's Magazine, 89[1] (May 1819), 432.
    (Baldwin's) London Magazine, 1 (Mar. 1820), 254-63.

Plunkett, Mrs. _____.
  See Elizabeth Gunning.

Pocock, James.
  Yes, or No? A Musical Farce. (D)
    Poetical Register, 7 (1809), 619.

  Hit or Miss! A Musical Farce. (D)
    British Critic, 38 (Aug. 1811), 191.
    Poetical Register, 8 (1810), 599.

  Twenty Years Ago! A New Melodramatic Entertainment. 1810.
  (D)
    British Critic, 38 (Sept. 1811), 296.
    Poetical Register, 8 (1810), 598.

  Anything New. A Musical Farce. 1811. (D)
    British Critic, 40 (Dec. 1812), 640.
    Poetical Register, 8 (1811), 643.

  Robinson Crusoe; or, the Bold Bucaniers: a Romantic Melo-
  Drama. (D)
    Theatrical Inquisitor, 10 (May 1817), 369-70.

  Rob Roy Macgregor; or Auld Lang Syne! A Musical Drama. (D)
    Monthly Review, ns,v85 (Mar. 1818), 323.

Polidori, G.
  Two Tragedies. 1798. (D)
    Monthly Review, ns,v28 (Mar. 1799), 352-53.

  Gernando. (D)
    Monthly Magazine, Suppl. v8 (Jan. 20, 1800), 1057.

  Isabella. (D)
    Monthly Magazine, Suppl. v8 (Jan. 20, 1800), 1057.

Polidori, John William.
  The Vampyre. A Tale. 1819. (F)
    La Belle Assemblée, Suppl. v20 (1819), 334-37.

British Lady's Magazine, s3,v3 (July 1819), 31-34.
Edinburgh Monthly Review, 1 (May 1819), 618-20.
Fireside Magazine (quoting Monthly Review and Monthly
   Magazine), 1 (June 1819), 231, 233-34.
Fireside Magazine (quoting Monthly Review), 1 (July 1819),
   265.
Kaleidoscope, 1 (Apr. 13, 1819), 149-50.
Lady's Monthly Museum, s3,v9 (May 1819), 282-87.
Literary Journal and General Miscellany, 2 (Apr. 3, 1819),
   214.
Literary Journal and General Miscellany, 2 (May 8, 1819),
   267-73.
Monthly Magazine, 47 (May 1819), 345.
Monthly Review, ns,v89 (May 1819), 87-96.
New Monthly Magazine, 11 (Apr. 1819), 195-206.
Theatre; or Dramatic and Literary Mirror, 1 (May 1, 15,
   1819), 149-52, 166-69.

Ernestus Berchtold; or, the Modern Oedipus. A Tale. 1819.
(F)
   La Belle Assemblée, ns,v20 (Dec. 1819), 280-83.
   Edinburgh Monthly Review, 4 (Dec. 1820), 727-35.
   European Magazine, 76 (Dec. 1819), 534-36.
   Literary Gazette, Aug. 28, 1819), pp. 546-48.
   Monthly Review, ns,v91 (Feb. 1820), 215.

Ximenes, the Wreath, and Other Poems. 1819. (P)
   European Magazine, 75 (Mar. 1819), 250-51.
   Fireside Magazine (quoting New Monthly Magazine and Gen-
      tleman's Magazine), 1 (May, Sept. 1819), 199, 360.
   Gentleman's Magazine, 89^1 (June 1819), 552.
   Monthly Review, 90 (Sept. 1819), 92-94.
   New Monthly Magazine, 11 (Apr. 1819), 246-51.

Pollexfen, William.
   Rhapsodies Patriotic, and in Verse. 1810. (P)
      Satirist, 7 (Dec. 1810), 585-90.

Polwhele, Richard.
   Sketches in Verse, with Prose Illustrations. 1797. (P)
      Antijacobin Review, 3 (June 1799), 174.
      Gentleman's Magazine, 69^1 (Jan. 1799), 47.

   The Old English Gentleman, a Poem. 1797. (P)
      Analytical Review, 28 (Sept. 1798), 276-79.
      Antijacobin Review, 3 (June 1799), 171-74.
      Antijacobin Review, 6 (June 1800), 230-33.
      British Critic, 11 (Apr. 1798), 367-70.
      Critical Review, s2,v22 (Mar. 1798), 251-53.
      European Magazine, 33 (Apr. 1798), 251-54.
      Gentleman's Magazine, 69^1 (Jan. 1799), 58.
      Monthly Magazine, Suppl. v5 (July 15, 1798), 507.
      Monthly Review, 25 (Apr. 1798), 396-98.

Polwhele, Richard (continued)

The Unsexed Females, a Poem; Addressed to the Author of
"The Pursuits of Literature." (Anon.) 1798. (P)
  Antijacobin Review, 3 (May 1799), 27-33.
  British Critic, 14 (July 1799), 70-71.
  Critical Review, s2,v27 (Oct. 1799), 231-32.
  Gentleman's Magazine, 71^2 (Aug. 1801), 730.
  Monthly Magazine, Suppl. v8 (Jan. 20, 1800), 1051.
  Monthly Review, 30 (Sept. 1799), 102-03.
  New Annual Register, 20 (1799), [268-69].
  New London Review, 2 (July 1799), 83.

The Influence of Local Attachment with Respect to Home. A
New Edition, with Large Additions, and Odes, with Other
Poems. 1798. (F)
  Analytical Review, 27 (June 1798), 604-07.
  Antijacobin Review, 5 (Feb. 1800), 200-04.
  Antijacobin Review, 37 (Sept. 1810), 87-89. (3rd ed.)
  British Critic, 12 (Sept. 1798), 254-56.
  Critical Review, s2,v24 (Nov. 1798), 296-98.
  European Magazine, 34 (Oct. 1798), 252-53.
  Gentleman's Magazine, 68^1 (Apr. 1798), 322-24.
  Monthly Magazine, Suppl. v5 (July 15, 1798), 507.
  Monthly Mirror, 6 (Dec. 1798), 345-46.
  Monthly Review, 27 (Oct. 1798), 228.
  New Annual Register, 19 (1798), [307-08].

Grecian Prospects, a Poem. 1799. (P)
  Antijacobin Review, 5 (Apr. 1800), 428-30.
  British Critic, 15 (Mar. 1800), 260-63.
  Critical Review, s2,v29 (Aug. 1800), 448-52.
  European Magazine, 37 (Mar. 1800), 220.
  Gentleman's Magazine, 70^1 (May 1800), 458-59.
  Monthly Magazine, Suppl. v9 (July 20, 1800), 638.
  Monthly Review, 31 (Apr. 1800), 433.
  New Annual Register, 21 (1800), [326].
  New London Review, 3 (Mar. 1800), 284-85.

Warlike Ode to Faithful Cornwall. (Anon.) 1803. (P)
  Antijacobin Review, 16 (Oct. 1803), 178-81.

Poems. 1806. (P)
  Annual Review, 5 (1806), 535.
  Antijacobin Review, 30 (May 1808), 75-77.
  British Critic, 31 (Mar. 1808), 265-68.
  Critical Review, s3,v13 (Jan. 1808), 53-56.
  Poetical Register, 6 (1806), 503.
  Satirist, 5 (July 1809), 95-96. (Excerpts from other re-
    views.)

The Family Picture, or Domestic Education. A Poetic Epistle from a Country Gentleman to His College Friend. (Anon.)
1808. (P)

Polwhele, Richard (concluded)
  Annual Review, 7 (1808), 530.
  Antijacobin Review, 32 (Jan. 1809), 61-76.
  British Critic, 33 (Feb. 1809), 181-83.
  Critical Review, s3,v16 (Apr. 1809), 437-38.
  Eclectic Review, 5 (Mar. 1809), 281-82.
  European Magazine, 54 (Dec. 1808), 455-56.
  Gentleman's Magazine, 79¹ (Jan. 1809), 47.
  Monthly Review, 58 (Mar. 1809), 326-27.
  Poetical Register, 7 (1808), 566.

  Poems. Chiefly the Local Attachment; the Unsexed Females;
  the Old English Gentleman; the Pneumatic Revellers; and
  the Family Picture. 1810. (P)
    British Critic, 37 (Apr. 1811), 341-44.
    European Magazine, 60 (Aug. 1811), 119-22.
    Poetical Register, 8 (1810), 555.

  The Deserted Village School; a Poem. (Anon.) 1813. (P)
    British Critic, 42 (Aug. 1813), 190-92.
    European Magazine, 65 (Mar. 1814), 227-28.
    Gentleman's Magazine, 83² (Oct. 1813), 347-48.
    Monthly Review, 71 (June 1813), 109 [209].

  The Fair Isabel of Cotchele, a Cornish Romance. By the
  Author of Local Attachments and Translator of Theocritus.
  1815. (P)
    Antijacobin Review, 50 (Apr. 1816), 341-48.
    Augustan Review, 3 (Sept. 1816), 255-60.
    British Critic, ns,v6 (July 1816), 90-92.
    Gentleman's Magazine, 85² (July, Oct. 1815), 50-53, 330-
      35.
    Monthly Review, 78 (Nov. 1815), 317-19.
    Quarterly Review, 14 (Jan. 1816), 402-05.

Polypus.
  See Eaton Stannard Barrett.

Poole, Mrs. _____.
  The Lily. (F?)
    European Magazine, 53 (Feb. 1808), 127.

Poole, John.
  Hamlet Travestie. With Burlesque Annotations after the
  Manner of Dr. Johnson and George Stevens, Esq. and the
  Various Commentators. 1810. (D)
    British Critic, 40 (Oct. 1812), 409-10.
    Critical Review, s3,v21 (Nov. 1810), 333-34.
    European Magazine, 58 (Nov. 1810), 369-71.
    General Chronicle, 1 (Jan. 1811), 61-63.
    Monthly Mirror, ns,v8 (Dec. 1810), 444-49.
    Monthly Review, ns,v63 (Nov. 1810), 325-26.
    Poetical Register, 8 (1811), 637.

Intrigue, a Comic Interlude. 1814. (D)
　　Monthly Review, ns,v74 (May 1814), 102.

Who's Who? or, the Double Imposture. 1815. (D)
　　Augustan Review, 2 (Jan. 1816), 55-59.
　　Monthly Review, ns,v80 (May 1816), 103-05.
　　Theatrical Inquisitor, 7 (Dec. 1815), 461-62.

A Short Reign and a Merry One. A Petite Comedy. (D)
　　Theatrical Inquisitor, 16 (Jan. 1820), 31.

Porden, Eleanor Ann (later Franklin).
　The Veils; or the Triumph of Constancy. A Poem. 1815. (P)
　　British Critic, ns,v7 (Feb. 1817), 163-70.
　　Blackwood's Edinburgh Magazine, 1 (June 1817), 298.
　　Gentleman's Magazine, 86¹ (Jan. 1816), 45-49.
　　Monthly Review, 85 (Jan. 1818), 39-54.
　　Quarterly Review, 16 (Jan. 1817), 387-96.

　The Arctic Expeditions. A Poem. 1818. (P)
　　Antijacobin Review, 54 (May 1818), 250-52.
　　La Belle Assemblée, ns,v18 (July 1818), 34-35.
　　British Critic, ns,v9 (May 1818), 513-17.
　　Eclectic Review, s2,v10 (Dec. 1818), 601-04.
　　Fireside Magazine (quoting Monthly Review and Eclectic
　　　Review), 1 (Jan. 1819), 34, 36.
　　Literary Gazette, Apr. 18, 1818, pp. 246-47.
　　Monthly Review, 87 (Nov. 1818), 324-25.

Porter, Anna Maria.
　Octavia. 1798. (F)
　　Analytical Review, 28 (Nov. 1798), 517-18.
　　British Critic, 13 (Mar. 1799), 311.
　　Critical Review, ns,v24 (Dec. 1798), 471-72.
　　Monthly Magazine, Suppl. v6 (1798), 516.
　　Monthly Magazine, Suppl. v7 (July 20, 1799), 543.
　　Monthly Mirror, 7 (Mar. 1799), 165-66.
　　New London Review, 1 (Apr. 1799), 406.

　The Lake of Killarney. 1804. (F)
　　British Critic, 25 (Mar. 1805), 321.
　　Imperial Review, 3 (Oct. 1804), 303.
　　Lady's Monthly Museum, 14 (May 1805), 345.
　　Literary Journal, a Review..., 4 (Aug. 1804), 207.
　　Monthly Magazine, Suppl. v18 (Jan. 28, 1805), 595.
　　Monthly Review, ns,v47 (June 1805), 205-06.

　The Hungarian Brothers. 1807. (F)
　　Annual Review, 7 (1808), 603.
　　Critical Review, s3,v13 (Apr. 1808), 442-43.
　　Gentleman's Magazine, 79² (Oct. 1809), 954-55.
　　Monthly Magazine, Suppl. v23 (July 30, 1807), 644.
　　Monthly Pantheon, 1 (Nov. 1808), 575-76.

446

Monthly Review, ns,v58 (Aug. 1808), 432-33.

Don Sebastian; or, the House of Braganza, an Historical Romance. 1809. (F)
  Le Beau Monde, 2 (Dec. 1809), 192-93.
  Critical Review, s3,v18 (Dec. 1809), 356-63.
  Monthly Mirror, ns,v7 (Feb. 1810), 29-33.

Ballad Romances, and Other Poems. 1811. (P)
  British Critic, 40 (Sept. 1812), 301.
  Critical Review, s4,v1 (Feb. 1812), 164-65.
  Eclectic Review, 8 (Apr. 1812), 430-32.
  Edinburgh Monthly Magazine and Review (Scotish Review),
    1 (Sept. 1812), 133-41.
  European Magazine, 64 (Dec. 1813), 521.
  Gentleman's Magazine, 83² (Dec. 1813), 576.
  Monthly Review, 67 (Mar. 1812), 325-26.
  Poetical Register, 8 (1811), 614.

The Recluse of Norway. 1814. (F)
  Augustan Review, 1 (June 1815), 106-10.
  British Lady's Magazine, 1 (Mar. 1815), 203-08.
  Champion, Jan. 8, 1815, p. 15.
  Critical Review, s5,v1 (Apr. 1815), 423-24.
  Monthly Review, ns,v77 (June 1815), 212.
  New Monthly Magazine, 2 (Dec. 1814), 444.

The Knight of St. John, a Romance. 1817. (F)
  British Critic, ns,v8 (Dec. 1817), 621-25.
  European Magazine, 73 (Jan. 1818), 47-50.
  Gentleman's Magazine, Suppl. 87² (July-Dec. 1817), 614-
    15.
  Monthly Magazine, 44 (Nov. 1817), 346-47.
  Monthly Review, ns,v85 (Mar. 1818), 328-29.

The Fast of St. Magdalen. A Romance. 1819. (F)
  La Belle Assemblée, ns,v18 (1818), 331-33.
  Champion, Jan. 10, 1819, p. 28.
  Edinburgh Monthly Review, 1 (May 1819), 531-37.
  European Magazine, 74 (Nov. 1818), 435-36.
  Fireside Magazine (quoting Monthly Review), 1 (May 1819),
    188.
  Fireside Magazine, 1 (Jan. 1819), 31.
  Fireside Magazine (quoting Monthly Magazine), 1 (Jan.
    1819), 37.
  Monthly Magazine, 46 (Dec. 1818), 444.
  Monthly Review, ns,v88 (Mar. 1819), 329.

Porter, J.
  The Two Princes of Persia. Addressed to Youth. 1801. (F)
    Antijacobin Review, 8 (Apr. 1801), 421.
    Monthly Visitor, 13 (May 1801), 93.

Porter, Jane.
  Thaddeus of Warsaw. 1803. (F)
    Annual Review, 2 (1803), 604-05.
    Antijacobin Review, 19 (Sept. 1804), 77-78.
    Critical Review, ns,v39 (Sept. 1803), 120.
    Flowers of Literature, 2 (1803), 461.
    Imperial Review, 1 (Feb. 1804), 309-14.
    Monthly Magazine, Suppl. v16 (Jan. 25, 1804), 634.
    Monthly Register, 3 (May 1803), 16.
    Monthly Review, ns,v43 (Feb. 1804), 214-15.

  The Scottish Chiefs, a Romance. 1810. (F)
    British Critic, 37 (Mar. 1811), 247-56.
    Gentleman's Magazine, 80^2 (Oct. 1810), 345-46.
    Glasgow Magazine, 1 (Sept. 1810), 67-74.
    Lady's Monthly Museum, ns,v9 (Aug. 1810), 100-08.
    Monthly Magazine, Suppl. v30 (Jan. 31, 1811), 676.
    Scots Magazine, 72 (Apr. 1810), 278-83.

  The Pastor's Fire-Side, a Novel. 1817. (F)
    British Critic, ns,v7 (June 1817), 633-40.
    British Lady's Magazine, 5 (Mar. 1817), 165-69.
    Critical Review, s5,v5 (Feb. 1817), 173-86.
    European Magazine, 71 (Feb. 1817), 140-43.
    Gentleman's Magazine, 87 (Feb. 1817), 145-47.
    Literary Gazette, Mar. 8, 1817, pp. 100-01.
    Monthly Magazine, 43 (Feb. 1817), 64.
    Monthly Review, ns,v83 (May 1817), 97-98.

Porter, Stephen.
  Lover's Vows; or, the Child of Love. (D)
    Analytical Review, ns,v1 (Mar. 1799), 317.
    British Critic, 14 (July 1799), 73.

Potter, Matilda.
  Mount Erin; an Irish Tale. 1813. (F)
    Antijacobin Review, 45 (Oct. 1813), 346-49.
    British Critic, 42 (Aug. 1813), 196.
    Critical Review, s4,v4 (Sept. 1813), 329.
    Monthly Review, ns,v73 (Jan. 1814), 105-06.
    New Review, 2 (Sept. 1813), 297-98.

Poulett, W. H.
  Adversity; or, the Miseries of the Seduced, a Poem. 1804.
  (P)
    Antijacobin Review, 17 (Apr. 1804), 434.
    British Critic, 23 (June 1804), 673-74.
    Imperial Review, 1 (Apr. 1804), 636.
    Monthly Mirror, 18 (Dec. 1804), 394-95.
    Monthly Review, 45 (Nov. 1804), 317-18.

Powell, Thomas.
  Daphne, a Poem. (P)

Monthly Review, 26 (May 1798), 94-95.

Power, T. F.
The Outlaw; or the Eve of St. Ann, a Tale. 1816. (P)
Dublin Examiner, 1 (Aug. 1816), 305-10.

Pratt, Peter.
Elegy on the National Character. (P)
Monthly Review, 80 (June 1816), 216.

Pratt, Samuel Jackson.
Family Secrets. 2nd ed. 1798. (F)
Analytical Review, 27 (May 1798), 519.
European Magazine, 33 (June 1798), 392.
Gentleman's Magazine, 68[1] (May 1798), 414-15.
Monthly Mirror, 6 (Aug. 1798), 93-94.

Pity's Gift; a Collection of Interesting Tales....From the
Writings of Mr. Pratt. Selected by a Lady. (P)
Monthly Visitor, 5 (Sept. 1798), 102-04.

Gleanings in England, Descriptive of the Countenance, Mind,
and Character of the Country. 1799-1803. 3 vols. (P)
British Critic, 18 (Aug. 1801), 165-73. (Vol. II.)
Critical Review, s2,v27 (Oct. 1799), 167-73. (Vol. I.)
Imperial Review, 3 (Dec. 1804), 580-85. (Vol. III.)

Bread; or, the Poor, a Poem. 1801. (P)
Antijacobin Review, 11 (Mar. 1802), 285-90.
British Critic, 19 (Apr. 1802), 416-18.
Critical Review, s2,v34 (Jan. 1802), 80-87.
Edinburgh Review, 1 (Oct. 1802), 108-12.
European Magazine, 41 (Jan. 1802), 29-32.
European Magazine, 41 (Apr. 1802), 289.
Flowers of Literature, 1 (1801-02), 448-49.
Gentleman's Magazine, 71[2] (Suppl. 1801), 1189-91.
Monthly Magazine, Suppl. v13 (July 20, 1802), 658.
Monthly Mirror, 13 (Jan. 1802), 31-32.
Monthly Mirror, 13 (Apr. 1802), 250.
Monthly Review, 37 (Mar. 1802), 310-14.
New Annual Register, 22 (1801), [313-14].
Poetical Register, 1 (1801), 441-42.
Union Magazine and Imperial Register, 3 (Apr. 1802), 246-
50.

The Paternal Present: Being a Sequel to Pity's Gift.
Chiefly Selected from the Writings of Mr. Pratt. (P)
Annual Review, 1 (1802), 723.
British Critic, 20 (Aug. 1802), 200.

Cottage Pictures; or the Poor, a Poem. (P)
Annual Review, 1 (1802), 660-61.
European Magazine, 44 (1803), 129-30.

Pratt, Samuel Jackson (continued)
John and Dame; or the Loyal Cottagers. 1803. (P)
  Antijacobin Review, 16 (Dec. 1803), 421.
  British Critic, 22 (Sept. 1803), 312.
  Critical Review, s2,v39 (Nov. 1803), 357.
  European Magazine, 44 (Sept. 1803), 217.
  Gentleman's Magazine, 73^2 (Oct. 1803), 951.
  Monthly Mirror, 16 (Oct. 1803), 256-57.
  Monthly Review, 42 (Sept. 1803), 102.
  Poetical Register, 3 (1803), 454.

Harvest Home: Consisting of Supplementary Gleanings, Origi-
nal Dramas and Poems. Contributions of Literary Friends,
and Selected Re-publications.... 1805. (P)
  Annual Review, 4 (1805), 736-38.
  Antijacobin Review, 20 (Mar. 1805), 275-83.
  British Critic, 25 (May 1805), 545-49.
  Critical Review, s3,v5 (June 1805), 198-211.
  European Magazine, 47 (June 1805), 437-40.
  Flowers of Literature, 4 (1805), 424.
  Imperial Review, 5 (Sept. 1805), 291-96.
  Lady's Monthly Museum, 15 (Aug. 1805), 129.
  Literary Journal, a Review..., 5 (Apr. 1805), 347-53.
  Monthly Mirror, 19 (Mar. 1805), 173-77.
  Monthly Review, 48 (Sept. 1805), 23-35
  Universal Magazine, ns,v4 (Dec. 1805), 531-36.

Landscapes in Verse; Tears of Genius; Cottage Pictures;
"Sympathy"; and Other Poems. A New Edition. 1807. (P)
  Antijacobin Review, 28 (Oct. 1807), 188-90.

Sympathy, and Other Poems, Including Landscapes, in Verse,
and Cottage Pictures, Revised, Corrected, and Enlarged.
1807. (P)
  British Critic, 33 (May 1809), 520.
  Cabinet, 1 (July 1807), 330-31.
  Eclectic Review, 3 (Sept. 1807), 820-22.
  Flowers of Literature, 5 (1806), 512.
  Gentleman's Magazine, 77^1 (May 1807), 447.
  Monthly Magazine, Suppl. v23 (July 30, 1807), 642.
  Monthly Mirror, ns,v2 (Aug. 1807), 115.
  Oxford Review, 2 (Aug. 1807), 192-93.
  Satirist, 1 (Nov. 1807), 210.
  Satirist, 1 (Dec. 1807), 299-300.

The Contrast, a Poem; Including Comparative Views of Brit-
ain, France, and Spain, at the Present Moment. 1808. (P)
  Antijacobin Review, 31 (Nov. 1808), 307-08.
  British Critic, 36 (Nov. 1810), 519-20.
  Cabinet, 4 (Dec. 1808), 399-400.
  Cyclopaedian Magazine, 3 (Jan. 1809), 27-29.
  Eclectic Review, 4 (Dec. 1808), 1095-1100.
  European Magazine, 54 (Oct. 1808), 300-01.

Pratt, Samuel Jackson (concluded)
Gentleman's Magazine, 78² (Oct. 1808), 920-21.
Literary Panorama, 5 (Nov. 1808), 276-79.
Monthly Review, 57 (Oct. 1808), 210-11.
New Annual Register, 29 (1808), [406].
Satirist, 2 (May 1808), 322-23.
Universal Magazine, ns,v10 (Nov. 1808), 416-20.

The Lower World, a Poem. 1810. (P)
Antijacobin Review, 38 (Apr. 1811), 428-29.
La Belle Assemblée, ns,v1 (June 1810), 271-72.
British Critic, 36 (Aug. 1810), 181-82.
Critical Review, s3,v21 (Oct. 1810), 179-86.
Eclectic Review, 6 (Nov. 1810), 1047.
European Magazine, 57 (June 1810), 450-52.
Gentleman's Magazine, 80¹ (May 1810), 454-57.
Lady's Monthly Museum, s2,v10 (Feb. 1811), 103-07.
Literary Panorama, 8 (June 1810), 223-29.
Monthly Magazine, Suppl. v30 (Jan. 31, 1811), 675-76.
Monthly Mirror, ns,v8 (Sept. 1810), 203-08.
Monthly Review, 62 (May 1810), 91-94.
Poetical Register, 8 (1810), 572.
Satirist, 9 (Dec. 1811), 492. (Excerpts from other reviews.)
Universal Magazine, ns,v13 (June 1810), 481-87.

Prescott, Miss _____.
Poems. 1812. (P)
British Critic, 42 (Sept. 1813), 295.
Critical Review, s4,v4 (Oct. 1813), 441-42.
Monthly Review, 73 (Feb. 1814), 208-09.

Price, Richard.
The Works of Richard Price, Esq. Consisting of Poems, Letters, and Essays. (P-Pr)
Critical Review, s3,v4 (Jan. 1805), 111.
Literary Journal, a Review..., 4 (July 1804), 93.

Price, Uvedale.
Essay on the Picturesque, as Compared with the Sublime and Beautiful; and on the Use of Studying Pictures, for the Purpose of Improving Real Landscape. 1810. (Original ed., 2 vols., 1794-98.) (Pr)
Quarterly Review, 4 (Nov. 1810), 372-82.

Prichett, Miss _____.
Warwick Castle, an Historical Novel. 1815. (F)
Critical Review, s5,v1 (June 1815), 635.
Monthly Review, ns,v78 (Oct. 1815), 217.

Prim, Obadiah.
Ludicrous Debates among the Gods and Goddesses, in a Grand Council on the...Use of Gas-Lights. (P)
Monthly Review, 53 (July 1807), 320.

Pringle, Thomas.
  The Autumnal Excursion; or Sketches in Teviotdale. With
  Other Poems. 1819. (P)
    Eclectic Review, s2,v13 (May 1820), 481-84.
    Edinburgh Magazine and Literary Miscellany (Scots Maga-
      zine), ns,v4 (Apr. 1819), 319-23.
    Fireside Magazine (quoting Monthly Review), 1 (Sept.
      1819), 345.
    Literary and Statistical Magazine, 3 (Feb. 1819), 75-78.
    Monthly Review, 89 (July 1819), 326.

Proby, John Joshua.
  Dramatic and Narrative Poems. 1810. (P)
    British Critic, 36 (July 1810), 52-55.
    Eclectic Review, 7 (Mar. 1811), 273-74.
    Monthly Review, 64 (Mar. 1811), 265-72.
    New Annual Register, 32 (1811), [365].
    Poetical Register, 8 (1810), 555-56.

Proby, William Charles.
  The Mysterious Seal. A Romance. 1799. (F)
    Analytical Review, ns,v1 (June 1799), 602.
    British Critic, 14 (July 1799), 75.
    Critical Review, ns,v26 (July 1799), 358.
    Lady's Monthly Museum, 3 (July 1799), 70-71.
    Monthly Magazine, Suppl. v8 (Jan. 20, 1800), 1054.
    Monthly Mirror, 8 (July 1799), 28.
    Monthly Review, ns,v30 (Dec. 1799), 471.
    New London Review, 1 (June 1799), 615.

  The Spirit of the Castle. A Romance. 1800. (F)
    Monthly Mirror, 9 (Mar. 1800), 159.
    New London Review, 3 (Jan. 1800), 83.

Procter, Bryan Waller (Barry Cornwall).
  Dramatic Scenes, and Other Poems. 1819. (P)
    Blackwood's Edinburgh Magazine, 5 (June 1819), 310-16.
    British Stage and Literary Cabinet, 3 (Aug. 1819), 231-33.
    Eclectic Review, s2,v14 (Nov. 1820), 323-33.
    Edinburgh Magazine and Literary Miscellany (Scots Maga-
      zine), ns,v5 (Aug. 1819), 121-25.
    Examiner, May 23, 31, 1819, pp. 333-34, 345-46.
    Fireside Magazine (quoting Monthly Magazine), 1 (Aug.
      1819), 319.
    Literary Gazette, May 22, 1819, pp. 321-23.
    Literary Gazette, Apr. 8, 1820, pp. 227-28.
    Monthly Magazine, 47 (July 1819), 539-40.
    Monthly Review, 90 (Nov. 1819), 296-99.
    Theatrical Inquisitor, 16 (June 1820), 366-73.

  Marcian Colonna, an Italian Tale, with Three Dramatic
  Scenes, and Other Poems. 1820. (P)
    Dublin Magazine, 2 (July 1820), 60-70.

Eclectic Review, s2,vl4 (Nov. 1820), 323-33.
Edinburgh Magazine and Literary Miscellany (Scots Magazine), ns,v7 (July 1820), 7-14.
Edinburgh Review, 34 (Nov. 1820), 449-60.
Examiner, Sept. 17, 1820, pp. 603-04.
Literary Chronicle, 2 (July 15, 1820), 452-54.
Literary Gazette, June 10, 1820, pp. 369-71.
Literary Gazette, June 17, 1820, p. 389.
(Baldwin's) London Magazine, 2 (July 1820), 75-81.
(Gold's) London Magazine, 2 (July, Aug., 1820), 81-83, 183-92.
Monthly Magazine, 50 (Aug. 1820), 65.
Monthly Review, 92 (July 1820), 310-19.
New Monthly Magazine, 14 (July 1820), 76-77.
Talisman, 1 (June 24, 1820), 5-6.
Theatrical Inquisitor, ns,vl (July-Sept. 1820), 53-57, 126-31, 216-20.

A Sicilian Story, with Diego de Montilla, and Other Poems.
1820. (P)
La Belle Assemblée, Suppl. ns,v22 (1820), 342-44.
Blackwood's Edinburgh Magazine, 6 (Mar. 1820), 643-50.
British Stage and Literary Cabinet, 4 (Nov. 1819), 74-75.
British Stage and Literary Cabinet, 4 (Mar. 1820), 133-34.
Champion, Jan. 15, 1820, pp. 44-45.
Dublin Magazine, 1 (Mar. 1820), 209-32.
Eclectic Review, s2,vl4 (Nov. 1820), 323-33.
Edinburgh Magazine and Literary Miscellany (Scots Magazine), ns,v6 (Mar. 1820), 212-16.
Edinburgh Monthly Review, 3 (Mar. 1820), 271-76.
Edinburgh Review, 33 (Jan. 1820), 144-55.
Examiner, Jan. 2, 1820, pp. 11-12.
Literary Gazette, Dec. 4, 11, 1819, pp. 771-72, 788-89.
(Baldwin's) London Magazine, 1 (Jan. 1820), 84-86.
(Gold's) London Magazine, 1 (Mar. 1820), 302-09.
Monthly Magazine, 49 (June 1820), 447.
Monthly Review, 91 (Mar. 1820), 291-96.
New Monthly Magazine, 13 (Jan. 1820), 178-83.
Theatrical Inquisitor, 16 (Jan. 1820), 40-43 [40-45].

Procter, William.
Rosamond, Memory's Musings, and Other Poems. 1819. (P)
Gentleman's Magazine, 90[1] (Mar. 1820), 240.
Literary Chronicle, 1 (Sept. 18, 1819), 276-77.
Monthly Review, 92 (May 1820), 96-98.
New Monthly Magazine, 12 (Nov. 1819), 457.

Proctor, W. T.
Joseph. A Sacred Drama. 1802. (D)
British Critic, 21 (Mar. 1803), 313-14.
Critical Review, ns,v37 (Apr. 1803), 477.
Monthly Magazine, Suppl. vl5 (July 28, 1803), 631.
New Annual Register, 23 (1802), [320].

453

Poetical Register, 2 (1802), 451.

Prowett, Rev. J.
The Voluspa, or Speech of the Prophetess, with Other Poems.
1816. (P)
British Critic, ns,v5 (June 1816), 670-73.
Monthly Review, 80 (July 1816), 319-20.

Pry, Peter.
See Thomas Hill.

Pryme, George.
Ode Graeda Praemio Dignata, Quod Donavit Academiae Canbrig-
iensi Vir Reverendus Claudius Buchanan.... 1804. (P)
Monthly Review, 48 (Sept. 1805), 36-37.

The Conquest of Canaan, a Seatonian Prize Poem. 1810. (P)
British Critic, 35 (Feb. 1810), 185-86.
British Critic, 37 (June 1811), 629-30.
Eclectic Review, 6 (Mar. 1810), 279.
Monthly Review, 62 (July 1810), 328-30.
Poetical Register, 8 (1810), 580.

Ode to Trinity College, Cambridge. (Anon.) (P)
British Critic, ns,v1 (Jan. 1814), 102.
Critical Review, s4,v2 (Oct. 1812), 440-42.
Monthly Review, 74 (Aug. 1814), 434-35.

Purcell, Mrs. _____.
The Orientalist; or, Electioneering in Ireland. 1820. (F)
Lady's Monthly Museum, s3,v12 (July 1820), 35.
Monthly Review, ns,v92 (July 1820), 321.

Pybus, Charles Small.
The Sovereign. Addressed to His Imperial Majesty, Paul,
Emperour of All the Russias. 1800. (P)
British Critic, 17 (Feb. 1801), 149-51.
Critical Review, s2,v29 (May 1800), 12-18.
Gentleman's Magazine, 70[2] (Sept. 1800), 854-55.
Monthly Magazine, Suppl. v9 (July 20, 1800), 639.
Monthly Review, 33 (Dec. 1800), 378-80.
New Annual Register, 21 (1800), [324-25].

Pye, Henry James (see also Henry James Pye and James Petit
Andrews; also Henry James Pye and Samuel James Arnold).
Naucratia; or Naval Dominion, a Poem. 1798. (P)
British Critic, 11 (Feb. 1798), 179-83.
British Critic, 12 (Dec. 1798), 664-65.
Critical Review, s2,v23 (July 1798), 294-97.
European Magazine, 33 (Apr. 1798), 259.
Monthly Magazine, Suppl. v5 (July 15, 1798), 506.
Monthly Mirror, 5 (June 1798), 349-50.
Monthly Review, 26 (May 1798), 63-68.

Monthly Visitor, 4 (May 1798), 87-90.
Scientific Magazine (Freemason's Magazine, 1 (Aug. 1798), 126-27.

The Aristocrat. By the Author of The Democrat. 1799. (F)
    Analytical Review, ns,v1 (Apr. 1799), 416.
    Antijacobin Review, 6 (May 1800), 55-56.
    Critical Review, ns,v26 (July 1799), 358.
    Monthly Magazine, Suppl. v7 (July 20, 1799), 543.
    Monthly Mirror, 7 (Apr. 1799), 221.
    Monthly Review, ns,v29 (Aug. 1799), 468-69.
    New London Review, 1 (Apr. 1799), 408-09.

Adelaide, a Tragedy. 1800. (D)
    British Critic, 15 (Feb. 1800), 182-85.
    Critical Review, ns,v29 (June 1800), 208-15.
    Monthly Magazine, Suppl. v10 (Jan. 20, 1801), 612.
    Monthly Review, ns,v33 (Nov. 1800), 316-17.
    New London Review, 3 (Feb. 1800), 183-84.

Carmen Seculare for the Year 1800. 1800. (P)
    British Critic, 15 (Jan. 1800), 73-75.
    Critical Review, s2,v28 (Mar. 1800), 299-305.
    European Magazine, 37 (Apr. 1800), 302.
    Gentleman's Magazine, 70^1 (Jan. 1800), 65-67.
    Monthly Magazine, Suppl. v9 (July 20, 1800), 639.
    Monthly Review, 31 (Mar. 1800), 304-07.
    New London Review, 3 (Apr. 1800), 353-54.

Alfred; an Epic Poem. 1801. (P)
    Antijacobin Review, 9 (July, Aug. 1801), 232-34, 340-47;
        10 (Sept. 1801), 12-21.
    British Critic, 18 (July 1801), 27-33.
    Critical Review, s2,v34 (Apr. 1802), 361-70.
    Monthly Magazine, Suppl. v13 (July 20, 1802), 657.
    Monthly Review, 37 (Feb. 1802), 179-83.
    New Annual Register, 22 (1801), [309].
    Poetical Register, 1 (1801), 423.

Verses on Several Subjects, Written in the Vicinity of
Stoke Park, in the Summer and Autumn of 1801. 1802. (P)
    British Critic, 20 (July 1802), 69-71.
    Monthly Mirror, 14 (Aug. 1802), 102.
    Monthly Review, 41 (Aug. 1803), 361-65.
    New Annual Register, 23 (1802), [316].
    Poetical Register, 2 (1802), 431.

Pye, Henry James, and James Petit Andrews.
The Inquisitor, a Tragedy. Altered from the German. 1798.
(D)
    British Critic, 12 (July 1798), 73.

Pye, Henry James, and Samuel James Arnold.

A Prior Claim, a Comedy. 1803. (D)
   Antijacobin Review, 22 (Dec. 1805), 422-23.
   Critical Review, s3,v8 (May 1806), 99.
   European Magazine, 48 (Nov. 1805), 378-79.
   Monthly Magazine, 21 (July 25, 1806), 609.
   Poetical Register, 5 (1805), 504.

Pyke, Sarah Leigh.
   The Triumph of Messiah. 1813. (P)
   Eclectic Review, 10 (Dec. 1813), 601-10.

Q in the Corner.
   See Thomas Haynes Bayley.

Q. Q. and W. W.
   Leaves of Laurel; or, New Probationary Odes for the Vacant
   Laureatship. 1813. (P)
      Critical Review, s4,v4 (Sept. 1813), 319-21.
      Monthly Review, 72 (Sept. 1813), 103-05.

Queen Mab.
   The Modern Minerva; or the Bat's Seminary for Young Ladies.
   A Satire on Female Education. 1810. (P)
      Antijacobin Review, 40 (Sept. 1811), 91.
      British Critic, 38 (Sept. 1811), 294-95.
      Critical Review, s3,v24 (Sept. 1811), 104-05.
      Monthly Review, 66 (Oct. 1811), 216-18.
      Poetical Register, 8 (1810), 588.

Quillinan, Edward.
   Ball Room Votaries; or, Canterbury and Its Vicinity. 2nd
   ed. (P)
      Poetical Register, 8 (1810), 583.

   Monthermer: A Poem. 1815. (P)
      Gentleman's Magazine, 85[2] (Aug. 1815), 149-52.
      Monthly Review, 79 (Jan. 1816), 99-100.
      New Monthly Magazine, 4 (Sept. 1815), 154.
      Tradesman, 15 (Sept. 1815), 231-36.

   The Sacrifice of Isabel, a Poem. 1816. (P)
      Critical Review, s5,v4 (Oct. 1816), 390-94.
      Gentleman's Magazine, 86[1] (June 1816), 527-31.
      Monthly Review, 82 (Apr. 1817), 433-34.

   Dunlace Castle. 1818. (P)
      Blackwood's Edinburgh Magazine, 4 (Feb. 1819), 574-79.
      Man of Kent, Dec. 12, 19, 1818, pp. 198-200, 213.

Quin, Thomas.
   The City of Refuge; a Poem. (P)
      Baptist Magazine, 11 (May 1819), 212.

Quince, Peter, the Younger.
  The Cheltenham Mail Bag; or Letters from Gloucestershire.
  1820. (P)
    Gentleman's Magazine, 90[2] (Nov. 1820), 440.
    Literary Chronicle, 2 (Sept. 23, 1820), 609-11.
    New Monthly Magazine, 14 (Dec. 1820), 686-87.

Quiz, Jeremiah.
  The Ass on Parnassus; and from Scotland, Ge Ho!! Comes Rod-
  erigh Vich Neddy Dhu, Ho! Ieroe!!! A Prophetic Tale Written in Imitation of The Lady of the Lake. 1811. (P)
    Antijacobin Review, 39 (May 1811), 77-80.
    British Critic, 38 (Oct. 1811), 405.
    Poetical Register, 8 (1810), 586-87.

Quondam Oxonian & Carthusian, A.
  See Daniel Cabanel.

Rabelais, Robert, the Younger.
  A Nineteenth Century and Familiar History of the Lives,
  Loves, and Misfortunes of Abeillard and Heloisa. 1819. (P)
    La Bella Assemblée, ns,v20 (July 1819), 32-33.
    Fireside Magazine (quoting New Monthly Magazine and
      Monthly Magazine), 1 (May, June 1819), 198, 233.
    Literary Gazette, Jan. 16, 1819, p. 37.
    Monthly Magazine, 47 (May 1819), 344-45.
    Monthly Review, 90 (Oct. 1819), 212-13.
    New Monthly Magazine, 11 (Feb. 1819), 66.
    Theatre; or Dramatic and Literary Mirror, 2 (Aug. 7,
      1819), 37-38.

Radcliffe, Ann.
  The Italian; or the Confessional of the Black Penitents.
  A Romance. 1797. (F)
    Critical Review, ns,v23 (June 1798), 166-69.

Radcliffe, Mary Ann.
  Manfroni; or the One-Handed Monk, a Romance. (F)
    Le Beau Monde, 2 (Oct. 1809), 45.

Raffles, Thomas, James Baldwin Brown, and Jeremiah H. Wiffen.
  Poems. By Three Friends. 1813. (P)
    Critical Review, s4,v4 (Nov. 1813), 554-56.
    Critical Review, s5,v3 (Jan. 1816), 93-94. (2nd ed.)
    Eclectic Review, s2,v1 (Feb. 1814), 195-96.
    Gentleman's Magazine, 84[2] (Nov. 1814), 466-67.
    Literary Panorama, 14 (Jan. 1814), 940-43.
    Monthly Review, 72 (Dec. 1813), 438-41.
    Monthly Review, 80 (May 1816), 96. (2nd ed.)
    New Review, 2 (Dec. 1813), 647-49.

Rag, Matthew.
  The New Eldorado; or, Triumphs of Elba. (P)
    La Belle Assemblée, ns,v10 (Oct. 1814), 177-79.

Rannie, John.
  Musical Dramas, with Select Poems and Ballads. 1807. (P-D)
    Antijacobin Review, 26 (Feb. 1807), 175.
    British Critic, 30 (Sept. 1807), 314.
    Literary Annual Register, 1 (July 1807), 320.
    Literary Panorama, 2 (Sept. 1807), 1198.
    Monthly Magazine, Suppl. v23 (July 30, 1807), 643.
    Monthly Review, 55 (Feb. 1808), 222.
    Poetical Register, 7 (1808), 578.
    Satirist, 1 (Feb. 1808), 526-29.
    Satirist, 2 (May 1808), 322-23.

Rayner, W. H.
  Virtue and Vice. 1806. (F)
    Literary Journal, a Review..., ns,v1 (Jan. 1806), 108.
    Monthly Mirror, 21 (Apr. 1806), 259.

Read, William.
  The Hill of Caves, with Other Poems. (P)
    Literary Gazette, Apr. 11, 1818, pp. 228-29.
    Monthly Review, 92 (May 1820), 96.

Redding, Cyrus.
  Mount Edgcumbe, a Poem. 1811. (P)
    Critical Review, s4,v1 (Apr. 1812), 443-44.
    Monthly Review, 68 (May 1812), 107.
    Poetical Register, 8 (1811), 625-26.

Reeve, Mrs. _____.
  The Flowers at Court. 1809. (P)
    Antijacobin Review, 32 (Feb. 1809), 191-92.
    British Critic, 33 (Feb. 1809), 183-84.
    Critical Review, s3,v16 (Feb. 1809), 211.
    Lady's Monthly Museum, s2,v6 (Mar. 1809), 154-55.
    Literary Panorama, 6 (May 1809), 231.
    Monthly Review, 59 (Aug. 1809), 439-40.

Reeve, Clara.
  Destination; or Memoirs of a Private Family. 1799. (F)
    British Critic, 14 (Sept. 1799), 313.
    Critical Review, ns,v27 (Sept. 1799), 115.
    Monthly Magazine, Suppl. v8 (Jan. 20, 1800), 1053.
    Monthly Mirror, 8 (July 1799), 28.
    Monthly Review, ns,v30 (Sept. 1799), 97.

Reeve, Sophia.
  The Mysterious Wanderer. 1807. (F)
    British Critic, 30 (Oct. 1807), 444.
    Critical Review, s3,v11 (July 1807), 326.
    European Magazine, 51 (Mar. 1807), 218.
    Monthly Magazine, Suppl. v24 (Jan. 30, 1808), 630.
    Monthly Mirror, ns,v3 (Jan. 1808), 30.
    Monthly Review, ns,v59 (July 1809), 321.

Satirist, 5 (Oct. 1809), 414.

Relph, Rev. Josiah.
  Poems. With the Life of the Author. 1798. (P)
    Analytical Review, ns,v1 (Apr. 1799), 406-08.
    Monthly Magazine, Suppl. v7 (July 20, 1799), 537-38.
    Monthly Review, 29 (Aug. 1799), 448-49.

Rendell, Sophia.
  The Village Minstrel; or Simple Lays. (P)
    Literary Annual Register, 2 (June 1808), 264-65.

Rennell, Thomas.
  Ode Praemio a Reverendo Viro, Claudio Buchanan. 1804. (P)
    Monthly Review, 40 (Sept. 1805), 36-37.

Repton, Humphrey.
  Odd Whims and Miscellanies. 1804. (D)
    Critical Review, s3,v5 (May 1805), 106-07.
    Flowers of Literature, 4 (1805), 430.
    Lady's Monthly Museum, 14 (May 1805), 346.

Reynolds, Frederick.
  The Will, a Comedy. 1797. (D)
    British Critic, 12 (Sept. 1798), 304.

  Cheap Living. A Comedy. 1797. (D)
    British Critic, 11 (May 1798), 561.
    Monthly Magazine, Suppl. v5 (July 15, 1798), 508.
    Monthly Magazine, Suppl. v7 (July 20, 1798), 538.
    Monthly Mirror, 6 (July 1798), 38.

  Laugh When You Can. A Comedy. 1799. (D)
    British Critic, 13 (May 1799), 549.
    Critical Review, ns,v26 (May 1798), 115-16.
    Monthly Magazine, Suppl. v8 (Jan. 20, 1800), 1055.
    Monthly Mirror, 7 (May 1799), 292-93.
    Monthly Review, ns,v29 (June 1799), 232-33.
    New London Review, 1 (Mar. 1799), 303.

  Management. A Comedy. 1800. (D)
    Antijacobin Review, 6 (May 1800), 57.
    British Critic, 15 (Apr. 1800), 432.
    Critical Review, ns,v28 (Apr. 1800), 475.
    Monthly Mirror, 10 (July 1800), 38.
    Monthly Review, ns,v31 (Jan. 1800), 95-97.
    New London Review, 2 (Dec. 1799), 604-05.

  Life. A Comedy. 1800. (D)
    Antijacobin Review, 8 (Jan. 1801), 60.
    British Critic. 17 (May 1801), 540.
    Monthly Magazine, Suppl. v11 (July 20, 1801), 607.
    Monthly Review, ns,v35 (July 1801), 323.

Reynolds, Frederick (continued)

Folly As It Flies. A Comedy. 1802. (D)
  Annual Review, 1 (1802), 694.
  Critical Review, ns,v36 (Sept. 1802), 115-17.
  Monthly Magazine, Suppl. v13 (July 20, 1802), 660.
  Monthly Magazine, Suppl. v14 (Jan. 25, 1803), 600.
  Monthly Mirror, 13 (Mar. 1802), 202 [192].
  Monthly Review, ns,v39 (Nov. 1802), 322-24.
  New Annual Register, 23 (1802), [320].
  Poetical Register, 2 (1802), 453.

Delays and Blunders. A Comedy. 1803. (D)
  Annual Review, 2 (1803), 595.
  British Critic, 23 (Apr. 1803), 434.
  Critical Review, ns,v37 (Mar. 1803), 355.
  Flowers of Literature, 2 (1803), 446.
  Monthly Magazine, Suppl. v15 (July 28, 1803), 631.
  Monthly Mirror, 15 (Feb. 1803), 115.
  Monthly Review, ns,v40 (Mar. 1803), 329-30.
  Poetical Register, 3 (1803), 464.

The Caravan; or, the Driver and His Dog. A Grand Serio-
Comic Romance. 1803. (D)
  Annual Review, 2 (1803), 596.
  British Critic, 23 (May 1804), 555.
  Critical Review, s3,v1 (Jan. 1804), 118.
  Monthly Mirror, 17 (Feb. 1804), 115.
  Poetical Register, 3 (1803), 466.

The Blind Bargain; or Hear It Out. A Comedy. 1805. (D)
  Annual Review, 4 (1805), 641.
  British Critic, 25 (Apr. 1805), 442.
  Critical Review, s3,v4 (Feb. 1805), 210-11.
  Flowers of Literature, 4 (1805), 417.
  Literary Journal, a Review..., 26 (Feb. 1805), 205-06.
  Monthly Mirror, 19 (Jan. 1805), 43.
  Monthly Review, ns,v49 (Feb. 1806), 217.
  Poetical Register, 5 (1805), 505.

The Delinquent; or Seeing Company. A Comedy. 1805. (D)
  Annual Review, 4 (1805), 643.
  Antijacobin Review, 23 (Feb. 1806), 206-07.
  Critical Review, s3,v7 (Jan. 1806), 99-100.
  Flowers of Literature, 5 (1806), 500.
  General Review, 1 (Jan. 1806), 91.
  Monthly Magazine, Suppl. v21 (July 25, 1806), 609.
  Monthly Mirror, 21 (Jan. 1806), 42.
  Monthly Review, ns,v50 (May 1806), 102.
  Poetical Register, 5 (1805), 503.

The Deserts of Arabia. A Grand Spectacle. 1806. (D)
  Flowers of Literature, 5 (1806), 500.

Reynolds, Frederick (concluded)
  Begone Dull Care. A Comedy. 1808. (D)
    Poetical Register, 7 (1808), 580.

  The Free Knights; or the Edict of Charlemagne. 1810. (D)
    Poetical Register, 8 (1810), 597.

  What's a Man of Fashion? A Farce. 1815. (D)
    Augustan Review, 2 (Jan. 1816), 55-59.
    Monthly Review, ns,v79 (Jan. 1816), 96-97.

Reynolds, John Hamilton.
  Safie, an Eastern Tale. 1814. (P)
    Antijacobin Review, 46 (Feb. 1814), 150-52.
    La Belle Assemblée, ns,v9 (Mar. 1814), 129-31.
    British Critic, ns,v1 (Feb. 1814), 210-12.
    Critical Review, s4,v5 (Mar. 1814), 318-22.
    Monthly Review, 75 (Sept. 1814), 60-65.
    New Annual Register, 35 (1814), [363].
    New Review, 3 (Mar. 1814), 293-95.
    Theatrical Inquisitor, 4 (Apr. 1814), 229-32.
    Universal Magazine, ns,v21 (Feb. 1814), 136.

  The Eden of Imagination. A Poem. 1814. (P)
    British Critic, ns,v4 (July 1815), 95-97.
    Critical Review, s4,v6 (Nov. 1814), 479-81.

  The Naiad, a Tale. (Anon.) 1816. (P)
    Augustan Review, 3 (Oct. 1816), 345-50.
    British Critic, ns,v8 (Oct. 1817), 415-20.
    Critical Review, s5,v4 (Oct. 1816), 344-50.
    Eclectic Review, 9 (Nov. 1816), 489-99.
    European Magazine, 70 (Sept. 1816), 250.
    Gentleman's Magazine, 86^2 (Nov. 1816), 436-37.
    Literary Panorama, ns,v5 (Feb. 1817), 758-61.
    Monthly Review, 82 (Mar. 1817), 323.

  Peter Bell; a Lyrical Ballad. (Anon.) 1819. (P)
    British Lady's Magazine, s3,v3 (July 1819), 35-36.
    Eclectic Review, s2,v11 (May 1819), 473-78.
    Examiner, Apr. 25, 1819, p. 270.
    Fireside Magazine (quoting Eclectic Review and Gentle-
      man's Magazine), 1 (June, July, 1819), 228-29, 275.
    Gentleman's Magazine, 89^1 (May 1819), 442.
    Literary Gazette, May 1, 1819, pp. 275-76.
    Literary Journal and General Miscellany, 2 (Apr. 24,
      1819), 243-44.
    Monthly Review, 89 (Aug. 1819), 422-23.
    Theatrical Inquisitor, 14 (June 1819), 449-50.

  Benjamin the Waggoner, a Righte Merrie and Conceitede Tale
  in Verse. A Fragment. (Anon.) 1819. (P)
    Fireside Magazine (quoting Monthly Magazine), 1 (Sept.

461

1819), 355.
Gentleman's Magazine, 89[2] (Aug. 1819), 144.
Monthly Magazine, 48 (Aug. 1819), 38.
Monthly Review, 90 (Sept. 1819), 40-42.

The Fancy: A Selection from the Poetical Remains of the
Late Peter Corcoran. 1820. (P)
   Blackwood's Edinburgh Magazine, 7 (June 1820), 294-306.
   Literary Chronicle, 2 (July 8, 1820), 437-40.
   (Baldwin's) London Magazine, 2 (July 1820), 71-75.
   New Monthly Magazine, 14 (Aug. 1820), 174-77.

Rhinde, William.
   The Ratiad, a Serio-Comic Poem. By an Anti-Hudibrastian.
   1807. (P)
   British Critic, 32 (Dec. 1808), 635-36.
   Cabinet, 2 (Dec. 1807), 325.
   Critical Review, s3,v10 (Apr. 1807), 439-40.
   Eclectic Review, 3 (July 1807), 644.
   Gentleman's Magazine, 78[1] (May 1808), 429-30.
   Monthly Mirror, ns,v2 (Nov. 1807), 331.
   Monthly Review, 54 (Oct. 1807), 209.
   Satirist, 4 (Feb. 1809), 206.

Rhodes, George Ambrose.
   Dion, a Tragedy; with Miscellaneous Poetry. 1806. (D-P)
   Annual Review, 5 (1806), 536.
   British Critic, 29 (Jan. 1807), 75-77.
   Critical Review, s3,v8 (July 1806), 322-23.
   Poetical Register, 6 (1806), 525.
   Theatrical Inquisitor, 16 (June 1820), 359-66.

   The Gentleman: A Satire. (Anon.) 1818. (P)
   Antijacobin Review, 55 (Dec. 1818), 299-305.
   Fireside Magazine (quoting Monthly Review and Antijacobin
      Review), 1 (Jan., Feb. 1819), 34, 77.
   Gentleman's Magazine, 89[1] (Feb. 1819), 144-45.
   Monthly Review, 87 (Nov. 1818), 321-23.
   Monthly Review, 91 (Feb. 1820), 213-14.

Rhodes, Henrietta.
   Rosalie, or the Castle of Montalbretti. (Anon.) 1811. (F)
   British Critic, 40 (Nov. 1812), 530.
   Monthly Review, ns,v67 (Mar. 1812), 320-21.

Rhodes, William Barnes.
   Epigrams. 1803. (P)
   Annual Review, 2 (1803), 558.
   Literary Journal, a Review..., 2 (July 16, 1803), 24-25.
   Monthly Visitor, ns,v4 (June 1803), 204-05.
   New Annual Register, 24 (1803), [327].
   Poetical Register, 3 (1803), 448-49.

Eccentric Tales in Verse. By Cornelius Crambo. 1808. (P)
  Annual Register, 7 (1808), 522.
  Antijacobin Review, 30 (Aug. 1808), 413-14.
  British Critic, 34 (Aug. 1809), 184-85.
  British Critic, 41 (Jan. 1813), 71.
  Critical Review, s3,v15 (Sept. 1808), 102.
  Critical Review, s4,v3 (Jan. 1813), 104-05.
  Monthly Review, 58 (Feb. 1809), 207-09.
  Poetical Register, 7 (1808), 562.
  Satirist, 10 (Mar. 1812), 232-33. (Excerpts from other
    reviews.)

Rice, Mrs. _____.
  Montieth, a Novel, Founded on Scottish History. By Mrs.
  Rice, Author of The Deserted Wife. 1806. (F)
    Literary Journal, a Review..., 5 (Dec. 1805), 1320.
    Literary Journal, a Review..., ns,v2 (Oct. 1806), 446.
    Monthly Mirror, 22 (Dec. 1806), 399.

Richards, G. P.
  Carmen Praemio, à Reverendo Viro Claudio Buchanan. 1805.
  (P)
    Imperial Review, 5 (July 1805), 66-68.

Richards, George.
  Poems. 1804. (P)
    Annual Review, 3 (1804), 585-86.
    British Critic, 23 (Apr. 1804), 403-10.
    Critical Review, s3,v2 (Aug. 1804), 435-42.
    Edinburgh Review, 4 (July 1804), 337-43.
    Gentleman's Magazine, 74^1 (May 1804), 434.
    Imperial Review, 1 (Mar. 1804), 459-65.
    Literary Journal, a Review..., 4 (Sept. 1804), 291-97.
    Monthly Magazine, Suppl. v17 (July 28, 1804), 664-65.
    Monthly Review, 47 (June 1805), 188-92.
    New Annual Register, 25 (1804), [352].
    Poetical Register, 4 (1804), 489.

  Monody on Admiral Lord Viscount Nelson.... 1805. (P)
    British Critic, 27 (May 1806), 549.
    Gentleman's Magazine, 76^1 (Feb. 1806), 142.
    Literary Journal, a Review..., 5 (Nov. 1805), 1220-21.
    Monthly Review, 49 (Jan. 1806), 96-97.
    Poetical Register, 5 (1805), 495.

Richardson, Mrs. _____.
  The Husband and the Lover. An Historical and Moral Romance. 1809. (F)
    Monthly Mirror, ns,v6 (Aug. 1809), 99.

Richardson, Charlotte Caroline.
  Poems Written on Different Occasions. 1806. (P)
    British Critic, 31 (May 1808), 547-48.

Critical Review, s3,v8 (June 1806), 217-22.
Eclectic Review, 2 (Dec. 1806), 938.
Guardian of Education, 5 (Mar. 1806), 180-86.
Literary Journal, a Review..., ns,v2 (July 1806), 108-09.
Monthly Repository, 1 (July 1806), 380-82.
Poetical Register, 6 (1806), 509.

Harvest, a Poem; with Other Poetical Pieces. (P)
Fireside Magazine (quoting Monthly Magazine), 1 (Apr.
1819), 160.
Monthly Magazine, 47 (Feb. 1819), 61.
Monthly Review, 91 (Apr. 1820), 440.

Richardson, Mrs. Joseph.
Original Poems, Intended for the Use of Young Persons.
1808. (P)
Annual Review, 7 (1808), 540.
Antijacobin Review, 30 (Aug. 1808), 414.
British Critic, 34 (Nov. 1809), 521-22.
Eclectic Review, 5 (Oct. 1809), 973.
European Magazine, 53 (May 1808), 370.
Gentleman's Magazine, 79^2 (Dec. 1809), 1137.
Monthly Magazine, Suppl. v25 (July 30, 1808), 596.
Monthly Mirror, ns,v4 (Aug. 1808), 99.
Monthly Review, 58 (Feb. 1809), 211.
Poetical Register, 7 (1808), 559.
Satirist, 5 (Dec. 1809), 623.

Richardson, William.
The Maid of Lochlin, a Lyrical Drama; with Legendary Odes
and Other Poems. 1801. (P-D)
Antijacobin Review, 12 (May 1802), 18-21.
British Critic, 19 (May 1802), 478-83.
Critical Review, s2,v34 (Feb. 1802), 164-70.
European Magazine, 40 (Dec. 1801), 433-35.
Gentleman's Magazine, 72^2 (Dec. 1802), 1138-39.
Monthly Magazine, Suppl. v13 (July 20, 1802), 659-60.
Monthly Mirror, 13 (Jan. 1802), 39-41.
Monthly Review, 38 (July 1802), 309-11.
New Annual Register, 22 (1801), [314].
Poetical Register, 1 (1801), 457.

Poems and Plays. 1805. (P)
Annual Review, 4 (1805), 565.
Antijacobin Review, 29 (Mar. 1808), 238-49.
British Critic, 28 (Sept. 1806), 335-36.
Critical Review, s3,v10 (Jan. 1807), 1-13.
General Review, 1 (Jan. 1806), 90.
Gentleman's Magazine, 78^2 (July 1808), 609-11.
Monthly Mirror, 20 (Aug. 1805), 102-05.
Poetical Register, 5 (1805), 491.

Rickman, Thomas Clio.
  Poetical Scraps. 1803. (P)
    Poetical Register, 3 (1803), 453.
    Universal Magazine, ns,v2 (July 1804), 57-60.

  An Ode, in Celebration of the Emancipation of the Blacks
  of St. Domingo, November 29, 1803. 1804. (P)
    Annual Review, 3 (1804), 572.
    British Critic, 23 (June 1804), 674.
    Monthly Review, 46 (Mar. 1805), 322-23.
    Poetical Register, 4 (1804), 497-98.
    Universal Magazine, ns,v1 (June 1804), 615-16.

  Corruption, a Satire. 1806. (P)
    Critical Review, s3,v8 (Aug. 1806), 440-41.
    Monthly Mirror, 22 (Oct. 1806), 250.
    Monthly Review, 52 (Jan. 1807), 92-94.
    Poetical Register, 6 (1806), 519.

  Elegy to the Memory of Thomas Paine; to Which Is Added His
  Epitaph and a Sonnet. 1810. (P)
    Poetical Register, 8 (1810), 576-77.
    Satirist, 7 (Sept. 1810), 295-98.
    Universal Magazine, ns,v13 (June 1810), 481.

Riddell, Mrs. Maria.
  The Metrical Miscellany. (P)
    Annual Review, 1 (1802), 667-68.

Rigshaw, Cincinnatus.
  Sans Culotides. 1800.
    Antijacobin Review, 6 (July 1800), 292-301.
    British Critic, 16 (Aug. 1800), 198-99.
    Critical Review, s2,v30 (Oct. 1800), 224-25.

Ring, John.
  The Commemoration of Handel, and Other Poems. (P)
    Fireside Magazine (quoting Gentleman's Magazine), 1
    (Sept. 1819), 360.
    New Monthly Magazine, 12 (Sept. 1819), 208.

Ringletub, Jeremiah.
  See John Styles.

Ripley, J. J.
  Adhelm and Ethelfled, a Metrical Story. (P)
    European Magazine, 74 (July 1818), 56.

Ripon, John Scott.
  See John Scott Byerley.

Ritson, Mrs. Anne.
  A Poetical Picture of America, Being Observations Made

during a Residence of Several Years, at Alexandria and Norfolk in Virginia.... 1809. (P)
  Antijacobin Review, 35 (Mar. 1810), 300.
  British Critic, 34 (Dec. 1809), 625.
  Critical Review, s3,v17 (June 1809), 218-19.
  Eclectic Review, 5 (Apr. 1809), 378-79.
  Literary Panorama, 6 (May 1809), 233-38.
  Monthly Review, 59 (July 1809), 326-27.
  Poetical Register, 7 (1809), 596-97.

The Poetical Chain, Consisting of Miscellaneous Poems, Moral, Sentimental, and Descriptive.... 1811. (P)
  British Critic, 38 (Dec. 1811), 633-34.
  Critical Review, s4,v1 (Feb. 1812), 217.
  Eclectic Review, 8 (Feb. 1812), 219.
  European Magazine, 61 (Jan. 1812), 42-43.
  Monthly Review, 67 (Mar. 1812), 323-24.
  Poetical Register, 8 (1811), 625.

Rivers, David.
  Lord Mayor's Day: An Heroic Poem. (Anon.) 1797. (P)
    British Critic, 11 (June 1798), 676.
    Monthly Mirror, 5 (Jan. 1798), 32.

  Poems; to Which Is Annexed Lord Mayor's Day, a Mock-Heroic Poem. 1800. (P)
    Antijacobin Review, 8 (Jan. 1801), 64.
    British Critic, 17 (May 1801), 538.
    Critical Review, s2,v32 (May 1801), 98-99.
    European Magazine, 38 (Nov. 1800), 361-62.
    Monthly Magazine, Suppl. v11 (July 20, 1801), 606.
    Monthly Mirror, 12 (Oct. 1801), 257-58.
    Poetical Register, 1 (1801), 439-40.

Robb, Rev. William.
  Poems, Illustrative of the Genius and Influence of Christianity. 1810. (P)
    British Critic, 36 (Sept. 1810), 301-02.

Roberdeau, John Peter.
  Fugitive Verse and Prose: Consisting of Poems, Lyric, Obituary, Dramatic, Satiric, and Miscellaneous. 1803. (P)
    Annual Review, 2 (1803), 582-83.
    European Magazine, 47 (Jan. 1805), 54.
    Gentleman's Magazine, 75[1] (Feb. 1805), 152-53.
    Imperial Review, 3 (Dec. 1804), 603-04.
    Literary Journal, a Review..., 2 (Sept. 16, 1803), 271-72.
    Poetical Register, 3 (1803), 442.

Roberts, Mrs. Margaret.
  Rose and Emily, or Sketches of Youth. 1812. (F)
    Monthly Review, ns,v69 (Nov. 1812), 332.
    Universal Magazine, ns,v20 (Aug. 1813), 140.

Duty, a Novel. 1814. (F)
    British Critic, ns,v3 (May 1815), 553.
    Monthly Review, ns,v77 (June 1815), 212-13.

Roberts, Samuel.
    The State Lottery. 1817. (P)
        Gentleman's Magazine, 87[1] (May 1817), 438-39.
        Literary Panorama, ns,v6 (May 1817), 245-49.
        Monthly Review, 85 (Feb. 1818), 220.

Roberts, Thomas.
    Carmen Seculare. A Sacred Poem, on the Commencement of
    the Present Century. 1800. (P)
        Monthly Review, 34 (Apr. 1801), 438-39.

Roberts, William Isaac.
    Poems and Letters. With Some Account of His Life. 1811.
    (P)
        British Critic, 39 (Feb. 1812), 193-95.
        Eclectic Review, 8 (June 1812), 644.
        Monthly Review, 67 (Jan. 1812), 60-66.
        Poetical Register, 8 (1811), 621.

Robertus.
    Poems. 1805. (P)
        Annual Review, 4 (1805), 622.
        British Critic, 26 (Nov. 1805), 564.
        Critical Review, s3,v6 (Dec. 1805), 435-36.
        Gentleman's Magazine, 78[1] (May 1808), 431.
        Monthly Review, 49 (Apr. 1806), 437.
        Poetical Register, 5 (1805), 488.
        Universal Magazine, ns,v4 (Nov. 1805), 436-37.

Robins, John, Jr.
    Sensibility, with Other Poems. 1806. (P)
        British Critic, 28 (Oct. 1806), 445.
        British Critic, 32 (Nov. 1808), 516-17.
        Critical Review, s3,v8 (May 1806), 102-03.
        Monthly Magazine, Suppl. v21 (July 25, 1806), 608.
        Monthly Review, 50 (May 1806), 101-02.

Robinson, G.
    The Mysterious Protector. (F)
        Literary Journal, a Review..., 5 (Nov. 1805), 1222.

Robinson, Mary ("Perdita").
    Hubert de Sevrac. A Romance of the Eighteenth Century.
    1796. (F)
        Critical Review, ns,v23 (Aug. 1798), 472.

    Walsingham; or, the Pupil of Nature. A Domestic Story.
    1797. (F)
        Analytical Review, 27 (Jan. 1798), 80-83.

Antijacobin Review, 1 (Aug. 1798), 160-64.
Critical Review, ns,v22 (Appendix, 1798), 553-58.
Monthly Magazine, Suppl. v5 (July 15, 1798), 508.
Monthly Mirror, 5 (Mar. 1798), 163-64.
Monthly Review, ns,v26 (Aug. 1798), 441-44.
Monthly Visitor, 3 (Jan. 1798), 86-87.

The False Friend. A Domestic Story. 1799. (F)
Analytical Review, ns,v1 (Feb. 1799), 209-10.
Antijacobin Review, 3 (May 1799), 39-42.
British Critic, 14 (July 1799), 74-75.
Critical Review, ns,v26 (May 1799), 117.
Monthly Magazine, Suppl. v7 (July 20, 1799), 541.
Monthly Mirror, 7 (Mar. 1799), 166-67.
Monthly Review, ns,v30 (Sept. 1799), 98.
Monthly Visitor, 7 (Aug. 1799), 420.
New London Review, 1 (Mar. 1799), 298.

The Natural Daughter; with Portraits of the Leadenhead Family. 1799. (F)
British Critic, 16 (Sept. 1800), 320-21.
Critical Review, ns,v28 (Apr. 1800), 477.
European Magazine, 37 (Feb. 1800), 138-39.
Monthly Magazine, Supp. v9 (July 20, 1800), 640.
Monthly Review, ns,v32 (May 1800), 93-94.
New London Review, 2 (Sept. 1799), 285-86.

Lyrical Tales. 1800. (P)
British Critic, 18 (Aug. 1801), 193.
European Magazine, 38 (Nov. 1800), 362.
Monthly Review, 36 (Sept. 1801), 26-30.
Monthly Visitor, 12 (Apr. 1801), 416.

Memoirs of the Late Mrs. Robinson, Written by Herself, with Some Posthumous Pieces. 1801. (Pr-P)
Monthly Review, 36 (Dec. 1801), 344-50.
Poetical Register, 1 (1801), 433.

The Poetical Works of the Late Mrs. Mary Robinson. 1806. (P)
Annual Review, 5 (1806), 516-19.
British Critic, 30 (July 1807), 78-79.
Flowers of Literature, 5 (1806), 511.
New Annual Register, 27 (1806), [371].
Poetical Register, 6 (1807), 540.

Robinson, T.
The Tyrolese Villagers; or, a Prospect of War, an Epistolary Tale. With Other Poems. 1810. (P)
British Critic, 38 (Dec. 1811), 632-33.
Monthly Review, 67 (Feb. 1812), 186-89.
Poetical Register, 8 (1810), 562-63.

Robinson, Rev. Thomas.
  Sketches in Verse. (P)
    Critical Review, s2,v22 (Apr. 1798), 474.

Robinson, Thomas Romney.
  Juvenile Poems. 1806. (P)
    Critical Review, s3,v9 (Dec. 1806), 440-46.
    Eclectic Review, 4 (June 1808), 569.
    Poetical Register, 6 (1807), 547.

Robson, Mary (later Mrs. Hughes).
  The Ornaments Discovered, a Story. By the Author of Aunt
  Mary's Tales. 1815. (F)
    British Critic, ns,v5 (May 1816), 556.
    Gentleman's Magazine, 86[1] (Mar. 1816), 250.
    New Monthly Magazine, 4 (Dec. 1815), 445.

Roby, John.
  Jokeby, a Burlesque on Rokeby. By an Amateur of Fashion.
  1813. (P)
    British Critic, 42 (Oct. 1813), 408-09.
    Country Magazine, 1 (July 1813), 319-23.
    European Magazine, 64 (Oct. 1813), 329.
    Monthly Review, 71 (July 1813), 318.
    New Review, 2 (Sept. 1813), 230-32.
    Town Talk, 4 (July 1813), 439-40.

  The Lay of the Poor Fiddler, a Parody on "The Lay of the
  Last Minstrel." By an Admirer of Walter Scott. 1814. (P)
    British Critic, ns,v4 (Nov. 1815), 542-44.
    Monthly Review, 78 (Oct. 1815), 215.

  Sir Bertram, a Poem. 1815. (P)
    La Belle Assemblée, Suppl. ns,v14 (1816), 343-44.
    Critical Review, s5,v3 (Feb. 1816), 120-28.
    Monthly Review, 80 (June 1816), 212-13.

  Lorenzo; or the Tale of Redemption. (Anon.) (P)
    Christian's Pocket Magazine, 3 (Nov. 1820), 251-52.

Roche, Hamilton.
  Salamanca, a Poem. 1812. (P)
    New Review, 1 (Jan. 1813), 4-5.
    Town Talk, 3 (Dec. 1812), 367-72.

  France; a Heroic Poem. 1814. (P)
    Critical Review, s4,v6 (Sept. 1814), 313.
    New Monthly Magazine, 2 (Nov. 1814), 350.

Roche, Regina Maria.
  The Children of the Abbey, a Tale. 1797. (F)
    British Critic, 11 (Jan. 1798), 77.

Clermont. A Tale. 1798. (P)
Critical Review, ns,v24 (Nov. 1798), 356.

The Discarded Son. (F)
Annual Review, 6 (1807), 666-67.

The Monastery of St. Columb; or, the Atonement. (F)
La Belle Assemblée, Suppl. ns,v6 (1812), 371-77.

Trecothick Bower, or the Lady of the West Country, a Tale.
1814. (F)
Critical Review, s4,v5 (Jan. 1814), 99-101.

Anna, or Edinburgh. 1815. (F)
Critical Review, s5,v1 (Feb. 1815), 208.

The Munster Cottage, a Tale. 1820. (F)
Edinburgh Monthly Review, 3 (Apr. 1820), 418-28.

Rodd, Thomas.
Ancient Ballads, from the Civil Wars of Granada, and the
Twelve Peers of France. 1801. (P)
Antijacobin Review, 9 (Aug. 1801), 412-13.
British Critic, 18 (Oct. 1801), 422-24.

An Elegy on His Grace Francis, the Late Duke of Bedford.
1802. (P)
Antijacobin Review, 14 (Jan. 1803), 80.
Critical Review, s2,v36 (Dec. 1802), 476.
Monthly Review, 38 (May 1802), 99-100.
New Annual Register, 23 (1802), [318].

Sonnets, Amatory, Descriptive, and Religious; Odes, Songs,
and Ballads. 1814. (P)
British Critic, ns,v3 (Feb. 1815), 207-08.
Monthly Review, 79 (Jan. 1816), 97-98.

Roe, F.
Warwick Castle, a Poem. 1812. (P)
Antijacobin Review, 43 (Nov. 1812), 242-48.
British Critic, 41 (Feb. 1813), 187-88.
Monthly Review, 71 (May 1813), 96-97.

Rogers, John Benjamin.
The Days of Harold. A Metrical Tale. 1816. (P)
British Critic, ns,v6 (Sept. 1816), 318-20.
Critical Review, s5,v3 (Apr. 1816), 351-52.
European Magazine, 69 (May 1816), 435-37.
Fireside Magazine (quoting Gentleman's Magazine), 1
(Sept. 1819), 359.
Gentleman's Magazine, 89[1] (June 1819), 546-47.
Lady's Monthly Museum, s3,v3 (Feb. 1816), 99-101.
Monthly Review, 80 (July 1816), 318-19.

Rogers, Samuel.
An Epistle to a Friend, with Other Poems. By the Author of
The Pleasures of Memory. 1798. (P)
    Analytical Review, 27 (Apr. 1798), 419-20.
    Antijacobin Review, 5 (Jan. 1800), 71-75.
    British Critic, 11 (June 1798), 652-54.
    Critical Review, s2,v23 (July 1798), 351-52.
    Monthly Magazine, Suppl. v5 (July 15, 1798), 506.
    Monthly Mirror, 6 (July 1798), 35-36.
    Monthly Review, 25 (Apr. 1798), 361-64.
    Monthly Visitor, 4 (May 1798), 85-87.
    New Annual Register, 19 (1798), [308-09].
    Scientific Magazine (Freemason's Magazine), 1 (Aug. 1798),
        127.

Poems; Including Fragments of a Poem Called The Voyage of
Columbus. 1812. (P)
    La Belle Assemblée, Suppl. ns,v8 (1813), 322.
    Edinburgh Review, 22 (Oct. 1813), 32-50.
    Quarterly Review, 9 (Mar. 1813), 207-18.
    Town Talk, 5 (Aug. 1813), 50-54.

Jacqueline, a Tale. 1814. (P)
    La Belle Assemblée, ns,v10 (Sept. 1814), 132-33.
    British Critic, ns,v2 (Oct. 1814), 401-13.
    Critical Review, s4,v6 (Aug. 1814), 203.
    Eclectic Review, s2,v2 (Oct. 1814), 393-400.
    Entertaining Magazine, 2 (Aug., Sept. 1814), 432-36,
        486-90.
    Lady's Monthly Museum, s2,v17 (Nov. 1814), 290-94.
    Monthly Museum, 2 (Sept. 1814), 220-24.
    Monthly Review, 75 (Sept. 1814), 83-92.
    New Monthly Magazine, 2 (Sept. 1814), 156-57.
    New Universal Magazine, 1 (Aug. 1814), 123-26.
    Theatrical Inquisitor, 5 (Aug. 1814), 101-13.

Human Life, a Poem. 1819. (P)
    La Belle Assemblée, Suppl. ns,v20 (1819), 342-43.
    Blackwood's Edinburgh Magazine, 4 (Feb. 1819), 553-58.
    British Critic, ns,v11 (Apr. 1819), 437-43.
    British Lady's Magazine, s3,v2 (Apr. 1819), 166-69.
    British Review, 13 (May 1819), 372-77.
    Christian's Pocket Magazine, 1 (May-July 1819), 39, 93,
        182. (Digests from other reviews.)
    Christian's Pocket Magazine, 1 (July 1819), 184-88.
    Eclectic Review, s2,v11 (Mar. 1819), 218-26.
    Edinburgh Monthly Review, 1 (Apr. 1819), 427-34.
    Edinburgh Review, 31 (Mar. 1819), 325-36.
    Fireside Magazine (quoting 8 other reviews), 1 (Apr.
        1819), 155, 186-87, 194, 197, 198, 227, 258-59, 307-08.
    Fireside Magazine, 1 (July 1819), 256-57.
    Gentleman's Magazine, 89¹ (Feb. 1819), 157.
    Literary Annual Register, 1 (Jan. 1807), 22-23.

Literary Gazette, Feb. 13, 1819, pp. 97-98.
Monthly Magazine, 47 (Apr. 1819), 254-55.
Monthly Review, 88 (Mar. 1819), 307-18.
New Monthly Magazine, 11 (Mar. 1819), 153-58.
Theatrical Inquisitor, 14 (Mar. 1819), 210-12.

Rolleston, Matthew.
The Anti-Corsicàn, a Poem. (Anon.) 1805. (P)
    Annual Review, 4 (1805), 597-98.
    Critical Review, s3,v5 (June 1805), 219.
    Lady's Monthly Museum, 14 (June 1805), 418.
    Monthly Magazine, Suppl. v19 (July 28, 1805), 659.
    Monthly Mirror, 19 (May 1805), 325-26.
    Monthly Review, 46 (Apr. 1805), 440-43.

Mahomet: A Prize Poem, Recited in the Theatre, Oxford.
(Anon.) 1808. (P)
    Eclectic Review, 4 (Dec. 1808), 1134-35.

Rolls, Mrs. Henry.
Sacred Sketches from Scripture History. 1815. (P)
    Critical Review, s5,v2 (Aug. 1815), 213-15.
    Gentleman's Magazine, 86^2 (Nov. 1816), 434.
    Literary Panorama, ns,v3 (Oct. 1815), 66-70.
    Monthly Review, 78 (Dec. 1815), 434.

Moscow, a Poem. 1816. (P)
    Antijacobin Review, 51 (Dec. 1816), 375-77.
    Gentleman's Magazine, 86^2 (July 1816), 54.
    Lady's Monthly Museum, s3,v3 (Apr. 1816), 222.
    Literary Panorama, ns,v4 (May 1816), 244-45.
    Monthly Review, 79 (Apr. 1816), 433.
    New Monthly Magazine, 5 (Apr. 1816), 242.

The Home of Love, a Poem. 1817. (P)
    Antijacobin Review, 51 (Feb. 1817), 622-24.
    Critical Review, s5,v5 (Mar. 1817), 319-20.
    Literary Gazette, Mar. 1, 1817, p. 85.
    Literary Panorama, ns,v5 (Mar. 1817), 947-48.
    Monthly Review, 83 (May 1817), 96.
    New Monthly Magazine, 7 (Apr. 1817), 250-51.

Rondeau, James.
Leopold's Loss; or, England's Tears O'er the Urn of Her
Beloved Princess. (P)
    Monthly Review, 85 (Jan. 1818), 103-04.

Humourous Recitations in Verse. 1820. (P)
    Literary Chronicle, 2 (Jan. 15, 1820), 37.
    Monthly Magazine, 49 (May 1820), 358.
    Monthly Review, 91 (Apr. 1820), 364-69.

Rosa Matilda.
    See Charlotte Dacre.

Roscoe, Jane Elizabeth.
  Poems. By One of the Authors of Poems for Youth, by a Family Circle. 1820. (P)
     British Critic, ns,v14 (Nov. 1820), 493-99.
     Kaleidoscope, ns,v1 (Sept. 19, 1820), 92.
     Monthly Magazine, 50 (Oct. 1820), 267.
     Monthly Repository, 15 (Aug. 1820), 477-79.
     New Monthly Magazine, 14 (Dec. 1820), 687.

Roscoe, Robert.
  Chevy Chase, a Poem, Founded on the Ancient Ballad; with
  Other Poems. (Anon.) 1813. (P)
     Critical Review, s4,v5 (Mar. 1814), 241-47.
     Monthly Magazine, 49 (May 1820), 357.
     Monthly Review, 92 (July 1820), 327-30.
     New Monthly Magazine, 13 (June 1820), 734.

Roscoe, Thomas.
  Gonzalo, the Traitor; a Tragedy. 1820. (D)
     Monthly Magazine, 49 (July 1820), 555.
     Monthly Review, ns,v92 (July 1820), 330-31.
     Theatrical Inquisitor, 16 (May 1820), 290-97.

Roscoe, William.
  The Butterfly's Ball, and the Grasshopper's Feast. 1807.
  (P)
     British Critic, 30 (Nov. 1807), 554-55.
     Monthly Review, 54 (Dec. 1807), 446-47.

Roscoe, William, and Other Members of His Family.
  Poems for Youth. By a Family Circle. 1820. (P)
     Literary Gazette, Sept. 16, 1820, pp. 596-97.
     Monthly Magazine, 49 (Apr. 1820), 259.
     Monthly Repository, 15 (July 1820), 425.

Rose, Edward.
  The Sea-Devil; or, the Son of a Bellows-Mender. A Tragi-
  Comic Romance. 1811. (F)
     British Critic, 39 (Feb. 1812), 197-98.
     Monthly Review, ns,v67 (Mar. 1812), 320.

Rose, William Stewart.
  The Crusade of St. Lewis and King Edward the Martyr.
  1811. (P)
     British Critic, 38 (Oct. 1811), 406.
     Critical Review, s3,v22 (Apr. 1811), 376-79.
     Poetical Register, 8 (1810), 578.

Ross, Mrs. _____.
  The Marchioness!! or, "The Matured Enchantress." By Lady
  _____. 1813. (F)
     New Review, 2 (Oct. 1813), 337-41.

The Strangers of Lindenfeldt; or, Who Is My Father? (F)
New Review, 3 (Mar. 1814), 263-64.

Paired--Not Matched; or, Matrimony of the Nineteenth Century. 1815. (F)
Critical Review, s5,v2 (Aug. 1815), 216-17.

Rough, William.
Lorenzino di Medici, and Other Poems. (Anon.) 1797. (P)
Critical Review, s2,v23 (Aug. 1798), 466-67.

The Conspiracy of Gowrie, a Tragedy. (Anon.) 1800. (D)
British Critic, 17 (June 1801), 614-17.
Monthly Mirror, 13 (Mar. 1802), 201-02 [191-92].
Monthly Review, 35 (July 1801), 321-22.

Lines on the Death of the Late Sir Ralph Abercromby. By
the Author of The Conspiracy of Gowrie. 1801. (P)
British Critic, 18 (Sept. 1801), 307-08.
Critical Review, s2,v34 (Mar. 1802), 352-53.
Monthly Mirror, 12 (Aug. 1801), 100.
Monthly Review, 36 (Oct. 1801), 215-16.
Poetical Register, 1 (1801), 442.

Rouviere, Henrietta.
Lushington Abbey. (F)
Literary Journal, a Review..., 4 (Aug. 1804), 207.

The Heirs of Villeroy; a Romance. (F)
Literary Journal, 5 (Nov. 1805), 1222.

Rover, Sir George.
Caelebs Suited, or the Opinion and Part of the Life of
Caleb Caelebs, Esq. 1809. (F)
British Critic, 37 (Feb. 1811), 191-92.

Rowden, Frances Arabella.
A Poetical Introduction to the Study of Botany. 1801.
2nd ed., 1812. (P)
Antijacobin Review, 10 (Dec. 1801), 356-67.
Augustan Review, 2 (Jan. 1816), 23-28.
British Critic, 19 (Mar. 1802), 303-04.
Critical Review, s4,v1 (May 1812), 559.
Eclectic Review, 8 (Aug. 1812), 854.
European Magazine, 61 (May 1812), 359-60.
Flowers of Literature, 1 (1801-02), 455.
Literary Panorama, 11 (May 1812), 831-33.
Monthly Magazine, 13 (July 20, 1802), 658.
Monthly Review, 40 (Jan. 1803), 30-32.
Monthly Review, 70 (Jan. 1813), 98-99.
New Review, 1 (Jan. 1813), 103-06.
Poetical Register, 1 (1801), 435-36.

The Pleasures of Friendship, a Poem. 1810. 2nd ed. 1812.
(P)
    Augustan Review, 2 (Jan. 1816), 23-28.
    British Critic, 36 (July 1810), 69-70.
    Eclectic Review, 6 (July 1810), 659-60.
    European Magazine, 61 (Apr. 1812), 287.
    Monthly Review, 67 (Apr. 1812), 434.
    New Review, 1 (Jan. 1813), 60-63.
    Poetical Register, 8 (1810), 561.

Rowe, Rev. Henry.
  Fables in Verse. 1810. (P)
    Antijacobin Review, 37 (Sept. 1810), 87.
    British Critic, 36 (Nov. 1810), 522.
    Eclectic Review, 6 (Dec. 1810), 1139.
    Poetical Register, 8 (1810), 556-57.
    Satirist, 10 (Mar. 1812), 234. (Excerpts from other re-
      views.)

Rowlandson, T.
  Petticoat Loose: A Fragmentary "Tale of the Castle." 1812.
  (P)
    British Critic, 40 (Aug. 1812), 184-85.
    Literary Panorama, 11 (Apr. 1812), 645-51.

Rowse, Elizabeth.
  Outlines of English History, in Verse. 1808. (P)
    British Critic, 31 (Jan. 1808), 81.
    Eclectic Review, 4 (Jan. 1808), 84-85.
    Literary Annual Register, 2 (Apr. 1808), 158.
    Monthly Magazine, Suppl. v25 (July 30, 1808), 596.
    Monthly Review, 56 (June 1808), 209-10.

Rowson, Susanna.
  Reuben and Rachel; or, Tales of Old Times. 1799. (F)
    Critical Review, ns,v28 (Jan. 1800), 116-17.
    New London Review, 1 (May 1799), 508.

Rushton, Edward.
  Poems. 1806. (P)
    Annual Review, 5 (1806), 523-25.
    Antijacobin Review, 23 (Mar. 1806), 336.
    British Critic, 28 (Nov. 1806), 561-62.
    Critical Review, s3,v7 (Apr. 1806), 439-41.
    Literary Journal, a Review..., ns,v1 (May 1806), 558-59.
    Monthly Magazine, Suppl. v21 (July 25, 1806), 608.
    Monthly Review, 50 (May 1806), 95-96.
    New Annual Register, 27 (1806), [370].
    Poetical Register, 6 (1806), 505.

Russell, George.
  Letters, Essays, and Poems, on Religious Subjects. 1810.
  (P)

Baptist Magazine, 4 (Feb. 1812), 72-75.
Monthly Review, 63 (Dec. 1810), 440.

Russell, Joshua (Joseph?).
  Poems. 1819. (P)
    Evangelical Magazine, 28 (Oct. 1820), 422.
    Monthly Review, 92 (June 1820), 210.

Ryley, Samuel William.
  The Itinerant; or Memoirs of an Actor. 1808. (F)
    Annual Review, 7 (1808), 621-23.
    British Critic, 34 (Oct. 1809), 410-11.

Rymer, M.
  The Spaniard; or the Pride of Birth. A Tale. (F)
    Monthly Literary Recreations, 1 (Nov. 1806), 406.
    Monthly Review, ns,v57 (Sept. 1808), 100-01.

Ryves, Mrs. _____.
  Cambrian Legends; or, Tales of Other Times. (P)
    European Magazine, 66 (Oct. 1814), 331.
    Monthly Review, 76 (Feb. 1815), 211.

S_____, Mrs.
  Gotha; or, Memoirs of the Wurtzburg Family. 1811. (F)
    Antijacobin Review, 42 (Aug. 1812), 430.
    Monthly Review, ns,v66 (Oct. 1811), 208.

S., I. T.
  See John Talwyn Shewell.

S., J. J.
  See John Anstey.

S., R., Esq.
  The New Monk. A Romance. 1798. (F)
    Critical Review, ns,v24 (Nov. 1798), 356-57.
    Monthly Mirror, 6 (Dec. 1798), 345.

S., R., a Passenger in the Hector.
  The Life and Adventures of Peter Wilkins, a Cornish-Man.
  1816. (F)
    Monthly Review, ns,v81 (Nov. 1816), 331.

St. Ann.
  The Castles of Wolfnorth and Monteagle. 1812. (F)
    Antijacobin Review, 44 (Jan. 1813), 49-53.
    British Critic, 42 (Aug. 1813), 195.
    Critical Review, s4,v2 (Oct. 1812), 444-45.
    Monthly Review, ns,v69 (Nov. 1812), 332.

St. George Catherine.
  Maria, a Domestic Tale. 1817. (F)

Antijacobin Review, 52 (Aug. 1817), 566.
Gentleman's Magazine, 88² (Aug. 1818), 146.

St. John, A.
  Tales of Former Times. (F)
    Annual Review, 7 (1808), 607-08.

St. Leon, Count Reginald de.
  See Edward Du Bois.

St. Raphael, Felix.
  Fatal Love; or, Letters from a Village. 1812. (F)
    Antijacobin Review, 42 (July 1812), 297-99.

Sanders, Charlotte.
  The Little Family, Written for the Amusement and Instruc-
    tion of Young Persons. 1797. (F)
    British Critic, 11 (Jan. 1798), 77.
    Monthly Visitor, 4 (June 1798), 216.
    New London Review, 3 (Apr. 1800), 374.

Sanderson, Thomas. (See also Josiah Relph's Poems.)
  Original Poems. 1800. (P)
    Antijacobin Review, 10 (Sept. 1810), 81-83.
    British Critic, 17 (Jan. 1801), 78-79.
    Critical Review, s2,v32 (June 1801), 228-30.
    Monthly Review, 35 (July 1801), 318-20.

Sandham, Mrs. Elizabeth.
  The Twin Sisters; or, the Advantages of Religion. 1st ed.,
    1788. 2nd ed., 1805?. (F)
    Antijacobin Review, 28 (Dec. 1807), 422-23.
    British Critic, 32 (Oct. 1808), 413.
    Critical Review, s3,v12 (Dec. 1807), 446.
    Guardian of Education, 4 (Dec. 1805), 70-79.
    Monthly Review, ns,v59 (July 1809), 321.
    Satirist, 4 (July 1809), 97.

  The Adventures of a Bullfinch. 1809. (F)
    Gentleman's Magazine, 80¹ (Jan. 1810), 52.

  The Adventures of Poor Puss. 1809. (F)
    Gentleman's Magazine, 80¹ (Jan. 1810), 52.

  The History of William Selwyn. 1815. (F)
    Gentleman's Magazine, 86¹ (Mar. 1816), 250.

  The School-fellows. A Moral Tale. 1818. (F)
    Antijacobin Review, 55 (Dec. 1818), 346-53.
    Fireside Magazine (quoting Antijacobin Review and Monthly
      Review), 1 (Feb., Sept. 1819), 78, 346.

  Lucilla; or the Reconciliation. 1819. (F)

Gentleman's Magazine, 90[1] (Jan. 1820), 54.

Friendship, a Tale. 1820. (F)
  Literary Gazette, July 29, 1820, p. 488.

Sanon, George.
  The Causes of the French Revolution; and the Science of
  Governing an Empire. 1806. (P)
    British Critic, 28 (Oct. 1806), 443-44.
    Critical Review, s3,v10 (Apr. 1807), 370-75.
    Poetical Register, 6 (1806), 502-03.

Sansom, James.
  Greenwich, a Poem, Descriptive and Historical. 1808. (P)
    Le Beau Monde, 4 (Jan. 1809), 327-31.
    Monthly Review, 59 (May 1809), 102-03.

Sappho.
  Elephantasmagoria, or the Covent Garden Elephant's Entrance
  into Elysium; Being a Letter from the Shade of Garrick to
  J. P. Kemble. 1812. (P)
    Antijacobin Review, 41 (Mar. 1812), 262-64.
    British Critic, 40 (Aug. 1812), 187.
    Critical Review, s4,v1 (June 1812), 663.
    Monthly Review, 69 (Oct. 1812), 213-14.

Sargant, Jane Alice.
  Sonnets and Other Poems. (P)
    Gentleman's Magazine, 87[2] (Aug. 1817), 151-53.

Sargent, Winthrop.
  Boston. (P)
    Monthly Magazine, 17 (1804), 134-35.

Savory, Martha.
  Inspiration. A Poetical Essay. 1805. (P)
    British Critic, 27 (Jan. 1806), 78.
    Literary Journal, a Review..., 5 (May 1805), 547.
    Monthly Magazine, Suppl. v20 (Jan. 31, 1806), 615.

  Poetical Tales. 1808. (P)
    Annual Review, 7 (1808), 521-22.
    British Critic, 31 (May 1808), 546.
    Cabinet, 4 (Nov. 1808), 336.
    Monthly Review, 57 (Sept. 1808), 92-94.
    Poetical Register, 7 (1808), 567.

  Life's Vicissitudes, or Winter's Tears. 1811. (P)
    British Critic, 38 (Aug. 1811), 191.
    Poetical Register, 8 (1810), 564-65.

Sayers, Frank.
  Nugae Poeticae. 1803. (P)

Annual Review, 2 (1803), 561-62.
Critical Review, s2,v39 (Dec. 1803), 477-79.
Eclectic Review, 5 (Apr. 1809), 364-67.
Critical Review, s3,v2 (Aug. 1804), 468-71.
Monthly Magazine, Suppl. v16 (Jan. 25, 1804), 633.
Monthly Review, 44 (Aug. 1804), 429.
New Annual Register, 24 (1803), [327].
Poetical Register, 3 (1803), 444.

Sayers, James.
All the Talents Garland; or a Few Rockets Let Off at a
Celebrated Ministry. (Anon.) 1807. (P)
Antijacobin Review, 27 (June 1807), 186-93.
Antijacobin Review, 27 (Aug. 1807), 421-25.
British Critic, 32 (Aug. 1808), 106 07.
Monthly Mirror, ns,v2 (Nov. 1807), 327-28.
Monthly Review, 53 (July 1807), 326-27.
Poetical Register, 6 (1807), 556.

Elijah's Mantle: A Poem. (Anon.) 1807. (P)
Le Beau Monde, 1 (May 1807), 382.
British Critic, 29 (May 1807), 557-58.
Flower's Political Review, 1 (June 1807), 464.
Monthly Mirror, ns,v2 (Aug. 1807), 109.
Monthly Review, 52 (Apr. 1807), 439.

Uti Possidetis, and Status Quo: a Political Satire. (Anon.)
1807. (P)
British Critic, 31 (Jan. 1808), 80-81.
Literary Annual Register, 2 (Mar. 1808), 119.
Monthly Mirror, ns,v2 (Sept. 1807), 184.
Monthly Review, 52 (Apr. 1807), 439.

Hints to J. Nollekens, Esq. R. A., on His Modelling a Bust
of Lord G******le. (Anon.) 1808. (P)
Antijacobin Review, 30 (Aug. 1808), 410-12.
Literary Annual Register, 2 (Sept. 1808), 407.

Scafe, John.
King Coal's Levee, or Geological Etiquette; and the Council
of the Metals. (Anon.) 1819. (P)
Literary Gazette, Nov. 13, 1819, pp. 723-25.
Monthly Magazine, 49 (Apr. 1820), 259-60.

Court News; or the Peers of King Coal and the Errants; or
a Survey of British Strata. (Anon.) (P)
Gentleman's Magazine, 90^2 (July-Dec. 1820), 613.

A Geological Primer in Verse, with a Poetical Geognosy and
Sundry Right Pleasant Poems. (Anon.) (P)
European Magazine, 78 (Oct. 1820), 334-37.
Literary Gazette, Mar. 18, 1820, pp. 186-87.
Monthly Magazine, 49 (May 1820), 358-59.

Schlegel, Augustus William.
  A Course of Lectures on Dramatic Art and Literature. Translated from the Original German, by John Black. 1815. (Pr)
     Augustan Review, 2 (Mar. 1816), 297-308.
     Champion, Jan. 21, 1816, pp. 22-23.
     Edinburgh Review, 26 (Feb. 1816), 67-107.
     Liverpool Magazine, 1 (Feb. 1816), 68-72.

Scot, Elizabeth.
  Alonzo and Cora, with Other Original Poems, Principally
  Elegiac. 1801. (P)
     Antijacobin Review, 10 (Sept. 1801), 77-79.
     British Critic, 18 (Dec. 1801), 663.
     Critical Review, s2,v34 (Feb. 1802), 229-30.
     Monthly Magazine, Suppl. v13 (July 20, 1802), 658.
     Monthly Review, 38 (Aug. 1802), 436-37.
     Poetical Register, 1 (1801), 434.

Scott, Honoria.
  A Winter in Edinburgh; or, the Russian Brothers. 1810. (F)
     Satirist, 6 (Feb. 1810), 193-97.

Scott, John.
  The House of Mourning, a Poem; with Some Smaller Pieces.
  1817. (P)
     British Critic, ns,v7 (Apr. 1817), 426-27.
     British Lady's Magazine, 5 (May 1817), 300-01.
     Critical Review, s5,v5 (Apr. 1817), 349-55.
     Eclectic Review, s2,v7 (June 1817), 609-15.
     European Magazine, 75 (Apr. 1819), 347-48.
     Gentleman's Magazine, 87[1] (Apr. 1817), 339-40.
     Literary Gazette, Apr. 5, 1817, p. 163.
     Monthly Magazine, 43 (May 1817), 355.
     Monthly Review, 83 (Aug. 1817), 432.
     Thanet Magazine, 1 (Aug. 1817), 108-10.

Scott, Richard.
  The Battle of Maida, an Epic Poem. 1808. (P)
     Antijacobin Review, 33 (Aug. 1809), 396-99.
     British Critic, 32 (Nov. 1808), 519.
     Critical Review, s3,v15 (Dec. 1808), 439-40.
     Literary Panorama, 5 (Jan. 1809), 697-701.
     Monthly Review, 59 (June 1809), 216.
     Universal Magazine, ns,v10 (Dec. 1808), 518-20.

Scott, Sir Walter.
  Minstrelsy of the Scottish Border: Consisting of Historical
  and Romantic Ballads.... 1802-03. (P)
     Annual Review, 1 (1802), 635-43.
     Annual Review, 2 (1803), 533-38.
     British Critic, 19 (June 1802), 570-76.
     British Critic, 23 (Jan. 1804), 36-43.
     Critical Review, s2,v39 (Nov. 1803), 250-59.

Scott, Sir Walter (continued).
  Edinburgh Review, 1 (Jan. 1803), 395-406.
  Literary Journal, a Review..., 2 (Aug. 16, 1803), 144-47.
  Monthly Magazine, Suppl. v14 (Jan. 25, 1803), 598.
  Monthly Magazine, Suppl. v17 (July 28, 1804), 666.
  Monthly Mirror, 13 (Mar. 1802), 168-69.
  Monthly Register, 3 (Aug. 1803), 133-34.
  Monthly Review, 42 (Sept. 1803), 21-33.
  Monthly Review, 45 (Oct. 1804), 126-34.
  Poetical Register, 2 (1802), 447.
  Poetical Register, 3 (1803), 462.
  Scots Magazine, 64 (Jan. 1802), 68-71.

  Sir Tristrem; a Metrical Romance of the Thirteenth Century.
  1804. (P)
    Annual Review, 3 (1804), 555-63.
    British Critic, 25 (Apr. 1805), 361-68.
    Critical Review, s3,v3 (Sept. 1804), 45-52.
    Edinburgh Review, 4 (July 1804), 427-44.
    Monthly Magazine, Suppl. v18 (Jan. 28, 1805), 593.
    Monthly Review, 48 (Oct. 1805), 196-203.
    Poetical Register, 6 (1806-07), 557-58.

  The Lay of the Last Minstrel, a Poem. 1805. (P)
    Annual Review, 3 (1804), 600-04.
    British Critic, 26 (Aug. 1805), 154-60.
    Critical Review, s3,v5 (July 1805), 225-42.
    Eclectic Review, 2 (Mar. 1806), 193-200.
    Edinburgh Review, 6 (Apr. 1805), 1-20.
    Imperial Review, 4 (Feb. 1805), 90-104.
    Lady's Monthly Museum, 15 (Oct. 1805), 270-71.
    Lady's Monthly Museum, 16 (June 1806), 412-13.
    Literary Journal, a Review..., 5 (Mar. 1805), 271-80.
    Monthly Magazine, Suppl. v19 (July 28, 1805), 658.
    Monthly Mirror, 22 (Dec. 1806), 385-95.
    Monthly Review, 49 (Mar. 1806), 295-303.
    New Annual Register, 25 (1804), [351].
    Poetical Register, 5 (1805), 484.
    Scots Magazine, 67 (Jan. 1805), 37-45.

  Ballads and Lyrical Pieces. 1806. (P)
    Annual Review, 5 (1806), 494-97.
    Le Beau Monde, 1 (Feb. 1807), 206-12.
    La Belle Assemblée, Suppl. v2 (1807), 33-34.
    British Critic, 32 (July 1808), 72.
    Critical Review, s3,v9 (Dec. 1806), 342-48.
    Eclectic Review, 3 (May 1807), 374-80.
    Flowers of Literature, 5 (1806), 498.
    Literary Annual Register, 1 (July 1807), 320-21.
    Monthly Magazine, Suppl. v22 (Jan. 25, 1807), 641-42.
    Monthly Mirror, 22 (Dec. 1806), 401-04.
    Monthly Review, 53 (June 1807), 183-91.
    Oxford Review, 1 (Jan. 1807), 74-83.

Scott, Sir Walter (continued).
   Poetical Register, 6 (1806), 499-500.
   Scots Magazine, 68 (Oct. 1806), 767-68.

   Marmion, a Tale of Flodden Field. 1808. (P)
   Annual Review, 7 (1808), 462-73.
   Antijacobin Review, 38 (Mar. 1811), 225-48.
   Le Beau Monde, 3 (May, June 1808), 263-70, 315-21.
   Belfast Monthly Magazine, 1 (Sept. 1808), 57-60.
   La Belle Assemblée, 4 (Apr. 1808), 177-83.
   British Critic, 31 (June 1808), 640-48.
   British Critic, 36 (Oct. 1810), 375.
   Cabinet, 3 (May 1808), 321-32; 4 (July 1808), 333-36.
   Cabinet, ns,v2 (Aug. 1809), 115-23.
   Critical Review, s3,v13 (Apr. 1808), 387-401.
   Cyclopaedian Magazine, 2 (Aug. 1808), 449-52.
   Eclectic Review, 4 (May 1808), 407-22.
   Edinburgh Review, 12 (Aug. 1808), 1-35.
   English Censor, 1 (Feb. 1809), 144-50.
   Literary Panorama, 4 (Apr. 1808), 53-63.
   London Review, 1 (Feb. 1809), 82-121.
   Monthly Magazine, Suppl. v25 (July 30, 1808), 594-95.
   Monthly Mirror, ns,v4 (Aug. 1808), 85-92.
   Monthly Review, 56 (May 1808), 1-19.
   New Annual Register, 29 (1808), [405].
   Poetical Register, 7 (1808), 547.
   Satirist, 2 (Apr. 1808), 186-93.
   Satirist, 4 (Apr. 1809), 410-16. (Excerpts from other
      reviews.)
   Scots Magazine, 70 (Mar. 1808), 195-202.
   Universal Magazine, ns,v9 (May 1808), 410-20.

   The Works of John Dryden. 1808. (Pr)
   Annual Review, 7 (1809), 765-75.
   British Critic, 35 (Feb.-Mar., May-June 1810), 97-109,
      272-88, 465-74, 574-84.
   Edinburgh Review, 13 (Oct. 1808), 116-35.
   London Review, 1 (Feb. 1809), 42-65.
   Monthly Magazine, 26 (Jan. 30, 1809), 636-37.
   Monthly Review, 58 (Feb. 1809), 137-60.
   Satirist, 2 (July 1808), 518-26; 3 (Aug. 1808), 66-71.
   Scots Magazine, 70 (May 1808), 355-59.

   The Lady of the Lake, a Poem. 1810. (P)
   Antijacobin Review, 38 (Mar. 1811), 225-48.
   La Belle Assemblée, s2,v1 (May 1810), 245-52.
   La Belle Assemblée, Suppl. s2,v2 (1811), 351-52.
   British Critic, 36 (Aug. 1810), 119-24.
   Christian Observer, 9 (June 1810), 366-89.
   Critical Review, s3,v20 (Aug. 1810), 337-57.
   Eclectic Review, 6 (July 1810), 577-602.
   Edinburgh Review, 16 (Aug. 1810), 263-93.
   European Magazine, 58 (Nov.-Dec. 1810), 363-69, 443-48.

Scott, Sir Walter (continued).
  Hibernia Magazine, 2 (July 1810), 59.
  Literary Panorama, 8 (Nov. 1810), 1231-43.
  Monthly Magazine, Suppl. v29 (July 31, 1810), 631-32.
  Monthly Mirror, ns,v8 (July 1810), 36-51.
  Monthly Review, 62 (June 1810), 178-94.
  Poetical Register, 8 (1810), 548.
  Quarterly Review, 3 (May 1810), 492-517.
  Satirist, 10 (Apr. 1812), 313-14.
  Scots Magazine, 72 (May 1810), 359-64.
  Universal Magazine, ns,v15 (May 1811), 393-97.
  Walker's Hibernian Magazine, 26 (Jan.-Feb. 1811), 6-16,
    67-68.
  Weekly Register, 2 (June 30, 1810), 1451-52.

The Poetical Works of Anna Seward.
  See Anna Seward, below.

The Vision of Don Roderick, a Poem. 1811. (P)
  British Critic, 38 (Sept. 1811), 280-84.
  Christian Observer, 11 (Jan. 1812), 29-33.
  Critical Review, s3,v23 (Aug. 1811), 337-49.
  Eclectic Review, 7 (Aug. 1811), 672-88.
  Edinburgh Monthly Magazine and Review, 1 (Sept. 1811),
    411-27.
  Edinburgh Review, 18 (Aug. 1811), 379-92.
  General Chronicle, Suppl. v2 (1811), 503-18.
  Glasgow Magazine, 2 (July 1811), 205-10.
  Military Panorama, 1 (Jan.-Mar. 1813), 329-32, 456-59,
    537-46.
  Monthly Review, 65 (July 1811), 293-307.
  New Annual Register, 32 (1811), [363].
  Poetical Register, 8 (1811), 603-04.
  Quarterly Review, 6 (Oct. 1811), 221-35.
  Scourge, 2 (Sept. 1811), 224-35.
  Universal Magazine, ns,v16 (Aug. 1811), 126-34.

The Border Antiquities of England and Scotland. 1812-17.
  Antijacobin Review, 42 (Aug. 1812), 337-43.
  Eclectic Review, s2,v10 (Oct. 1818), 305-22.
  Edinburgh Magazine, s2,v1 (Dec. 1817), 450-55.

Rokeby, a Poem. 1813. (P)
  Antijacobin Review, 44 (Apr. 1813), 377-90.
  La Belle Assemblée, ns,v7 (Mar. 1813), 126-33.
  British Critic, 42 (Aug. 1813), 110-23.
  British Review, 4 (May 1813), 270-82.
  Country Magazine, 1 (Apr., July 1813), 203-07, 319-23.
  Critical Review, s4,v3 (Mar. 1813), 240-58.
  Drakard's Paper, Jan. 31, 1813, pp. 31-32.
  Dublin Magazine, 1 (Apr.-May 1813), 329-40, 393-94.
  Eclectic Review, 9 (June 1813), 587-605.
  European Magazine, 63 (Mar. 1813), 223-26.

Scott, Sir Walter (continued).
 Literary Panorama, 13 (June 1813), 737-53.
 Monthly Review, 70 (Feb.-Mar. 1813), 113-32, 225-40.
 New Annual Register, 34 (1813), [408].
 New Review, 2 (Sept. 1813), 228-30.
 Quarterly Review, 8 (Dec. 1812), 485-507.
 Satirist, ns,v2 (May 1813), 464-73.
 Scots Magazine, 75 (Jan. 1813), 46-51.
 Scourge, 5 (Feb. 1813), 154-62.
 Theatrical Inquisitor, 2 (Feb. 1813), 41-51.

 The Bridal of Triermain; or, the Vale of St. John. 1813.
 (P)
 Critical Review, s4,v3 (May 1813), 473-82.
 Drakard's Paper, Dec. 18, 1813, pp. 398-99.
 Eclectic Review, 10 (Oct. 1813), 368-78.
 Lady's Monthly Museum, s2,v17 (Dec. 1814), 340-43.
 Monthly Magazine, 48 (Oct. 1819), 255-56.
 Monthly Review, 73 (Mar. 1814), 237-44.
 Quarterly Review, 9 (July 1813), 480-97.
 Scots Magazine, 75 (Apr. 1813), 282-86.
 Town Talk, 4 (July 1813), 437-39.

 Waverley; or 'Tis Sixty Years Since. (Anon.) 1814. (F)
 Antijacobin Review, 47 (Sept. 1814), 217-47.
 British Critic, ns,v2 (Aug. 1814), 189-211.
 Champion, July 24, 1814, pp. 238-39.
 Critical Review, s5,v1 (Mar. 1815), 288-83 [288-93].
 Edinburgh Review, 24 (Nov. 1814), 208-43.
 Edinburgh Review, 33 (Jan. 1820), 1-54.
 Monthly Museum, 2 (Sept. 1814), 225-30.
 Monthly Review, ns,v75 (Nov. 1814), 275-89.
 New Annual Register, 35 (1814), [365].
 New Monthly Magazine, 2 (Sept. 1814), 156.
 Quarterly Review, 11 (July 1814), 354-77.
 Scots Magazine, 76 (July 1814), 524-33.
 Scourge, 8 (Oct. 1814), 291-97.

 The Life and Works of Jonathan Swift. 1814. (Pr)
 Edinburgh Review, 27 (Sept. 1816), 1-58.
 Scots Magazine, 76 (Nov. 1814), 847-54.

 The Lord of the Isles, a Poem. 1815. (P)
 Antijacobin Review, 50 (Feb. 1816), 105-27.
 Augustan Review, 1 (May 1815), 1-11.
 La Belle Assemblée, ns,v11 (Mar. 1815), 125-28.
 British Critic, ns,v3 (Feb. 1815), 130-47.
 British Lady's Magazine, 1 (Feb. 1815), 118-23.
 British Review, 6 (Aug. 1815), 87-107.
 Champion, Jan. 15, 1815, p. 21.
 Critical Review, s5,v2 (July 1815), 58-77.
 Eclectic Review, s2,v3 (May 1815), 469-80.
 Edinburgh Review, 24 (Feb. 1815), 273-94.

Scott, Sir Walter (continued).
   European Magazine, 67 (Jan. 1815), 48-50.
   Gentleman's Magazine, 85[1] (Feb. 1815), 148-50.
   Literary Panorama, ns,v2 (Apr. 1815), 12-26.
   Mentor, 1 (Oct. 11, 25, Nov. 1, 1817), 245-52, 269-72,
     281-86.
   Monthly Magazine, Suppl. v38 (Jan. 30, 1815), 649-58.
   Monthly Review, 76 (Mar. 1815), 262-81.
   New Monthly Magazine, 3 (Feb. 1815), 54.
   Quarterly Review, 13 (July 1815), 287-309.
   Scots Magazine, 77 (Jan. 1815), 42-49.
   Theatrical Inquisitor, 6 (Jan. 1815), 55-67.
   Tradesman, ns,v15 (Apr. 1815), 313-17.

Guy Mannering; or the Astrologer. By the Author of Waver-
ley. 1815. (F)
   Antijacobin Review, 48 (June 1815), 544-50.
   Augustan Review, 1 (July 1815), 228-33.
   British Critic, ns,v3 (Apr. 1815), 399-409.
   British Lady's Magazine, 1 (May 1815), 355-58.
   Champion, Apr. 9, 1815, p. 118.
   Critical Review, s5,v1 (June 1815), 600-03.
   Edinburgh Review, 33 (Jan. 1820), 1-54.
   Monthly Review, ns,v77 (May 1815), 85-94.
   New Annual Register, 36 (1815), [432].
   New Monthly Magazine, 3 (Apr. 1815), 256.
   Quarterly Review, 12 (Jan. 1815), 501-09.
   Scots Magazine, 77 (Aug. 1815), 608-14.

The Field of Waterloo; a Poem. 1815.
   Antijacobin Review, 49 (Nov.-Dec., 1815), 471-79, 521-37.
   Augustan Review, 1 (Nov. 1815), 785-94.
   La Belle Assemblée, Suppl. ns,v12 (1815), 340-42.
   British Critic, ns,v4 (Nov. 1815), 528-32.
   British Lady's Magazine, 2 (Dec. 1815), 393-94.
   Champion, Nov. 5, 1815, p. 358.
   Christian Observer, 14 (Nov. 1815), 750-60.
   Critical Review, s5,v2 (Nov. 1815), 457-63.
   Eclectic Review, s2,v4 (Dec. 1815), 570-78.
   European Magazine, 69 (Feb. 1816), 141-42.
   Lady's Monthly Museum, s2,v3 (Dec. 1815), 329-31.
   Literary Panorama, ns,v3 (Dec. 1815), 392-98.
   Liverpool Magazine, 1 (Jan. 1816), 24-28.
   Monthly Review, 78 (Nov. 1815), 251-60.
   Scourge, 10 (Dec. 1815), 437-51.
   Theatrical Inquisitor, 7 (Dec. 1815), 452-59.

The Antiquary. By the Author of Waverley and Guy Manner-
ing. 1816. (F)
   Antijacobin Review, 50 (July 1816), 625-32.
   Augustan Review, 3 (Aug. 1816), 155-77.
   British Critic, ns,v5 (June 1816), 633-57.
   British Lady's Magazine, 4 (Aug. 1816), 103-05.

Scott, Sir Walter (continued).
  Critical Review, s5,v3 (May 1816), 485-500.
  Dublin Examiner, 1 (June 1816), 81-92.
  Edinburgh Review, 33 (Jan. 1820), 1-54.
  European Magazine, 70 (Sept. 1816), 248-50.
  Gentleman's Magazine, 86[1] (June 1816), 521-23.
  Monthly Review, ns,v82 (Jan. 1817), 38-52.
  New Monthly Magazine, 5 (June 1816), 444.
  Quarterly Review, 15 (Apr. 1816), 125-39.
  Scots Magazine, 78 (May 1816), 365-73.

Paul's Letters to His Kinsfolk. (Anon.) 1816.
  Antijacobin Review, 50 (July 1816), 661-79.
  Augustan Review, 2 (Apr. 1816), 360-75.
  British Critic, ns,v5 (Apr. 1816), 421-30.
  British Lady's Magazine, 3 (Mar. 1, 1816), 169-78.
  Eclectic Review, ns,v5 (Apr. 1816), 346-57.
  Gentleman's Magazine, 86[1] (Mar. 1816), 247-48.
  Monthly Review, ns,v80 (Aug. 1816), 337-55.
  Monthly Review, ns,v81 (Sept. 1816), 30-52.
  Scots Magazine, 78 (Feb. 1816), 125-34.
  Theatrical Inquisitor, 8 (Feb. 1816), 139-49.

Tales of My Landlord. Collected and Arranged by Jedediah
Cleishbotham. 1816. (F)
  British Critic, ns,v7 (Jan. 1817), 73-97.
  British Lady's Magazine, 5 (Feb. 1817), 94-101.
  British Review, 9 (Feb. 1817), 184-204.
  Critical Review, s5,v4 (Dec. 1816), 614-25.
  Eclectic Review, ns,v7 (Apr. 1817), 309-36.
  Edinburgh Christian Instructor, 14 (Jan.-Mar. 1817), 41-
    73, 100-40, 170-201.
  Edinburgh Review, 28 (Mar. 1817), 193-259.
  Edinburgh Review, 33 (Jan. 1820), 1-54.
  Independent, no3 (1816), 318-34.
  Monthly Magazine, 42 (Jan. 1817), 546.
  Monthly Review, ns,v82 (Apr. 1817), 383-91.
  New Monthly Magazine, 6 (Jan. 1817), 533-34.
  Portfolio, Political and Literary, Dec. 14, 21, 1816,
    pp. 145-52, 173-79.
  Quarterly Review, 16 (Jan. 1817), 430-80.
  Scots Magazine, 78 (Dec. 1816), 928-34.

Harold the Dauntless, a Poem. By the Author of The Bridal
of Triermain. 1817. (P)
  Blackwood's Edinburgh Magazine, 1 (Apr. 1817), 76-78.
  Critical Review, s5,v5 (Apr. 1817), 379-84.
  Dublin Examiner, 2 (Jan. 1817), 218-26.
  Eclectic Review, s2,v7 (May 1817), 457-63.
  Literary Gazette, Mar. 15, 1817, pp. 117-18.
  Monthly Magazine, 48 (Oct. 1819), 255-56.
  Monthly Review, 84 (Sept. 1817), 10-18.
  New Monthly Magazine, 7 (Apr. 1817), 251.

Scott, Sir Walter (continued)
  Scots Magazine, 79 (Feb. 1817), 131-34.

  Rob Roy; a Novel. By the Author of Waverley, Guy Mannering,
  and The Antiquary. 1818. (F)
    Antijacobin Review, 53 (Jan. 1818), 417-31.
    Anti-Unionist, 1 (Jan. 31-Feb. 7, 1818), 7-10, 24-28.
    British Critic, ns,v9 (May 1818), 528-40.
    British Lady's Magazine, ns,v2 (Mar., June 1818), 119-23,
      264-68.
    British Review, 11 (Feb. 1818), 192-225.
    Edinburgh Magazine and Literary Miscellany (Scots Maga-
      zine), ns,v2 (Jan.-Feb. 1818), 41-50, 148-53.
    Edinburgh Observer, 1 (Mar. 7, 1818), 269.
    Edinburgh Review, 29 (Feb. 1818), 403-32.
    Edinburgh Review, 33 (Jan. 1820), 1-54.
    European Magazine, 73 (Feb. 1818), 137-39.
    Gentleman's Magazine, 88^1 (Mar. 1818), 243.
    Literary and Political Examiner, 1 (Feb. 1818), 14-28.
    Literary and Statistical Magazine, 2 (Feb. 1818), 45-60.
    Literary Gazette, Jan. 17, 1818, pp. 34-36.
    Monthly Magazine, 45 (Feb. 1818), 63.
    Monthly Review, ns,v85 (Mar. 1818), 261-75.
    Northern Star, 2 (Feb. 1818), 126-35.
    Quarterly Review, 26 (Oct. 1812), 109-28.
    Scotsman, Jan. 3, 1818, p. 7.
    Theatrical Inquisitor, 12 (Jan. 1818), 36-40.
    Visitor; or Literary Miscellany, 1 (1817), 177-83.

  Tales of My Landlord. Second Series. Collected and Arranged by Jedediah Cleishbotham. 1818. (F)
    Antijacobin Review, 55 (Nov. 1818), 212-18.
    Blackwood's Edinburgh Magazine, 3 (Aug. 1818), 567-74.
    British Critic, ns,v10 (Sept. 1818), 246-60.
    British Lady's Magazine, s3,v1 (Dec. 1818), 268-73.
    British Review, 12 (Nov. 1818), 396-406.
    Clydesdale Magazine, 1 (July-Sept. 1818), 125-27, 169-71,
      218-19.
    Eclectic Review, ns,v12 (Nov. 1819), 422-52.
    Edinburgh Advertiser, Aug. 14, 1818, p. 100. (Reprinted
      from New Times.)
    Edinburgh Magazine and Literary Miscellany (Scots Maga-
      zine), 3 (Aug. 1818), 107-17.
    Edinburgh Reflector, Aug. 5-19, 1818, pp. 42-47, 53-56,
      63.
    Edinburgh Review, 33 (Jan. 1820), 1-54.
    Fireside Magazine (quoting Antijacobin Review and Monthly
      Review), 1 (Jan.-Feb. 1819), 32, 69-70.
    Gentleman's Magazine, 88^2 (Nov. 1818), 426-29.
    Green Man, Dec. 12, 1818, pp. 68-69.
    Literary and Statistical Magazine, 2 (Aug. 1818), 314-22.
    Literary Gazette, Aug. 8, 1818, pp. 497-500.
    Literary Journal and General Miscellany, 1 (Aug. 8-15,

Scott, Sir Walter (continued)
1818), 304-06, 324-27.
Monthly Magazine, 46 (Sept. 1818), 158.
Monthly Review, ns,v87 (Dec. 1818), 356-70.
New Monthly Magazine, 10 (Oct. 1818), 250.
Quarterly Review, 26 (Oct. 1821), 109-48.
Scotsman, Aug. 1, 1818, p. 247.

Provincial Antiquities of Scotland. 1819-26. (Pr)
Literary Chronicle, Nov. 27, 1819, pp. 433-34.

Tales of My Landlord. Third Series. Collected and Arrang-
ed by Jedediah Cleishbotham. 1819. (F)
Antijacobin Review, 56 (Aug. 1819), 507-14.
Blackwood's Edinburgh Magazine, 5 (June 1819), 340-53.
British Lady's Magazine, s3,v3 (Aug.-Oct. 1819), 80-82,
127-33, 178-80.
British Review, 14 (Aug. 1819), 233-47.
Eclectic Review, s2,v12 (Nov. 1819), 422-52.
Edinburgh Magazine and Literary Miscellany (Scots Maga-
zine), ns,v5 (July 1819), 38-45.
Edinburgh Monthly Review, 2 (Aug. 1819), 160-84.
Edinburgh Review, 33 (Jan. 1820), 1-54.
Fireside Magazine, 1 (Sept. 1819), 342.
Fireside Magazine (quoting Monthly Review and New Monthly
Magazine), 1 (Sept. 1819), 351, 355-56.
Kaleidoscope, 1 (July 6, 1819), 198-99.
Literary Chronicle, 1 (June 26-July 3, 1819), 81-86, 101-
04.
Literary Chronicle, 1 (Nov. 13, 1819), 409.
Literary Chronicle, 1 (Dec. 18-25, 1819), 481-83, 499-502.
Literary Chronicle, 2 (Dec. 9, 1820), 785.
Literary Gazette, June 26, 1819, pp. 401-05.
Literary Gazette, July 3, 1819, pp. 419-23.
Literary Gazette, Dec. 18, 1819, pp. 802-06.
(Gold's) London Magazine, 1 (Jan. 1820), 55-57.
Man of Kent, 2 (July 10, 1819), 677-82.
Miniature Magazine, 3 (July 1819), 85-93.
Miniature Magazine, 3 (Sept. 1819), 184-93.
Monthly Magazine, 47 (July 1819), 539.
Monthly Magazine, 48 (Jan. 1820), 538-39.
Monthly Review, ns,v89 (Aug. 1819), 387-403.
New Monthly Magazine, 12 (Aug. 1819), 67-73.
Quarterly Review, 26 (Oct. 1821), 109-48.
Scotsman, June 26, 1819, p. 207.

Ivanhoe; a Romance. By the Author of Waverley. 1820. (F)
Blackwood's Edinburgh Magazine, 6 (Dec. 1819), 262-72.
British Review, 15 (June 1820), 393-454.
Champion, Jan. 9-15, 1820, pp. 27-28, 42-44.
Comet, 1 (1820), 101-11, 171-81, 235-47.
Dublin Magazine, 1 (Jan. 1820), 27-44.
Eclectic Review, ns,v13 (June 1820), 526-40.
Edinburgh Magazine and Literary Miscellany (Scots Maga-

Scott, Sir Walter (continued)
   zine), ns,v6 (Jan. 1820), 7-16.
   Edinburgh Monthly Review, 3 (Feb. 1820), 163-99.
   Edinburgh Review, 33 (Jan. 1820), 1-54.
   Lady's Monthly Museum, s3,v11 (Feb. 1820), 97-101.
   Literary Chronicle, 2 (Jan. 1-8, 1820), 1-4, 21-24.
   Literary Gazette, Dec. 25, 1819, pp. 817-23.
   (Baldwin's) London Magazine, 1 (Jan. 1820), 79-84.
   (Gold's) London Magazine, 1 (Jan.-Feb. 1820), 79-84, 154-
      71.
   Lonsdale Magazine, 1 (Feb. 1820), 78-85.
   Monthly Magazine, 49 (Feb. 1820), 71.
   Monthly Review, ns,v91 (Jan. 1820), 71-89.
   New Monthly Magazine, 13 (Jan. 1820), 73-82.
   Quarterly Review, 26 (Oct. 1821), 109-49.

The Monastery; a Romance. By the Author of Waverley. 1820.
   Antijacobin Review, 58 (Apr. 1820), 174-83.
   La Belle Assemblée, ns,v21 (Apr. 1820), 186-88.
   Blackwood's Edinburgh Magazine, 6 (Mar. 1820), 692-704.
   British Review, 15 (June 1820), 393-454.
   Dublin Magazine, 1 (Apr. 1820), 301-14.
   Eclectic Review, ns,v14 (Oct. 1820), 244-68.
   Edinburgh Magazine and Literary Miscellany (Scots Maga-
      zine), ns,v6 (Mar.-Apr. 1820), 254-56, 297-304.
   Edinburgh Monthly Review, 4 (Dec. 1820), 691-717.
   European Magazine, 77 (Apr. 1820), 344-47.
   Gentleman's Magazine, 90^1 (Apr. 1820), 334-36.
   Lady's Monthly Museum, s3,v11 (May 1820), 273-80.
   Literary Chronicle, 2 (Apr. 1, 1820), 209-14.
   Literary Gazette, Mar. 25, 1820, pp. 193-200.
   (Baldwin's) London Magazine, 1 (May 1820), 565-68.
   (Gold's) London Magazine, 1 (Apr.-May, 1820), 414-22,
      506-14.
   Lonsdale Magazine, 1 (May 1820), 218-27.
   Monthly Magazine, 49 (May 1820), 354-55.
   Monthly Review, ns,v91 (Apr. 1820), 404-26.
   New Monthly Magazine, 13 (Apr. 1820), 486-87.
   Quarterly Review, 26 (Oct. 1821), 109-48.
   Scotsman, Mar. 25, 1820, p. 101.

Trivial Poems and Triolets. By Patrick Carey. (Ed. by
Walter Scott.) 1820.
   Lady's Monthly Museum, s3,v12 (July 1820), 35.
   Literary Chronicle, 2 (June 3, 1820), 355-57.
   Literary Gazette, May 27, 1820, pp. 337-38.
   Monthly Review, 95 (June 1821), 212-15.

The Abbot. By the Author of Waverley. 1820. (F)
   Antijacobin Review, 59 (Sept. 1820), 49-66.
   La Belle Assemblée, ns,v22 (Sept. 1820), 138.
   Blackwood's Edinburgh Magazine, 7 (Sept. 1820), 663-67.
   Dublin Magazine, 2 (Sept. 1820), 195-207.

Scott, Sir Walter (concluded)
  Eclectic Review, ns,v14 (Oct. 1820), 254-68.
  Edinburgh Magazine and Literary Miscellany (Scots Maga-
    zine), ns,v7 (Sept. 1820), 248-56.
  Edinburgh Monthly Review, 4 (Dec. 1820), 691-717.
  European Magazine, 78 (Sept. 1820), 241-46.
  Gentleman's Magazine, 90² (Nov. 1820), 433-36.
  Glasgow Magazine, 1 (Oct. 1820), 26-38.
  Kaleidoscope, ns,v1 (Sept. 19, 1820), 92-93.
  Lady's Monthly Museum, s3,v12 (Oct. 1820), 213-15.
  Literary Chronicle, 2 (Sept. 9, 1820), 577-85.
  Literary Gazette, Sept. 2, 1820, pp. 561-69.
  (Baldwin's) London Magazine, 2 (Oct. 1820), 427-37.
  (Gold's) London Magazine, 2 (Oct.-Nov. 1820), 414-16,
    493-503.
  Lonsdale Magazine, 1 (Oct. 1820), 450-58.
  Monthly Magazine, 50 (Oct. 1820), 266-67.
  Monthly Review, ns,v93 (Sept. 1820), 67-83.
  New Monthly Magazine, 14 (Oct. 1820), 421-30.
  Newcastle Magazine, 1 (Nov. 1820), 178-94.
  Quarterly Review, 26 (Oct. 1821), 109-48.
  Scotsman, Sept. 9, 1820, p. 295.
  Scottish Episcopal Review (Literary and Statistical Mag-
    azine), 1 (Nov. 1820), 372-81.

Scott, William.
  Signs of the Times, a Poem; or the Downfall of the Pope
  and the Papal Hierarchy. 1800. (P)
    British Critic, 18 (July 1801), 83.
    Critical Review, s2,v32 (June 1801), 230.
    Monthly Review, 35 (June 1801), 212.

Scrutator.
  All the Talents in Ireland; a Satirical Poem. 1807. (P)
    Annual Review, 6 (1807), 585.
    Antijacobin Review, 28 (Sept. 1807), 26-39.
    Poetical Register, 6 (1807), 556.

Sculptor, Satiricus.
  See William Henry Ireland.

Sea Lark, A.
  See A. Clark.

Search, Sappho.
  See Rev. John Black.

Sebright, Paul.
  Coincidence; or, the Soothsayer. (F)
    Lady's Monthly Museum, s3,v11 (Mar. 1820), 156-58.

Secundus, Junius.
  See Charles Kelsall.

Sedley, Charles.
  The Infidel Mother; or Three Winters in London. (F)
    Monthly Magazine, Suppl. v23 (July 30, 1807), 645.
    Satirist, 1 (Nov. 1807), 181-85.

  The Barouche Driver and His Wife, a Tale for the Haut Ton,
  Containing a Curious Biography of Living Characters. (F)
    Le Beau Monde, 2 (Oct. 1807), 142-45.
    Satirist, 1 (Oct. 1807), 69-70.

  A Winter in Dublin, a Descriptive Tale. (F)
    Satirist, 1 (Dec. 1807), 291-97.

  Asmodeus; or, the Devil in London. (Anon.) (F)
    Lady's Monthly Museum, ns,v6 (May 1809), 269-70.

Seldon, Catharine.
  Villa Nova; or the Ruined Castle. A Romance. (F)
    Literary Journal, a Review..., 5 (Mar. 1805), 321.

Sellon, Martha Sellon.
  Individuality; or the Causes of Reciprocal Misapprehension.
  1814. (P)
    British Critic, ns,v2 (Nov. 1814), 545-47.
    Eclectic Review, s2,v2 (Nov. 1814), 513-14.
    Literary Panorama, 15 (July 1814), 905.
    Monthly Review, 77 (Aug. 1815), 350-56.

Semple, Robert.
  Charles Ellis; or, the Friends. Comprising the Incidents
  and Observations Occurring on a Voyage to the Brazils and
  West Indies. 1806. (F)
    Antijacobin Review, 25 (Nov. 1806), 260-67.
    British Critic, 29 (Feb. 1807), 202.
    Cabinet, 2 (Dec. 1807), 324.
    Critical Review, s3,v10 (Jan. 1807), 102.
    Flowers of Literature, 5 (1806), 499.
    Literary Journal, a Review..., ns,v2 (Nov. 1806), 523-27.
    Monthly Literary Recreations, 1 (Nov. 1806), 406.
    Monthly Mirror, ns,v1 (Mar. 1807), 192.
    Monthly Review, ns,v54 (Oct. 1807), 212.
    New Annual Register, 28 (1807), ⌊379⌋.

Senwod, Joseph.
  One Lay of a Night Harper to His Queen. 1820. (P)
    Monthly Review, 93 (Sept. 1820), 96-97.

Serle, Thomas James.
  Raffaelle Cimaro, a Tragedy. 1819. (D)
    British Stage and Literary Cabinet, 3 (June 1819), 167-
    69.

Serres, Mrs. John Thomas.

Flights of Fancy. Poems. 1805. (P)
    Antijacobin Review, 22 (Sept. 1805), 77-78.
    British Critic, 26 (Sept. 1805), 316-17.
    Critical Review, s3,v6 (Oct. 1805), 213.
    European Magazine, 50 (July 1806), 50.
    Flowers of Literature, 4 (1805), 423.
    Literary Journal, a Review..., 5 (Oct. 1805), 1104.
    Monthly Magazine, Suppl. v20 (Jan. 31, 1806), 615.
    Monthly Mirror, 20 (Nov. 1805), 328.
    Monthly Review, 50 (June 1806), 206-08.

St. Julian. In a Series of Letters. 1805. (F)
    Antijacobin Review, 22 (Sept. 1805), 72.
    British Critic, 26 (Sept. 1805), 322.
    Critical Review, s3,v6 (Nov. 1805), 326-27.
    Flowers of Literature, 4 (1805), 433-34.
    Literary Journal, a Review..., 5 (Oct. 1805), 1104-05.
    Monthly Magazine, Suppl. v20 (Jan. 31, 1806), 616.
    Monthly Review, ns,v50 (July 1806), 318-19.

Service, David.
  The Caledonian Herd Boy, a Rural Poem. 1802. (P)
    British Critic, 20 (Sept. 1820), 320.
    European Magazine, 42 (Sept. 1802), 210.

  Crispin; or, the Apprentice Boy, a Poem. (P)
    European Magazine, 48 (Oct. 1805), 298.

  The Wild Harp's Murmurs; or, Rustic Strains. 1806. (P)
    Annual Review, 5 (1806), 530-31.
    British Critic, 29 (Jan. 1807), 74-75.
    European Magazine, 50 (Aug. 1806), 129.
    Literary Annual Register, 2 (July 1808), 320-21.
    Literary Journal, a Review..., ns,v2 (July 1806), 106-08.
    Monthly Literary Recreations, 1 (Aug. 1806), 166.
    Monthly Magazine, Suppl. v22 (Jan. 25, 1807), 641.
    Monthly Review, 53 (May 1807), 98.
    New Annual Register, 27 (1806), [370].
    Poetical Register, 6 (1806), 509.

Several Hands.
  See Joshua Edkins.

Several Young Persons.
  See Ann and Jane Taylor.

Seward, Anna.
  Original Sonnets on Various Subjects; and Odes Paraphrased
  from Horace. 1799. (P)
    Analytical Review, ns,v1 (May-June 1799), 517-22, 624-27.
    Antijacobin Review, 4 (Nov. 1799), 327-30.
    British Critic, 14 (Aug. 1799), 166-71.
    Critical Review, s2,v26 (May 1799), 33-38.

European Magazine, 35 (May 1799), 323-25.
Gentleman's Magazine, 69[2] (Dec. 1799), 1065-66.
Monthly Magazine, Suppl. v7 (July 20, 1799), 536.
Monthly Mirror, 7 (May 1799), 283-84.
Monthly Review, 29 (Aug. 1799), 361-69.
Monthly Visitor, 10 (July 1800), 320-21.
New Annual Register, 20 (1799), [265].
New London Review, 2 (July-Sept. 1799), 59-72, 113-20,
    252-56.

The Poetical Works of Anna Seward, with Extracts from Her
Literary Correspondence.   Edited by Walter Scott. 1810. (P)
    Antijacobin Review, 41 (Apr. 1812), 372-86.
    British Critic, 37 (May 1811), 493-500.
    British Review, ? (Sept. 1811), 171-81.
    Critical Review, s3,v23 (July 1811), 225-38.
    Eclectic Review, 7 (Jan. 1811), 19-32.
    European Magazine, 58 (Aug.-Oct. 1810), 119-24, 201-04,
        291-93.
    Literary Panorama, 9 (Mar. 1811), 466-74.
    Monthly Review, 69 (Sept. 1812), 20-34.
    Poetical Register, 8 (1810), 560.
    Scots Magazine, 73 (July 1811), 520-35.

Sewell, Mrs. George.
    Poems.   1803.   (P)
    Annual Review, 2 (1803), 591.
    British Critic, 22 (Nov. 1803), 553-54.
    British Critic, 28 (Dec. 1806), 675-76.
    Gentleman's Magazine, 75[1] (Feb. 1805), 139.
    Monthly Magazine, Suppl. v16 (Jan. 25, 1804), 633.
    Monthly Mirror, 17 (Jan. 1804), 35.
    Monthly Review, 44 (May 1804), 101-02.
    Poetical Register, 3 (1803), 453-54.

Sextus Scriblerus.
    See Pindar Minimus.

Seymour, Miss Charlotte.
    The Powers of Imagination, a Poem.   1803.   (P)
    Annual Review, 2 (1803), 591-92.
    British Critic, 22 (Oct. 1803), 432-33.
    Monthly Magazine, Suppl. v16 (Jan. 25, 1804), 633.
    Monthly Mirror, 16 (Nov. 1803), 326-27.
    Monthly Review, 43 (Feb. 1804), 183-85.
    Poetical Register, 3 (1803), 440.

Shakleton, Elizabeth.
    See Mary Leadbeater and Tales for Cottagers.

Sharp, Charles.
    Zopheir; a Tragedy.   1819.   (D)
    British Stage and Literary Cabinet, 3 (July 1819), 197-99.

Sharpe, Charles Kirkpatrick.
  Metrical Legends, and Other Poems. 1807. (P)
    Annual Review, 7 (1808), 473-74.
    Critical Review, s3,v16 (Apr. 1809), 369-75.
    Monthly Review, 56 (Aug. 1808), 382-85.
    Poetical Register, 6 (1807), 539.

Sharpe, Richard Scrafton.
  The Margate New Guide; or Memoirs of Five Families Out of
  Six. (Anon.) 1799. (P)
    British Critic, 14 (Aug. 1799), 184.
    Critical Review, s2,v27 (Dec. 1799), 472.
    Lady's Monthly Museum, 3 (Aug. 1799), 152-55.
    Monthly Review, 29 (July 1799), 340-41.
    Monthly Visitor, 7 (Aug. 1799), 416-20.
    New London Review, 2 (Oct. 1799), 391-92.

  Theodore; or the Gamester's Progress. (Anon.) 1799. (P)
    Analytical Review, ns,v1 (Feb. 1799), 203-04.
    British Critic, 14 (July 1799), 72-73.
    Lady's Monthly Museum, 2 (Feb. 1799), 151.
    Monthly Magazine, Suppl. v7 (July 20, 1799), 537.
    Monthly Mirror, 7 (Jan. 1799), 32-33.
    Monthly Review, 28 (Mar. 1799), 353-54.
    Monthly Visitor, 6 (Apr. 1799), 422.
    Monthly Visitor, 8 (Sept. 1799), 38.
    New London Review, 1 (Jan. 1799), 100.

  Parodies on Gay. To Which Is Added The Battle of the
  Busts, a Fable. (Anon.) 1800. (P)
    British Critic, 18 (Aug. 1801), 196.
    Monthly Mirror, 10 (Nov. 1800), 312.
    Monthly Review, 33 (Sept. 1800), 105.

  Matilda, or the Welch Cottage, a Poetic Tale. (Anon.)
  1801. (P)
    Antijacobin Review, 9 (June 1801), 185.
    Antijacobin Review, 11 (Apr. 1802), 397.
    Critical Review, s2,v33 (Sept. 1801), 110.
    Monthly Mirror, 11 (May 1801), 327.
    Monthly Review, 36 (Sept. 1801), 99-100.
    Monthly Visitor, 13 (June 1801), 206.
    Union Magazine, 2 (Sept. 1801), 184.

  Old Friends in a New Dress; or, Familiar Fables in Verse.
  (Anon.) 1807. (P)
    Cabinet, 3 (May 1808), 333-34.
    Monthly Mirror, ns,v2 (July 1807), 35.
    Monthly Review, 55 (Apr. 1808), 440-41.

  The Conjuror; or the Turkey and the Ring. A Comic Tale.
  (Anon.) (P)
    Antijacobin Review, 31 (Sept. 1808), 58.

<u>Monthly Review</u>, 61 (Mar. 1810), 326-27.

<u>Little Thumb and the Ogre, Being a Versification of One of
the Celebrated Tales of Mother Goose</u>. (Anon.) 1808. (P)
  <u>Antijacobin Review</u>, 31 (Sept. 1808), 58.
  <u>Monthly Review</u>, 61 (Mar. 1810), 327.

<u>The Master Cat; or, Puss in Boots</u>. (Anon.) 1808. (P)
  <u>Antijacobin Review</u>, 31 (Sept. 1809), 58.
  <u>Monthly Review</u>, 61 (Mar. 1810), 326-27.

<u>The Fairy; Being the Second of the Mother Goose Tales</u>.
(Anon.) (P)
  <u>Monthly Review</u>, 61 (Mar. 1810), 326-27.

Shaw, L. O.
  <u>The Duel, a Satirical Poem, in Four Cantos</u>. <u>With Other
Poems</u>. 1815. (P)
    <u>Antijacobin Review</u>, 49 (Oct. 1815), 380-83.
    <u>British Critic</u>, ns,v5 (Feb. 1816), 219.
    <u>Critical Review</u>, s5,v2 (Aug. 1815), 213.
    <u>Literary Panorama</u>, ns,v2 (Sept. 1815), 970-72.
    <u>Monthly Review</u>, 78 (Oct. 1815), 215.

Shee, John.
  <u>Lines on the Battle of Waterloo</u>. 1816. (P)
    <u>Dublin Examiner</u>, 2 (Dec. 1816), 152-58.

Shee, Martin Archer.
  <u>Rhymes on Art; or, the Remonstrance of a Painter</u>. <u>With
Notes, and a Preface, Including Strictures on the State of
the Arts, Criticism, Patronage, and Public Taste</u>. 1805.
(P)
    <u>Annual Review</u>, 4 (1805), 592-96.
    <u>British Critic</u>, 26 (Sept. 1805), 268-76.
    <u>Critical Review</u>, s3,v4 (Apr. 1805), 444-46.
    <u>Eclectic Review</u>, 1 (July 1805), 489-95.
    <u>Edinburgh Review</u>, 8 (Apr. 1806), 213-22.
    <u>European Magazine</u>, 47 (May 1805), 363-66.
    <u>Flowers of Literature</u>, 4 (1805), 432.
    <u>Flowers of Literature</u>, 5 (1806), 511-12.
    <u>Lady's Monthly Museum</u>, 15 (July 1805), 59.
    <u>Lady's Monthly Museum</u>, 15 (Sept. 1805), 200-01.
    <u>Lady's Monthly Museum</u>, 15 (Nov. 1805), 347.
    <u>Literary Journal, a Review...</u>, 5 (July 1805), 714-22.
    <u>Monthly Magazine</u>, Suppl. v20 (Jan. 31, 1806), 614.
    <u>Monthly Mirror</u>, 19 (Apr. 1805), 243-48.
    <u>Monthly Pantheon</u>, 2 (Feb.-Mar. 1809), 106-09, 199-204.
    <u>Monthly Review</u>, 47 (July 1805), 262-70.
    <u>New Annual Register</u>, 26 (1805), [355].
    <u>Poetical Register</u>, 5 (1805), 497.

  <u>Elements of Art</u>. <u>With Notes and Preface, Including Stric-</u>

tures on the State of the Arts, Criticism, Patronage, and
Public Taste. 1809. (P)
  Le Beau Monde, 1 (June 1809), 246-49.
  British Critic, 36 (Sept. 1810), 228-40.
  Critical Review, s3,v18 (Nov. 1809), 225-46.
  Eclectic Review, 7 (July 1811), 612-19.
  Literary Panorama, 6 (July 1809), 637-47.
  London Review, 2 (Nov. 1809), 372-406.
  Monthly Mirror, ns,v7 (Feb., May 1810), 115-27, 362-68.
  Monthly Review, 64 (Apr. 1811), 401-17.
  Poetical Register, 7 (1809), 591-92.
  Quarterly Review, 3 (May 1810), 407-17.

The Commemoration of Reynolds. With Notes, and Other Poems.
1815. (P)
  Antijacobin Review, 47 (July 1814), 20-29.
  British Critic, ns,v2 (Oct. 1814), 436-37.
  Eclectic Review, s2,v2 (Aug. 1814), 186-91.
  Gentleman's Magazine, 85^1 (May 1815), 435-37.
  Monthly Review, 76 (Mar. 1815), 294-301.
  Theatrical Inquisitor, 4 (May 1814), 289-91.

Sheil, Richard Lalor.
  Adelaide, a Tragedy. 1814. 2nd ed., 1816. (D)
    British Lady's Magazine, 4 (July 1816), 39-43.
    Monthly Review, ns,v84 (Nov. 1817), 236-39.
    New Monthly Magazine, 5 (July 1816), 534.
    Theatrical Inquisitor, 9 (Sept. 1816), 205-06.

  The Apostate, a Tragedy. 1817. (D)
    British Critic, ns,v8 (Dec. 1817), 644-48.
    Monthly Magazine, 43 (June 1817), 452.
    Monthly Review, ns,v84 (Nov. 1817), 239-43.
    Theatrical Inquisitor, 11 (July 1817), 48-55.
    Quarterly Review, 17 (Apr. 1817), 248-60.

  Bellamira; or the Fall of Tunis. 1818. (D)
    The Anti-Unionist, 1 (May 16, 1818), 343-46.
    Literary Journal and General Miscellany, 1 (Aug. 29,
      1818), 357.

  Evadne; or the Statue. A Tragedy. 1819. (D)
    Fireside Magazine (quoting Monthly Review), 1 (June
      1819), 225.
    Monthly Review, ns,v88 (Apr. 1819), 440-44.
    Quarterly Review, 22 (Jan. 1820), 402-15.
    Theatre, or Dramatic and Literary Mirror, 1 (Feb. 27,
      1819), 21-24.

Shelley, Mary.
  Frankenstein; or the Modern Prometheus. 1818. (F)
    Blackwood's Edinburgh Magazine, 2 (Mar. 1818), 613-20.
    British Critic, ns,v9 (Apr. 1818), 432-38.

Gentleman's Magazine, 88[1] (Apr. 1818), 334-35.
Monthly Review, 85 (Apr. 1818), 439.
Quarterly Review, 18 (Jan. 1818), 379-85.
Scots Magazine, ns,v2 (Mar. 1818), 249-53.

Shelley, Percy Bysshe.
Zastrossi, a Romance. By P. B. S. 1810. (F)
Critical Review, s3,v21 (Nov. 1810), 329-31.
Gentleman's Magazine, 80[2] (Sept. 1810), 258.

Original Poetry; by Victor and Cazire. 1810. (P)
Antijacobin Review, 37 (Oct. 1810), 206.
British Critic, 37 (Apr. 1811), 408-09.
Literary Panorama, 8 (Oct. 1810), 1063-66.
Poetical Register, 8 (1811), 617.

St. Irvyne; or the Rosicrucian: a Romance. By a Gentleman
of the University of Oxford. 1811. (F)
Antijacobin Review, 41 (Jan. 1812), 69-71.
British Critic, 37 (Jan. 1811), 70-71.
Literary Panorama, 9 (Feb. 1811), 252-54.

Queen Mab; a Philosophical Poem. 1813. (P)
Theological Enquirer, 1 (Mar.-May, July 1815), 34-39,
105-10, 205-09, 358-62.

Alastor; or, the Spirit of Solitude: and Other Poems. 1816.
(P)
Blackwood's Edinburgh Magazine, 6 (Nov. 1819), 148-54.
British Critic, ns,v5 (May 1816), 545-46.
Eclectic Review, s2,v6 (Oct. 1816), 391-93.
Monthly Review, 79 (Apr. 1816), 433.

Laon and Cythna, or the Revolution of the Golden City. A
Vision of the Nineteenth Century. 1818. (P)
Quarterly Review, 21 (Apr. 1819), 460-71.

The Revolt of Islam, a Poem. 1818. (P)
Blackwood's Edinburgh Magazine, 4 (Jan. 1819), 475-82.
Examiner, Feb. 1, 22, Mar. 1, 1818, pp. 75-76, 121-22,
139-41.
Fireside Magazine (quoting Monthly Review), 1 (May 1819),
187.
Man of Kent (from a Correspondent), Nov. 21, 1818, 157-60.
Monthly Magazine, 45 (Mar. 1818), 154.
Monthly Review, 88 (Mar. 1819), 323-24.
Quarterly Review, 21 (Apr. 1819), 460-71.

Rosalind and Helen, a Modern Eclogue; with Other Poems.
1819. (P)
Blackwood's Edinburgh Magazine, 5 (June 1819), 268-74.
Examiner, May 9, 1819, pp. 302-03.
Commercial Chronicle, June 3, 1819, p. 1.

Gentleman's Magazine (quoting New Times), 89¹ (Suppl. Jan.-June 1819), 625-26.
London Chronicle (identical with Commercial Chronicle and Gentleman's Magazine), June 1, 1819, p. 521.
Monthly Review, 90 (Oct. 1819), 207-09.

The Cenci; a Tragedy. 1819. (D-P)
  British Review, 17 (June 1821), 380-89.
  Edinburgh Review, 3 (May 1820), 591-604.
  Examiner, Mar. 19, 1820, pp. 190-91.
  Independent, Feb. 17, 1821, pp. 99-103.
  Indicator, July 19-26, 1820, pp. 321-28, 329-36.
  Literary Gazette, Apr. 1, 1820, pp. 209-10.
  (Baldwin's) London Magazine, 1 (May 1820), 546-55.
  (Gold's) London Magazine, 1 (Apr. 1820), 401-07.
  Monthly Magazine, 49 (Apr. 1820), 260.
  Monthly Review, 94 (Feb. 1821), 161-68.
  New Monthly Magazine, 13 (May 1820), 550-53.
  Theatrical Inquisitor, 16 (Apr. 1820), 205-18.

Prometheus Unbound; a Lyrical Drama; with Other Poems.
1820. (P)
  Blackwood's Edinburgh Magazine, 7 (Sept. 1820), 679-87.
  Literary Gazette, Sept. 9, 1820, pp. 580-82.
  (Baldwin's) London Magazine, 1 (June 1820), 706.
  (Gold's) London Magazine, 2 (Sept.-Oct. 1820), 306-07, 382-91.
  Lonsdale Magazine, 1 (Nov. 1820), 498-500.
  Monthly Review, 94 (Feb. 1821), 168-73.
  Quarterly Review, 26 (Oct. 1821), 168-80.

Sheridan, Richard Brinsley.
  Clio's Protest; or, "The Picture" Varnished; with Other Poems. 1819. (P)
    Fireside Magazine (quoting Monthly Review), 1 (July 1819), 266.
    Literary Journal and General Miscellany, 2 (Mar. 27, 1819), 193-94.
    Monthly Review, 89 (May 1819), 97-101.

  Ode to Scandal; to Which Are Added, Stanzas on Fire. 1819. (P)
    British Lady's Magazine, s3,v2 (Feb. 1819), 80.
    Fireside Magazine (quoting Monthly Review), 1 (Apr. 1819), 152.
    Green Man, Jan. 23, 1819, pp. 103-04.
    Literary Gazette, Jan. 16, 1819, p. 34.
    Monthly Review, 88 (Feb. 1819), 210-11.
    Theatre; or Dramatic and Literary Mirror, 1 (May 29, 1819), 199-200.

Sherston, Peter.
  The Months, Commencing with Early Spring; a Poem Descripti

of Rural Scenes and Village Characters. (P)
   Poetical Register, 8 (1810), 579.

Shewell, John Talwyn.
   A Tribute to the Memory of William Cowper, and Other Poems.
   By J. T. S. (P)
   Monthly Review, 63 (Sept. 1810), 95-96.
   Poetical Register, 8 (1810), 576.

Shilton, R. P.
   Jephtha's Sacrifice, a Poem. (P)
   Monthly Review, 93 (Dec. 1820), 435-36.

Shirley, Thomas.
   A Tribute to the Memory of the Right Honourable William
   Pitt. 1806. (P)
   Antijacobin Review, 24 (June 1806), 196-97.
   British Critic, 29 (Feb. 1807), 201.
   Critical Review, s3,v8 (July 1806), 330.
   Literary Journal, a Review..., ns,v2 (July 1816), 104.
   Poetical Register, 6 (1806), 514.

Shuffleton, Tom.
   See Sir Lumley St. George Skeffington.

Sicklemore, Richard.
   Edgar; or the Phantom of the Castle. 1798. (F)
   Critical Review, ns,v23 (Aug. 1798), 473.
   Monthly Mirror, 6 (Sept. 1798), 161.

   Agnes and Lenora, a Novel. (F)
   New London Review, 1 (Apr. 1799), 405-06.

   Mary-Jane, a Novel. 1800. (F)
   Critical Review, ns,v31 (Feb. 1801), 236.

   Rashleigh Abbey; or, the Ruin of the Rock. (F)
   Literary Journal, a Review..., 5 (Dec. 1805), 1327-28.

Siddons, Henry.
   A Tale of Terror; a Dramatic Romance. (D)
   Annual Review, 2 (1803), 595.
   Poetical Register, 3 (1803), 465-66.

   Virtuous Poverty, a Tale. 1804. (F)
   Flowers of Literature, 3 (1804), 467.
   Imperial Review, 2 (May 1804), 143.
   Monthly Review, ns,v45 (Nov. 1804), 314.
   North British Magazine, Sept. 1805(4?), pp.175-77.

   The Maid, Wife, and Widow. A Tale. 1806. (F)
   Flowers of Literature, 5 (1806), 506.
   Monthly Magazine, Suppl. v21 (July 25, 1806), 609.

Practical Illustrations of Theatrical Gesture and Action, Adapted to the Business of the English Stage, and to the Characters of the English Drama, from the Original Work of M. Engel. (Pr)
  Monthly Magazine, Suppl. v25 (July 30, 1808), 597.
  Oxford Review, 1 (Mar. 1807), 305-14.

  Time's a Tell-Tale, a Comedy. 1807. (D)
  Annual Review, 7 (1808), 570.
  Monthly Mirror, ns,v2 (Dec. 1807), 415.
  Monthly Review, ns,v57 (Sept. 1808), 100.
  New Annual Register, 28 (1807), [379].
  Oxford Review, 3 (Feb. 1808), 169.
  Poetical Register, 6 (1807), 564-65.

Sigourney, Lydia Huntley.
  Moral Pieces in Prose and Verse. 1815. (P)
    Critical Review, s5,v2 (Nov. 1815), 544.

Sikes, Mrs. S.
  Hymns and Poems on Moral Subjects. 1815. (P)
    British Lady's Magazine, 2 (Sept. 1815), 181-82.
    Monthly Review, 79 (Jan. 1816), 101.

Simple, Tristram.
  The People. 1811. (P)
    Eclectic Review, 7 (July 1811), 650.

  The Age; or the Consolations of Philosophy. 1811. (P)
    British Critic, 38 (Nov. 1811), 519-20.
    Critical Review, s3,v23 (Aug. 1811), 442-43.
    Eclectic Review, 7 (July 1811), 650.
    Gentleman's Magazine, 81^2 (Oct. 1811), 343-44.
    Monthly Review, 68 (May 1812), 105-06.
    Poetical Register, 8 (1811), 611-12.

Sinclair, Harvey.
  A Peep at the World, or the Children of Providence. (F)
    Critical Review, s3,v2 (June 1804), 235.
    Lady's Monthly Museum, 14 (Jan. 1805), 64.
    Monthly Review, ns,v45 (Nov. 1804), 314.

Singleton, William.
  Mentor and Amander; or, a Visit to Ackworth School. By a Late Teacher. 1814. (P)
    Critical Review, s4,v6 (July 1814), 92.
    Monthly Review, 76 (Feb. 1815), 211.

Sister, A.
  See Miss _____ Walsh.

Skeffington, Sir Lumley St. George.
  The Amatory Works of Tom Shuffleton. 1814. (P)

Augustan Review, 1 (Oct. 1815), 609-10.
Critical Review, s5,v1 (May 1815), 531.
Gentleman's Magazine, Suppl. v85[1] (Jan.-June 1815), 611-12.
Monthly Review, 76 (Apr. 1815), 437.

Skurray, Rev. Francis.
    Bidcombe Hill, with Other Rural Poems. 1808. (P)
        Antijacobin Review, 32 (Jan. 1808), 55-61.
        Antijacobin Review, 40 (Nov. 1811), 318-24.
        British Critic, 35 (Apr. 1810), 397-99.
        Critical Review, s3,v17 (July 1809), 328-29.
        Eclectic Review, 5 (Sept. 1809), 872-74.
        Monthly Review, 64 (Mar. 1811), 272-76.
        Poetical Register, 7 (1808), 554.
        Universal Magazine, ns,v11 (June 1809), 524-26.

Sleath, Mrs. Eleanor.
    The Orphan of the Rhine. A Romance. 1798. (F)
        Critical Review, ns,v27 (Nov. 1799), 356.

    Who's the Murderer? (F)
        Monthly Magazine, Suppl. v15 (July 28, 1803), 639.

    The Bristol Heiress; or, Errors of Education. (F)
        Le Beau Monde, 2 (Oct. 1809), 45-46.

Small, Richard.
    Poems, Chiefly Amatory. 1811. (P)
        British Critic, 40 (July 1812), 73-74.

Smallpiece, Anna Maria.
    Original Sonnets, and Other Small Poems. 1805. (P)
        General Review, 1 (Jan. 1806), 90-91.
        Literary Journal, a Review..., ns,v1 (Mar. 1806), 329-30.
        Poetical Register, 5 (1805), 489-90.

Smallshot, Jasper.
    See Major Ware.

Smedley, Rev. Edward, Sr.
    Erin, a Geographical and Descriptive Poem. 1810. (P)
        British Critic, 35 (June 1810), 599-600.
        Gentleman's Magazine, 80[2] (July 1810), 57-60.
        Hibernia Magazine, 2 (Aug. 1810), 121-22.
        Poetical Register, 8 (1810), 574.

Smedley, Edward, Jr.
    A Few Verses; English and Latin. 1812. (P)
        British Critic, 40 (July 1812), 71-72.
        Critical Review, s4,v3 (Apr. 1813), 383-86.
        Gentleman's Magazine, 82[2] (Aug. 1812), 151-52.
        Monthly Review, 70 (Mar. 1813), 322-24.

The Death of Saul and Jonathan. A Poem. (P)
  Gentleman's Magazine, 84^1 (Apr. 1814), 361-62.

Jephthah, a Poem. 1814. (P)
  Antijacobin Review, 47 (Dec. 1814), 587-91.
  British Critic, ns,v3 (Jan. 1815), 96-97.
  Christian Observer, 14 (May 1815), 328-36.
  Eclectic Review, s2,v3 (Feb. 1815), 205-09.
  Gentleman's Magazine, 84^2 (Dec. 1814), 566-67.
  Literary Panorama, ns,vl (Jan. 1815), 505-09.
  Monthly Review, 77 (May 1815), 100-01.

Jonah, a Poem. 1815. (P)
  Eclectic Review, s2,v5 (Mar. 1816), 289-92.
  Gentleman's Magazine, 86^1 (Jan. 1816), 44-45.
  Monthly Review, 81 (Nov. 1816), 289-99.
  New Monthly Magazine, 6 (Sept. 1816), 149-50.

Prescience; or the Secrets of Divination. A Poem. 1816.
  (P)
  Augustan Review, 2 (June 1816), 639-41.
  British Critic, ns,v8 (Aug. 1817), 190-99.
  Eclectic Review, s2,v5 (May 1816), 472-77.
  Gentleman's Magazine, 86^1 (June 1816), 523-26.
  Literary Panorama, ns,v7 (Oct. 1817), 62-64.
  Monthly Review, 82 (Feb. 1817), 184-93.
  New Monthly Magazine, 6 (Nov. 1816), 347.

Religio Clerici, a Churchman's Epistle. 1818. (P)
  British Critic, ns,v9 (Apr. 1818), 438-44.
  Eclectic Review, s2,v9 (Apr. 1818), 370-73.
  Gentleman's Magazine, 88^1 (June 1818), 529-31.
  Literary Gazette, Mar. 21, 1818, pp. 177-78.
  Monthly Review, 86 (July 1818), 323-26.

A Churchman's Second Epistle. By the Author of Religio
  Clerici. 1819. (P)
  Antijacobin Review, 56 (Apr. 1819), 122-25.
  British Critic, ns,vll (Feb. 1819), 186-200.
  Monthly Review, 89 (May 1819), 64-70.

Smellfungus, Geoffrey.
  The Augustan Chief, a Poem. 1819. (P)
  Literary Chronicle, 1 (Nov. 13, 1819), 406-07.

Smith, Mr. _____.
  A Family Story. 1800. (F)
  Critical Review, ns,v28 (Apr. 1800), 477.
  Monthly Magazine, Suppl. v9 (July 20, 1800), 640.
  New Monthly Review, 3 (Mar. 1800), 281.

  The Runaway; or, the Seat of Benevolence. 1800. (F)
  British Critic, 17 (Apr. 1801), 434.

    Critical Review, ns,v31 (Apr. 1801), 474.
    Monthly Mirror, 11 (May 1801), 324.
    Monthly Review, ns,v34 (Feb. 1801), 204.

Smith, Charles.
  A Day at Rome: A Musical Entertainment. 1798.   (D)
    Analytical Review, 28 (Nov. 1798), 515.
    British Critic, 14 (July 1799), 74.
    Monthly Mirror, 6 (Nov. 1798), 299.
    Monthly Review, ns,v27 (Nov. 1798), 346.

  A Trip to Bengal: A Musical Entertainment. 1802.   (D)
    Annual Review, 1 (1802), 693.
    Critical Review, ns,v36 (Nov. 1802), 356.
    Monthly Mirror, 13 (Mar. 1802), 202[192].

  The Mosiad, or Israel Delivered; a Sacred Poem.   1815. (P)
    Literary Panorama, ns,v4 (Apr. 1816), 47-54.
    Monthly Review, 79 (Feb. 1816), 185-90.

Smith, Charlotte.
  Elegiac Sonnets, and Other Poems. 1797. 1st ed., 1784. (P)
    Monthly Mirror, 5 (Jan. 1798), 32-33.

  The Young Philosopher, a Novel. 1798.   (F)
    Analytical Review, 28 (July 1798), 73-77.
    Antijacobin Review, 1 (Aug. 1798), 187-90.
    Critical Review, ns,v24 (Sept. 1798), 77-84.
    Monthly Magazine, Suppl. v6 (1798), 516.

  Minor Morals, Interspersed with Sketches of Natural History, Historical Anecdotes, and Original Stories.   (P)
    Monthly Visitor, 6 (Feb. 1799), 214-16.

  What Is She? A Comedy. (Anon.) 1799.   (D)
    Antijacobin Review, 3 (June 1799), 150-55.
    Critical Review, ns,v27 (Nov. 1799), 355.
    Monthly Magazine, Suppl. v8 (Jan. 20, 1800), 1055.
    Monthly Mirror, 8 (July 1799), 32.
    Monthly Review, ns,v29 (Aug. 1799), 451.
    New London Review, 2 (Aug. 1799), 192.

  Letters of a Solitary Wanderer. 1800 & 1802.   (F)
    Annual Review, 1 (1802), 720.
    Flowers of Literature, 1 (1801-02), 452.
    Monthly Magazine, Suppl. v11 (July 20, 1801), 606.
    Monthly Magazine, Suppl. v12 (Jan. 20, 1802), 584.
    Monthly Magazine, Suppl. v15 (July 28, 1803), 639.
    Monthly Review, ns,v35 (July 1801), 332.
    Monthly Review, ns,v39 (Dec. 1802), 428.
    New Annual Register, 23 (1802), [321].

  Conversations, Introducing Poetry; Chiefly on Subjects of

Natural History; for the Use of Children and Young Persons.
1804. (P)
  Eclectic Review, 1 (May 1805), 330-33.
  Lady's Monthly Museum, 16 (Mar. 1806), 202-03.
  Monthly Review, 49 (Jan. 1806), 79-82.

Beachy Head; with Other Poems. 1807. (P)
  Annual Review, 6 (1807), 536-38.
  British Critic, 30 (Aug. 1807), 170-74.
  Cabinet, 2 (Aug. 1807), 40-41.
  Cyclopaedian Magazine, 1 (Aug. 1807), 481.
  Literary Annual Register, 1 (Mar. 1807), 129-31.
  Literary Panorama, 2 (May 1807), 294-95.
  Monthly Review, 56 (May 1808), 99-101.
  Poetical Register, 6 (1807), 541-42.
  Universal Magazine, ns,v7 (Mar. 1807), 228-31.

Emmeline, or the Orphan of the Castle. (F)
  Guide, a Moral and Economical Weekly Family Paper, 1
    (July 7, 1808), 286.

Smith, Eaglesfield.
  The Scath of France; or, the Death of St. Just and His
  Sons. To Which Is Added, Sir Mordac and Balma. 1797. (P)
    Critical Review, s2,v22 (Jan. 1798), 101.
    Gentleman's Magazine, 68^2 (Nov. 1798), 973.
    Monthly Magazine, Suppl. v5 (July 15, 1798), 507.

  Sir John Butt: A Farce. (Anon.) 1798. (D)
    Critical Review, ns,v28 (Feb. 1800), 235.
    Monthly Mirror, 9 (Jan. 1800), 41.
    New London Review, 2 (Dec. 1799), 604.

  The Poetical Works of Eaglesfield Smith. 1802. (P)
    British Critic, 19 (June 1802), 643-44.
    European Magazine, 41 (Feb. 1802), 122.
    Monthly Review, 40 (Jan. 1803), 103-04.
    Poetical Register, 2 (1802), 433-34.

  Legendary Tales. 1807. (P)
    Antijacobin Review, 30 (May 1808), 77-78.
    British Critic, 31 (Mar. 1808), 311-12.
    Critical Review, s3,v13 (Mar. 1808), 334-35.
    Monthly Review, 56 (May 1808), 101-02.
    Oxford Review, 2 (Sept. 1807), 315-17.
    Poetical Register, 6 (1807), 543.
    Satirist, 2 (June 1808), 445.

  On the Tragic Ballad: with Some Account of Legendary Tales.
  (Pr)
    Scots Magazine, 69 (Aug. 1807), 588-91.

  Rudigar the Dane, a Legendary Tale. 1809. (P)

Antijacobin Review, 33 (June 1809), 187.
Critical Review, s3,v18 (Sept. 1809), 108-09.
Eclectic Review, 5 (Nov. 1809), 1067.
Gentleman's Magazine, 80^1 (Mar. 1810), 246.
Monthly Review, 60 (Dec. 1809), 433-34.
Poetical Register, 7 (1809), 600.
Satirist, 7 (Dec. 1810), 598-99.

Smith, Edward, Jr.
  Morcar and Elfina. A Legendary Tale. 1799. (P)
    Critical Review, s2,v28 (Jan. 1800), 109.
    Monthly Review, 33 (Sept. 1800), 105.

Smith, Elizabeth.
  Fragments, in Prose and Verse. 1808; 1810. (P-Pr)
    British Critic, 33 (Mar. 1809), 217-23.
    Critical Review, s3,v23 (June 1811), 140-50.
    Cyclopaedian Magazine, 2 (Oct.-Nov. 1808), 569-71, 618-
      21.
    Eclectic Review, 4 (Sept. 1808), 827-32.
    Edinburgh Monthly Magazine, 1 (Sept. 1811), 449-58.
    Monthly Review, 64 (Jan. 1811), 67-79.
    Poetical Register, 7 (1808), 553-54.
    Satirist, 9 (Aug. 1811), 162-63.

Smith, Emelius Felix.
  Fugitive Pieces in Verse. 1804. (P)
    European Magazine, 49 (June 1806), 444-46.

Smith, Horatio.
  First Impressions; or Trade in the West. A Comedy. 1813.
  (D)
    Monthly Review, ns,v73 (Jan. 1814), 99-100.
    New Annual Register, 35 (1814), [365].
    New Review, 3 (Apr. 1814), 362-65.

  Amarynthus the Nympholept; Lucy Milford, and Other Poems.
  (Anon.) 1820. (P)
    Literary Gazette, Dec. 16, 1820, pp. 804-06.

Smith, Horatio, and James Smith.
  Rejected Addresses; or the New Theatrum Poetarum. (Anon.)
  1812. (P)
    British Critic, 40 (Nov. 1812), 527-28.
    Critical Review, s4,v2 (Nov. 1812), 541-48.
    Eclectic Review, 9 (Jan. 1813), 94-107.
    Edinburgh Review, 20 (Nov. 1812), 434-51.
    Gentleman's Magazine, 82^2 (Nov. 1812), 468-69.
    Lady's Monthly Museum, s2,v13 (Dec. 1812), 341-43.
    Literary Panorama, 12 (Jan. 1813), 1173-81.
    Monthly Review, 69 (Nov. 1812), 288-98.
    New Review, 1 (Feb. 1813), 201-06.
    Quarterly Review, 8 (Sept. 1812), 172-81.

Satirist, ns,v1 (Nov. 1812), 452-56.
Scourge, 5 (Jan. 1813), 18-23.
Theatrical Inquisitor, 1 (Nov. 1812), 161-67.

Horace in London; Consisting of Imitations of the First Two
Books of the Odes of Horace. By the Authors of the Rejected Addresses. 1813. (P)
    British Critic, 41 (May 1813), 517-19.
    Critical Review, s4,v3 (Mar. 1813), 280-84.
    Eclectic Review, 9 (May 1813), 479-84.
    Monthly Review, 70 (Mar. 1813), 319-21.
    New Annual Register, 34 (1813), [409].
    New Review, 1 (May 1813), 581-83.
    Scots Magazine, 75 (July 1813), 531-33.
    Scourge, 5 (Apr. 1813), 335-39.
    Theatrical Inquisitor, 2 (Apr. 1813), 160-67.

Smith, James.
See Horatio Smith and James Smith.

Smith, John.
    Metrical Remarks on Modern Castles and Cottages, and Archi-
    tecture in General. (Anon.) 1813. (P)
        British Critic, 42 (Sept. 1813), 295-96.
        Gentleman's Magazine, 85^2 (July 1815), 53-55.
        Monthly Review, 72 (Sept. 1813), 106-07.

Smith, John.
    The House of Atreus, and the House of Laius; Tragedies
    Founded on the Greek Drama. With a Preface on the Peculi-
    arities of Its Structure and Moral Principles; and Other
    Poems. 1819. (D)
        Fireside Magazine (quoting British Critic), 1 (Aug. 1819),
        314.
        Monthly Review, 92 (May 1820), 87-95.

Smith, John William.
    Terrors of Imagination, and Other Poems. 1814. (P)
        British Critic, ns,v2 (Nov. 1814), 547-48.
        Critical Review, s4,v6 (Sept. 1814), 314.
        Monthly Review, 75 (Sept. 1814), 99-100.
        New Review, 3 (June 1814), 544-46.
        Theatrical Inquisitor, 5 (July 1814), 45-50.

Smith, Mrs. Julia.
    Letters of the Swedish Court. Written Chiefly in the Early
    Part of the Reign of Gustavus III. (Anon.) (F)
        British Critic, 34 (Nov. 1809), 524.

    The Prison of Montauban; or Times of Terror. A Reflective
    Tale. (Anon.) 1819. (F)
        Antijacobin Review, 38 (Apr. 1811), 430-34.
        British Critic, 35 (May 1810), 522.

Critical Review, s3,v20 (July 1810), 329-31.
Monthly Review, ns,v63 (Oct. 1810), 218.

Smith, Thomas.
  Poems. 1797. (P)
    British Critic, 14 (July 1799), 73.
    Critical Review, s2,v26 (July 1799), 349-50.
    Critical Review, s2,v32 (Aug. 1801), 465-66.
    European Magazine, 36 (July 1799), 41.
    Monthly Visitor, 7 (June 1799), 200-04.

Smith, Rev. Thomas.
  The Shepherd's Son; or, the Wish Accomplished: A Moral Tale.
  (F)
    European Magazine, 38 (Dec. 1800), 441.

  Lucinda; or, Virtue Triumphant: A Moral Tale. (F)
    European Magazine, 40 (Aug. 1801), 116.

Smith, William.
  British Heroism, Exemplified in the Character of His Grace,
  Arthur, Duke, and Marquis of Wellington, and the Brave Offi-
  cers Serving under His Command.... 1815. (P)
    Critical Review, s5,v2 (July 1815), 101.

Smithers, Henry.
  Affection, with Other Poems. 1807. (P)
    Annual Review, 6 (1807), 570-71.
    Le Beau Monde, 3 (Jan. 1808), 34-37.
    British Critic, 32 (July 1808), 73.
    Cabinet, 2 (Aug., Oct. 1807), 42-45, 180-85.
    Critical Review, s3,v12 (Dec. 1807), 411-18.
    Critical Review, s5,v2 (Dec. 1815), 635-40. (2nd ed.)
    Eclectic Review, 3 (Oct. 1807), 904-08.
    Monthly Review, 56 (Aug. 1808), 430.
    Poetical Register, 6 (1807), 538.
    Satirist, 2 (Mar. 1808), 94-95. (Excerpts from other re-
      views.)

Smyth, L.
  Slavery, a Poem. 1820. (P)
    Monthly Magazine, 49 (May 1820), 356.
    Monthly Review, 92 (Aug. 1820), 438.

Smyth, Philip.
  Rhyme and Reason; Short and Original Poems. (Anon.) 1803.
  (P)
    Annual Review, 1 (1802), 650.
    Antijacobin Review, 13 (Dec. 1802), 418-21.
    British Critic, 21 (Feb. 1803), 188-89.
    Critical Review, s2,v37 (Apr. 1803), 475-76.
    Flowers of Literature, 2 (1803), 459.
    Monthly Magazine, Suppl. v15 (July 28, 1803), 637.

Monthly Mirror, 14 (Dec. 1802), 402.
Monthly Mirror, 16 (Aug. 1803), 114.
Monthly Review, 41 (July 1803), 327-29.
Poetical Register, 2 (1802), 427.

Smyth, William.
  English Lyrics. 1806. (P)
    Annual Review, 4 (1805), 613-15.
    Annual Review, 5 (1806), 525.
    British Critic, 28 (Aug. 1806), 179-81.
    Critical Review, s3,v8 (Aug. 1806), 404-11.
    Edinburgh Review, 8 (Apr. 1806), 154-58.
    Monthly Literary Recreations, 1 (July 1806), 85.
    Monthly Magazine, Supp. v21 (July 25, 1806), 608.
    New Annual Register, 26 (1805), [356].
    New Annual Register, 27 (1806), [371].
    Poetical Register, 6 (1806), 502.

Snow, Joseph.
  Misanthropy, and Other Poems. 1819. (P)
    British Critic, ns,v13 (Jan. 1820), 65-70.
    Literary Chronicle, 1 (Nov. 1819), 389-91.
    Monthly Review, 91 (Jan. 1820), 100-01.

Soame, Esq., _____.
  Epistle in Rhyme, to M. G. Lewis, Esq. 1798; 1800. (P)
    British Critic, 12 (Aug. 1798), 180-81.
    Critical Review, s2,v24 (Sept. 1798), 110.
    Critical Review, s2,v30 (Oct. 1800), 226-27.
    Gentleman's Magazine, 69^1 (Jan. 1799), 53.
    Monthly Magazine, Suppl. v6 (1798), 514.
    Monthly Mirror, 10 (Dec. 1800), 384.
    Monthly Review, 26 (Aug. 1798), 460.
    Monthly Review, 33 (Nov. 1800), 312-13.

Soane, George.
  The Peasant of Lucern, a Melo-Drama. 1815. (D)
    Critical Review, s5,v2 (Oct. 1815), 399-408.
    Theatrical Inquisitor, 7 (Aug. 1815), 133-41.

  The Bohemian. A Tragedy. 1817. (D)
    New Monthly Magazine, 8 (Oct. 1817), 244.
    Thanet Magazine, 1 (Oct. 1817), 186-94.
    Theatrical Inquisitor, 11 (Aug. 1817), 127-32.

  The Falls of Clyde, a Melo-Drama. 1817. (D)
    Monthly Review, ns,v85 (Jan. 1818), 102.

  The Innkeeper's Daughter, a Melo-Drama. (D)
    Theatrical Inquisitor, 10 (May 1817), 347-69[367-69].

  The Dwarf of Naples. A Tragi-Comedy. (D)
    Fireside Magazine (quoting Monthly Review), 1 (June

1819), 225.
Monthly Review, ns,v88 (Apr. 1819), 444.

Self-Sacrifice; or the Maid of the Cottage. A Melo-Drama.
(D)
Theatrical Inquisitor, 13 (Aug. 1819), 91-92.

The Hebrew. A Drama. (D)
Theatrical Inquisitor, 16 (Mar. 1820), 150-56.

Somebody, E.
Poems. 1806. (P)
Antijacobin Review, 28 (Oct. 1807), 190-92.
British Critic, 30 (Nov. 1807), 550-51.
Critical Review, s3,v12 (Oct. 1807), 330.
Eclectic Review, 3 (Dec. 1807), 1123.
Monthly Review, 55 (Apr. 1808), 438-40.
Satirist, 2 (May 1808), 335.

Somerville, Elizabeth.
Flora; or, the Deserted Child. 1800. (F)
European Magazine, 39 (Apr. 1801), 278.

The Village Maid; or, Dame Burton's Moral Stories for the
Amusement of Youth. 1801. (F)
Antijacobin Review, 10 (Nov. 1801), 311.

Mabel Woodbine, and Her Sister Lydia; a Tale. 1802. (F)
Monthly Review, ns,v39 (Dec. 1802), 425.
Union Magazine and Imperial Register, 3 (June 1802), 394.

The New Children in the Wood; or the Welsh Cottagers, a
Tale. 1802. (F)
Monthly Review, ns,v39 (Dec. 1802), 425.

Aurora and Maria; or the Advantages of Adversity. A Moral
Tale. 1809. (F?)
Antijacobin Review, 32 (Mar. 1809), 309.

Sophia, Mary.
Poems, on Various Subjects. (P)
Poetical Register, 8 (1810), 573.

Sotheby, Miss _____.
Patient Griselda, a Tale. From the Italian of Boccaccio.
1798. (P)
British Critic, 14 (Aug. 1799), 182-83.
New Annual Register, 20 (1799), [265-66].

Sotheby, William.
The Battle of the Nile, a Poem. 1799. (P)
Analytical Review, ns,v1 (Feb. 1799), 204-05.
Antijacobin Review, 2 (Feb. 1799), 151-55.

Sotheby, William (continued)
    British Critic, 13 (Feb. 1799), 187-88.
    Critical Review, s2,v25 (Mar. 1799), 351-52.
    Gentleman's Magazine, 69^1 (Apr. 1799), 321.
    Monthly Magazine, Suppl. v7 (July 20, 1799), 536-37.
    Monthly Mirror, 7 (May 1799), 287.
    Monthly Review, 28 (Feb. 1799), 227-28.
    New Annual Register, 20 (1799), [270].

The Siege of Cuzco, a Tragedy. 1800. (D)
    Antijacobin Review, 7 (Sept. 1800), 62-63.
    British Critic, 15 (May 1800), 552.
    Critical Review, ns,v32 (May 1801), 100-02.
    European Magazine, 37 (May 1800), 383.
    Gentleman's Magazine, 70^2 (Aug. 1800), 758.
    Monthly Magazine, Suppl. v9 (July 20, 1800), 641.
    Monthly Mirror, 11 (June 1801), 399.
    Monthly Review, ns,v33 (Sept. 1800), 106.
    New London Review, 3 (May 1800), 475-76.

Julian and Agnes; or, the Monks of the Great St. Bernard,
a Tragedy. 1801. (D)
    Critical Review, ns,v33 (Nov. 1801), 328-34.
    Monthly Review, ns,v37 (Jan. 1802), 97-99.
    Poetical Register, 1 (1801), 461.

A Poetical Epistle to Sir George Beaumont, Bart. on the En-
couragement of the British School of Painting. 1801. (P)
    Antijacobin Review, 9 (June 1801), 182-85.
    British Critic, 18 (July 1801), 78-81.
    Critical Review, s2,v36 (Nov. 1802), 349-52.
    Flowers of Literature, 1 (1801-02), 456.
    Gentleman's Magazine, 75^1 (Feb. 1805), 147.
    Monthly Magazine, Suppl. v13 (July 20, 1802), 657.
    Monthly Review, 37 (Apr. 1802), 436-38.
    New Annual Register, 22 (1801), [312].
    Poetical Register, 1 (1801), 447.

Oberon: or Huon de Bourdeaux, a Mask. And Orestes, a Tragedy. 1802. (D)
    Annual Review, 1 (1802), 648-49.
    British Critic, 20 (July 1802), 62-66.
    Imperial Review, 3 (Nov. 1804), 379-92.
    Monthly Review, ns,v42 (Dec. 1803), 432-36.
    New Annual Register, 23 (1802), [319].
    Poetical Register, 2 (1802), 450.

Saul, a Poem. 1807. (P)
    Annual Review, 6 (1807), 532-36.
    Le Beau Monde, 2 (Aug. 1807), 28-33.
    La Belle Assemblée, Suppl. v2 (1807), 40-42.
    British Critic, 30 (Oct. 1807), 381-89.
    Eclectic Review, 3 (July 1807), 594-607.

Sotheby, William (concluded)
    Edinburgh Review, 10 (Apr. 1807), 206-17.
    Literary Annual Register, 2 (Mar. 1808), 119-23.
    Literary Panorama, 3 (Oct. 1807), 32-42.
    Monthly Magazine, Suppl. v23 (July 30, 1807), 642-43.
    Monthly Repository, 2 (June 1807), 322-26.
    Monthly Review, 55 (Apr. 1808), 400-05.
    New Annual Register, 28 (1807), [378].
    Poetical Register, 6 (1807), 535.
    Satirist, 2 (July 1808), 544-45.

    Constance de Castile, a Poem. 1810. (P)
    British Critic, 36 (Nov. 1810), 433-47.
    Critical Review, s3,v20 (July 1810), 242-48.
    Eclectic Review, 6 (Oct. 1810), 904-17.
    Monthly Magazine, Suppl. v30 (Jan. 31, 1811), 677[673].
    Monthly Review, 63 (Oct. 1810), 145-52.
    Poetical Register, 8 (1810), 548.
    Satirist, 9 (Dec. 1811), 494-95. (Excerpts from other re-
    views.)

    A Song of Triumph. 1814. (P)
    Eclectic Review, s2,v1 (June 1814), 622-27.
    Monthly Review, 74 (May 1814), 101-02.

    Tragedies, by William Sotheby. The Death of Darnley, Ivan,
    Zamorin and Zama, The Confession, Orestes. 1814. (D)
    Augustan Review, 2 (June 1816), 622-30.
    Eclectic Review, ns,v4 (Nov. 1815), 473-86.
    Gentleman's Magazine, 85[1] (May 1815), 434.
    Monthly Review, ns,v77 (May 1815), 54-64.
    New Monthly Magazine, 2 (Sept. 1814), 153.
    Universal Magazine, s3,v1 (Sept. 1814), 211-13.

    Ellen, or the Confession, a Tragedy. 1816. (D)
    Augustan Review, 2 (June 1816), 622-30.
    British Critic, ns,v8 (July 1817), 100-09.
    British Lady's Magazine, 3 (May 1816), 326-32.
    Monthly Review, ns,v80 (May 1816), 97.

    Ivan, a Tragedy. 1816. (D)
    Augustan Review, 2 (June 1816), 622-30.
    British Critic, ns,v8 (July 1817), 100-09.
    British Lady's Magazine, 3 (Apr. 1816), 253-57.
    Critical Review, s5,v4 (Sept. 1816), 293-301.
    Monthly Review, ns,v80 (May 1816), 97.
    Theatrical Inquisitor, 9 (Sept. 1816), 207-08.

Southey, Caroline Anne (née Bowles).
    Ellen Fitzarthur: A Metrical Tale. 1820. (P)
    Literary Gazette, May 27, 1820, pp. 342-44.
    Monthly Review, 93 (Dec. 1820), 430-33.
    New Monthly Magazine, 14 (July 1820), 35-40.

Southey, Robert.
   Letters Written during a Short Residence in Spain and Portugal. With Some Account of Spanish and Portuguese Poetry.
   1797. (Pr)
      British Critic, 11 (Apr. 1798), 362-67.

   Joan of Arc. 1798. 2nd ed. (1st ed. 1796.) (P)
      Analytical Review, ns,v1 (Apr. 1799), 397-403.
      Antijacobin Review, 3 (June 1799), 120-28.
      Critical Review, s2,v23 (June 1798), 196-200.
      Monthly Magazine, Suppl. v5 (July 15, 1798), 506.
      Monthly Review, 28 (Jan. 1799), 57-62.
      Monthly Visitor, 5 (Sept. 1798), 91-93.
      New Annual Register, 19 (1798), [307].

   Poems. Vol. II. 1799. (P)
      Analytical Review, ns,v1 (Apr. 1799), 403-06.
      Antijacobin Review, 3 (June 1799), 120-28.
      Critical Review, s2,v26 (June 1799), 161-64.
      Monthly Magazine, Suppl. v7 (July 20, 1799), 535.
      Monthly Review, 31 (Mar. 1800), 261-67.
      Monthly Visitor, 7 (May 1799), 92-98.
      New Annual Register, 20 (1799), [264].
      New London Review, 1 (Apr. 1799), 363-66.

   Thalaba the Destroyer, a Metrical Romance. 1801. (P)
      British Critic, 18 (Sept. 1801), 309-10.
      Critical Review, s2,v39 (Dec. 1803), 369-79.
      Edinburgh Review, 1 (Oct. 1802), 63-83.
      Monthly Magazine, Suppl. v12 (Jan. 20, 1802), 581-84.
      Monthly Mirror, 12 (1801), 243-47.
      Monthly Review, 39 (Nov. 1802), 240-51.
      Monthly Visitor, 13 (Aug. 1801), 419-20.
      Poetical Register, 1 (1801), 427-28.

   Amadis of Gaul. 1803. (Pr)
      Annual Review, 2 (1803), 600-03.
      British Critic, 24 (Nov. 1804), 471-81.
      Critical Review, s3,v1 (Jan. 1804), 45-52.
      Edinburgh Review, 3 (Oct. 1803), 109-36.
      Literary Journal, a Review..., 2 (Sept. 16, 1803), 263-64.
      Monthly Magazine, 16 (Jan. 25, 1804), 636.
      Monthly Mirror, 16 (Nov. 1803), 318-20.
      Monthly Mirror, 47 (May 1805), 13-25.

   The Works of Thomas Chatterton. 1803. (Pr)
      Annual Review, 1 (1802), 672.
      British Critic, 21 (Apr. 1803), 367-73.
      Edinburgh Review, 4 (Apr. 1804), 214-30.
      Monthly Magazine, 15 (July 28, 1803), 636.

   Madoc, a Poem. 1805. (P)
      Annual Review, 4 (1805), 604-13.

Southey, Robert (continued)
  British Critic, 28 (Oct.-Nov. 1806), 395-410, 486-94.
  Critical Review, s3,v7 (Jan. 1806), 72-83.
  Eclectic Review, 1 (Dec. 1805), 899-908.
  Edinburgh Review, 7 (Oct. 1805), 1-29.
  European Magazine, 48 (Oct. 1805), 279-82.
  General Review, 1 (June 1806), 505-26.
  Imperial Review, 5 (Oct.-Nov. 1805), 417-26, 465-73.
  Literary Journal, a Review..., 5 (June 1805), 621-36.
  Monthly Magazine, Suppl. v19 (July 28, 1805), 656-58.
  Monthly Review, 48 (Oct. 1805), 113-22.
  New Annual Register, 26 (1805), [354-55].
  Poetical Register, 5 (1805), 483-84.
  Universal Magazine, ns,v4 (Aug. 1805), 149-53.

Metrical Tales, and Other Poems. 1805. (P)
  Annual Review, 4 (1805), 579-81.
  British Critic, 25 (May 1805), 553-55.
  Critical Review, s3,v4 (Feb. 1805), 118-21.
  Eclectic Review, 1 (Apr. 1805), 279-81.
  Literary Journal, a Review..., 5 (Feb. 1805), 157-65.
  Monthly Mirror, 19 (May 1805), 316-18.
  Monthly Review, 48 (Nov. 1805), 323-24.
  New Annual Register, 26 (1805), [355].
  Poetical Register, 5 (1805), 487.

Letters from England. By Don Manuel Alvarez Espriella.
Translated from the Spanish. 1807. (Pr)
  Annual Review, 6 (1807), 637-42.
  Antijacobin Review, 34 (Nov. 1809), 274-89.
  British Critic, 31 (Feb. 1808), 168-78.
  Cabinet, 3 (Apr. 1808), 260-62.
  Critical Review, s3,v13 (Mar. 1808), 282-83.
  Edinburgh Review, 11 (Jan. 1808), 370-90.
  Gentleman's Magazine, 78² (1808), 1169-74.
  Monthly Magazine, Suppl. v24 (Jan. 20, 1808), 633-34.
  Monthly Mirror, s2,v2 (Sept. 1807), 177-82.
  Monthly Review, 55 (Apr. 1808), 380-86.
  Oxford Review, 2 (Sept. 1807), 284-97.
  Universal Magazine, s2,v9 (Jan. 1808), 42-43.

Palmerin of England. By Francisco de Moraes. From the
Original Portuguese. 1807. (Pr)
  Annual Review, 7 (1808), 575-85.
  Critical Review, s3,v12 (Dec. 1807), 431-37.
  Gentleman's Magazine, 79¹ (May 1809), 438-43.
  Monthly Magazine, Suppl. v24 (Jan. 30, 1808), 630.
  Monthly Review, 60 (Oct. 1809), 157-59.
  Satirist, 2 (June 1808), 448.

Specimens of the Later English Poets, with Preliminary
Notices. 1807. (Pr)
  Annual Review, 6 (1807), 557-60.

Southey, Robert (continued)
   British Critic, 30 (Sept. 1807), 245-49.
   Eclectic Review, 3 (Oct. 1807), 845-55.
   Edinburgh Review, 11 (Oct. 1807), 31-40.
   Literary Annual Register, 1 (Oct. 1807), 467-68.
   Monthly Magazine, 23 (July 30, 1807), 640-41.
   Oxford Review, 1 (May 1807), 558-65.
   Poetical Register, 8 (1811), 558.
   Universal Magazine, ns,v8 (July 1807), 32-36.

The Remains of Henry Kirke White. With an Account of His
Life. 1808.
See Henry Kirke White, below.

Chronicle of the Cid. From the Spanish. 1808. (Pr)
   Annual Review, 7 (1808), 91-99.
   Antijacobin Review, 31 (Oct.-Nov. 1808), 151-65, 234-45.
   Le Beau Monde, 4 (Dec., 1808-Jan. 1809), 282-85, 331-32.
   British Critic, 33 (May-June 1809), 458-67, 610-18.
   Critical Review, s3,v16 (Jan.-Feb. 1809), 1-18, 155-69.
   Eclectic Review, 5 (Mar. 1809), 201-18.
   Gentleman's Magazine, 79^1 (Mar. 1809), 236-45.
   Monthly Review, 64 (Feb. 1811), 131-44.
   Quarterly Review, 1 (Feb. 1809), 134-53.

The Curse of Kehama. 1810. (P)
   La Belle Assemblée, Suppl. ns,v4 (1811), 373-76.
   British Critic, 39 (Mar. 1812), 272-82.
   Critical Review, s3,v22 (Mar. 1811), 225-51.
   Eclectic Review, 7 (Mar.-Apr. 1811), 185-205, 334-50.
   Edinburgh Review, 17 (Feb. 1811), 429-65.
   General Chronicle, 1 (Mar. 1811), 273-85.
   Glasgow Magazine, 2 (May 1811), 62-63.
   Literary Panorama, 9 (June 1811), 1044-59.
   Monthly Magazine, Suppl. v30 (Jan. 31, 1811), 677[673]-
     75.
   Monthly Mirror, ns,v9 (Feb. 1811), 122-35.
   Monthly Review, 65 (May-June 1811), 55-69, 113-28.
   Poetical Register, 8 (1810), 547.
   Quarterly Review, 5 (Feb. 1811), 40-61.
   Satirist, 8 (Feb.-Mar. 1811), 168-74, 249-56.

History of Brazil. Three Parts. 1810-29. (Pr)
   British Critic, s2,v9 (Mar.-Apr. 1818), 225-45, 369-91.
   Critical Review, s3,v21 (Sept. 1810), 27-43.
   Critical Review, s5,v5 (Apr. 1817), 327-49.
   Eclectic Review, 6 (Sept. 1810), 788-800.
   Gentleman's Magazine, 81^1 (May 1811), 458-60.
   Gentleman's Magazine, 87 (June 1817), 528-29.
   Literary Chronicle, 1 (Dec. 11-25, 1819), 467-69, 486-87,
     503-05.
   Literary Gazette, Apr. 26, 1817, p. 213.
   Literary Gazette, Oct. 30-Nov. 20, 1819, 689-90, 710-11,

Southey, Robert (continued)
    727-29, 743.
  Monthly Magazine, 30 (Jan. 31, 1811), 654-55.
  Monthly Review, 69 (Dec. 1812), 337-52.
  Monthly Review, 87 (Nov. 1818), 267-78.
  Quarterly Review, 4 (Nov. 1810), 454-74.
  Quarterly Review, 18 (Oct. 1817), 99-128.

Omniana; or, Horae Otiosiores. 1812. (Pr)
  British Critic, 40 (Nov. 1812), 540-41.
  Critical Review, s4,v3 (Feb. 1813), 205-09.
  European Magazine, 65 (Feb. 1814), 130.
  Monthly Review, 73 (Jan. 1814), 108-11.

The Life of Nelson. 1813. (Pr)
  Antijacobin Review, 45 (July-Aug. 1813), 72-89, 138-60.
  British Critic, 42 (Oct. 1813), 360-66.
  British Review, 5 (Oct. 1813), 167-96.
  Critical Review, s4,v4 (July 1813), 11-26.
  Eclectic Review, s2,v1 (June 1814), 606-22.
  Gentleman's Magazine, 83² (Aug. 1813), 137-38.
  Literary Panorama, 13 (July 1813), 959-61.

Carmen Triumphale, for the Commencement of the Year 1814.
1814. (P)
  Critical Review, s4,v5 (Feb. 1814), 203-08.
  Eclectic Review, s2,v1 (Apr. 1814), 431-36.
  Edinburgh Review, 22 (Jan. 1814), 447-54.
  European Magazine, 66 (Nov. 1814), 427-28.
  Monthly Review, 73 (Apr. 1814), 428-31.
  Scourge, 7 (Feb. 1, 1814), 122-30.
  Theatrical Inquisitor, 4 (Feb. 1814), 103-04.

Odes to the Prince Regent, the Emperor of Russia, and the
King of Prussia. 1814. (P)
  British Critic, ns,v2 (July 1814), 95-98.
  Critical Review, s4,v6 (Sept. 1814), 313.
  Eclectic Review, s2,v2 (Aug. 1814), 179-81.
  Gentleman's Magazine, 84² (Oct. 1814), 359.
  Literary Panorama, 15 (Aug. 1814), 1045-52.
  New Annual Register, 35 (1814), [360-61].
  Satirist (Tripod), 15 (July 1814), 42-52.

Roderick, the Last of the Goths. 1814. (P)
  Augustan Review, 1 (Aug. 1815), 380-93.
  British Critic, ns,v3 (Apr. 1815), 353-89.
  British Review, 6 (Nov. 1815), 287-306.
  Catholicon, 3 (Nov.-Dec. 1816), 175-79, 225-27.
  Champion, Jan. 1, 1815, pp. 423-24.
  Christian Observer, 14 (Sept. 1815), 592-616.
  Critical Review, s5,v1 (Jan. 1815), 28-38.
  Eclectic Review, s2,v3 (Apr. 1815), 352-68.
  Edinburgh Review, 25 (June 1815), 1-31.

Southey, Robert (continued)
   Monthly Review, 76 (Mar. 1815), 225-40.
   New Annual Register, 35 (1814), [359].
   New Monthly Magazine, 2 (Jan. 1815), 549.
   Quarterly Review, 13 (Apr. 1815), 83-113.
   Theatrical Inquisitor, 5 (Dec. 1814), 389-93.

The Minor Poems of Robert Southey. 1815. (P)
   Monthly Review, 78 (Oct. 1815), 181-85.

The Poet's Pilgrimage to Waterloo. 1816. (P)
   Antijacobin Review, 50 (June 1816), 521-37.
   Augustan Review, 3 (July 1816), 45-54.
   British Critic, ns,v6 (July 1816), 27-40.
   Champion, May 19, 1816, p. 158.
   Critical Review, s5,v3 (May 1816), 470-82.
   Eclectic Review, s2,v6 (July 1816), 1-18.
   European Magazine, 70 (Nov. 1816), 438-39.
   Monthly Review, 80 (June 1816), 189-99.
   Scourge and Satirist, 12 (Aug. 1816), 129-41.

The Lay of the Laureate. Carmen Nuptiale. 1816. (P)
   Augustan Review, 3 (Aug. 1816), 151-55.
   British Critic, ns,v6 (July 1816), 40-45.
   British Review, 8 (Aug. 1816), 189-93.
   Champion, June 30, 1816, p. 206.
   Critical Review, s5,v4 (July 1816), 16-26.
   Eclectic Review, s2,v6 (Aug. 1816), 196-204.
   Edinburgh Review, 26 (June 1816), 441-49.
   Examiner, July 7-14, 1816, pp. 426-28, 441-43.
   Monthly Review, 82 (Jan. 1817), 91-97.
   New Monthly Magazine, 6 (Aug. 1816), 55.

A Letter to William Smith, Esq. M. P. 1817. (Pr)
   British Critic, s2,v7 (May 1817), 437-38.
   Critical Review, s5,v5 (Apr. 1817), 390-95.
   Edinburgh Review, 28 (Mar. 1817), 151-74.
   Examiner, May 4-18, 1817, pp. 284-87, 298-300, 315-18.
   Monthly Repository, 12 (May 1817), 274-76, 301-02.
   Monthly Review, 83 (June 1817), 223-24.
   New Monthly Magazine, 7 (June 1817), 444.

Wat Tyler, a Dramatic Poem. (Anon.) 1817. (P)
   Black Dwarf, Mar. 26, 1817, pp. 139-43.
   British Critic, ns,v7 (May 1817), 437-48.
   Critical Review, s5,v5 (Feb. 1817), 187-89.
   Edinburgh Review, 28 (Mar. 1817), 151-74.
   Examiner, Mar. 9, 1817, pp. 157-59.
   Literary Gazette, Mar. 29, 1817, pp. 147-48.
   Monitor, a Collection of Essays, 1 (Apr. 1817), 37-43.
   Monthly Repository, 12 (Mar. 1817), 172-74.
   Monthly Review, 82 (Mar. 1817), 313-17.
   New Monthly Magazine, 7 (Apr. 1817), 250.

Southey, Robert (concluded)
　　Theatrical Inquisitor, 10 (May 1817), 370-75.

　　The Byrth, Lyf, and Actes of Kyng Arthur. 1817. (Pr)
　　　Monthly Review, 87 (Dec. 1818), 370-82.

　　The Life of Wesley; and the Rise and Progress of Methodism.
　　1820. (Pr)
　　　Antijacobin Review, 58 (May-June, Aug. 1820), 257-66,
　　　　329-44, 505-17.
　　　Blackwood's Edinburgh Magazine, 15 (Feb. 1824), 208-19.
　　　British Critic, ns,v14 (July-Aug. 1820), 1-32, 164-85.
　　　British Review, 15 (June 1820), 455-92.
　　　Christian Observer, 19 (Nov. 1820), 738-60.
　　　Eclectic Review, s2,v15 (Jan. 1821), 1-30.
　　　Edinburgh Magazine and Literary Miscellany (Scots Maga-
　　　　zine), s2,v6 (May 1820), 405-08.
　　　Gentleman's Magazine, 90¹ (June 1820), 532-35.
　　　Imperial Magazine, 2 (June-Sept. 1820), 475-79, 546-54,
　　　　759-65.
　　　Investigator, 1 (Sept. 1820), 367-409.
　　　Lady's Monthly Museum, s3,v11 (June 1820), 333-34.
　　　Literary and Statistical Magazine, 4 (Aug. 1820), 282-300.
　　　Literary Gazette, Mar. 25-Apr. 22, 1820, pp. 203-06, 213-
　　　　15, 231-33, 246-48, 263-66.
　　　(Baldwin's) London Magazine, 2 (Aug. 1820), 190-94.
　　　(Gold's) London Magazine, 1 (May 1820), 529-33.
　　　Monthly Magazine, 49 (June 1820), 448-49.
　　　Monthly Review, 96 (Sept. 1821), 26-43.
　　　Quarterly Review, 24 (Oct. 1820), 1-55.

Southwood, T.
　　Delworth; or Elevated Generosity. 1808. (F)
　　　British Critic, 33 (Feb. 1809), 185-86.
　　　Critical Review, s3,v15 (Oct. 1808), 221.
　　　Monthly Review, ns,v59 (June 1809), 220.
　　　Satirist, 6 (June 1810), 623-24.

Spalding, Mrs. _____.
　　Lines on Seeing His Royal Highness the Duke of York's Let-
　　ter of the 24th of September, 1799. (P)
　　　British Critic, 16 (Aug. 1800), 201.

Spence, Elizabeth Isabella.
　　Helen Sinclair. 1799. (F)
　　　Critical Review, ns,v26 (Aug. 1799), 477.
　　　Monthly Review, ns,v29 (May 1799), 89.

　　The Nobility of the Heart, a Novel. 1805. (F)
　　　Critical Review, s3,v5 (June 1805), 218.
　　　Lady's Monthly Museum, 15 (Sept. 1805), 200.
　　　Lady's Monthly Museum, 15 (Oct. 1805), 270.
　　　Literary Journal, a Review..., 4 (Dec. 1804), 650-51.

Monthly Magazine, Suppl. v19 (July 28, 1805), 660.
Monthly Mirror, 20 (July 1805), 34.
Monthly Review, ns,v49 (Feb. 1806), 207-08.

The Wedding Day, a Novel. 1807. (F)
    Annual Review, 6 (1807), 667.
    Antijacobin Review, 30 (May 1808), 70-72.
    British Critic, 32 (Nov. 1808), 521.
    Critical Review, s3,v11 (Aug. 1807), 437-38.
    Monthly Magazine, Suppl. v25 (July 30, 1808), 597.
    Monthly Review, ns,v59 (July 1809), 321.

The Curate and His Daughter, a Cornish Tale. 1813. (F)
    British Critic, 41 (Apr. 1813), 411.
    Critical Review, s4,v4 (Sept. 1813), 327-29.
    Monthly Review, ns,v71 (June 1813), 212.

A Traveller's Tale of the Last Century. 1819. (F)
    European Magazine, 75 (May 1819), 440-41.
    Gentleman's Magazine, 89^1 (Suppl. Jan.-June 1819), 627.
    Monthly Review, ns,v90 (Oct. 1819), 215.

Spencer, Mrs. Walter.
    Commemorative Feelings, or Miscellaneous Poems. 1812. (P)
    British Critic, 40 (Aug. 1812), 183-84.

Spencer, William Robert.
    Urania; or the Illuminé. A Comedy. 1802. (D)
    Annual Review, 1 (1802), 693-94.
    British Critic, 22 (July 1803), 82-83.
    Critical Review, ns,v35 (Aug. 1802), 476.
    Monthly Magazine, Suppl. v14 (Jan. 25, 1803), 600.
    Monthly Review, ns,v39 (Nov. 1802), 324-25.
    New Annual Register, 23 (1802), [320].
    Poetical Register, 2 (1802), 454.

The Year of Sorrow, Written in the Spring of 1803. 1804.
(P)
    Annual Review, 3 (1804), 574-75.
    British Critic, 23 (Apr. 1804), 431-32.
    Lady's Monthly Museum, 14 (Feb. 1805), 129-30.
    Literary Journal, a Review..., 3 (Apr. 16, 1804), 412-13.
    Monthly Magazine, Suppl. v17 (July 28, 1804), 666.
    Monthly Review, 45 (Nov. 1804), 288-92.
    New Annual Register, 25 (1804), [352].
    Poetical Register, 4 (1804), 499.

Poems. 1811. (P)
    Antijacobin Review, 40 (Sept. 1811), 32-37.
    British Critic, 38 (Sept. 1811), 224-27.
    Critical Review, s3,v24 (Nov. 1811), 317-23.
    Glasgow Magazine, 2 (Sept. 1811), 386.
    Monthly Review, 67 (Jan. 1812), 54-60.

Poetical Register, 8 (1811), 605.
Quarterly Review, 7 (June 1812), 438-40.
Satirist, 9 (Dec. 1811), 476-81.

Spenser, Edmund, the Younger.
　The Ugly Club. A Dramatic Caricature. (D)
　　Critical Review, ns,v28 (Jan. 1800), 116.
　　Monthly Review, ns,v31 (Feb. 1800), 210-11.

Stanhope, Louisa Sidney.
　The Crusaders; an Historical Romance of the Twelfth Century.
　1820. (F)
　　Monthly Review, ns,v93 (Dec. 1820), 437.

Stanley, Rev. Jacob.
　The Hunting Vicar; and the Commissioners, alias the Wood-
　cock and the Snipes. 1820. (P)
　　Imperial Magazine, 2 (Dec. 1820), 1045-46.

Stanley, William.
　The Rejected Addresses; or, the Triumph of the Ale-King.
　A Farce. 1813. (P)
　　Critical Review, s4,v4 (Aug. 1813), 216-17.
　　Gentleman's Magazine, 83^2 (Aug. 1813), 150-51.
　　Monthly Review, 74 (May 1814), 103.
　　New Review, 2 (Nov. 1813), 479-82.

Starke, Mariana.
　The Tournament, a Tragedy. 1800. (D)
　　British Critic, 16 (Oct. 1800), 438.
　　Monthly Magazine, Suppl. v9 (July 20, 1800), 641.
　　Monthly Mirror, 9 (Jan. 1800), 39-40.

　The Beauties of Carlo Maria Maggi Paraphrased. To Which
　Are Added Sonnets. 1811. (P)
　　British Critic, 37 (Apr. 1811), 411-12.
　　Critical Review, s3,v22 (Apr. 1811), 442.
　　Monthly Review, 66 (Nov. 1811), 324-25.
　　Poetical Register, 8 (1811), 635.

Stebbing, Henry.
　The Minstrel of the Glen, and Other Poems. 1818. (P)
　　Fireside Magazine (quoting New Monthly Magazine), 1 (Apr.
　　　1819), 160.
　　Fireside Magazine (quoting Monthly Review and Gentleman's
　　　Magazine), 1 (Sept. 1819), 345-360.
　　Gentleman's Magazine, 89^1 (June 1819), 547-48.
　　Literary Gazette, Dec. 19, 1818, pp. 804-05.
　　Monthly Review, 89 (July 1819), 328-29.
　　New Monthly Magazine, 11 (Feb. 1819), 61-62.

Steers, H.
　Elegy to the Memory of Francis, Late Duke of Bedford.

1802. (P)
  Antijacobin Review, 13 (Oct. 1802), 180.
  British Critic, 20 (Sept. 1802), 320.
  Critical Review, s2,v36 (Dec. 1802), 476.
  Gentleman's Magazine, 72^2 (Sept. 1802), 846.
  Monthly Mirror, 14 (Aug. 1802), 103.
  Monthly Review, 38 (Aug. 1802), 439.
  New Annual Register, 23 (1802), [318].

Aesop's Fables, Now Versified from the Best English Editions. 1803. (P)
  British Critic, 22 (Aug. 1803), 192-93.

Steers, W.
  Leisure Hours, or Morning Amusements. 1811. (P)
    British Critic, 39 (Jan. 1812), 79.
    Critical Review, s3,v24 (Dec. 1811), 442-43.
    Eclectic Review, 8 (Mar. 1812), 318.
    Monthly Review, 67 (Mar. 1812), 324-25.
    Poetical Register, 8 (1811), 621.

Stephenson, Benjamin.
  Attempts at Poetry, or Trifles in Verse. By Ebn Osn.
  1807. (P)
    Critical Review, s3,v12 (Oct. 1807), 220-21.
    Gentleman's Magazine, 77^2 (Sept. 1807), 844.
    Monthly Mirror, ns,v2 (Nov. 1807), 331-32.
    Monthly Review, 57 (Sept. 1808), 97.
    Universal Magazine, ns,v8 (Dec. 1807), 511.

Sterndale, Mary.
  The Panorama of Youth. 1807. (P)
    Antijacobin Review, 26 (Apr. 1807), 397-99.
    Literary Panorama, 2 (May 1807), 257-58.

Sternhold and Hopkins.
  The Canonization of Thomas ****, Esq. Who Has Lately Erect-
  ed at East L***h, Dorset, a Monastery.... 1801. (P)
    Antijacobin Review, 10 (Oct. 1801), 205-06.
    British Critic, 19 (Feb. 1802), 189.
    Critical Review, s2,v32 (June 1801), 230.
    Monthly Review, 35 (Aug. 1801), 436-37.

Stevens, Mrs. Grace Buchanan.
  Llewellen; or, the Vale of Phlinlimmon. 1818. (F)
    Fireside Magazine (quoting Monthly Review), 1 (Aug.
      1819), 311.
    Monthly Review, ns,v89 (June 1819), 210.
    Scots Magazine, ns,v2 (May 1818), 457-58.

Stevens, J. L.
  Fancy's Wreath; a Collection of Poems. (P)
    Gentleman's Magazine, 90^2 (Oct. 1820), 346.

Monthly Magazine, 50 (Dec. 1820), 458.
New Monthly Magazine, 14 (Dec. 1820), 687.

Stewart, Rev. Charles Edward.
A Collection of Trifles in Verse. 1797.
Antijacobin Review, 2 (Feb. 1799), 146-49.

Critical Trifles, in a Familiar Epistle to John Fisher, Esq.
1797. (P)
Antijacobin Review, 2 (Feb. 1799), 149-51.
British Critic, 11 (Apr. 1798), 436.
Monthly Mirror, 5 (Jan. 1798), 31-32.

Extracts from the Regicide; an Heroic Poem. (Anon.) 1801.
(P)
Antijacobin Review, 9 (May 1801), 73-76.
Critical Review, s2,v33 (Dec. 1801), 460.

The Argument (in Verse) of the Foxiad; an Historical Poem.
By the Author of The Regicide. 1803. (P)
Antijacobin Review, 14 (Apr. 1803), 418-25.
British Critic, 21 (May 1803), 551-52.
Flowers of Literature, 2 (1803), 441-42.

Charles's Small Clothes. A National Ode. By the Author of
The Foxiad. 1808. (P)
Antijacobin Review, 30 (June 1808), 178-83.
British Critic, 32 (July 1808), 72.
Critical Review, s3,v14 (June 1808), 217.
Gentleman's Magazine, 78[2] (Nov. 1808), 1015.
Satirist, 3 (Oct. 1808), 320-23.
Satirist, 5 (Dec. 1809), 624. (Excerpts from other re-
views.)

Last Trifles in Verse. (P)
Antijacobin Review, 46 (May 1814), 462-70.
British Critic, 41 (Apr. 1813), 406.
Gentleman's Magazine, 83[2] (Dec. 1813), 583.
Satirist, ns,v2 (June 1813), 575.

The Aliad, an Heroic Epistle to Clootz Redivivus. By the
Author of The Regicide, The Foxiad, and Charles's Small-
Clothes. 1815. (P)
Antijacobin Review, 49 (Aug. 1815), 147-51.
Gentleman's Magazine, Suppl. 85[1] (Jan.-June 1815), 610-11.

The Political Works, in Verse, of the Rev. Charles Edward
Stewart; Consisting of The Regicide, The Foxiad, Charles's
Small-Clothes. 1816. (P)
Critical Review, s5,v3 (Mar. 1816), 283-300.

Stewart, Jessie.
Ode to Dr. Thomas Percy, Lord Bishop of Dromore; Occasioned

521

by Reading the Reliques of Ancient English Poetry. 1804. (P)
   Annual Review, 3 (1804), 597.
   British Critic, 26 (July 1805), 76-77.
   Imperial Review, 4 (Mar. 1805), 341-45.
   Monthly Mirror, 18 (Aug. 1804), 103-05.
   North British Magazine and Review, 3 (Jan. 1805), 38-39.
   Poetical Register, 4 (1804), 497.

Stewart, John.
   Britons United, or Britannia Roused. In Humble Verse, upon
   Different Subjects before and Subsequent to the Battle of
   the Nile. 1800. (P)
   Antijacobin Review, 7 (Dec. 1800), 417.
   British Critic, 17 (Feb. 1801), 190.
   Monthly Review, 35 (June 1801), 211-12.

   The Challenge Accepted. A Poem. 1801. (P)
   Antijacobin Review, 8 (Apr. 1801), 416.

   The Pleasures of Love. A Poem. 1806. (P)
   Annual Review, 4 (1805), 591.
   British Critic, 28 (Aug. 1806), 197-98.
   Critical Review, s3,v7 (Feb. 1806), 183-87.
   Literary Journal, a Review..., 5 (Dec. 1805), 1247-51.
   Monthly Magazine, Suppl. v20 (Jan. 31, 1806), 614.
   Monthly Mirror, 21 (Apr. 1806), 257.
   Monthly Review, 50 (June 1806), 209-10.
   New Annual Register, 26 (1805), [356].
   Poetical Register, 6 (1806), 500.

   The Resurrection. A Poem. 1808. (P)
   Annual Review, 7 (1808), 537.
   Antijacobin Review, 32 (Mar. 1809), 306-07.
   British Critic, 31 (Feb. 1808), 192-93.
   Critical Review, s3,v15 (Sept. 1808), 101-02.
   Eclectic Review, 4 (Apr. 1808), 365-69.
   Monthly Magazine, Suppl. v25 (July 30, 1808), 595.
   Monthly Pantheon, 1 (June 1808), 80-81.
   Monthly Review, 59 (June 1809), 174-79.
   New Annual Register, 29 (1808), [405-06].
   Oxford Review, 3 (Mar. 1808), 274-79.
   Poetical Register, 7 (1808), 552-53.
   Satirist, 2 (May 1808), 310-14.
   Satirist, 5 (Oct. 1809), 414-15.

   Genevieve; or, the Spirit of the Drave. A Poem. With Odes
   and Other Poems. (P)
   Poetical Register, 8 (1810), 569.

Stiver, Alexander.
   Love and War; an Historical Romance. 1814. (P)
   Critical Review, s4,v5 (June 1814), 648.

Stockdale, Mary.
  The Effusions of the Heart. 1798. (P)
    British Critic, 11 (Feb. 1798), 193-94.
    Critical Review, s2,v22 (Mar. 1798), 352.
    Monthly Mirror, 5 (Apr. 1798), 225-26.
    Monthly Visitor, 3 (Feb. 1798), 216.

  Sincerity's Offering: An Ode on His Majesty, Written during
  a Period of Public Affliction. 1804. (P)
    Poetical Register, 4 (1804), 499-500.

  The Widow and Her Orphan Family, an Elegy. 1812. (P)
    Antijacobin Review, 42 (May 1812), 68.
    Critical Review, s4,v1 (Jan. 1812), 107-08.
    Eclectic Review, 8 (Mar. 1812), 319.
    Monthly Review, 67 (Mar. 1812), 323.

  A Plume for Sir Samuel Romilly; or, the Offering of the
  Fatherless: An Elegy. (P)
    Gentleman's Magazine, 89^2 (Oct. 1819), 338.

  A Shroud for Sir Samuel Romilly: An Elegy. (P)
    Gentleman's Magazine, 89^2 (Oct. 1819), 338.

Stockdale, John Joseph, Jr.
  Albio-Hibernia; or the Isle of Erin. A Poem. 1799. (P)
    Antijacobin Review, 4 (Nov. 1799), 330.
    British Critic, 14 (Oct. 1799), 428.
    Critical Review, s2,v28 (Feb. 1800), 232.
    Monthly Magazine, Suppl. v8 (Jan. 20, 1800), 1052.
    Monthly Mirror, 8 (Nov. 1799), 284.

Stockdale, Percival.
  The Invincible Island: a Poem. With Introductory Observations on the Present War. 1797. (P)
    Analytical Review, 27 (Jan. 1798), 74-75.
    British Critic, 11 (Feb. 1798), 194-95.
    Critical Review, s2,v22 (Feb. 1798), 231.
    European Magazine, 33 (Jan. 1798), 41.
    Gentleman's Magazine, 68^1 (Jan. 1798), 57-59.
    Monthly Mirror, 5 (Mar. 1798), 165.
    Monthly Review, 26 (May 1798), 92.
    Monthly Visitor, 3 (Jan. 1798), 88-94.

  Poems. 1800. (P)
    British Critic, 17 (Mar. 1801), 311-13.
    Monthly Mirror, 10 (Sept. 1800), 154-55.

  Lectures on the Truly Eminent English Poets. 1807. (P1)
    Annual Review, 6 (1807), 654-58.
    British Critic, 33 (May 1809), 512-15.
    Critical Review, s3,v14 (Feb. 1808), 142-48.
    Eclectic Review, 4 (Mar. 1808), 227.

Edinburgh Review, 12 (Apr. 1808), 62-82.
London Review, 2 (Aug. 1809), 118-37.
New Annual Register, 29 (1808), [403-04].
Universal Magazine, ns,v9 (June 1808), 511-14.

The Poetical Works of Percival Stockdale. (P)
Poetical Register, 8 (1811), 608.

Stone, Anne.
Features of the Youthful Mind; or, Tales for Juvenile Read-
ers. 1802. (F)
British Critic, 21 (May 1803), 556.

Stone, John Moore.
The Vale of Trent; a Poem. (Anon.) 1801. (P)
Antijacobin Review, 9 (July 1801), 305.
British Critic, 17 (Apr. 1801), 432.
Critical Review, s2,v32 (July 1801), 348-49.
Monthly Magazine, 11 (July 20, 1801), 605.
Monthly Review, 35 (May 1801), 110-11.

Stoney, T. U.
The Tears of Granta, a Satire; Addressed to the Undergrad-
uates in the University of Cambridge. (Anon.) 1812. (P)
Antijacobin Review, 43 (Dec. 1812), 326-35.
Critical Review, s4,v3 (Feb. 1813), 216-18.

Strange, T.
A Hint to Britain's Arch-Enemy Buonaparte. 1804. (P)
Antijacobin Review, 17 (Mar. 1804), 308.
British Critic, 24 (Oct. 1804), 437.
European Magazine, 45 (Mar. 1804), 220.
Imperial Review, 1 (Apr. 1804), 635.
Literary Journal, 3 (Apr. 2, 1804), 358.
Monthly Mirror, 18 (Nov. 1804), 321-22.
Monthly Review, 43 (Apr. 1804), 437.

Straubenzee, George Van.
The Impetus, a Poem; on the Threatened Invasion. 1803.
(P)
Literary Journal, a Review..., 2 (Oct. 1, 1803), 352.
Monthly Mirror, 16 (Sept. 1803), 192.

Strong, Elizabeth Kirkham.
Poems. (P)
Gentleman's Magazine, 68[2] (Aug. 1798), 700-01.

Struthers, John.
The Poor Man's Sabbath. A Poem. 1804. (P)
Eclectic Review, 2 (Sept. 1806), 745-46.
North British Magazine and Review, 2 (Oct. 1804), 240-42.
Poetical Register, 7 (1808), 562-63.
Scots Magazine, 67 (Oct. 1805), 774-75.

The Peasant's Death; and Other Poems. 1806. (P)
   Cabinet, 1 (Apr. 1807), 114-16.
   Cyclopaedian Magazine, 1 (Apr. 1807), 220-21.
   Eclectic Review, 4 (Mar. 1808), 247-49.
   Literary Annual Register, 2 (Oct. 1808), 455-56.

   Poems, Moral and Religious. 1814. (P)
   Christian Observer, 13 (Aug. 1814), 520-25.

Strutt, Joseph.
   The Test of Guilt; or, Traits of Antient Superstition. A
   Dramatic Tale. 1808. (P)
   British Critic, 31 (June 1808), 658-59.
   Cabinet, 3 (Feb.-Mar. 1808), 119-20, 183-88.
   Critical Review, s3,v14 (May 1808), 56-58.
   European Magazine, 53 (Mar. 1808), 194-98.
   Gentleman's Magazine, 78[1] (Feb. 1808), 137-39.
   Literary Annual Register, 2 (Apr. 1808), 156.
   Literary Panorama, 3 (Mar. 1808), 1193-96.
   Monthly Magazine, Suppl. v25 (July 30, 1808), 597.
   Poetical Register, 7 (1808), 577-78.

   Queenhoo-Hall, a Romance; and Ancient Times, a Drama. 1808.
   (P-D)
   Annual Review, 7 (1808), 605-07.
   British Critic, 32 (July 1808), 75.
   Critical Review, s3,v14 (Aug. 1808), 406-09.
   European Magazine, 54 (July-Aug. 1808), 27-32, 118-23.
   Gentleman's Magazine, 78[2] (Oct. 1808), 919-20.
   Lady's Monthly Museum, ns,v5 (July 1808), 34-41.
   Literary Panorama, 4 (Aug. 1808), 874-82.
   Monthly Review, ns,v58 (Jan. 1809), 40-45.
   Scots Magazine, 70 (Oct. 1808), 752-56.
   Universal Magazine, ns,v10 (Aug. 1808), 130-40.

Stuart, James.
   Poems on Various Subjects. 1811. (P)
   Monthly Review, 67 (Mar. 1812), 323.

Student of Divinity in the University, A.
   See Rev. Hamilton Paul.

Styles, John.
   An Essay on the Character [and the] Immoral and Anti-Chris-
   tian Tendency of the Stage. 1806. (Pr)
   Annual Review, 5 (1806), 569-74.
   Critical Review, s5,v2 (Nov. 1815), 528-34.
   Eclectic Review, 3 (Apr. 1807), 335-39.

   The Legend of the Velvet Cushion, in a Series of Letters
   to My Brother Jonathan, Who Lives in the Country. By
   Jeremiah Ringletub. 1815. (F)
   Eclectic Review, ns,v4 (July 1815), 75-86.

Monthly Review, ns,v78 (Sept. 1815), 57-61.

A New Covering to the Velvet Cushion. (Anon.) 1815. (F)
   Antijacobin Review, 49 (Oct. 1815), 313-18.
   Baptist Magazine, 7 (July 1815), 296-300.
   Critical Review, s5,v1 (Mar. 1815), 317.
   Eclectic Review, ns,v3 (June 1815), 595-99.
   Monthly Review, ns,v77 (May 1815), 110.
   Quarterly Review, 13 (Apr. 1815), 113-19.

Styrke, Issachar.
   Euripides's Alcestis Burlesqued. (P)
      Gentleman's Magazine, 86[1] (Apr. 1816), 342-43.

Sullivan, Mary Ann.
   Owen Castle, or Which Is the Heroine? 1816. (F)
      Critical Review, s5,v4 (July 1816), 91.

Sullivan, Michael John (or O'Sullivan?).
   The Prince of the Lake, or O'Donoghue of Rosse. 1815. (P)
      Monthly Review, 84 (Nov. 1817), 319-20.

Sullivan, William Francis.
   The Test of Union and Loyalty, on the Long-Threatened
   French Invasion. 1803. 4th ed. (1st ed. 1797) (P)
      Antijacobin Review, 17 (Feb. 1804), 189.
      Monthly Review, 42 (Nov. 1803), 328.

   The Recluse, or the Hermit of Windermere. 1819. (F)
      Theatrical Inquisitor, 14 (Feb. 1819), 137-38.

Summersett, Henry.
   Probable Incidents; or, Scenes in Life. 1797. (F)
      Critical Review, ns,v22 (Mar. 1798), 357-58.
      Monthly Mirror, 5 (Apr. 1798), 224.

   Mad Man of the Mountain, a Tale. 1799. (F)
      Antijacobin Review, 6 (May 1800), 55.
      Critical Review, ns,v29 (May 1800), 115.

   Martyn of Fenrose; or, the Wizard of the Sword. A Romance.
   1801. (F)
      British Critic, 18 (Aug. 1801), 197-98.
      Critical Review, ns,v33 (Sept. 1801), 112.
      Monthly Mirror, 15 (May 1803), 329.
      Monthly Review, ns,v40 (Feb. 1803), 207.
      Union Magazine and Imperial Register, 2 (Aug. 1801), 116.

   The Worst of Stains, a Novel. (F)
      Imperial Review, 2 (May 1804), 143.

   Maurice, the Rustic; and Other Poems. 1805. (P)
      Annual Review, 4 (1805), 622.

British Critic, 27 (Mar. 1806), 317-18.
Critical Review, s3,v7 (Feb. 1806), 214-15.
Literary Journal, a Review..., 5 (Nov. 1805), 1221-22.
Monthly Mirror, 19 (May 1805), 318-21.
Poetical Register, 6 (1806), 506.

Surr, Thomas Skinner.
  Christ's Hospital, a Poem. 1797. (P)
    British Critic, 11 (Jan. 1798), 73.
    Critical Review, s2,v22 (Jan. 1798), 102.
    Gentleman's Magazine, 68^1 (June 1798), 509.
    Monthly Mirror, 6 (July 1798), 35.
    Monthly Review, 26 (May 1798), 97.

  George Barnwell. A Novel. 1798. (F)
    Critical Review, ns,v24 (Dec. 1798), 472.
    Monthly Magazine, Suppl. v7 (July 20, 1799), 541.
    Monthly Mirror, 7 (Mar. 1799), 164.
    Monthly Visitor, 6 (Feb. 1799), 203.

  Splendid Misery. A Novel. 1801. (F)
    Critical Review, ns,v35 (May 1802), 112.
    Monthly Magazine, Suppl. v14 (Jan. 25, 1803), 599.

  A Winter in London; or, Spectacles of Fashion. 1806. (F)
    La Belle Assemblée, Suppl. v1 (1806), 28-32.
    British Critic, 27 (June 1806), 672.
    Critical Review, s3,v8 (July 1806), 318-20.
    European Magazine, 50 (July 1806), 44-47.
    Flowers of Literature, 5 (1806), 497, 518.
    Literary Journal, a Review..., ns,v1 (Jan. 1806), 107.
    Monthly Magazine, Suppl. v21 (July 25, 1806), 609.
    Monthly Mirror, 22 (Sept. 1806), 181.
    Monthly Review, ns,v49 (Feb. 1806), 207.

  The Mask of Fashion. A Plain Tale, with Anecdotes Foreign
  and Domestic. 1807. (F)
    Flowers of Literature, 5 (1806), 505.
    Monthly Literary Recreations, 1 (Dec. 1806), 487.

  The Magic of Wealth, a Novel. 1815. (F)
    Antijacobin Review, 48 (Apr. 1815), 357-68.
    British Critic, ns,v4 (July 1815), 106-07.
    British Lady's Magazine, 1 (June 1815), 426-27.
    Monthly Review, ns,v79 (Feb. 1816), 213.

Surrebutter, John J.
  See John Anstey.

Susurr, Simon.
  Sir Christopher Hatton's Ghost; or, a Whisper to the Fair.
  1806. (P)
    Antijacobin Review, 24 (June 1806), 194-95.

British Critic, 29 (Mar. 1807), 314-15.
Literary Journal, a Review..., ns,v2 (July 1806), 104-06.
Monthly Mirror, 22 (Aug. 1806), 108.
Poetical Register, 6 (1806), 515.

Swammerdam, Martin Gribaldus.
See William Mudford.

Swan, Charles.
The Counterfeit Saints; or, Female Fanaticism; with Other
Poems. 1819. (P)
    La Belle Assemblée, ns,v20 (Aug. 1819), 80-82.
    Literary Chronicle, 1 (Aug. 22, 1819), 228-29.
    Literary Gazette, June 19, 1819, pp. 386-87.

Epistle Dedicatory. (P)
    Monthly Magazine, 49 (May 1820), 357.

Retribution, a Poem; Addressed to Woman. 1820. (P)
    Gentleman's Magazine, 90^2 (July 1820), 54.
    Imperial Magazine, 2 (June 1820), 464-67.
    Literary Chronicle, 2 (Apr. 8, 1820), 229-30.
    Monthly Magazine, 49 (May 1820), 357.
    Monthly Review, 93 (Oct. 1820), 213-14.

Swan, James, Sr.
Stanzas Secred to the Memory of Mr. James Swan, Jun.... (P)
    Monthly Review, 86 (Aug. 1818), 445.

Swan, Simon, Barrister.
See Joseph Fawcett.

Swift, Edmund L.
Anacreon in Dublin. (Anon.) 1814. (P)
    Antijacobin Review, 46 (June 1814), 533-46.
    British Critic, ns,v2 (July 1814), 98-100.
    New Annual Register, 35 (1814), [364].
    New Review, 3 (June 1814), 528-31.

Waterloo, and Other Poems. 1815. (P)
    Antijacobin Review, 49 (Nov. 1815), 471-79.
    Augustan Review, 1 (Nov. 1815), 785-94.
    British Critic, ns,v4 (Dec. 1815), 669-70.
    Monthly Review, 80 (June 1816), 206-07.

Woman's Will--A Riddle! An Operatic Drama. 1820. (D)
    Monthly Review, ns,v93 (Dec. 1820), 434.
    Theatrical Inquisitor, ns,v1 (Aug. 1820), 139-43.

Symmons, Caroline. (See also Francis Wrangham, The Raising of
    Jairus's Daughter; also Caroline and Charles Symmons.)
The Cottage of the Var, a Tale. 1809. (F)
    British Critic, 33 (May 1809), 524.

        Critical Review, s3,v17 (July 1809), 330.
        Monthly Review, ns,v60 (Sept. 1809), 97.

Symmons, Caroline, and Charles Symmons.
    Poems. 1812. (P)
        British Critic, 42 (July 1813), 75.
        Critical Review, s4,v3 (June 1813), 594-99.
        Eclectic Review, 9 (June 1813), 624-36.
        Monthly Review, 72 (Oct. 1813), 182-91.
        New Review, 3 (Mar. 1814), 237-44.

Symmons, Charles. (See also Caroline and Charles Symmons.)
    Inez, a Tragedy. 1796. (D)
        Critical Review, ns,v22 (Mar. 1798), 326-30.

Sympson, Rev. J.
    Science Revived, or the Vision of Alfred. 1802. (P)
        British Critic, 19 (Apr. 1802), 388-94.
        Critical Review, s2,v35 (May 1802), 39-52.
        Monthly Magazine, Suppl. v13 (July 20, 1802), 656-57.
        Monthly Review, 40 (Jan. 1803), 27-30.
        New Annual Register, 23 (1802), [313].
        Poetical Register, 2 (1802), 425.

Syntax, Doctor.
    See William Combe.

Taafe, J.
    Padilla: A Tale of Palestine. 1816. (P)
        Literary Panorama, ns,v6 (June 1817), 413-16.

Talfourd, Thomas Noon.
    Poems on Various Subjects, Including a Poem on the Educa-
    tion of the Poor, an Indian Tale, and the Offering of
    Isaac, a Sacred Drama. 1811. (P-D)
        British Critic, 38 (Sept. 1811), 291-92.
        Critical Review, s3,v24 (Oct. 1811), 215-16.
        Eclectic Review, 7 (Sept. 1811), 845.
        Gentleman's Magazine, 81^2 (Oct. 1811), 341-43.
        Monthly Review, 66 (Dec. 1811), 436.
        Poetical Register, 8 (1811), 618.

Tangible, Timothy.
    The Mixture; or Too True a Tale; Being a Combination of
    Unfortunate and Fortunate Events; Proving That Playing Too
    Deep, or Gambling, Is Pernicious. 1809. (P)
        Antijacobin Review, 36 (July 1810), 312-13.
        British Critic, 36 (Nov. 1810), 519.
        Eclectic Review, 6 (July 1810), 655-57.

Tarpaulin, Timothy.
    See A. Clark.

Tartt, William Macdowal.
  Odes, Sonnets, and Other Poems. 1808. (P)
    Critical Review, s3,v14 (Aug. 1808), 444.
    Eclectic Review, 6 (Oct. 1810), 951.
    Monthly Review, 58 (Mar. 1809), 326.

Tasker, Rev. William.
  Aviragus; or, the Roman Invasion, an Historical Tragedy.
  1798. (P)
    Critical Review, ns,v22 (Feb. 1798), 231-32.
    European Magazine, 34 (Aug. 1798), 111.

  Extracts from Poems, on Naval and Military Subjects. 1799.
  (P)
    Antijacobin Review, 3 (Aug. 1799), 438.
    New London Review, 2 (July 1799), 82.

Tatlock, Eleanor.
  Poems. 1811. (P)
    Eclectic Review, 7 (May 1811), 466-67.

Taylor, Ann (née Taylor).
  The Family Mansion. A Tale. (F)
    Christian's Pocket Magazine, 2 (May 1820), 273. (Digeste
      from Eclectic Review.)
    New Monthly Magazine, 13 (Feb. 1820), 218.

Taylor, Ann (afterwards Gilbert). (Also see Ann & Jane Taylor.)
  The Wedding among the Flowers. By One of the Authors of
  Original Poems. 1808. (P)
    Literary Panorama, 6 (May 1809), 231-33.

Taylor, Ann, and Jane Taylor.
  Original Poems for Infant Minds. By Several Young Persons.
  (Anon.) 1805. (P)
    British Critic, 27 (Apr. 1806), 431.
    Critical Review, s3,v6 (Nov. 1805), 333.
    Eclectic Review, 1 (May 1805), 391.
    Eclectic Review, 1 (Dec. 1805), 952-53.
    Imperial Review, 2 (Aug. 1804), 622.
    Monthly Review, 50 (July 1806), 329.

  Rhymes for the Nursery. By the Authors of Original Poems.
  1806. (P)
    Critical Review, s3,v8 (Aug. 1806), 440.
    Monthly Mirror, 22 (Oct. 1806), 253.

  Hymns for Infant Minds. By the Authors of Original Poems,
  Rhymes for the Nursery, &c. 1810. (P)
    Literary Panorama, 8 (Oct. 1810), 1062-63.

  Correspondence between a Mother and Her Daughter at School.
  1817. (Pr)

Literary Panorama, ns,v6 (Aug. 1817), 769-72.

Taylor, Anna Maria.
Walsh Colville, or a Young Man's Entrance into Life. 1797.
(F)
British Critic, 11 (Mar. 1798), 315-16.

Taylor, George.
An Elegy on the Lamented Though Glorious Death of Admiral
the Right Honourable Horatio Viscount Nelson. (P)
Eclectic Review, 2 (Feb. 1806), 161.

The Spirit of the Mountains, with Other Poems. 1806. (P)
British Critic, 29 (Feb. 1807), 200-01.
Literary Annual Register, 1 (July 1807), 317.
Literary Journal, a Review..., ns,v2 (Sept. 1806), 331-33.
Monthly Mirror, ns,v1 (Apr. 1807), 265-66.

Taylor, George Watson.
Equanimity in Death, a Poem. 1813. (P)
New Review, 2 (Dec. 1813), 606-08.

The Cross Bath Guide; Being the Correspondence of a Respec-
table Family upon the Subject of a Late Unexpected Dis-
pensation of Honours. By Sir Joseph Cheakill. 1815. (P)
La Belle Assemblée, ns,v12 (Dec. 1815), 271-73.
British Critic, ns,v3 (June 1815), 653-54.
Critical Review, s5,v1 (May 1815), 429-34.
Eclectic Review, s2,v3 (Apr. 1815), 397-98.
Gentleman's Magazine, Suppl. v85[1] (Jan.-June 1815), 609-
10.
Monthly Review, 76 (Apr. 1815), 433-35.
New Monthly Magazine, 3 (Apr. 1815), 257.

Taylor, Jane. (See also Ann and Jane Taylor above; and Josi-
ah Conder, His Wife, and Jane Taylor above.)
Display, a Tale for Young People. 1815. (F)
British Critic, ns,v4 (July 1815), 107-08.
Critical Review, s5,v2 (Aug. 1815), 215-16.
Eclectic Review, ns,v4 (Aug. 1815), 158-67.
Gentleman's Magazine, 86[1] (Mar. 1816), p. 250.
Literary Panorama, ns,v2 (June 1815), 417-20.
Monthly Review, ns,v79 (Mar. 1816), 325.

Essays in Rhyme, on Morals and Manners. 1816. (P)
Augustan Review, 3 (Nov. 1816), 459-73.
Champion, Aug. 4, 1816, p. 246.
Christian Observer, 17 (Feb. 1818), 115-24.
Critical Review, s5,v4 (Sept. 1816), 269-76.
Eclectic Review, s2,v6 (Sept. 1816), 263-76.
Evangelical Magazine, 24 (Nov. 1816), 435-36.
Gentleman's Magazine, 86[2] (Nov. 1816), 434-35.
Literary Panorama, ns,v4 (Aug. 1816), 757-63.

Monthly Review, 82 (Apr. 1817), 432-33.

Taylor, Jefferys.
Harry's Holiday, or the Doings of One Who Had Nothing To
Do. 1818. (F)
Literary Panorama, ns,v8 (Dec. 1818), 1475.

Taylor, John.
The Caledonian Comet. (Anon.) 1810. (P)
Antijacobin Review, 36 (July 1810), 310-12.
British Critic, 36 (Aug. 1810), 180.
Eclectic Review, 6 (Oct. 1810), 951-52.
Gentleman's Magazine, 80[1] (June 1810), 554-56.
Literary Panorama, 8 (Aug. 1810), 649-51.
Monthly Mirror, ns,v7 (June 1810), 442-46.
Monthly Review, 64 (Mar. 1811), 315-16.

Poems on Several Occasions; Consisting of Sonnets, Miscel-
laneous Pieces, Prologues and Epilogues, Tales, and Imita-
tions. 1811. (P)
Antijacobin Review, 47 (July 1814), 63-68.
British Critic, 38 (Sept. 1811), 270-73.
Eclectic Review, 7 (Sept. 1811), 841.
Satirist, 10 (May 1812), 373-79.

Taylor, Joseph.
Anecdotes of Remarkable Insects; Selected from Natural His-
tory, and Interspersed with Poetry. 1817. (P)
Monthly Review, 86 (May 1818), 93-97.

Taylor, P.
Poems, or Miscellaneous Metricals, Amatory, Moral, Pathe-
tic, &c. 1814. (P)
Monthly Review, 74 (Aug. 1814), 431-32.

Taylor, Thomas.
Miscellanies in Prose and Verse. (P-Pr)
Annual Review, 5 (1806), 552-53.

Taylor, William.
Parnassian Wild Shrubs: Consisting of Odes; the Moralist,
a Series of Poetical Essays; Sonnets; and Miscellaneous
Pieces. 1814. (P)
British Critic, ns,v4 (Aug. 1815), 211-12.
Critical Review, s4,v6 (July 1814), 93.
Eclectic Review, s2,v2 (Aug. 1814), 182-83.
Lady's Monthly Museum, s2,v17 (Aug. 1814), 113-14.
Literary Panorama, ns,v1 (Oct. 1814), 82-83.
Monthly Review, 74 (Aug. 1814), 435-36.

Taylor, Rev. William Cooper.
The Seasons in England. Descriptive Poems. 1806. (P)
British Critic, 30 (Sept. 1807), 313-14.

Literary Annual Register, 2 (June 1808), 263-64.
Poetical Register, 6 (1806), 506.

Tegg, Thomas.
The Rise, Progress, and Termination of the O. P. War, in
Poetic Epistles, or Hudibrastic Letters, from Ap Simkins
in Town, to His Friend Ap Davies in Wales.... 1810. (P)
  Antijacobin Review, 35 (Feb. 1810), 200-01.
  Critical Review, s3,v19 (Mar. 1810), 333.
  Monthly Review, 62 (June 1810), 215-17.
  Poetical Register, 8 (1810), 573-74.

Temple, Mrs. _____.
Ferdinand Fitzormond; or, the Fool of Nature. 1806. (F)
  Flowers of Literature, 5 (1806), 502.
  Monthly Magazine, Suppl. v20 (Jan. 31, 1806), 616.

Temple, Henry John, Third Viscount Palmerston.
The New Whig Guide. (Anon.) 1819. (P-Pr)
  Blackwood's Edinburgh Magazine, 5 (Apr. 1819), 89-96.
  Blackwood's Edinburgh Magazine, 5 (May 1819), 197-204.
  Literary Gazette, Apr. 3, 1819, pp. 210-12.
  Monthly Magazine, 49 (May 1820), 356-57.

The Fudger Fudged; or, the Devil and T***y M***e. By the
Editor of The New Whig Guide. 1819. (P)
  Gentleman's Magazine, 89[2] (Sept. 1819), 249.
  Literary Chronicle, 1 (Aug. 14, 1819), 199-200.
  Literary Gazette, Sept. 11, 1819, pp. 584-85.
  Monthly Review, 91 (Mar. 1820), 326-27.

Temple, Laura Sophia.
Poems. 1805. (P)
  Annual Review, 4 (1805), 615.
  Antijacobin Review, 20 (Feb. 1805), 169-70.
  British Critic, 25 (May 1805), 557-59.
  Eclectic Review, 1 (Aug. 1805), 578-81.
  Imperial Review, 5 (Aug. 1805), 202.
  Lady's Monthly Museum, 14 (Apr. 1805), 275.
  Lady's Monthly Museum, 14 (June 1805), 419.
  Monthly Mirror, 19 (Apr. 1805), 241-43.
  Monthly Review, 51 (Sept. 1806), 102-03.
  Poetical Register, 5 (1805), 492.

Lyric and Other Poems. 1808. (P)
  Annual Review, 7 (1808), 528-29.
  Antijacobin Review, 34 (Nov. 1809), 289-95.
  British Critic, 32 (Sept. 1808), 297-98.
  Critical Review, s3,v14 (May 1808), 107.
  Monthly Review, 57 (Sept. 1808), 94-96.
  Poetical Register, 7 (1808), 557.
  Satirist, 6 (Feb. 1810), 205. (Excerpts from other re-
    views.)

The Siege of Zaragosa, and Other Poems. 1812. (P)
   British Critic, 39 (Apr. 1812), 413-14.
   Critical Review, s4,v1 (Mar. 1812), 324-25.
   Literary Panorama, 11 (Apr. 1812), 651-56.
   Monthly Review, 68 (July 1812), 323.

Templeman, James.
   Alphonso and Clementina, or the Triumph of Reason; together
   with a Variety of Other Entertaining Tales and Ballads. (P)
   Annual Review, 7 (1808), 518.

   Alcander and Lavinia, or the Mysterious Shriek; a Metrical
   Romance. (P)
   Annual Review, 7 (1808), 518-19.

   Gilbert, or the Young Carrier. An Amatory Rural Poem.
   (Anon.) 1808. (P)
   Annual Review, 7 (1808), 519-20.
   British Critic, 34 (July 1809), 72-73.
   Poetical Register, 7 (1808), 564.

Templeton, James.
   Poems. (P)
   Cyclopaedian Magazine, 3 (Jan. 1809), 27-29.

Tennant, William.
   Anster Fair. (Anon.) 1812. (P)
   British Critic, 40 (Sept. 1812), 300-01.
   Critical Review, s4,v2 (Aug. 1812), 217.
   Eclectic Review, s2,v4 (Aug. 1815), 125-35.
   Edinburgh Review, 24 (Nov. 1814), 174-82.
   Monthly Review, 69 (Dec. 1812), 432.
   New Monthly Magazine, 2 (Aug. 1814), 58.
   Scots Magazine, 74 (July 1812), 540-43.
   Tradesman, 14 (May-June 1815), 317-24, 483-90.

Terrot, Charles Hughes.
   Common Sense, a Poem. (Anon.) 1819. (P)
   Antijacobin Review, 57 (Feb. 1820), 523-27.
   British Review, 15 (Mar. 1820), 31-44.
   Christian's Pocket Magazine, 2 (Feb., Apr. 1820), 94, 209.
      (Digests from Eclectic Review and British Review.)
   Christian's Pocket Magazine, 3 (July 1820), 27. (Digest
      from Monthly Review.)
   Eclectic Review, s2,v13 (Jan. 1820), 85-92.
   Edinburgh Magazine and Literary Miscellany (Scots Maga-
      zine), ns,v5 (Dec. 1819), 499-502.
   Edinburgh Monthly Review, 2 (Dec. 1819), 670-84.
   Literary and Statistical Magazine, 4 (Feb. 1820), 77-82.
   Monthly Review, 92 (May 1820), 98-100.

Terry, Daniel.
   Guy Mannering; or, the Gipsey's Prophecy. A Musical Play.

1816. (D)
Theatrical Inquisitor, 8 (June 1816), 440-42.

The Antiquary, a Musical Play. (D)
Theatrical Inquisitor, 16 (Mar. 1820), 158-59.

Thackwell, Paul.
A Collection of Miscellaneous and Religious Poems. To
Which Is Added A Series of Odes. 1820. (P)
Gentleman's Magazine, 90² (Aug. 1820), 147-48.
Monthly Magazine, 50 (Sept. 1820), 168.
Monthly Review, 93 (Nov. 1820), 331-32.

Tharmott, Maria.
Sans Souci Park, or the Melange. (F)
Monthly Literary Recreations, 2 (Feb. 1807), 151.

Thelwall, John.
Poems Written Chiefly in Retirement. Effusions of Social
and Relative Feelings, &c. &c. With a Prefatory Memoir of
the Life of the Author. 1802. 2nd ed. (P)
Edinburgh Review, 2 (Apr. 1803), 197-202.

The Trident of Albion, an Epic Effusion; and an Oration on
the Influence of Elocution on Martial Enthusiasm; with an
Address to the Shade of Nelson.... 1805. (P)
Monthly Review, 49 (Feb. 1806), 218-21.

The Vestibule of Eloquence. Original Articles, Oratorical
and Poetical, Intended as Exercises in Recitation. 1810.
(P-Pr)
Antijacobin Review, 40 (Nov. 1811), 298-304.
Monthly Review, 70 (Mar. 1813), 293-305.

Thicknesse, Mrs. Ann.
The School for Fashion. 1800. (F)
British Critic, 16 (Sept. 1800), 320.
European Magazine, 38 (Aug. 1800), 123.
Flowers of Literature, 1 (1801-02), 457.
Monthly Magazine, Suppl. v10 (Jan. 20, 1801), 611.
Monthly Mirror, 10 (Oct. 1800), 232-33.
Monthly Review, ns,v35 (Aug. 1801), 430-31.

Thinks-I-to-Myself Who.
See Edward Nares.

Thirlwall, Connop.
Primitiae; or Essays and Poems, on Various Subjects, Reli-
gious, Moral, and Entertaining. 1809. (P)
Antijacobin Review, 34 (Sept. 1809), 66-75.
Le Beau Monde, 1 (May 1809), 138-39.
Critical Review, s3,v16 (Apr. 1809), 442-44.
Eclectic Review, 5 (Oct. 1809), 958-60.

European Magazine, 55 (May 1809), 392-93.
Gentleman's Magazine, 79[2] (Sept. 1809), 834-36.
Monthly Review, 60 (Oct. 1809), 220-21.

Thomas, Mrs. Elizabeth.
Purity of Heart; or the Ancient Costume, a Tale. Addressed
to the Author of Glenarvon. (Anon.) 1816. (F)
British Lady's Magazine, 4 (Dec. 1816), 397-99.
Critical Review, s5,v4 (Dec. 1816), 661.
European Magazine, 71 (Apr.-May 1817), 333-36, 432-34.
Literary Panorama, ns,v7 (Dec. 1817), 419-20.
Theatrical Inquisitor, 9 (Dec. 1816), 417-18.

The Confession; or, the Novice of St. Clare. And Other
Poems. By the Author of Purity of Heart. 1818. (P)
Antijacobin Review, 54 (May 1818), 256-60.
La Belle Assemblée, ns,v17 (June 1818), 272-74.
Gentleman's Magazine, 88[1] (June 1818), 528-29.
Literary Panorama, ns,v8 (July 1818), 587-89.
Monthly Magazine, 45 (June 1818), 436.
Monthly Review, 89 (Aug. 1819), 432.
New Monthly Magazine, 10 (Sept. 1818), 169-70.
Theatrical Inquisitor, 14 (Feb. 1819), 133-37.

Thomas, Francis Tracy.
Monk-Wood Priory. 1799. (F)
Critical Review, ns,v31 (Feb. 1801), 236.
Monthly Mirror, 8 (Nov. 1799), 284.
Monthly Review, ns,v31 (Jan. 1800), 82.
New London Review, 2 (Oct. 1799), 389.

Thomas, George.
Freedom; with Other Poems. 1816. (P)
British Critic, ns,v6 (Oct. 1816), 440-41.
Critical Review, s5,v4 (July 1816), 93.
Monthly Review, 82 (Jan. 1817), 102-03.

Thompson, Rev. Benjamin.
Original Poems. 1799. (P)
British Critic, 14 (Oct. 1799), 426-27.
Monthly Magazine, Suppl. v8 (Jan. 20, 1800), 1052.

The Happy Family. 1799. (D)
British Critic, 15 (Apr. 1800), 431.

La Perouse. 1799. (D)
British Critic, 15 (Apr. 1800), 431.

The Recal of Momus, a Bagatelle. 1804. (D)
Annual Review, 3 (1804), 606.
British Critic, 23 (June 1804), 673.
Literary Journal, a Review..., 3 (June 16, 1804), 681.
Monthly Mirror, 17 (June 1804), 397-99.

New Annual Register, 25 (1804), [354].
Poetical Register, 4 (1804), 498-99.

Oberon's Oath; or, the Paladin and the Princess. A Melo-
Dramatic Romance. 1816. (D)
   Theatrical Inquisitor, 9 (July 1816), 43-45.

Thompson, Gilbert.
   Select Translations from the Works of Homer and Horace;
   with Original Poems. 1802. (P)
      Antijacobin Review, 12 (Aug. 1802), 422-23.
      Critical Review, s2,v36 (Sept. 1802), 107-09.

Thomson, Alexander.
   Pictures of Poetry: Historical, Biographical, and Critical.
   1799. (P)
      British Critic, 16 (Nov. 1800), 510-14.
      Critical Review, s2,v27 (Nov. 1799), 260-68.
      Monthly Magazine, Suppl. v8 (Jan. 20, 1800), 1050.
      Monthly Mirror, 8 (Aug. 1799), 97-98.
      New Annual Register, 20 (1799), [264-65].
      New London Review, 2 (Sept. 1799), 288-90.

   The British Parnassus, at the Close of the Eighteenth Century, a Poem. 1801. (P)
      British Critic, 19 (Apr. 1802), 415-16.
      Critical Review, s2,v35 (May 1802), 110-11.
      Monthly Magazine, Suppl. v13 (July 20, 1802), 657-58.
      Monthly Mirror, 11 (May 1801), 317-20.
      Monthly Review, 39 (Nov. 1802), 318-20.
      Poetical Register, 1 (1801), 444.

   Sonnets, Odes, and Elegies. 1801. (P)
      Antijacobin Review, 13 (Oct. 1802), 179-80.
      Critical Review, s2,v36 (Sept. 1802), 109-11.
      Monthly Mirror, 13 (Mar. 1802), 177-79.
      Monthly Review, 39 (Nov. 1802), 320-21.
      Poetical Register, 1 (1801), 428-29.

Thomson, Mrs. William.
   Emily Dundorne; or, the Effects of Early Impressions. A
   Novel. (F)
      New London Review, 1 (Feb. 1799), 197.

   The Pride of Ancestry; or, Who Is She? 1804. (F)
      Antijacobin Review, 19 (Sept. 1804), 78-81.
      Critical Review, s3,v2 (June 1804), 235.
      Flowers of Literature, 3 (1804), 461.
      Lady's Monthly Museum, 13 (Sept. 1804), 203.
      Literary Journal, a Review..., 3 (Feb. 16, 1804), 164.
      Monthly Magazine, Suppl. v18 (Jan. 28, 1805), 595.
      Monthly Review, ns,v45 (Oct. 1804), 212.

Thomson, Anthony Todd.
  Ode to the Memory of Sir Ralph Abercromby. 1801. (P)
    Critical Review, s2,v34 (Mar. 1802), 353-54.
    Monthly Review, 36 (Oct. 1801), 216.
    Poetical Register, 1 (1801), 442.

Thomson, James.
  De Courci, a Tale; with Other Poems. (P)
    European Magazine, 71 (June 1817), 519-24.
    Fireside Magazine (quoting Monthly Review), 1 (Sept.
      1819), 345.
    Literary Gazette, (Feb. 28, 1818), 135.
    Literary Journal, 1 (Nov. 1, 1818), 541-42.
    Monthly Review, 89 (July 1819), 324.
    New Monthly Magazine, 8 (Aug. 1817), 52-53.

  A Cure for Romance. An Operatic Farce. (D)
    Theatrical Inquisitor, 15 (Oct. 1819), 205-06.

  The Shroud of Royalty; a Prince's and a Monarch's Dirge. (P)
    Literary Chronicle, 2 (Feb. 12, 1820), 99[103].
    Monthly Magazine, 49 (Mar. 1820), 165.

Thomson, Thomas.
  The Immortality of the Soul, and Other Poems. (P)
    Fireside Magazine (quoting New Monthly Magazine and
      Monthly Review), 1 (Jan., Sept. 1819), 38, 345.
    Gentleman's Magazine, 89¹ (Mar. 1819), 239.
    Monthly Review, 89 (July 1819), 324-25.
    New Monthly Magazine, 10 (Dec. 1818), 439.

Thomson, William.
  An Enquiry into the Elementary Principle of Beauty, in the
  Works of Nature and Art. To Which Is Prefixed an Introduc-
  tory Discourse on Taste. 1798.
    Monthly Mirror, 10 (Sept. 1800), 162-63.
    New London Review, 3 (May 1800), 413-15.

Thorn, Romaine Joseph.
  Lodon and Miranda. To Which Is Added, The Poor Boy, a Tale.
  1799. (P)
    Antijacobin Review, 5 (Apr. 1800), 432-334[434].
    British Critic, 14 (July 1799), 71.
    Critical Review, s3,v27 (Sept. 1799), 110-12.
    Monthly Magazine, Suppl. v8 (Jan. 20, 1800), 1052.
    Monthly Mirror, 8 (Aug. 1799), 94.
    Monthly Review, 33 (Sept. 1800), 105.
    New London Review, 2 (July 1799), 82-83.

Thornhill, Frederick.
  Poems. 1814. (P)
    Antijacobin Review, 48 (Jan. 1815), 65.
    British Critic, ns,v3 (Mar. 1815), 307-08.

Critical Review, s4,v5 (May 1814), 545-46.
Monthly Review, 76 (June 1815), 99-100.
Universal Magazine, ns,v21 (May 1814), 401-02.

Three Friends.
See Thomas Raffles, James Baldwin Brown, and Jeremiah Wiffen.

Thurlow, Edward, Lord, later Hovell-Thurlow.
Hermilda in Palestine; with Other Poems. (Anon.) 1812. (P)
British Critic, 40 (Dec. 1812), 576-81.

Althea, a Poem. (Anon.) (P)
Gentleman's Magazine, 83[1] (June 1813), 549-50.

Poems on Several Occasions. 1813. (P)
Antijacobin Review, 45 (July 1813), 61-72.
Critical Review, s4,v6 (July 1814), 60-63.
Eclectic Review, 10 (July 1813), 74-77.
Edinburgh Review, 23 (Sept. 1814), 411-24.
European Magazine, 64 (Sept. 1813), 233-35.
Gentleman's Magazine, 83[1] (Jan. 1813), 41-42.
Gentleman's Magazine, 83[2] (Oct. 1813), 353-54.
Gentleman's Magazine, 83[2] (Dec. 1813), 579.
Monthly Review, 71 (May 1813), 31-35.
New Review, 2 (Aug. 1813), 132-35.
Satirist, ns,v3 (Sept. 1813), 209-19.
Theatrical Inquisitor, 3 (Aug. 1813), 50-52.
Town Talk, 5 (Sept. 1813), 107-14.

Ariadne, a Poem. 1814. (P)
British Critic, ns,v2 (Sept. 1814), 321-24.
Edinburgh Review, 23 (Sept. 1814), 411-24.
Gentleman's Magazine, 84[2] (Aug. 1814), 149.
Monthly Review, 75 (Sept. 1814), 30-36.

Carmen Britannicum; or the Song of Britain; Written in Hon-
our of His Royal Highness George Augustus Frederick, Prince
Regent. 1814. (P)
Gentleman's Magazine, 84[2] (Sept. 1814), 252-54.
Monthly Review, 76 (Apr. 1815), 419-22.
New Monthly Magazine, 2 (Nov. 1814), 350.

The Doge's Daughter, a Poem; with Several Translations from
Anacreon and Horace. 1814. (P)
British Critic, ns,v2 (Sept. 1814), 321-24.
Edinburgh Review, 23 (Sept. 1814), 411-24.
Gentleman's Magazine, 84[1] (Apr. 1814), 357-58.
Monthly Review, 75 (Sept. 1814), 30-36.

Moonlight, a Poem; with Several Copies of Verses. 1814.
(P)
British Critic, ns,v1 (Feb. 1814), 212-15.
Champion, Jan. 23, 1814, pp. 30-31.

Critical Review, s4,v6 (July 1814), 63-65.
Edinburgh Review, 23 (Sept. 1814), 411-24.
Gentleman's Magazine, 84[1] (Jan. 1814), 53-56.
Literary Panorama, 15 (May 1814), 529-31.
Monthly Review, 75 (Sept. 1814), 30-36.
New Annual Register, 35 (1814), [362-63].
New Review, 3 (Apr. 1814), 377-79.

Thurtle, Mrs. Frances.
  Ashford Rectory; or the Spoiled Child Reformed. 1818. (F)
    Antijacobin Review, 54 (Aug. 1818), 533-37.
    Fireside Magazine (quoting Monthly Review), 1 (Sept.
      1819), 346.
    Literary Gazette, Sept. 12, 1818, p. 583.

Tierney, T.
  An Ode to Scandal. (P)
    Antijacobin Review, 15 (May 1803), 97-101.

Tighe, Mrs. Henry.
  Psyche, with Other Poems. 1811. (P)
    British Critic, 38 (Dec. 1811), 631-32.
    British Review, 1 (June 1811), 277-98.
    Critical Review, s4,v1 (June 1812), 606-09.
    Eclectic Review, 9 (Mar. 1813), 217-29.
    Gentleman's Magazine, 82[2] (Nov. 1812), 464-67.
    Glasgow Magazine, 2 (Aug. 1811), 304-05.
    Monthly Review, 66 (Oct. 1811), 138-52.
    New Annual Register, 32 (1811), [364].
    Poetical Register, 8 (1811), 604.
    Quarterly Review, 5 (May 1811), 471-85.

Tighe, William.
  The Plants, a Poem. Cantos I and II, with Notes and Occasional Poems. 1808. (P)
    Annual Review, 7 (1808), 509-12.
    Antijacobin Review, 32 (Jan. 1809), 40-49.
    British Critic, 35 (May 1810), 516-17.
    Critical Review, s3,v15 (Sept. 1808), 72-76.
    Eclectic Review, 5 (July 1809), 654-59.
    Literary Annual Register, 2 (Nov. 1808), 499-500.
    Monthly Review, 58 (Jan. 1809), 20-23.
    Poetical Register, 7 (1808), 553.

  The Plants, a Poem. Cantos III and IV, with Notes and Observations. 1811. (P)
    British Critic, 38 (Aug. 1811), 185-87.
    Critical Review, s3,v23 (July 1811), 309-16.
    Monthly Review, 66 (Nov. 1811), 250-54.
    New Annual Register, 32 (1811), [364].
    Poetical Register, 8 (1811), 608.

Tindal, Rev. William.

The Evils and Advantages of Genius Contrasted, a Poetical
Essay. 1803. (P)
  British Critic, 24 (July 1804), 77-78.
  Critical Review, s3,v1 (Jan. 1804), 114-15.
  Gentleman's Magazine, 75[1] (Feb. 1805), 140.
  Monthly Review, 44 (May 1804), 101.

Tit, Tom.
  The Eagle's Masque. 1808. (P)
    Critical Review, s3,v14 (Aug. 1808), 445.
    Monthly Review, 57 (Sept. 1809), 97.

Tobin, John.
  The Honey Moon, a Comedy. 1805. (D)
    Annual Review, 4 (1805), 641-42.
    Antijacobin Review, 21 (May 1805), 69.
    British Critic, 26 (Aug. 1805), 202-03.
    Critical Review, s3,v4 (Apr. 1805), 442-44.
    Flowers of Literature, 4 (1805), 424.
    Literary Journal, 5 (Feb. 1805), 205.
    Monthly Magazine, Suppl. v20 (Jan. 31, 1806), 616.
    Monthly Mirror, 20 (Oct. 1805), 262.
    Poetical Register, 5 (1805), 502-03.

  The Curfew, a Play. 1807. (D)
    Annual Review, 6 (1807), 593-98.
    Cabinet, 1 (June 1807), 262-63.
    Critical Review, s3,v11 (June 1807), 219-22.
    Monthly Magazine, Suppl. v23 (July 30, 1807), 643-44.
    Oxford Review, 1 (Apr. 1807), 454-56.
    Poetical Register, 6 (1807), 563.

  The School for Authors, a Comedy. 1809. (D)
    British Critic, 34 (Oct. 1809), 406-07.
    Poetical Register, 7 (1808), 581.

  The Faro Table; or the Guardians. A Comedy. 1816. (D)
    Monthly Review, ns,v82 (Jan. 1817), 103-04.
    Theatrical Inquisitor, 9 (Nov. 1816), 345-46.

  Memoirs of the Late John Tobin, with a Selection from His
  Unpublished Writings. By Miss Benger. (D-P)
    Gentleman's Magazine, 90[1] (Mar. 1820), 244-45.

Tomline, Edward Pretyman.
  Poema, Numismate Annuo Dignatum, et in Curia Cantabrigiensi
  Recitatum. (P)
    Monthly Review, 48 (Sept. 1805), 37-40.

Tomlins, Elizabeth Sophia.
  Tributes of Affection; with the Slave and Other Poems. By
  a Lady and Her Brother. 1797.
    British Critic, 11 (Feb. 1798), 192.

541

Critical Review, s2,v26 (May 1799), 109.

Rosalind de Tracey. A Novel. 1798. (F)
Analytical Review, 28 (Sept. 1798), 298.
Critical Review, ns,v25 (Jan. 1798), 118.
Monthly Review, ns,v27 (Nov. 1798), 331-32.

Torrens, Robert.
Caelibia Choosing a Husband. A Novel. (F)
Monthly Review, ns,v62 (Aug. 1810), 435-36.

The Victim of Intolerance; or, the Hermit of Killarney. A
Catholic Tale. 1814. (F)
Critical Review, s4,v5 (May 1814), 550.
Lady's Monthly Museum, ns,v16 (June 1814), 342-45.
Monthly Museum, 2 (Sept. 1814), 224-25.
Monthly Review, ns,v78 (Oct. 1815), 216-17.

Touch 'em, Timothy.
See Thomas Beck.

Toulmin, George Hoggart.
Illustrations of Affection; with Other Poems. 1819. (P)
British Stage and Literary Cabinet, 3 (July 1819), 200.
Fireside Magazine (quoting Monthly Magazine), 1 (July
1819), 276.
Fireside Magazine (quoting Monthly Review and Gentleman's
Magazine), 1 (Sept. 1819), 345, 359.
Gentleman's Magazine, 89¹ (June 1819), 547.
Literary Panorama, ns,v9 (May 1819), 543-44.
Monthly Magazine, 47 (June 1819), 443.
Monthly Review, 89 (July 1819), 329.
New Monthly Magazine, 11 (May 1819), 347.

Tovey, Thomas.
Things As They Were, as They Are, and as They Ought to Be,
a Poem. 1804. (P)
Critical Review, s3,v4 (Jan. 1805), 104-16.
Monthly Review, 48 (Sept. 1805), 103.

Towers, Joseph.
The History of Philip Waldegrave. (F)
New London Review, 2 (Aug. 1799), 179.

Townsend, Rev. George.
Poems. 1810. (P)
Satirist, 6 (Apr. 1810), 399-406.

Armageddon, a Poem. 1815. (P)
Augustan Review, 1 (June 1815), 89-97.
British Critic, ns,v5 (June 1816), 591-615.
British Lady's Magazine, 2 (Sept. 1815), 173-81.
Eclectic Review, s2,v4 (Oct. 1815), 392-95.

Literary Panorama, ns,v2 (July 1815), 564-71.
London Review, 1 (Feb. 1809), 73-82.
Monthly Repository, 10 (Oct. 1815), 649-52.
Monthly Review, 91 (Feb. 1820), 207-08.
New Annual Register, 36 (1815), [431].
New Monthly Magazine, 3 (July 1815), 546.

Townshend, Thomas.
  Poems. 1797. (P)
    Critical Review, s2,v22 (Feb. 1798), 185-88.

Trefusis, Miss _____.
  Poems and Tales. 1808. (P)
    Annual Review, 7 (1808), 524-25.
    Antijacobin Review, 30 (July 1808), 256-59.
    British Critic, 32 (Aug. 1808), 126-30.
    Cabinet, 4 (Dec. 1808), 396.
    Critical Review, s3,v14 (Aug. 1808), 442-43.
    Eclectic Review, 4 (Sept. 1808), 846.
    Monthly Review, 57 (Oct. 1808), 206-09.
    Poetical Register, 7 (1808), 557.

Trelawney, Ann.
  Characters at Brighton. 1808. (F)
    Critical Review, s3,v14 (Aug. 1808), 440-42.

Tremenheere, Rev. William. (See also Tremenheere & Zornlin.)
  Ode on the Fluctuations of Civil Society; to Which Is Added,
  an Ode to Fortune. (Anon.) 1797. (P)
    British Critic, 11 (Mar. 1798), 314.
    Critical Review, s2,v24 (Dec. 1798), 469-70.
    Gentleman's Magazine, 68[1] (Mar. 1798), 227.
    Monthly Review, 26 (June 1798), 229-30.

  Verses on the Victory of Trafalgar; and the Death of Admiral
  Lord Nelson. 1806. (P)
    Antijacobin Review, 23 (Feb. 1806), 209.
    Critical Review, s3,v7 (Mar. 1806), 332.
    Monthly Review, 49 (Mar. 1806), 317.

Tremenheere, William, and Elizabeth Zornlin.
  An Ode on the Victory and Death of Lord Viscount Nelson
  Off Trafalgar. To Which Are Added Lines Addressed to Him
  After the Celebrated Battle of the Nile. (Anon.) 1806. (P)
    British Critic, 27 (Feb. 1806), 185.
    Critical Review, s3,v7 (Mar. 1806), 332.
    Eclectic Review, 2 (Mar. 1806), 236.
    Gentleman's Magazine, 76[1] (Jan. 1806), 60.
    Lady's Monthly Museum, 16 (Apr. 1806), 260.
    Literary Journal, a Review..., ns,v1 (Jan. 1806), 106.
    Monthly Review, 49 (Jan. 1806), 95.

Trench, Mrs. Melesina Chevenix.

Mary Queen of Scots, an Historical Ballad; with Other
Poems. By a Lady. 1800. (P)
  British Critic, 17 (Feb. 1801). 187-88.

Campaspe, an Historical Tale; and Other Poems. (P)
  Literary Gazette, Oct. 14, 1820, pp. 661-62.

Laura's Dream; or the Moonlanders. (P)
  Literary Gazette, June 24, 1820, pp. 403-04.
  New Hibernian Magazine, 1 (Aug. 1820), 101-03.

A Monody on the Death of Mr. Grattan. (P)
  Literary Gazette, July 15, 1820, p. 456.

Tresham, Henry.
  Rome at the Close of the Eighteenth Century!!! a Poem.
  1799. (P)
    British Critic, 14 (Aug. 1799), 115-18.
    Critical Review, s2,v26 (June 1799), 232.
    Monthly Magazine, Suppl. v8 (Jan. 20, 1800), 1051.
    Monthly Mirror, 7 (June 1799), 348-49.
    Monthly Review, 30 (Oct. 1799), 194-98.
    Monthly Visitor, 10 (July 1800), 318-19.
    New Annual Register, 20 (1799), [267-68].
    New London Review, 1 (May 1799), 485-89.

  Recreations at Ramsgate. Poetical Effusions. 1801. (P)
    Monthly Mirror, 13 (May 1802), 333.
    Monthly Review, 37 (Apr. 1802), 439.

  Britannicus to Buonaparte, an Heroic Epistle. 1803. (P)
    Antijacobin Review, 16 (Dec. 1803), 415-16.
    British Critic, 23 (Jan. 1804), 82-83.
    European Magazine, 45 (Jan. 1804), 54.
    Literary Journal, a Review..., 2 (Dec. 1, 1803), 598-99.
    Monthly Review, 42 (Dec. 1803), 444-45.
    Poetical Register, 3 (1803), 456.

Trimmer, Mrs. Sarah.
  Instructive Tales. 1810. (F)
    British Critic, 36 (Oct. 1810), 426.
    Literary Panorama, 8 (Nov. 1810), 1267.

Triplet, Cosmo.
  Sonnets for the Year 1809. (P)
    Poetical Register, 7 (1809), 606-07.

Trotter, John Barnard.
  Stories for Calumniators; Interspersed with Remarks on the
  Disadvantages, Misfortunes, and Habits of the Irish. (F)
    Dublin Satirist, 1 (Jan. 1810), 167-72.
    Hibernia Magazine, 1 (Jan.-Mar. 1810), 48, 109-13, 177-81.

Trotter, Dr. Thomas.
  Suspiria Oceani; a Monody on the Death of Richard Earl Howe.
  1800. (P)
    Antijacobin Review, 8 (Jan. 1801), 56-58.
    British Critic, 17 (Mar. 1801), 309-11.
    Critical Review, s2,v31 (Feb. 1801), 229-30.
    Gentleman's Magazine, 71^2 (Aug. 1801), 739.
    Monthly Magazine, Suppl. v11 (July 20, 1801), 605.
    Monthly Mirror, 11 (Mar. 1801), 177.
    Monthly Review, 36 (Dec. 1801), 438-39.

  The Noble Foundling; or, the Hermit of the Tweed, a Tragedy.
  1812. (D)
    Monthly Review, ns,v71 (May 1813), 99-102.

Truman, J.
  The Review, a Poetic Epistle. (P)
    Ireland's Mirror, 1 (June 1804), 97-98.

Tuck, Elizabeth.
  The Juvenile Poetical Moralist. (P)
    New Evangelical Magazine, 6 (Mar. 1820), 87-88.

Tuckett, T. R.
  Urbino; or, the Vaults of Lepanto. 1813. (F)
    Critical Review, s4,v4 (Dec. 1813), 663.
    New Review, 3 (Mar. 1814), 267-69.

Turner, Charles.
  The Pleasures of Affection, a Poem. With the Adieu to
  School, and Other Poems. (P)
    Gentleman's Magazine, 87^2 (Oct. 1817), 344-46.

  An Elegy, with a Parody of the Bard of Gray. (P)
    Gentleman's Magazine, 88^1 (May 1818), 440-41.

Turner, Elizabeth.
  The Daisy; or Cautionary Verses Adapted to the Ideas of
  Children from Four to Eight Years Old. (Anon.) 1807. (P)
    Antijacobin Review, 27 (July 1807), 311.
    Monthly Review, 55 (Apr. 1808), 440.

Turner, Sharon.
  Sacred Meditations and Devotional Hymns. By a Layman.
  1811. (P)
    British Critic, 37 (June 1811), 623-24.
    Gentleman's Magazine, 81^1 (June 1811), 562-66.
    Monthly Review, 71 (July 1813), 328-29.
    Poetical Register, 8 (1811), 625.

  Prolusions on the Present Greatness of Britain; on Modern
  Poetry; and on the Present Aspect of the World. 1819. (P)
    Gentleman's Magazine, 89^2 (Sept. 1819), 242-43.

Literary Gazette, Sept. 4, 1819, pp. 562-64.
Monthly Magazine, 48 (Nov. 1819), 356.

Turner, William Henry.
   Essays on Subjects of a Miscellaneous Nature. 1803. (Pr)
      Flowers of Literature, 3 (1804), 451-52.

Turnour, Rev. Edward John.
   The Warning Voice, a Sacred Poem; Addressed to Infidel
   Writers of Poetry. (P)
      Gentleman's Magazine, 88[2] (Nov. 1818), 441.

Tweddell, H. Madison.
   Aquilhar, a Tragedy. 1820. (D)
      Monthly Review, ns,v93 (Oct. 1820), 212-13.
      Theatrical Inquisitor, 16 (May 1820), 284-89.

Twiss, Horace.
   St. Stephens's Chapel: A Satirical Poem. By Horatius.
   1807. (P)
      Annual Review, 6 (1807), 585.
      Antijacobin Review, 27 (June 1807), 183-86.
      British Critic, 30 (Dec. 1807), 673.
      Critical Review, s3,v11 (July 1807), 331-32.
      Cyclopaedian Magazine, 1 (July 1807), 417-18.
      Literary Annual Register, 1 (June 1807), 276.
      Monthly Magazine, Suppl. v23 (July 30, 1807), 643.
      Monthly Mirror, ns,v1 (June 1807), 403-06.
      Monthly Review, 53 (June 1807), 220-21.
      Oxford Review, 2 (Aug. 1807), 193-95.
      Poetical Register, 6 (1807), 552.
      Satirist, 1 (Nov. 1807), 206. (Excerpts from other re-
         views.)

   A Selection of Scotish Melodies, with Symphonies and Accom-
   paniments for the Piano Forte, by Henry R. Bishop, and
   Words by Horace Twiss. (P)
      Monthly Review, 74 (June 1814), 187-91.
      Theatrical Inquisitor, 1 (Sept. 1812), 34-38.

   Posthumous Parodies and Other Pieces, Composed by Several
   of Our Most Celebrated Poets, but Not Published in Any Former Edition of Their Works. (Anon.) 1814. (P)
      Critical Review, s4,v5 (Mar. 1814), 322-25.

   The Carib Chief, a Tragedy. 1819. (D)
      Champion, May 30, 1819, pp. 344-46.
      Literary Chronicle, 1 (May 22, 1819), 3-6.
      Literary Gazette, May 29, 1819, pp. 341-42.
      Monthly Review, ns,v89 (Aug. 1819), 423-29.
      Theatre, or Dramatic and Literary Mirror, 1 (May 29,
         1819), 181-83.

Tyler, Royall.
  The Algerine Captive; or, the Life and Adventures of Doctor
  Updike Underhill. 1802. (F)
    Critical Review, ns,v35 (May 1802), 113-14.
    Monthly Magazine, Suppl. v13 (July 20, 1802), 659.
    New Annual Register, 23 (1802), [321].

Type, Tom.
  See Rev. Richard Warner.

Tytler, H. W.
  The Voyage Home from the Cape of Good Hope; with Other
  Poems Relating to the Cape. 1803. (P)
    Annual Review, 2 (1803), 559.
    Antijacobin Review, 16 (Dec. 1803), 413-14.
    British Critic, 22 (Aug. 1803), 194.
    Literary Journal, a Review..., 2 (July 16, 1803), 23-24.
    Monthly Register, 3 (Aug. 1803), 140.
    Monthly Review, 44 (May 1804), 46-48.
    New Annual Register, 24 (1803), [327-28].
    Poetical Register, 3 (1803), 455.

Undergraduate, An.
  See T. U. Stoney.

Undergraduate of the University of Cambridge, An.
  See Thomas Dale.

Uneducated Youth, An.
  See John Jones.

Vandergoose, Peter.
  Gulliver and Munchausen Outdone. 1807. (F)
    Literary Panorama, 3 (Jan. 1808), 748-49.

Vardill, Anna Jane.
  Poems and Translations from the Minor Greek Poets and
  Others. By a Lady. 1809. (P)
    Antijacobin Review, 34 (Oct. 1809), 198-200.
    Critical Review, s3,v16 (Jan. 1809), 101.
    European Magazine, 55 (Feb. 1809), 140-42.
    European Magazine, 56 (Aug. 1809), 126-27.
    Gentleman's Magazine, 80^2 (Nov. 1810), 453.
    Monthly Magazine, Suppl. v27 (July 30, 1809), 658.
    Monthly Review, 62 (July 1810), 204-07.

  The Pleasures of Human Life, a Poem. 1812. (P)
    British Critic, 39 (Apr. 1812), 414-15.
    Critical Review, s4,v2 (Sept. 1812), 328-30.
    European Magazine, 61 (Apr. 1812), 275-80.
    Gentleman's Magazine, 83^1 (May 1813), 450-51.
    Monthly Review, 69 (Oct. 1812), 161-66.
    New Review, 1 (Mar. 1813), 331-32.

Varrot.
Sentimental Night Thoughts of a Young Man Retired from the
World. (P)
La Belle Assemblée, Suppl. ns,v14 (1816), 336-37.

Vartie, John.
Jephtha: A Dramatic Fragment. (D)
Theatrical Inquisitor, 16 (Mar. 1820), 138-43.

Vassar, J. J.
Poems on Several Occasions, Including the Petitioner, or a
Review of the Red-Book. 1799. (P)
British Critic, 18 (Aug. 1801), 193.
Critical Review, s2,v28 (Apr. 1800), 470-71.
New London Review, 3 (Feb. 1800), 178-79.

Vaughan, Thomas.
Playful Imitations, from the Greek and Roman Classics.
With Some Original Poems. (P)
Literary Journal, a Review, 4 (Dec. 1804), 650.

Vaux, F. B.
Domestic Pleasures, or the Happy Fire-side. 1816. (P)
British Critic, ns,v5 (Feb. 1816), 219-20.

Venning, Miss _____.
Simple Pleasures. (P)
New Annual Register, 32 (1811), [365].

Ventum, Harriet.
Justina; or, the History of a Young Lady. 1801. (F)
Antijacobin Review, 11 (Jan. 1802), 72.
British Critic, 19 (May 1802), 538.
Critical Review, ns,v33 (Dec. 1801), 460-61.
Monthly Review, ns,v38 (July 1802), 313.

The Good Aunt; Including the Story of Signor Aldersonini
and His Son. 1813. (F)
Monthly Review, ns,v73 (Mar. 1814), 318.

The Holiday Reward; or, Tales to Instruct and Amuse Good
Children, during the Christmas and Midsummer Vacations. (F)
Gentleman's Magazine, 84^2 (Oct. 1814), 364.

Venzee, Maria.
Fate; or, Spong Castle. 1813. (F)
British Critic, 23 (June 1804), 676.
Critical Review, s3,v2 (June 1804), 236.
Monthly Review, ns,v45 (Nov. 1804), 313.

Vere, Horace.
Guiscard, or the Accusation. A Romance. 1809. (F)
Critical Review, s3,v19 (Jan. 1810), 104-05.

Monthly Review, ns,v60 (Sept. 1809), 98.
Satirist, 8 (Mar. 1811), 274-75.

Verral, Charles.
The Pleasures of Possession; or, the Enjoyment of the Pres-
ent Moment, Contrasted with Those of Hope and Memory. A
Poem. 1810. (P)
    British Critic, 40 (Oct. 1812), 406-08.
    Critical Review, s3,v22 (Feb. 1811), 218-20.
    Monthly Review, 64 (Feb. 1811), 212.
    Poetical Register, 8 (1810), 572-73.
    Universal Magazine, ns,v14 (Oct. 1810), 296-300.

Victor and Cazire.
See Percy Bysshe Shelley.

Vigors, N. A.
An Enquiry into the Nature and Extent of Poetic Licence.
1813. (Pr)
    British Critic, ns,v2 (Aug. 1814), 109-27.
    Critical Review, s3,v21 (Dec. 1810), 407-18.

Villemer, P.
A Poem on Astronomy. 1808. (P)
    Critical Review, s3,v16 (Jan. 1809), 103.

Vincent, Rev. John.
Fowling; a Poem Descriptive of Grouse, Pheasant, Woodcock,
Duck, and Snipe Shooting. 1808. (P)
    Annual Review, 7 (1808), 505-06.
    Antijacobin Review, 35 (Feb. 1810), 134-37.
    Le Beau Monde, 4 (Dec. 1808), 289.
    Critical Review, s3,v16 (Feb. 1809), 148-55.
    Edinburgh Review, 13 (Oct. 1808), 69-76.
    Monthly Review, 60 (Nov. 1809), 320.
    New Annual Register, 29 (1808), [406].
    Poetical Register, 7 (1808), 565.
    Satirist, 3 (Nov. 1808), 425-27.

Volunteer, A.
See Thomas Jones.

W., W. W.
Camilla, or the Deserted Sister. A Poem. 1809. (P)
    Monthly Review, 61 (Jan. 1810), 108.

Wag, Walter.
The Fudge Committee; or Creditors Wanting MORE. A Hudibrastic Poem. 1819. (P)
    British Stage and Literary Cabinet, 3 (May 1819), 136-37.

Lake, William Rowland.
Poems. 1800. (P)

Critical Review, s2,v31 (Mar. 1801), 347-48.
London Review, 4 (Aug. 1800), 173.
Monthly Magazine, Suppl. v11 (July 20, 1801), 606.

Wakefield, Priscilla.
Sketches of Human Manners. (F)
Satirist, 3 (Oct. 1808), 335.

Waldron, Francis Godolphin.
The Prodigal, a Dramatic Piece. 1794. (D)
British Critic, 11 (Mar. 1798), 315.

The Virgin Queen. 1797. (D)
Monthly Magazine, Suppl. v5 (July 15, 1798), 508.

The Man with Two Wives; or Wigs For Ever! a Dramatic Fable.
1798. (D)
British Critic, 11 (May 1798), 561.

Il Luttuoso, ed Il Gaudioso, Il Giocoso, ed Il Diligente:
Poems on Music, the New Century, Sport, and Care. (Anon.)
1801. (P) [By Waldron?]
Antijacobin Review, 10 (Sept. 1801), 80.
British Critic, 20 (Nov. 1802), 557-58.
Critical Review, s2,v33 (Sept. 1801), 110-11.
European Magazine, 39 (Feb. 1801), 119.
Monthly Review, 36 (Oct. 1801), 218.
Union Magazine, 1 (Feb. 1801), 119-20.

Walker, Edward.
Raphael; or the Pupil of Nature. 1805. (P)
British Critic, 27 (Mar. 1806), 316-17.
Critical Review, s3,v6 (Sept. 1805), 101-02.
Monthly Magazine, Suppl. v20 (Jan. 31, 1806), 615.
Monthly Mirror, 20 (Oct. 1805), 257.

Walker, George.
Cinthelia, or a Woman of Ten Thousand. 1797. (F)
Analytical Review, 27 (Apr. 1798), 415-17.
Critical Review, ns,v23 (July 1798), 352-53.
Monthly Magazine, Suppl. v5 (July 15, 1798), 509.
Monthly Mirror, 5 (Jan. 1798), 30-31.
Monthly Review, ns,v26 (May 1798), 106-07.
Monthly Visitor, 3 (Jan. 1798), 94-95.

The Vagabond. 1799. (F)
Analytical Review, ns,v1 (Feb. 1799), 210-15.
Antijacobin Review, 2 (Feb. 1799), 137-40.
British Critic, 15 (Apr. 1800), 432.
Critical Review, ns,v26 (June 1799), 237.
Monthly Magazine, Suppl. v7 (July 20, 1799), 542.
Monthly Mirror, 9 (Mar. 1800), 158.
New London Review, 1 (Apr. 1799), 406.

The Three Spaniards; a Romance. (F)
   Antijacobin Review, 6 (May 1800), 52-53.
   New London Review, 3 (May 1800), 469.

Poems on Various Subjects. 1801. (P)
   Antijacobin Review, 10 (Dec. 1801), 422.
   British Critic, 18 (Nov. 1801), 541-42.
   Monthly Mirror, 12 (Dec. 1801), 397.
   Poetical Register, 1 (1801), 437.

Don Raphael, a Romance. 1803. (F)
   British Critic, 22 (Oct. 1803), 434.
   Critical Review, ns,v39 (Oct. 1803), 235-36.

The Battle of Waterloo, a Poem. 1815. (P)
   Augustan Review, 1 (Nov. 1815), 785-94.
   British Critic, ns,v5 (Apr. 1816), 441-42.
   Literary Panorama, ns,v3 (Nov. 1815), 242-45.
   Theatrical Inquisitor, 7 (Dec. 1815), 452-59.

Walker, Josiah.
   The Defence of Order, a Poem. 1803. (P)
   Annual Review, 2 (1803), 557.
   British Critic, 22 (Sept. 1803), 234-40.
   Edinburgh Review, 2 (July 1803), 421-28.
   Flowers of Literature, 2 (1803), 445.
   Monthly Review, 43 (Mar. 1804), 262-66.
   New Annual Register, 24 (1803), [327].
   Poetical Register, 3 (1803), 444.

Walker, W. S.
   Gustavus Vasa, and Other Poems. 1813. (P)
   British Lady's Magazine, ns,v1 (Dec. 1817), 348-50.
   Critical Review, s4,v4 (July 1813), 85-94.
   Gentleman's Magazine, 84[1] (Feb. 1814), 150-52.
   Monthly Review, 74 (July 1814), 289-93.
   Tradesman, 13 (July 1814), 52-54.

   The Heroes of Waterloo, an Ode. (P)
   Augustan Review, 1 (Nov. 1815), 785-94.
   Gentleman's Magazine, 86[1] (Mar. 1816), 243-44.

   The Appeal of Poland. An Ode. (P)
   Gentleman's Magazine, 86[2] (July 1816), 54-55.

Waller, Bryan.
   Epistle to Bennet Langton, Esq. in His Retirement. 1802.
   (P)
   Monthly Mirror, 14 (Aug. 1802), 104.

Wallis, Rev. Richard.
   The Happy Village, a Poem. 1802. (P)
   Annual Review, 1 (1802), 657.

British Critic, 21 (June 1803), 673-74.
Gentleman's Magazine, 72^1 (June 1802), 536.
Poetical Register, 2 (1802), 440.

Walpole, Horace.
  The Castle of Otranto. A Gothic Story. 1804.
    Monthly Mirror, 18 (Oct. 1804), 246.

Walsh, Miss _____.
  The Officer's Daughter, or a Visit to Ireland, in 1790.
  (Anon.) 1810. (F)
    British Critic, 36 (Aug. 1810), 184-85.
    Critical Review, s3,v21 (Sept. 1810), 43-49.
    Monthly Magazine, Suppl. v30 (Jan. 31, 1811), 676.

  Poems. By a Sister. (Anon.) (P)
    Gentleman's Magazine, 82^2 (Nov. 1812), 450.

Ward, Mr. _____.
  Oxoniana; a Didactic Poem, in Several Letters on the Late
  Improved Mode of Study, and Examination for Degrees in the
  University of Oxford. By a Cambridge Master of Arts.
  1812. (P)
    British Critic, 42 (July 1813), 76-77.
    Monthly Review, 71 (May 1813), 98-99.

Ward, Mary.
  Original Poetry. 1807. (P)
    Eclectic Review, 4 (Feb. 1808), 182-83.
    Monthly Review, 58 (Feb. 1809), 213-14.

Ware, Major.
  Squibs and Crackers, Serious, Comical, and Tender. By
  Jasper Smallshot. 1812. (P)
    British Critic, 38 (Dec. 1811), 634-35.
    Critical Review, s3,v24 (Nov. 1811), 328.
    Monthly Review, 67 (Feb. 1812), 219.
    Poetical Register, 8 (1811), 612-13.

Ware, Mrs. Major.
  Poems. Consisting of Translations, from the Greek, Latin,
  and Italian; with Some Originals. 1809. (P)
    Gentleman's Magazine, 79^2 (July 1809), 650-51.
    Literary Panorama, 7 (Feb. 1810), 891-93.
    Monthly Review, 60 (Nov. 1809), 250-53.
    Universal Magazine, ns,v13 (Mar. 1810), 216-19.

Waring, J.
  Scripture Versions, Hymns, and Reflections on Select Passages. 1808. (P)
    Critical Review, s3,v15 (Sept. 1808), 103.
    Monthly Review, 59 (June 1809), 216.

Warner, Rev. Richard.
  Bath Characters; or, Sketches from Life. Second Edition,
  with Many Additions.... By Peter Paul Pallet. 1808. (P)
    British Critic, 31 (Apr. 1808), 452-53.
    Critical Review, s3,v14 (June 1808), 222-23.
    European Magazine, 53 (Feb. 1808), 122-26.
    Monthly Review, 56 (Aug. 1808), 443.
    Satirist, 2 (May 1808), 305-10.

  Rebellion in Bath; or the Battle of the Upper-Rooms; an
  Heroico-Odico-Tragico-Comico Poem. By the Late Peter Paul
  Pallet. 1808. (P)
    Critical Review, s3,v18 (Oct. 1809), 214-17.
    Monthly Review, 62 (July 1810), 326-27.
    Poetical Register, 8 (1810), 587.

  The Restoration: Being the Second and Last Canto of Rebellion in Bath. By the Late Peter Paul Pallet. 1809. (P)
    Critical Review, s3,v18 (Oct. 1809), 214-17.
    Monthly Review, 62 (July 1810), 326-27.
    Poetical Register, 8 (1810), 587.

Warren, Caroline Matilda.
  Conrade; or, the Gamesters. A Novel. 1806. (F)
    Literary Journal, a Review..., ns,v2 (July 1806), 111.

Warren, E.
  The Poet's Day, or Imagination's Ramble, a Poem; with an
  Eulogy on Britain, Its Religion, Laws, and Liberties. 1803.
  (P)
    Annual Review, 3 (1804), 568.
    British Critic, 22 (Nov. 1803), 549-51.
    Evangelical Magazine, 14 (May 1806), 227.
    Imperial Review, 2 (July 1804), 463.
    Monthly Magazine, Suppl. v16 (Jan. 25, 1804), 633.
    Monthly Mirror, 16 (Dec. 1803), 400.
    Poetical Register, 4 (1804), 495.

Warren, Thomas Alston.
  Beneficence; or, Verses Addressed to the Patrons of the
  Society for Bettering the Condition and Encreasing the
  Comforts of the Poor. 1803. (P)
    Annual Review, 2 (1803), 579.
    Antijacobin Review, 15 (July 1803), 315-17.
    British Critic, 21 (June 1803), 672.
    Critical Review, s3,v1 (Mar. 1804), 356.
    European Magazine, 45 (Jan. 1804), 55.
    Monthly Mirror, 17 (Apr. 1804), 262.
    Monthly Review, 42 (Sept. 1803), 99-100.

Warrington, George.
  De Salkeld, Knight of the White Rose; a Tale of the Middle
  Ages. 1811. (P)

British Critic, 42 (Aug. 1813), 189-90.
Poetical Register, 8 (1811), 603.

Watkins, Miss H.
See Miss J. P. Watkins and Miss H. Watkins.

Watkins, Miss J. P., and Miss H. Watkins.
Poems on a Variety of Subjects. 1812. (P)
British Critic, 40 (Oct. 1812), 406.
Monthly Review, 69 (Nov. 1812), 329.

Watkins, William.
The Fall of Carthage; a Tragedy. 1802. (D)
Annual Review, 1 (1802), 685.
British Critic, 21 (Apr. 1803), 433-34.
Critical Review, ns,v37 (Apr. 1803), 477.
Monthly Magazine, Suppl. v15 (July 28, 1803), 630.
New Annual Register, 23 (1802), [320].

Watson, George.
See George Watson Taylor.

Watts, Susanna.
Original Poems and Translations. 1802. (P)
Annual Review, 1 (1802), 662-63.
Critical Review, s2,v37 (Apr. 1803), 434-39.
Monthly Magazine, Suppl. v14 (Jan. 25, 1803), 599.
New Annual Register, 23 (1802), [317].
Poetical Register, 2 (1802), 435-36.

Elegy on the Death of the Princess Charlotte-Augusta of
Wales. (P)
Gentleman's Magazine, 87^2 (Suppl. July-Dec. 1817), 610.

Weaver, W.
Melancholy Effusions, with a Few Miscellanies. 1818. (P)
Literary Panorama, ns,v8 (Oct. 1818), 1122.

Webb, Cornelius.
Heath-Flowers; or Songs, Odes, and Sonnets. (P)
Theatrical Inquisitor, 10 (Apr. 1817), 286-87.

Sonnets, Incidental and Descriptive; with Other Poems.
1820. (P)
British Stage and Literary Cabinet, 4 (Sept. 1820), 262-
63.
Gentleman's Magazine, 90^2 (Aug. 1820), 148.
Literary Chronicle, 2 (Dec. 16, 1820), 810.
Monthly Magazine, 50 (Sept. 1820), 166.
Monthly Review, 93 (Nov. 1820), 330-31.
New Monthly Magazine, 13 (June 1820), 733.
Theatrical Inquisitor, 16 (May 1820), 307-09.

Webb, Daniel.
  Miscellanies. 1802. (P)
    British Critic, 21 (Feb. 1803), 133-35.

Webb, Francis.
  Somerset, a Poem. 1811. (P)
    British Critic, 41 (Feb. 1813), 184-85.
    Eclectic Review, 7 (Aug. 1811), 742-43.
    Monthly Review, 67 (Feb. 1812), 220-21.
    Poetical Register, 8 (1811), 628.

Webb, John.
  Haverhill; a Descriptive Poem; and Other Poems. 1811. (P)
    British Critic, 38 (Aug. 1811), 190.
    Christian Observer, 10 (Apr. 1811), 241-48.
    Eclectic Review, 6 (Nov. 1810), 1050.
    Gentleman's Magazine, 80^2 (Dec. 1810), 546-48.
    Monthly Review, 62 (Aug. 1810), 443-48.
    Poetical Register, 8 (1810), 566-67.

Webster, J. Wedderburne.
  Waterloo, and Other Poems. 1816. (P)
    Augustan Review, 3 (Oct. 1816), 358-60.
    The Independent, no3 (1816), 295-97.
    Quarterly Review, 15 (July 1816), 345-50.

Wedderburn, Margaretta.
  Mary Queen of Scots; an Historical Poem, with Other Miscellaneous Pieces. (P)
    New Monthly Magazine, 8 (Dec. 1817), 435.

Weller, Mary Ann R.
  Poems, Pastoral and Descriptive. 1802. (P)
    Monthly Mirror, 14 (Oct. 1802), 255-56.

Wells, Helena (later Mrs. Whitford).
  The Step-Mother, a Domestic Tale. 1798. (F)
    Analytical Review, 28 (Sept. 1798), 298.
    Antijacobin Review, 3 (Aug. 1799), 421-23.
    British Critic, 12 (July 1798), 74.
    Critical Review, ns,v24 (Oct. 1798), 237.
    Gentleman's Magazine, 68^1 (June 1798), 516.
    Monthly Magazine, Suppl. v6 (1798), 517.
    Monthly Review, ns,v26 (Aug. 1798), 459.

  Constantia Neville; or, the West-Indian. 1800. (F)
    Annals of Philosophy, 1 (1801), 283.
    Antijacobin Review, 8 (Jan. 1801), 60.
    British Critic, 15 (June 1800), 676-77.
    Critical Review, ns,v29 (Aug. 1800), 472.
    Gentleman's Magazine, 70^2 (July 1800), 663.
    Monthly Mirror, 10 (Aug. 1800), 95.
    Monthly Review, ns,v33 (Oct. 1800), 206.

Monthly Visitor, 10 (June 1800), 193-202.
New London Review, 4 (July 1800), 86.

West, Miss _____.
  The Two Marillos; or the Mysterious Resemblance, a Romance.
  (F)
     Critical Review, s3,v1 (Mar. 1804), 357.

West, George.
  The Chieftain of the Vale. 1820. (P)
     Monthly Magazine, 50 (Sept. 1820), 167.
     Monthly Review, 93 (Nov. 1820), 328-30.

West, Jane.
  Elegy on the Death of the Right Honourable Edmund Burke.
  1797. (P)
     British Critic, 11 (Mar. 1798), 313.
     Critical Review, s2,v23 (June 1798), 227-28.
     Monthly Magazine, Suppl. v5 (July 15, 1798), 507.
     Monthly Mirror, 6 (July 1798), 34.

  A Tale of the Times. By the Author of A Gossip's Story.
  1799. (F)
     Analytical Review, ns,v1 (June 1799), 603-06.
     Gentleman's Magazine, 69¹ (Feb. 1799), 138.
     Lady's Monthly Museum, 2 (Feb. 1799), 152-54.
     Monthly Magazine, Suppl. v7 (July 10, 1799), 542.
     Monthly Mirror, 7 (Mar. 1799), 167.
     Monthly Review, ns,v29 (May 1799), 90-91.
     New London Review, 1 (Jan. 1799), 92.

  Poems and Plays. Vol. I-II. 1799. (P-D)
     British Critic, 14 (Sept. 1799), 279-84.
     Critical Review, s2,v27 (Oct. 1799), 131-36.
     Gentleman's Magazine, 69² (Oct. 1799), 881-82.
     Monthly Magazine, Suppl. v8 (Jan. 20, 1800), 1051.
     Monthly Mirror, 8 (Aug. 1799), 94-95.
     Monthly Review, 30 (Nov. 1799), 262-65.
     Monthly Visitor, 8 (Dec. 1799), 426-27.
     Monthly Visitor, 9 (Feb. 1800), 171.
     New Annual Register, 20 (1799), [266].
     New London Review, 2 (Aug. 1799), 164-66.

  The Infidel Father. By the Author of A Tale of the Times,
  A Gossip's Story, &c. 1802. (F)
     Annual Review, 1 (1802), 717-20.
     Antijacobin Review, 15 (May 1803), 41-48.
     British Critic, 21 (Apr. 1803), 406-11.
     Flowers of Literature, 2 (1803), 452.
     Imperial Review, 1 (Feb. 1804), 280-84.
     Literary Journal, a Review..., 1 (Jan. 13, 1803), 49.
     Monthly Magazine, Suppl. v15 (July 28, 1803), 639.

556

The Advantages of Education, or the History of Maria Wil-
liams. By the Author of A Gossip's Story, A Tale of the
Times, &c. Second Edition. 1803. (F)
  British Critic, 23 (Feb. 1804), 199.

Poems and Plays. Volumes III-IV. 1805. (P-D)
  Annual Review, 4 (1805), 602-04.
  British Critic, 28 (July 1806), 34-39.
  Guardian of Education, 4 (June 1805), 308-12.
  New Annual Register, 26 (1805), [356].
  Poetical Register, 5 (1805), 490.

The Mother, a Poem. 1809. (P)
  Le Beau Monde, 1 (June 1809), 245.
  British Critic, 33 (June 1809), 618-23.
  Critical Review, s3,v17 (July 1809), 218-21.
  Eclectic Review, 6 (Feb. 1810), 164-68.
  Gentleman's Magazine, 80² (Nov. 1810), 448-50.
  Literary Panorama, 7 (Nov. 1809), 256-62.
  Monthly Magazine, Suppl. v27 (July 30, 1809), 657.
  New Annual Register, 30 (1809), [371].
  Poetical Register, 7 (1809), 595.
  Satirist, 4 (Mar. 1809), 273-76.
  Universal Magazine, ns,v11 (Feb.-Mar. 1809), 139-43, 230-
  34.

The Refusal. By the Author of the Tale of the Times, Infi-
del Father, &c. 1810. (F)
  British Critic, 36 (July 1810), 59-65.
  Critical Review, s3,v20 (May 1810), 33-37.
  Edinburgh Quarterly Review, 1 (Dec. 1811), 609-21.
  Gentleman's Magazine, 80¹ (Apr. 1810), 355.
  Lady's Monthly Museum, ns,v9 (July 1810), 47.

The Loyalists, an Historical Novel. By the Author of Let-
ters to a Young Man, A Tale of the Times, &c. 1812. (F)
  British Critic, 40 (Oct. 1812), 354-59.
  Critical Review, s4,v2 (Sept. 1812), 277-81.
  Eclectic Review, 9 (Mar. 1813), 253-63.
  General Chronicle, 5 (July 1812), 340-42.
  Gentleman's Magazine, 82² (July 1812), 48.

Alicia de Lacy; an Historical Romance. By the Author of
The Loyalists, &c. 1814. (F)
  Antijacobin Review, 47 (Aug. 1814), 148-49.
  British Critic, ns,v2 (Nov. 1814), 549-52.
  Critical Review, s5,v2 (July 1815), 102-04.
  European Magazine, 66 (Nov. 1814), 421-23.
  Gentleman's Magazine, 84² (Aug. 1814), 137-38.

West, Joshua.
  A Sublime Monody, Sacred to the Memory of...Lord Nelson. (P)
  Monthly Review, 49 (Mar. 1806), 325-26.

Westall, Richard.
  A Day in Spring, and Other Poems. 1808. (P)
    Annual Review, 7 (1808), 509.
    Antijacobin Review, 30 (July 1808), 267-70.
    Le Beau Monde, 4 (Sept. 1808), 115-19.
    British Critic, 32 (Aug. 1808), 185-86.
    Critical Review, s3,v15 (Oct. 1808), 185-88.
    Eclectic Review, 4 (Aug. 1808), 749-51.
    Literary Annual Register, 2 (July 1808), 316-20.
    Literary Panorama, 4 (Aug. 1808), 883-86.
    Monthly Review, 57 (Oct. 1808), 148-53.
    New Annual Register, 29 (1808), [406].
    Poetical Register, 7 (1808), 552.

Weston, Ferdinand.
  Poems on Different Subjects. 1803. (P)
    British Critic, 22 (Sept. 1803), 312-13.
    Monthly Magazine, Suppl. v16 (Jan. 25, 1804), 632.
    Monthly Register, 3 (June 1803), 62-63.

Weston, Rev. Stephen.
  Werneria; or Short Characters of Earths and Minerals....
  With Tables of Their Genera, Species, Primitive Crystals,
  Specific Gravity, and Component Parts. By Terrae Filius
  Philagricola. Part I, 1805; Part II, 1806. (P)
    Critical Review, s3,v6 (Sept. 1805), 92-93.
    Critical Review, s3,v9 (Nov. 1806), 330.
    Eclectic Review, 3 (Feb. 1807), 176-77.
    Monthly Literary Recreations, 1 (Oct. 1806), 323.
    Monthly Review, 49 (Jan. 1806), 99-101.
    Monthly Review, 53 (May 1807), 92-93.

Whalley, Rev. Thomas Sedgwick.
  The Castle of Montval, a Tragedy. 1799. (D)
    Antijacobin Review, 4 (Sept. 1799), 62-67.
    British Critic, 14 (Oct. 1799), 429-30.
    Critical Review, ns,v27 (Nov. 1799), 352-53.
    Monthly Magazine, Suppl. v8 (Jan. 20, 1800), 1056.
    Monthly Mirror, 7 (June 1799), 354-56.
    Monthly Review, ns,v29 (Aug. 1799), 447-48.

  Kenneth and Fenella, a Legendary Tale. 1809. (P)
    Le Beau Monde, 1 (July 1809), 355-56.
    British Critic, 33 (June 1809), 629.
    Critical Review, s3,v17 (May 1809), 105-06.
    Monthly Review, 60 (Nov. 1809), 323.
    Poetical Register, 7 (1809), 605.

Wharton, R.
  Roncevalles: A Poem. 1812. (P)
    British Critic, 40 (Nov. 1812), 438-55.
    Critical Review, s4,v1 (Mar. 1812), 270-83.
    Monthly Review, 68 (June 1812), 113-30.

New Annual Register, 33 (1812), [377].

Wharton, Richard.
    Fables, Consisting of Select Parts from Dante, Berni, Chau-
    cer, and Ariosto, Imitated in English Heroic Verse. 1804.
    (P)
        British Critic, 23 (Apr. 1804), 432.

    Fables; Containing Cambuscan, an Heroic Poem. 1805. (P)
        Critical Review, s3,v5 (July 1805), 325-26.
        Lady's Monthly Museum, 15 (Oct. 1805), 269-70.
        Monthly Review, 50 (July 1806), 257-61.
        Poetical Register, 5 (1805), 485.

Wheelwright, Rev. C. A.
    Poems, Original and Translated. 1810? 2nd ed. 1011. (P)
        Eclectic Review, 7 (Aug. 1811), 715-20.
        Gentleman's Magazine, 80^2 (Oct. 1810), 340-43.
        Monthly Review, 67 (Mar. 1812), 261-72.
        Poetical Register, 8 (1811), 612.

Whistlecraft, William and Robert.
    See John Hookham Frere.

Whitby, Thomas.
    The Priory of Birkenhead; a Tale of the Fourteenth Century.
    1819. (P)
        European Magazine, 75 (Apr. 1819), 348.
        Fireside Magazine (quoting Monthly Magazine and New Month-
        ly Magazine), 1 (June 1819), 233, 235.
        Fireside Magazine (quoting Monthly Review), 1 (Aug. 1819),
        311.
        Gentleman's Magazine, 89^1 (Apr. 1819), 335.
        Literary Chronicle, 1 (July 24, 1819), 151.
        Monthly Magazine, 47 (May 1819), 345.
        Monthly Review, 89 (June 1819), 209-10.
        New Monthly Magazine, 11 (May 1819), 347.

    Retrospection. A Rural Poem. 1820. (P)
        Literary Chronicle, 2 (May 27, 1820), 344-45.
        (Gold's) London Magazine, 1 (Apr. 1820), 399-400.
        Monthly Magazine, 49 (Apr. 1820), 261-62.
        Monthly Review, 92 (Aug. 1820), 437.
        New Monthly Magazine, 13 (June 1820), 734.

Whitchurch, Samuel.
    Hispaniola, a Poem. To Which Are Added, Lines on the Cru-
    cifixion, and Other Poetical Pieces. 1804. (P)
        Annual Review, 4 (1805), 596-97.
        British Critic, 25 (Mar. 1805), 318-20.
        Critical Review, s3,v4 (Feb. 1805), 214-16.
        Eclectic Review, 1 (Apr. 1805), 298.
        Monthly Mirror, 19 (May 1805), 326.

Monthly Review, 46 (Apr. 1805), 438-40.
New Annual Register, 26 (1805), [356].

David Dreadnought; or, Nautical Tales and Adventures in
Verse. 1813. (P)
  Baptist Magazine, 8 (Feb. 1816), 80-81.
  Literary Panorama, 15 (Mar. 1814), 189-91.

The Sunday-School, a Poem. 1816. (P)
  Monthly Review, 86 (June 1818), 210.

White, Henry Kirke.
  Clifton Grove, a Sketch in Verse, with Other Poems.   1803.
  (P)
    Annual Review, 2 (1803), 552-54.
    Antijacobin Review, 17 (Jan. 1804), 97-98.
    British Critic, 22 (Sept. 1803), 310-11.
    Flowers of Literature, 3 (1804), 450.
    Literary Journal, a Review..., 2 (Nov. 1, 1803), 473.
    Monthly Magazine, Suppl. v16 (Jan. 25, 1804), 632.
    Monthly Mirror, 15 (June 1803), 385-88.
    Monthly Register, 3 (July 1803), 99.
    Monthly Review, 43 (Feb. 1804), 218.
    New Annual Register, 24 (1803), [328].
    Poetical Register, 3 (1803), 452-53.

  The Remains of Henry Kirke White...with an Account of His
  Life, by Robert Southey. 1807. (P-Pr)
    Annual Review, 6 (1807), 548-53.
    Antijacobin Review, 32 (Apr. 1809), 352-57.
    British Critic, 32 (Nov. 1808), 447-52.
    Cabinet, 3 (Mar. 1808), 177-82.
    Critical Review, s3,v13 (Mar. 1808), 320-26.
    Eclectic Review, 4 (Mar. 1808), 193-207.
    Gentleman's Magazine, 78[1] (Jan. 1808), 45-46.
    Monthly Mirror, ns,v5 (Mar. 1809), 149-55.
    Monthly Review, 61 (Jan. 1810), 71-84.
    New Annual Register, 29 (1808), [405].
    Poetical Register, 7 (1808), 550-51.

White, T. H.
  Bellgrove Castle; or, the Horrid Spectre!   A Romance.
  1803. (F)
    Monthly Mirror, 15 (Mar. 1803), 177.

White, Thomas.
  Saint Guerdun's Well, a Poem. 2nd ed. 1798. (P)
    Analytical Review, 28 (July 1798), 79-80.
    Antijacobin Review, 3 (Aug. 1799), 477-79.
    Antijacobin Review, 17 (Jan. 1804), 102.
    Gentleman's Magazine, 69[2] (Nov. 1799), 964.
    Monthly Review, 27 (Dec. 1798), 458-59.

Whitehouse, Rev. John.
 Hymn to Thanksgiving, on the Occasion of Our Late Victories
 and for Other Signal National Mercies and Deliverances.
 1814. (P)
   Antijacobin Review, 47 (July 1814), 75-78.
   Critical Review, s4,v5 (May 1814), 549.
   Monthly Review, 73 (Apr. 1814), 431-32.

 The Panegyric of Samuel Whitbread, Esq. M. P. 1816. (P)
   Eclectic Review, s2,v6 (Aug. 1816), 193-96.
   Monthly Review, 81 (Oct. 1816), 213-15.

 Tribute of Affection to the Memory of Mrs. Elizabeth
 Susanna Frederica Whitehouse. 1819. (P)
   Monthly Review, 92 (June 1820), 212-13.

Whitfield, Henry.
 The Christmas Holidays. 1803. (P)
   British Critic, 23 (Feb. 1804), 198-99.
   Critical Review, s3,v1 (Mar. 1804), 356.
   European Magazine, 45 (Jan. 1804), 57.
   Monthly Mirror, 16 (Dec. 1803), 400.
   Monthly Review, 46 (Mar. 1805), 323-24.

 The Christmas Holidays, and Black Monday; or, the Boy's
 Return to School. 1804. (P)
   Antijacobin Review, 17 (Mar. 1804), 308-09.
   Critical Review, s3,v2 (May 1804), 104.
   European Magazine, 45 (Mar. 1804), 220.
   Monthly Mirror, 17 (Feb. 1804), 111.

 Leopold; or, the Bastard. (Anon.) 1803. (F)
   Antijacobin Review, 19 (Sept. 1804), 81.
   Critical Review, ns,v38 (Aug. 1803), 441-44.
   European Magazine, 44 (July 1803), 49-50.
   Monthly Magazine, Suppl. v16 (Jan. 25, 1804), 634.
   Monthly Mirror, 16 (July 1803), 39.
   Monthly Mirror, 16 (Oct. 1803), 247.
   Monthly Register, 3 (Sept. 1803), 183.
   Monthly Review, ns,v44 (Aug. 1804), 424.

 A Picture from Life; or, the History of Emma Tankerville
 and Sir Henry Moreton. 1804. (F)
   Antijacobin Review, 18 (June 1804), 203-05.
   British Critic, 24 (July 1804), 80-81.
   Critical Review, s3,v2 (July 1804), 348.
   Imperial Review, 1 (Apr. 1804), 636.
   Literary Journal, a Review..., 3 (June 1, 1804), 610.
   Monthly Mirror, 17 (Mar.-Apr. 1804), 177-79, 259-61.
   Monthly Review, ns,v44 (Aug. 1804), 424.

 But Which? or Domestic Grievances of the Wolmore Family.
 By the Author of Leopold. 1807. (F)

British Critic, 30 (July 1807), 84.
Critical Review, s3,v11 (July 1807), 325-26.
European Magazine, 51 (Apr. 1807), 290.
Gentleman's Magazine, 77[1] (Apr. 1807), 346.
Monthly Mirror, ns,v2 (July 1807), 38-39.
Monthly Review, ns,v55 (Mar. 1808), 319.
Oxford Review, 3 (Feb. 1808), 169.

Whitmore, W.
The Fourth of June. England's Liberty's and Monarchy's Truly Triumphant Pageants, and Royal Birth-Day's Best Grace....
1799. (P)
British Critic, 15 (June 1800), 674.

Wickenden, W. S.
Count Glarus of Switzerland, Interspersed with Some Pieces
of Poetry. (P)
Gentleman's Magazine, 89[2] (Sept. 1819), 244-45.
Monthly Magazine, 50 (Oct. 1820), 269.

The Rustic's Lay, and Other Poems. (P)
Gentleman's Magazine, 89[2] (Sept. 1819), 244-45.

Wiffen, Jeremiah Holmes. (See also Thomas Raffles, James
Baldwin Brown, and Jeremiah Holmes Wiffen.)
Aonian Hours; and Other Poems. 1819. (P)
British Lady's Magazine, s2,v3 (Nov. 1819), 230-31.
Christian's Pocket Magazine, 3 (Nov. 1820), 252-60.
Eclectic Review, s2,v13 (Apr. 1820), 372-79.
European Magazine, 76 (Sept. 1819), 253-55.
Gentleman's Magazine, 89[2] (Aug.-Sept. 1819), 150-52, 238-
40.
Literary Chronicle, 1 (Oct. 9, 1819), 324-25.
Literary Gazette, Oct. 2, 1819, pp. 632-33.
Monthly Magazine, 48 (Sept. 1819), 157.
Monthly Review, 91 (Jan. 1820), 98.
New Monthly Magazine, 12 (Oct. 1819), 328-29.

Julia Alpinula; with the Captive of Stamboul, and Other
Poems. 1820. (P)
Christian's Pocket Magazine, 3 (Dec. 1820), 312-17.
European Magazine, 78 (Oct. 1820), 337-41.
Gentleman's Magazine, 90[2] (Nov. 1820), 437-39.
Literary Chronicle, 2 (July 22, 1820), 470-73.
Literary Gazette, Aug. 26, 1820, pp. 550-52.
(Gold's) London Magazine, 2 (Aug. 1820), 192-96.
Monthly Magazine, 50 (Sept. 1820), 168.
Monthly Review, 93 (Nov. 1820), 241-50.
New Monthly Magazine, 14 (Oct. 1820), 455.

Wilcocke, Samuel Hull.
Britannia, a Poem. 1798. (P)
British Critic, 11 (Mar. 1798), 314.

Critical Review, s2,v22 (Mar. 1798), 352.
Gentleman's Magazine, 68[1] (Jan. 1798), 55.

Wild, James.
Twenty One; an Operatic Afterpiece. (D)
Annual Review, 3 (1804), 605.

Wildman, Mr. _____.
The Force of Prejudice. A Moral Tale. (F)
Monthly Review, ns,v32 (Aug. 1800), 438-39.

Wilkinson, Sarah.
The Thatched Cottage; or, the Sorrows of Eugenia. 1806. (F)
Literary Journal, a Review..., ns,v1 (Feb. 1806), 222.
Monthly Mirror, 21 (Feb. 1806), 120.

Williams, Constantine.
The Campaign in Egypt. 1811. (P)
British Critic, 40 (Sept. 1812), 297-98.
Eclectic Review, 7 (Aug. 1811), 725-26.
Poetical Register, 8 (1811), 605-06.

Williams, John.
Nautical Odes, or Poetical Sketches, Designed to Commemorate
the Achievements of the British Navy. (Anon.) 1801. (P)
Antijacobin Review, 9 (June 1801), 169-71.
British Critic, 18 (Dec. 1801), 665.
Critical Review, s2,v32 (July 1801), 347-48.
European Magazine, 40 (July 1801), 44.
Flowers of Literature, 1 (1801-02), 454.
Monthly Review, 39 (Oct. 1802), 207-08.
Poetical Register, 1 (1801), 440.

Williams, Rev. John.
Sacred Allegories; or Allegorical Poems, Illustrative of
Subjects Moral and Divine; to Which Is Added, with an
Anacreontic, on the Discovery of Vaccination.... 1810. (P)
Baptist Magazine, 2 (Oct. 1810), 524.
British Critic, 38 (Aug. 1811), 190.
Critical Review, s3,v21 (Oct. 1810), 217.
Eclectic Review, 6 (Sept. 1810), 856.
Monthly Review, 64 (Feb. 1811), 214-15.
Poetical Register, 8 (1810), 566.
Satirist, 9 (Dec. 1811), 496.

Disappointment; or, the Hunt after Royalty. 1814. (P)
Monthly Review, 76 (Feb. 1815), 214.
New Monthly Magazine, 2 (Nov. 1814), 350.

Williams, John Ambrose.
Metrical Essays. 1815. (P)
British Critic, ns,v4 (Aug. 1815), 211.
Critical Review, s5,v1 (May 1815), 533.

<u>Monthly</u> <u>Review</u>, 78 (Nov. 1815), 323-24.

Williams, William Frederick.
  <u>Fitzmaurice</u>, <u>a</u> <u>Novel</u>. 1800. (F)
    <u>British</u> <u>Critic</u>, 15 (Feb. 1800), 193.
    <u>Critical</u> <u>Review</u>, ns,v30 (Nov. 1800), 351-52.
    <u>Monthly</u> <u>Mirror</u>, 9 (Mar. 1800), 157.
    <u>Monthly</u> <u>Review</u>, ns,v33 (Sept. 1800), 103.
    <u>New</u> <u>London</u> <u>Review</u>, 3 (Feb. 1800), 177.

  <u>Tales</u> <u>of</u> <u>an</u> <u>Exile</u>. (F)
    <u>Critical</u> <u>Review</u>, ns,v39 (Nov. 1803), 357.
    <u>Literary</u> <u>Journal</u>, <u>a</u> <u>Review</u>..., 2 (Sept. 16, 1803), 280.

  <u>The</u> <u>Witcheries</u> <u>of</u> <u>Craig</u> <u>Isaf</u>. 1804. (F)
    <u>Critical</u> <u>Review</u>, s3,v3 (Dec. 1804), 470.
    <u>Imperial</u> <u>Review</u>, 3 (Dec. 1804), 600-01.
    <u>Literary</u> <u>Journal</u>, <u>a</u> <u>Review</u>..., 4 (Oct. 1804), 435.

  <u>The</u> <u>World</u> <u>We</u> <u>Live</u> <u>In</u>. 1804. (F)
    <u>Literary</u> <u>Journal</u>, <u>a</u> <u>Review</u>..., 4 (July 1804), 92.

  <u>The</u> <u>Young</u> <u>Father</u>. 1805. (F)
    <u>Literary</u> <u>Journal</u>, 5 (Dec. 1805), 1328.

Williamson, Captain T.
  <u>The</u> <u>Dominican</u>, <u>a</u> <u>Romance</u>...<u>Relating</u> <u>to</u> <u>a</u> <u>Family</u> <u>of</u> <u>Distinc-</u>
  <u>tion</u> <u>Which</u> <u>Emigrated</u> <u>from</u> <u>France</u> <u>during</u> <u>the</u> <u>Revolution</u>.
  1809. (F)
    <u>Le</u> <u>Beau</u> <u>Monde</u>, 1 (July 1809), 348-49.
    <u>Critical</u> <u>Review</u>, s3,v17 (July 1809), 330-31.

Wills, Rev. William.
  <u>A</u> <u>Poetical</u> <u>Effigy</u> <u>on</u> <u>the</u> <u>Late</u> <u>Memorable</u> <u>Engagement</u>, <u>between</u>
  <u>the</u> <u>British</u> <u>and</u> <u>Combined</u> <u>Fleets</u> <u>of</u> <u>France</u> <u>and</u> <u>Spain</u>, <u>off</u>
  <u>Trafalgar</u>.... 1805. (P)
    <u>British</u> <u>Critic</u>, 27 (Apr. 1806), 431-32.

Willyams, James Brydges.
  <u>The</u> <u>Influence</u> <u>of</u> <u>Genius</u>, <u>a</u> <u>Poem</u>. 1816. (P)
    <u>Gentleman's</u> <u>Magazine</u>, 87[1] (Feb. 1817), 140.
    <u>Monthly</u> <u>Review</u>, 84 (Nov. 1817), 320-23.

Wilmot, Mrs. _____.
  <u>Ina</u>, <u>a</u> <u>Tragedy</u>. 1815. (D)
    <u>Augustan</u> <u>Review</u>, 1 (Sept. 1815), 483-88.
    <u>British</u> <u>Critic</u>, ns,v3 (Apr. 1815), 438-42.
    <u>British</u> <u>Lady's</u> <u>Magazine</u>, 2 (Nov. 1815), 321-24.
    <u>Lady's</u> <u>Monthly</u> <u>Museum</u>, s3,v2 (Nov. 1815), 284-86.
    <u>New</u> <u>Monthly</u> <u>Magazine</u>, 3 (July 1815), 544.
    <u>Scourge</u>, 9 (June 1815), 405-08.

Wilmot, R. H.

Scenes in Feudal Times. A Romance. 1809. (F)
  Critical Review, s3,v19 (Apr. 1810), 440-42.
  Monthly Review, ns,v63 (Sept. 1810), 102.

Wilmot, William.
  The Tale of Gismunda and Guiscardo, a Poem. 1819. (P)
  Literary Chronicle, 1 (July 31, 1819), 169.

Wilson, Miss _____,
  Lady Geraldine Beaufort. By a Daughter of the Late Ser-
  jeant Wilson. 1802. (F)
    Critical Review, ns,v35 (Aug. 1802), 477.
    Monthly Magazine, Suppl. v14 (Jan. 25, 1803), 599.
    Monthly Review, ns,v41 (May 1803), 103-04.
    New Annual Register, 23 (1802), [322].

  Scotch Law Suits; or a Tale of the Eighteenth and Nineteenth
  Centuries. By the Author of The Two Brothers. 1812. (F)
    British Critic, 41 (Jan. 1813), 74.
    Monthly Review, ns,v71 (June 1813), 213.

Wilson, Arthur.
  The Inconstant Lady, a Play. 1814. (D)
    Gentleman's Magazine, 84^2 (Sept. 1814), 254-57.

Wilson, C. H.
  Cambro Britons, an Historical Play. 1798. (D)
    British Critic, 13 (Mar. 1799), 310.

  The Irish Valet; or Whimsical Adventures of Paddy O'Haloran.
  1811. (D)
    Monthly Review, ns,v65 (Aug. 1811), 435-36.

Wilson, Mrs. Cornwall Baron, née Margaret Harries.
  Melancholy Hours; a Collection of Miscellaneous Poems.
  (Anon.) 1816. (P)
    Critical Review, s5,v4 (Oct. 1816), 430.
    Monthly Review, 82 (Jan. 1817), 100-01.
    Theatrical Inquisitor, 8 (May 1816), 351-56.

  Astarte, a Sicilian Tale; with Other Poems. By the Author
  of Melancholy Hours. 1818. (P)
    Antijacobin Review, 54 (June 1818), 362-63.
    La Belle Assemblée, ns,v17 (Apr. 1818), 177-78.
    Gentleman's Magazine, 88^2 (July 1818), 48.
    Literary Gazette, Mar. 28, 1818, pp. 194-95.
    Theatrical Inquisitor, 12 (May 1818), 346-55.

Wilson, John (Christopher North). (See also John Gibson
    Lockhart and John Wilson, above.)
  The Village Christening, a Poem; or Modern Christianity
  Displayed. (P)
    Monthly Review, 54 (Nov. 1807), 322.

Lines Sacred to the Memory of the Rev. James Grahame, Author of "The Sabbath." 1811. (P)
  Eclectic Review, 8 (Jan. 1812), 87-91.
  Edinburgh Christian Instructor, 5 (Dec. 1812), 399-409.
  Gentleman's Magazine, 81^2 (Dec. 1811), 555.

The Isle of Palms, and Other Poems. 1812. (P)
  British Critic, 42 (July 1813), 77-78.
  Critical Review, s4,v2 (Sept. 1812), 243-53.
  Eclectic Review, 9 (Jan. 1813), 22-34.
  Edinburgh Christian Instructor, 5 (July 1812), 39-48.
  Edinburgh Monthly Magazine and Review, 2 (Mar. 1812),
    165-87.
  Edinburgh Review, 19 (Feb. 1812), 373-88.
  Glasgow Magazine, 3 (Feb., May 1812), 131-41, 382-90.
  Literary Panorama, 12 (Aug. 1812), 215-20.
  Monthly Review, 68 (May 1812), 34-38.
  New Annual Register, 33 (1812), [377].

The City of the Plague, and Other Poems. 1816. (P)
  La Belle Assemblée, Suppl. ns,v14 (1816), 341-43.
  British Lady's Magazine, 4 (Sept. 1816), 177-80.
  Champion, Apr. 21, 1816, pp. 126-27.
  Critical Review, s5,v4 (Aug. 1816), 186-92.
  Eclectic Review, s2,v6 (Aug. 1816), 164-72.
  Edinburgh Review, 26 (June 1816), 458-76.
  Literary Panorama, ns,v5 (Nov. 1816), 241-45.
  Monthly Review, 82 (Mar. 1817), 244-57.
  New Monthly Magazine, 5 (May 1816), 344.
  Scots Magazine, 78 (Mar. 1816), 208-13.

Wilson, Susannah.
  Familiar Poems, Moral and Religious. 1814. (P)
    British Critic, ns,v4 (Nov. 1815), 540-42.
    Critical Review, s5,v1 (Jan. 1815), 81-82.
    Eclectic Review, s2,v3 (May 1815), 501-05.
    Literary Panorama, ns,v1 (Jan. 1815), 529-30.
    Monthly Review, 76 (Feb. 1815), 212.

Wilson, Thomas (?).
  Romance; a Poetical Capriccio. 1811. (P)
    British Critic, 37 (Apr. 1811), 412-13.
    Critical Review, s3,v23 (May 1811), 109.
    Eclectic Review, 7 (May 1811), 463-64.
    General Chronicle, 2 (May 1811), 62-64.
    Literary Panorama, 10 (Nov. 1811), 806.
    Poetical Register, 8 (1811), 629.

Wing, Rev. John.
  Waterloo; a Poetical Epistle. (Anon.) (P)
    Monthly Magazine, 50 (Dec. 1820), 456-57.

Wise, Rev. Joseph.

The System. A Poem. (P)
  Analytical Review, ns,vl (June 1799), 620-22.

Wodhull, Michael.
  The Equality of Mankind, a Poem. Revised and Corrected.
  1798. (P)
    Antijacobin Review, 2 (Mar. 1899), 287-89.
    Monthly Review, 29 (June 1799), 189-93.

Wolcot, John (Peter Pindar).
  An Ode to the Livery of London, on Their Petition to His
  Majesty for Kicking Out His Worthy Ministers.... 1797. (P)
    British Critic, 11 (Jan. 1798), 74.

  Tales of the Hoy; Interspersed with Song, Ode, and Dialogue.
  1798. (P)
    Analytical Review, 28 (Nov. 1798), 512-14.
    British Critic, 13 (June 1799), 663.
    Critical Review, s2,v25 (Apr. 1799), 475-77.
    Monthly Magazine, Suppl. v6 (1798), 514.
    Monthly Mirror, 6 (Oct. 1798), 223.
    Monthly Review, 27 (Oct. 1798), 228-29.
    Monthly Visitor, 5 (Oct. 1798), 199-204.

  Nil Admirari; or, a Smile at a Bishop, Occasioned by an Hy-
  perbolic Eulogy on Miss Hannah More....Moreover an Ode to
  the Blue-Stocking Club.... 1799. (P)
    Antijacobin Review, 4 (Nov. 1799), 321-27.
    Antijacobin Review, 5 (Jan. 1800), 80-81.
    British Critic, 14 (Nov. 1799), 547-48.
    Critical Review, s2,v28 (Feb. 1800), 230-32.
    Monthly Magazine, Suppl. v8 (Jan. 20, 1800), 1052.
    Monthly Mirror, 8 (Nov. 1799), 282.
    Monthly Review, 30 (Dec. 1799), 463-65.
    New London Review, 2 (Oct. 1799), 390-91.

  Lord Auckland's Triumph; or, the Death of Crim. Con. a Pair
  of Prophetic Odes. To Which Are Added an Address to Hymen;
  an Ode to the Passions; Advice to Young Woman.... 1800. (P)
    Antijacobin Review, 6 (July 1800), 306-10.
    British Critic, 16 (July 1800), 79-80.
    Critical Review, s2,v30 (Dec. 1800), 473-74.
    Literary and Masonic Magazine, 1 (June 1802), 251-52.
    Monthly Review, 32 (Aug. 1800), 436.
    Monthly Visitor, 10 (Aug. 1800), 426-28.

  Odes to Ins and Outs. 1801. (P)
    Critical Review, s2,v33 (Dec. 1801), 458-59.
    Monthly Magazine, Suppl. vll (July 20, 1801), 605.
    Monthly Review, 35 (May 1801), 106-07.

  Out at Last! or, the Fallen Minister. 1801. (P)
    Critical Review, s2,v32 (July 1801), 349-50.

Wolcot, John (continued)
    Monthly Magazine, Suppl. vll (July 20, 1801), 605.
    Monthly Mirror, 11 (June 1801), 397.
    Monthly Review, 35 (May 1801), 105-06.
    Monthly Visitor, 13 (June 1801), 205-06.

A Poetical Epistle to Benjamin Rumford, Knight of the White
Eagle, &c. 1801. (P)
    Monthly Review, 35 (Aug. 1801), 435-36.

Tears and Smiles, a Miscellaneous Collection of Poems.
1801. (P)
    British Critic, 18 (Oct. 1801), 424.
    Critical Review, s2,v33 (Dec. 1801), 457-58.
    Monthly Visitor, 14 (Sept. 1801), 93-95.
    Poetical Register, 1 (1801), 429-30.

The Works of Peter Pindar, Esq. (P)
    Poetical Register, 1 (1801), 448.

The Horrors of Bribery; a Penitential Epistle. 1802. (P)
    Critical Review, s2,v37 (Mar. 1803), 354-55.
    Monthly Magazine, Suppl. vl5 (July 28, 1803), 638.
    Monthly Review, 40 (Feb. 1803), 216.
    New Annual Register, 23 (1802), [318].
    Poetical Register, 2 (1802), 444.

Pitt and His Statue; an Epistle to the Subscribers. 1802.
(P)
    Critical Review, s2,v37 (Feb. 1803), 233-34.
    Monthly Epitome, 1 (Oct. 1802), 600.
    Monthly Review, 39 (Sept. 1802), 106-07.
    Poetical Register, 2 (1802), 444.

The Island of Innocence. A Poetical Epistle to a Friend.
1802. (P)
    Annual Review, 1 (1802), 653.
    Antijacobin Review, 12 (May 1802), 80-81.
    British Critic, 20 (Sept. 1802), 319.
    Critical Review, s2,v36 (Oct. 1802), 232-33.
    Monthly Magazine, Suppl. vl4 (Jan. 25, 1803), 597-98.
    Monthly Review, 38 (May 1802), 100-01.
    New Annual Register, 23 (1802), [318].
    Poetical Register, 2 (1802), 439-40.

The Middlesex Election; or, Poetical Epistles, in the
Devonshire Dialect. 1802. (P)
    Critical Review, s2,v37 (Feb. 1803), 234.
    Monthly Review, 40 (Mar. 1803), 326-27.
    New Annual Register, 23 (1802), [318].
    Poetical Register, 2 (1802), 444.

Great Cry and Little Wool; or, the Squads in an Uproar; or

Wolcot, John (continued)
the Progress of Politics; or Epistles, Poetical and Pic-
turesque. 1804. (P)
  British Critic, 24 (Nov. 1804), 558.
  Critical Review, s3,v4 (Jan. 1805), 103.
  Literary Journal, a Review..., 4 (July 1804), 91.
  Monthly Mirror, 18 (Sept. 1804), 181.
  Monthly Review, 45 (Sept. 1804), 101-03.
  Poetical Register, 4 (1804), 502-03.

An Instructive Epistle to John Perring, Esq. Lord Mayor of
London.... 1804. (P)
  British Critic, 24 (Oct. 1804), 438.
  Critical Review, s3,v4 (Jan. 1805), 102-03.
  Literary Journal, a Review..., 4 (Aug. 1804), 206-07.
  Monthly Mirror, 18 (Nov. 1804), 326.
  Monthly Review, 45 (Sept. 1804), 103.

Tristia, or the Sorrows of Peter; Elegies to the King,
Lords Grenville, Petty, Erskine, the Bishop of London,
Messrs. Fox, Sheridan, &c. 1806. (P)
  Le Beau Monde, 1 (Jan. 1807), 148-50.
  La Belle Assemblée, Suppl. vl (1806), 27-28.
  British Critic, 28 (Dec. 1806), 672-73.
  Monthly Mirror, ns,vl (Jan. 1807), 50-51.
  Monthly Review, 51 (Dec. 1806), 422-26.
  Poetical Register, 6 (1806), 510.

One More Peep at the Royal Academy; or Odes to Royal Acade-
micians, &c. 1808. (P)
  Monthly Review, 58 (Apr. 1809), 436-39.
  Poetical Register, 7 (1809), 610.

The Fall of Portugal; or, the Royal Exiles. 1808. (D)
  European Magazine, 53 (June 1808), 456-57.
  Monthly Magazine, Suppl. v25 (July 30, 1808), 596-97.
  Monthly Review, ns,v60 (Nov. 1809), 320-21.
  Poetical Register, 7 (1808), 579.

A Solemn, Sentimental, and Reprobating Epistle to Mrs.
Clarke. 1809.
  Monthly Review, 60 (Dec. 1809), 436-38.
  Poetical Register, 7 (1809), 603.

A Second Epistle to Mrs. Clarke. 1809. (P)
  Monthly Review, 60 (Dec. 1809), 436-38.
  Poetical Register, 8 (1810), 580.

Carlton House Féte, or the Disappointed Bard; in a Series
of Elegies. 1811. (P)
  Eclectic Review, 7 (Oct. 1811), 936.
  Monthly Review, 67 (Apr. 1812), 435-37.
  Poetical Register, 8 (1811), 628.

Wolcot, John (concluded)
  Lilliputian Navy!! The R*****t's Fleet, or John Bull at
  the Serpentine; a Poem. 2nd ed. 1814. (P)
    Critical Review, s4,v6 (July 1814), 92-93.

  Midnight Dreams; or Prophetic Visions of the R***l Blood.
  A Poem. (P)
    Monthly Review, 74 (July 1814), 320.

  More Kings! a Poem; to Which Is Prefixed an Epistle to the
  Reviewers. 2nd ed. 1814. (P)
    Critical Review, s4,v6 (July 1814), 95.

  The Regent and the King; or a Trip from Hartwell to Dover.
  A Poem. (P)
    Monthly Review, 74 (May 1814), 99-101.

  Royalty Fog-bound; or the Perils of a Night, and the Fro-
  lics of a Fortnight, a Poem. 1814. (P)
    Critical Review, s4,v5 (Feb. 1814), 214.
    Monthly Review, 73 (Feb. 1814), 208.

  A Most Solemn and Important Epistle to the Emperor of China
  on His Uncourtly and Impolitic Behaviour to the Sublime Am-
  bassadors of Great Britain. 1817. (P)
    Monthly Magazine, 43 (May 1817), 355.
    Monthly Review, 83 (June 1817), 222-23.

Wood, Henry Richard.
  Poems on Various Subjects. 1809. (P)
    Antijacobin Review, 33 (July 1809), 295-96.
    British Critic, 34 (Oct. 1809), 405.
    Critical Review, s3,v17 (May 1809), 104-05.
    Eclectic Review, 5 (June 1809), 587.
    Monthly Review, 60 (Dec. 1809), 435-36.
    Satirist, 7 (Oct. 1810), 399-400.

Wood, Rev. Thomas.
  The Conflagration, and Soliloquy. A Poem. 2nd ed. 1802.
  (P)
    Monthly Review, 38 (Aug. 1802), 439.

Woodfall, Sophia.
  Frederick Montravers, or the Adopted Son. 1802. (F)
    Critical Review, ns,v39 (Nov. 1803), 357.
    Flowers of Literature, 2 (1803), 466.

Woodhouse, James.
  Norbury Park, a Poem; with Several Others. 1803. (P)
    Annual Review, 2 (1803), 558-59.
    British Critic, 22 (Aug. 1803), 191-92.
    Critical Review, s3,v2 (May 1804), 106-08.
    Monthly Review, 48 (Jan. 1804), 93-95.

Poetical Register, 3 (1803), 448.

Love Letters to My Wife. 1804. (P)
Annual Review, 3 (1804), 596.
Monthly Review, 44 (Aug. 1804), 426-27.
New Annual Register, 25 (1804), [353].
Poetical Register, 4 (1804), 496.

Woodley, George.
The Church Yard; and Other Poems. 1808. (P)
Antijacobin Review, 35 (Mar. 1810), 301.
British Critic, 34 (Dec. 1809), 625.
Le Beau Monde, 1 (Oct. 1809), 44.
Critical Review, s3,v16 (Jan. 1809), 101-03.
Eclectic Review, 5 (Mar. 1809), 290-91.
Evangelical Magazine, 17 (Aug. 1809), 134.
Monthly Review, 59 (May 1809), 101-02.
New Annual Register, 30 (1809), [372].
Poetical Register, 7 (1808), 561.
Satirist, 4 (Feb. 1809), 194-97.

Portugal Delivered. 1812. (P)
Literary Panorama, 14 (Aug. 1813), 51-53.

Redemption, a Poem. 1816. (P)
Antijacobin Review, 50 (May 1816), 431-36.
Augustan Review, 2 (Apr. 1816), 389-94.
Monthly Review, 83 (May 1817), 58-61.

Woodward, George Moutard.
Familiar Verses from the Ghost of Willy Shakespeare to
Sammy Ireland. To Which Is Added, Prince Robert, an
Ancient Ballad. (Anon.) 1796. (P)
Critical Review, s2,v22 (Feb. 1798), 240.

The Bettyad, a Poem; Descriptive of the Progress of the
Young Roscius in London. 1805. (P)
Antijacobin Review, 20 (Mar. 1805), 302.
British Critic, 25 (Apr. 1805), 441.

The Comic Works, in Prose and Poetry, of G. M. Woodward.
1808. (P-Pr)
Antijacobin Review, 29 (Apr. 1808), 409.
British Critic, 32 (Aug. 1808), 203-04.
Cabinet, 3 (Apr. 1808), 254-55.
Critical Review, s3,v15 (Oct. 1808), 218.
European Magazine, 53 (Apr. 1808), 288-89.
Gentleman's Magazine, 78^1 (Apr. 1808), 338.

Woolsey, Robert.
An Elegy Sacred to the Memory of Lady Wright.... 1802. (P)
Antijacobin Review, 13 (Oct. 1802), 180.
British Critic, 20 (Aug. 1802), 200.

Critical Review, s2,v36 (Sept. 1802), 115.
European Magazine, 41 (Apr. 1802), 289.
Gentleman's Magazine, 73[1] (June 1803), 539.
Monthly Review, 40 (Feb. 1803), 215-16.

Wordsworth, William.
  Lyrical Ballad, with a Few Other Poems. (Anon.) 1798. (P)
    Analytical Review, 28 (Dec. 1798), 583-87.
    Antijacobin Review, 5 (Apr. 1800), 334[434].
    British Critic, 14 (Oct. 1799), 364-69.
    Critical Review, s2,v24 (Oct. 1798), 197-204.
    Monthly Magazine, Suppl. v6 (1798), 514.
    Monthly Mirror, 6 (Oct. 1798), 224-25.
    Monthly Review, 29 (June 1799), 202-10.
    New Annual Register, 19 (1798), [309-10].
    New London Review, 1 (Jan. 1799), 33-35.

  Lyrical Ballads, with Other Poems. Second Edition. 1800.
  (P)
    British Critic, 17 (Feb. 1801), 125-31.
    Literary and Masonic Magazine, 1 (Sept. 1802), 462.
    Monthly Mirror, 11 (June 1801), 389-92.
    Monthly Review, 38 (June 1802), 209.

  Poems, in Two Volumes. 1807. (P)
    Annual Review, 6 (1807), 521-29.
    Le Beau Monde, 2 (Oct. 1807), 138-42.
    British Critic, 33 (Mar. 1809), 298-99.
    Cabinet, 3 (Apr. 1808), 249-52.
    Critical Review, s3,v11 (Aug. 1807), 399-403.
    Eclectic Review, 4 (Jan. 1808), 35-43.
    Edinburgh Review, 11 (Oct. 1807), 214-31.
    Literary Annual Register, 1 (Oct. 1807), 468-69.
    Literary Panorama, 3 (Nov. 1807), 271-72.
    Monthly Literary Recreations, 3 (July 1807), 65-66.
    New Annual Register, 28 (1807), [378].
    Poetical Register, 6 (1807), 540-41.
    Satirist, 1 (Nov. 1807), 188-91.

  Concerning the Relations of Great Britain, Spain, and Portugal, to Each Other and the Common Enemy at This Crisis;
  and Specifically as Affected by the Convention of Cintra....
  1809. (Pr)
    British Critic, 34 (Sept. 1809), 305-06.
    Eclectic Review, 5 (Aug. 1809), 744-50.
    London Review, 2 (Nov. 1809), 231-75.

  The Excursion, Being a Portion of The Recluse, a Poem.
  1814. (P)
    Augustan Review, 1 (Aug. 1815), 343-56.
    La Belle Assemblée, 11 (May 1815), 224-25.
    British Critic, ns,v3 (May 1815), 449-67.
    British Review, 6 (Aug. 1815), 50-64.

Wordsworth, William (continued)
   Eclectic Review, s2,v3 (Jan. 1815), 13-39.
   Edinburgh Review, 24 (Nov. 1814), 1-30.
   Examiner, Aug. 21-28, Oct. 2, 1814, pp. 541-42, 555-58,
      636-38.
   Literary Gazette, Dec. 30, 1820, p. 837.
   Monthly Magazine, Suppl. v38 (Jan. 30, 1815), 638-49.
   Monthly Review, 76 (Feb. 1815), 123-36.
   New Monthly Magazine, 2 (Sept. 1814), 157.
   Philanthropist, 5 (1815), 342-63.
   Quarterly Review, 12 (Oct. 1814), 100-11.
   Variety, Sept. 10, 1814, pp. 5-16.

The White Doe of Rylstone, or the Fate of the Nortons.
1815. (P)
   Augustan Review, 1 (Aug. 1815), 343-56.
   La Belle Assemblée, ns,v12 (July 1815), 31-33.
   Blackwood's Edinburgh Magazine, 3 (July 1818), 369-81.
   British Lady's Magazine, 2 (July 1815), 33-37.
   British Review, 6 (Nov. 1815), 370-77.
   Champion, Jan. 25, 1815, pp. 205-06.
   Eclectic Review, s2,v5 (Jan. 1816), 33-45.
   Edinburgh Review, 25 (Oct. 1815), 355-63.
   European Magazine, 69 (Mar. 1816), 237-39.
   Gentleman's Magazine, 85^2 (Dec. 1815), 524-25.
   Monthly Review, 78 (Nov. 1815), 235-38.
   New Monthly Magazine, 3 (July 1815), 546.
   Quarterly Review, 14 (Oct. 1815), 201-25.
   Theatrical Inquisitor, 6 (June 1815), 445-50.

Poems by William Wordsworth, Including Lyrical Ballads, and
the Miscellaneous Pieces of the Author, with Additional
Poems, a New Preface and a Supplementary Essay.   1816.
(P-Pr)
   Augustan Review, 1 (Aug. 1815), 343-56.
   Monthly Review, 78 (Nov. 1815), 225-34.
   Quarterly Review, 14 (Oct. 1815), 201-25.

A Letter to a Friend of Robert Burns, Occasioned by an Intended Re-publication of the Account of the Life of Burns,
by Dr. Currie, and the Selection Made by Him from His Letters.   1816. (Pr)
   Blackwood's Edinburgh Magazine, 1 (June 1817), 261-66.
   Critical Review, s5,v4 (July 1816), 51-58.
   Monthly Review, 80 (June 1816), 221-22.

Thanksgiving Ode, January 18, 1816, with Other Short Pieces,
Chiefly Referring to Recent Public Events.   1816.   (P)
   British Critic, ns,v6 (Sept. 1816), 313-15.
   Champion, Oct. 20, 1816, pp. 334-35.
   Dublin Examiner, 2 (Nov. 1816), 18-25.
   Eclectic Review, s2,v6 (July 1816), 1-18.
   Monthly Review, 82 (Jan. 1817), 98-100.

Wordsworth, William (continued)
Peter Bell. A Tale in Verse. 1819. (P)
Blackwood's Edinburgh Magazine, 5 (May 1819), 130-36.
British Critic, ns,vll (June 1819), 584-603.
British Lady's Magazine, s3,v3 (July 1819), 34-35.
Eclectic Review, s2,vl2 (July 1819), 62-76.
Edinburgh Magazine and Literary Miscellany (Scots Magazine), s2,v4 (May 1819), 427-29.
Edinburgh Monthly Review, 2 (Dec. 1819), 654-61.
European Magazine, 75 (May 1819), 445-48.
Examiner, May 2, 1819, pp. 282-83.
Fireside Magazine (quoting Gentleman's Magazine and Monthly Magazine), 1 (July 1819), 275, 276.
Fireside Magazine (quoting British Critic and Eclectic Review), 1 (Aug. 1819), 314, 316.
Gentleman's Magazine, 89[1] (May 1819), 441-42.
Kaleidoscope, ns,vl (Mar. 6, 1821), 285-86.
Literary and Statistical Magazine, 3 (Aug. 1819), 314-19.
Literary Chronicle, 1 (May 29, 1819), 20-21.
Literary Gazette, May 1, 1819, pp. 273-75.
Monthly Magazine, 47 (June 1819), 442.
Monthly Review, 89 (Aug. 1819), 419-22.
Theatrical Inquisitor, 14 (May-June 1819), 369-76, 441-46.

The Waggoner, a Poem; to Which Are Added Sonnets. 1819.
(P)
Blackwood's Edinburgh Magazine, 5 (June 1819), 332-34.
British Critic, ns,vl2 (Nov. 1812), 464-79.
British Lady's Magazine, s3,v3 (Aug. 1819), 85-86.
Eclectic Review, s2,vl2 (July 1819), 62-76.
Edinburgh Monthly Review, 2 (Dec. 1819), 654-61.
European Magazine, 75 (June 1819), 531-33.
Fireside Magazine, 1 (Aug. 1819), 303-04.
Fireside Magazine (quoting New Monthly Magazine, 1 (Sept. 1819), 357.
Gentleman's Magazine, 89[2] (Aug. 1819), 143-44.
Literary and Statistical Magazine, 3 (Aug. 1819), 314-19.
Literary Gazette, June 12, 1819, pp. 369-71.
Monthly Magazine, 47 (July 1819), 540.
Monthly Review, 90 (Sept. 1819), 36-40.
New Monthly Magazine, 12 (Aug. 1819), 81.
Theatrical Inquisitor, 14 (June 1819), 447-49.

The River Duddon, a Series of Sonnets; Vaudracour and Julia; and Other Poems. To Which Is Annexed, a Topographical Description of the Country of the Lake, in the North of England. 1820. (P)
Blackwood's Edinburgh Magazine, 7 (May 1820), 206-13.
British Critic, s2,vl5 (Feb. 1821), 113-35.
British Review, 16 (Sept. 1820), 37-53.
Eclectic Review, s2,vl4 (Aug. 1820), 170-84.
European Magazine, 77 (June 1820), 523-25.

Wordsworth, William (concluded)
Gentleman's Magazine, 90² (Oct. 1820), 344-46.
Lady's Monthly Museum, s3,v12 (Aug. 1820), 95.
Literary and Statistical Magazine (Scottish Episcopal Review), 4 (Aug. 1820), 323-28.
Literary Chronicle, 2 (July 1, 1820), 420-22.
Literary Gazette, Mar. 25, 1820, pp. 200-03.
(Gold's) London Magazine, 1 (June 1820), 618-27.
Monthly Review, 93 (Oct. 1820), 132-43.

The Miscellaneous Poems of William Wordsworth. 1820. (P)
Literary Gazette, Oct. 7, 1820, p. 641.

Worgan, John Dawes.
Select Poems. To Which Are Added Some Particulars....
With a Preface by William Hayley. 1810. (P)
British Critic, 39 (Mar. 1812), 305-06.
Christian Guardian and Church of England Magazine, 2 (Suppl. 1810), 484-87.
Christian Observer, 9 (Apr. 1810), 229-36.
Critical Review, s3,v23 (June 1811), 140-50.
Eclectic Review, 7 (Oct. 1811), 894-900.
Evangelical Magazine, 18 (Dec. 1810), 481-82.
Poetical Register, 8 (1811), 617-18.
Quarterly Review, 3 (May 1810), 431-39.

Wrangham, Francis. (See also J. B. Papworth, Francis Wrangham, and William Combe, above.)
The Holy Land, a Poem. 1800. (P)
Antijacobin Review, 8 (Jan. 1801), 62-64.
British Critic, 17 (Feb. 1801), 186-87.
Critical Review, s2,v35 (July 1802), 349-51.
Gentleman's Magazine, 71¹ (Jan. 1801), 55.
Monthly Review, 34 (Mar. 1801), 321-23.
New Annual Register, 21 (1800), [326-27].

Poems. 1802. (P)
Annual Review, 1 (1802), 655-57.
British Critic, 20 (Dec. 1802), 675.
Critical Review, s2,v37 (Jan. 1803), 93-97.
Imperial Review, 5 (Dec. 1805), 681-83.
Monthly Magazine, Suppl. v15 (July 28, 1803), 638.
Monthly Review, 43 (Jan. 1804), 82-85.
Poetical Register, 2 (1802), 434-35.

The Raising of Jairus's Daughter. A Poem. To Which Is Annexed, a Short Memoir, Interspersed with a Few Poetical Productions, of the Late Caroline Symmons. 1804. (P)
British Critic, 24 (Sept. 1804), 283-86.
Eclectic Review, 1 (June 1805), 462-65.
Monthly Review, 45 (Dec. 1804), 436-39.
Poetical Register, 4 (1804), 500.

A Poem on the Restoration of Learning in the East. 1805.
(P)
   British Critic, 26 (Sept. 1805), 319-20.
   Christian Observer, 4 (July 1805), 424-28.
   Eclectic Review, 1 (May 1805), 383-86.
   European Magazine, 48 (Oct. 1805), 298.
   Gentleman's Magazine, 75^2 (Sept. 1805), 839.
   Monthly Magazine, Suppl. v19 (July 28, 1805), 659.
   Monthly Review, 47 (May 1805), 89-92.

Wright, Walter Rodwell.
  Horae Ionicae; a Poem, Descriptive of the Ionian Islands,
  and Part of the Adjacent Coast of Greece. 1809. (P)
   Antijacobin Review, 33 (May 1809), 70-79.
   Le Beau Monde, 1 (June 1809), 241-43.
   British Critic, 34 (Sept. 1809), 237-39.
   Eclectic Review, 5 (July 1809), 667-70.
   General Chronicle, 2 (Aug. 1811), 407-15.
   Literary Panorama, 6 (June 1809), 475-80.
   Monthly Mirror, ns,v6 (Sept. 1809), 149-51.
   Monthly Review, 60 (Sept. 1809), 98-101.
   New Annual Register, 30 (1809), [371].
   Poetical Register, 7 (1809), 592.
   Satirist, 5 (Dec. 1809), 595-600.

Yeates, Mrs. _____.
  Eliza, a Novel. 1800. (F)
   Critical Review, ns,v31 (Mar. 1801), 356-57.
   Monthly Magazine, Suppl. v11 (July 20, 1801), 606.

Yeman, Alexander.
  The Fisherman's Hut, in the Highlands of Scotland. With
  Other Poems. (P)
   Cyclopaedian Magazine, 1 (May 1807), 284.
   Monthly Literary Recreations, 2 (Jan. 1807), 72.
   Oxford Review, 1 (May 1807), 556-58.
   Poetical Register, 7 (1808), 561-62.

Young Hibernian, A.
  See E. Cummins.

Young Lady, A.
  See Elizabeth Smith; also Mary Panton; also Miss E. King.

Young, Hannah.
  An Elegy on the Death of Richard Reynolds. With Other
  Poems. 1818. (P)
   Fireside Magazine (quoting Monthly Review), 1 (Feb. 1819),
    71.
   Monthly Review, 87 (Dec. 1818), 439-40.

Young, Mary Julia.
  Rose-Mount Castle; or, False Report. A Novel. 1798. (F)
    Critical Review, ns,v24 (Dec. 1798), 470.

  Moss Cliff Abbey; or the Sepulchral Harmonist. 1803. (F)
    Critical Review, s3,v1 (Jan. 1804), 119.
    Monthly Magazine, Suppl. v17 (July 28, 1804), 667.

  Right and Wrong; or, the Kinsmen of Naples. A Romantic
  Story. (F)
    Antijacobin Review, 19 (Dec. 1804), 424-29.
    Critical Review, s3,v3 (Dec. 1804), 470.

  Donalda; or the Witches of Glenshiel. A Caledonian Legend.
  1805. (F)
    Monthly Mirror, 19 (June 1805), 393-94.

  A Summer at Brighton; Being a Continuation of The Winter
  in London. (Anon.) (F)
    Monthly Magazine, Suppl. v22 (Jan. 25, 1807), 643.

Young, Murdo.
  The Shades of Waterloo! a Vision, in Verse. 1817. (P)
    Critical Review, s5,v5 (Jan. 1817), 96-97.
    Fireside Magazine (quoting Monthly Review), 1 (Jan. 1819),
      34.
    Gentleman's Magazine, 87[1] (Feb. 1817), 154-55.
    Monthly Review, 87 (Nov. 1818), 326-27.

  Antonia; a Poem. 1818. (P)
    Antijacobin Review, 54 (June 1818), 316-29.
    La Belle Assemblée, ns,v18 (Aug. 1818), 81-84.
    Fireside Magazine (quoting Monthly Review), 1 (Sept.
      1819), 346.
    Gentleman's Magazine, 88[1] (Suppl. Jan.-June 1818), 610-13.
    Literary Gazette, June 13, 1818, pp. 369-72.
    Literary Journal and General Miscellany, 1 (Oct. 31-Nov.
      7, 1818), 493-94, 511-13.
    Literary Panorama, ns,v8 (Aug. 1818), 744-73.
    Monthly Magazine, 45 (July 1818), 535.
    Monthly Review, 89 (July 1819), 330.
    New Monthly Magazine, 10 (Aug. 1818), 61.

Ziegenhert, Mrs. Sophia F.
  Seabrook Village and Its Inhabitants; or, the History of
  Mrs. Worthy and Her Family. 1811. (F)
    British Critic, 38 (Nov. 1811), 523.
    Critical Review, s4,v1 (Mar. 1812), 331.
    Gentleman's Magazine, 82[1] (Jan. 1812), 59.
    Monthly Review, ns,v67 (Mar. 1812), 322.

  The Orphan of Tintern Abbey. 1816. (F)
    Monthly Review, ns,v79 (Apr. 1816), 439.

Zimmerman, J. G.
  Solitude. Vol. II. (F?)
    Lady's Monthly Museum, 3 (Oct. 1799), 313-19.

Zornlin, Mrs. Elizabeth.
  See Rev. William Tremenheere.

APPENDICES

A. General (Non-Review) Articles on Authors
   and Their Works

B. General and Genre Criticism
   B-1. Volumes of General and Genre Criticism
        Reviewed
   B-2. Articles of General Criticism
   B-3. Articles on Poetry
   B-4. Articles on Fiction
   B-5. Articles on Drama and Theatre

C. Reviews of Operas

(See Preface for comments introductory to Appendices)

APPENDIX A

GENERAL (NON-REVIEW) ARTICLES ON AUTHORS AND THEIR WORKS

Bloomfield, Robert.
"Memoirs of R. Bloomfield," Domestic Miscellany, 1 (Oct. 5, 1819), 25-27.
"Biographical Sketch of Robert Bloomfield," Monthly Mirror, 10 (Oct. 1800), 203-05.
"Melancholy Hours. No. VI," Monthly Mirror, 16 (Nov. 1803), 301-04.
"Sketch of the Memoirs of Robert Bloomfield," Monthly Visitor, 12 (Apr. 1801), 319-25.

Bowles, William Lisle.
"Gleaner. No. X. [On Coombe Ellen]," Edinburgh Magazine and Literary Miscellany, ns,v14 (Aug. 1799), 83-86.
"Mr. Bowles--as Editor of Pope," (Baldwin's) London Magazine, 2 (July 1820), 33-34.
"Melancholy Hours. Number V," Monthly Mirror, 16 (July 1803), 20-24.

Byron, George Gordon, Baron.
"A Critique on the Address Written by Lord Byron, Which Was Spoken at the Opening of the New Theatre Royal, Drury-Lane," Antijacobin Review, 43 (Dec. 1812), 359-73.
"Lines on Reading Lord Byron's Poem of Childe Harold," Antijacobin Review, 48 (Apr. 1815), 412-15.
"Lord Byron's Account of His Swimming Across the Hellespont," La Belle Assemblée, ns,v8 (Nov. 1813), 197.
"A Reply to Lord Byron's 'Fare Thee Well'," La Belle Assemblée, ns,v22 (July 1820), 35.
"[A summary of Edinburgh Review review of Childe Harold, III]," Blackwood's Edinburgh Magazine, 1 (Apr. 1817), 81.
"Marlowe's Tragical History of the Life and Death of Doctor Faustus," Blackwood's Edinburgh Magazine, 1 (July 1817), 388-94.
"Fragment of a Fifth Canto of Childe Harold's Pilgrimage. [A burlesque.]," Blackwood's Edinburgh Magazine, 3 (May 1818), 201-04.
"Note to the Editor, Enclosing a Letter to the Author of Beppo," Blackwood's Edinburgh Magazine, 3 (June 1818), 323.
"To the Author of Beppo," Blackwood's Edinburgh Magazine, 3 (June 1818), 323-29.

Byron, George Gordon, Baron (continued).

"The Story of Parisina," _Blackwood's Edinburgh Magazine_, 4 (Jan. 1819), 411-13.

"John Gilpin and Mazeppa," _Blackwood's Edinburgh Magazine_, 5 (July 1819), 434-39.

"Don Juan Unread. [A parody.]," _Blackwood's Edinburgh Magazine_, 6 (Nov. 1819), 194-95.

"Letter from Lord Byron, Enclosing the Commencement of Childe Daniel. [A parody.]," _Blackwood's Edinburgh Magazine_, 7 (May 1820), 186-87.

"Horae Germanicae. No. V. The Faustus of Goethe," _Blackwood's Edinburgh Magazine_, 7 (June 1820), 233-58.

"John and Joan, a New Poem. [A burlesque.]," _Blackwood's Edinburgh Magazine_, 7 (July 1820), 437-41.

"To the Editor. [Byron indiscriminately praised.]," _British Lady's Magazine_, 1 (Mar. 1815), 175-76.

"Engravings in Lord Byron's Works," _British Lady's Magazine_, 2 (Oct. 1815), 259-63.

"To Lord Byron," _British Lady's Magazine_, 4 (Aug. 1816), 118-19.

"Hebrew Melody. Not by Lord Byron," _British Lady's Magazine_, s3,v2 (Feb. 1819), 75.

"Byron vs. Elgin," _British Stage and Literary Cabinet_, 1 (Mar. 1817), 63-64.

"Miscellaneous Articles. Byron's Imitations," _British Stage and Literary Cabinet_, 1 (Oct. 1817), 232-35.

"Verse. Waltzing," _British Stage and Literary Cabinet_, 4 (Nov. 1819), 47-48.

"Lord and Lady Byron. [Letter to the Editor.]," _Busy Body_, 1 (May 1816), 127-29.

"The Minister in the Saloon at Covent Garden, an Hebrew Melody," _Busy Body_, 4 (Nov. 1, 1817), 97-100.

"Lines, Written in a Blank Leaf of Lord Byron's _Bride of Abydos_," _The Caledonian_, 1 (Jan. 2, 1819), 5.

"Portraits of Authors. No. VI. Lord Byron," _Champion_, May 7, 1814, pp. 150-51.

"Biographical Memoir of the Right Honourable George Gordon Byron," _The Comet, or Literary Wanderer_, 1 (1820), 129-37.

"Literary News. Lord Byron and _Don Juan_," _Déjeuné_, 1 (Oct. 21, 1820), 3.

"Literary News. Lord Byron," _Déjeuné_, 1 (Oct. 23, 1820), 12.

"Lines Supposed to Be Addressed by Lady B**** to Her Husband," _Dublin Examiner_, 1 (Oct. 1816), 431-32.

"Lord Byron's Poetry," _Dublin Magazine_, 1 (Jan., Apr. 1820), 55-59, 366-69.

"Lord Byron's _Corsair_," _Dublin Magazine_, 1 (Jan. 1820), 59.

"Illustration of a Passage in Lord Byron's Poem of _The Corsair_," _Dublin Magazine_, 2 (Nov. 1820), 411-12.

"On the Moral Constitution of Childe Harold," _Edinburgh Magazine and Literary Miscellany_, ns,v2 (Mar. 1818), 223-26.

Byron, George Gordon, Baron (continued).
"Epithets on Lord Byron," Edinburgh Reflector, 1 (Oct. 28,
1818), 153.
"Memoir of the Right. Hon. George Gordon Byron, Lord Byron
of Rochdale," European Magazine, 65 (Jan. 1814), 3-4.
"Defence of Lord Byron," European Magazine, 65 (Feb. 1814),
94-95.
"Agar's Portrait of Lord Byron," Examiner, Sept. 4, 1814,
pp. 570-71.
"Prints from the Designs of Mr. Stothard--Lord Byron's
Works," Examiner, Aug. 20, 1815, pp. 538-39.
"Distressing Circumstance in High Life," Examiner, Apr. 21,
1816, pp. 247-50.
"[Poem] To the Right Honourable Lord Byron, on His Depar-
ture for Italy and Greece," Examiner, Apr. 28, 1816,
pp. 266-67.
"Theatrical Examiner. No. 310 [on the production of The
Bride of Abydos]," Examiner, Feb. 8, 1818, pp. 90-91.
"[Lord Byron.]," Examiner, June 20, 1819, p. 395.
"Lord Byron," Examiner, Jan. 23, 1820, p. 56.
"Domestic Intelligence. Opening of Drury-Lane Theatre,"
General Chronicle, 6 (Nov. 1812), 393-95.
"Upon Reading Lord Byron's Reflections on the Battle of
Talavera in Childe Harold," Gentleman's Magazine, 82^1
(June 1812), 566.
"Sentiments on the First Perusal of The Giaour," Gentleman's
Magazine, 83^2 (July 1813), 4.
"To Lord Byron, on His Dog-Ditty," Gentleman's Magazine,
85^1(Apr. 1815), 350.
"To a Celebrated Noble Poet," Gentleman's Magazine, 86^1
(May 1816), 447-48.
"Reflections on Shipboard, by Lord Byron. [A hoax.]," Gentle-
man's Magazine, 86^1 (Suppl. Jan.-June 1816), 613.
"On Seeing Some Late Productions of a Noble Lord," Gentle-
man's Magazine, 86^1 (Suppl. Jan.-June 1816), 616.
"Lady Byron's Responsive 'Fare Thee Well'," Gentleman's
Magazine, 86^2 (July 1816), 62.
"Extracts from a Poem upon the Departure of a Great Poet
from This Country," Gentleman's Magazine, 86^2 (Aug.
1816), 160.
"On Reading the Third Canto of Childe Harold," Gentleman's
Magazine, 87^1 (Jan. 1817), 63-64.
"[Some Plagiarisms of Byron Noted in a Letter to the Edi-
tor]," Gentleman's Magazine, 88^1 (Feb. 1818), 121-22.
"[A Letter to the Editor on Stanzas to Geneva]," Gentle-
man's Magazine, 88^1 (Feb. 1818), 122.
"[A Letter to the Editor on Poetical Imitations by Byron],"
Gentleman's Magazine, 88^1 (May 1818), 389-90.
"The Ballad on Which the Poem of The Corsair is Founded,"
Gentleman's Magazine, 88^2 (Sept. 1818), 255.
"Remarks...on the Poetry of Byron and Scott," Gentleman's
Magazine, 89^2 (Nov. 1819), 397-400.
"The Radical Triumvirate; or Infidel Paine, Lord Byron, and

Byron, George Gordon, Baron (continued).
 Surgeon Lawrence...," <u>Gentleman's Magazine</u>, 90[1] (Mar. 1820), 250.
 "Remarks, Critical and Moral, on the Talents of Lord Byron, and the Tendencies of <u>Don Juan</u>," <u>Gentleman's Magazine</u>, 90[1] (Apr. 1820), 343-44.
 "Lord Byron. To the Editor of the <u>Gleaner</u>," <u>Gleaner</u>, 1 (1816), 613-20.
 "[Poem to Lord Byron]," <u>Green Man</u>, Nov. 14, 1818, pp. 23-24.
 "Reply to Lord Byron's Contemptible Assertion That Death's 'The First dark day of Nothingness'," <u>Green Man</u>, Dec. 12, 1818, p. 56.
 "Lines, Written in a Blank Leaf of Lord Byron's <u>Bride of Abydos</u>," <u>Green Man</u>, Jan. 9, 1819, p. 88.
 "Animadversions on Lord Byron's <u>Don Juan</u>," <u>Imperial Magazine</u>, 2 (May 1820), 373-78.
 "Lines Inscribed to Lord Byron, Occasioned by a Reception He Met at Cambridge, after a Long Absence," <u>Irish Magazine</u>, 2 (May 1820), 373-78.
 "Stanzas, Written after Reading the Fourth Canto of <u>Childe Harold</u>," <u>Kaleidoscope</u>, 1 (Jan. 26, 1819), 108.
 "Lord Byron's Travels in Greece," <u>Kaleidoscope</u>, 1 (June 22, 1819), 188.
 "[Concerning <u>The Vampyre</u>]," <u>Kaleidoscope</u>, 2 (July 20, 1819), 5-6.
 "Don Juan," <u>Kaleidoscope</u>, 2 (Aug. 24, 1819), 28.
 "Scott, Byron, Herbert, and Moore [Compared]," <u>Kaleidoscope</u>, 2 (Feb. 29, 1820), 135.
 "Lord Byron [from a French Critic]," <u>Kaleidoscope</u>, 2 (May 23, 1820), 178.
 "Lord Byron [from Baldwin's <u>London Magazine</u>]," <u>Kaleidoscope</u>, ns,vl (July 18, 1820), 23.
 "Hebrew Melody. No. 1. [An Imitation]," <u>Letter-Box</u>, March 21, 1818, p. 63.
 "Hebrew Melody. No. 2. [An Imitation]," <u>Letter-Box</u>, March 28, 1818, p. 79.
 "Hebrew Melody. No. 3. [An Imitation]," <u>Letter-Box</u>, July 27, 1818, pp. 303-04.
 "To a Grecian Girl [an imitation of Byron]," <u>Literary and Political Examiner</u>, 1 (May 1802), 230-31.
 "Upon Reading Lord Byron's Hebrew Melodies," <u>Literary and Statistical Magazine</u>, 4 (Aug. 1820), 329.
 "Original Correspondence. <u>Don Juan</u>," <u>Literary Chronicle</u>, 1 (July 17, 1819), 135-36.
 "Original Communications. Illustrations of a Passage in Lord Byron's Poem of <u>The Bride of Abydos</u>," <u>Literary Chronicle</u>, 1 (Sept. 18, 1819), 282.
 "Lord Byron," <u>Literary Chronicle</u>, 2 (Jan. 22, 1820), 59-60.
 "On the Poetical Style of Lord Byron," <u>Literary Gazette</u>, Mar. 29, 1817, p. 145.
 "On the Nature of Lord Byron's Poetry," <u>Literary Gazette</u>, Apr. 5, 1817, pp. 162-63.

Byron, George Gordon, Baron (continued).
 "Childe Harold in the Shades," Literary Gazette, Feb. 6,
   1819, p. 87.
 "Lord Byron," Literary Gazette, Mar. 27, 1819, p. 207.
 "Lord Byron," Literary Gazette, May 6, 1820, pp. 296-97.
 "Lord Byron's Tragedy [Marino Faliero]," Literary Gazette,
   Nov. 25, 1820, pp. 763-64.
 "Byron and Scott," Literary Journal and General Miscellany,
   1 (May 10, 1818), 104.
 "To Lord Byron. A Parody," Literary Journal and General
   Miscellany," 1 (May 17, 1818), 125.
 "Lord Byron's Residence to Mitylene," Literary Journal and
   General Miscellany, 1 (Nov. 28, 1818), 561-62.
 "Ode to Scandal and Lord Byron's Enigma," Literary Journal
   and General Miscellany, 2 (Jan. 30, 1819), 77.
 "Excerpts from the Notes to Lord Byron's Poem of Childe
   Harold," Literary Panorama, 11 (May 1812), 897-903.
 "Extract from Lord Byron's Journal," (Baldwin's) London
   Magazine, 1 (Mar. 1820), 295-96.
 "To the Author of Childe Harold," (Baldwin's) London Maga-
   zine, 1 (Apr. 1820), 415.
 "Lord Byron: His French Critics: the Newspapers: and the
   Magazines," (Baldwin's) London Magazine, 1 (May 1820),
   492-97.
 "The Lion's Head," (Baldwin's) London Magazine, 2 (July
   1820), 3-8.
 "Biographical Memoir of the Right Honourable George Gordon,
   Lord Byron," (Gold's) London Magazine, 1 (Jan.-Feb.
   1820), 1-11, 118-22.
 "Biographical Memoir of...Lord Byron," (Gold's) London
   Magazine, 1 (Feb. 1820), 120.
 "Original Poetry. Longinus o'er a Bottle [signed Byronius],"
   (Gold's) London Magazine, 1 (Feb.-June, 1820), 207-09,
   329-30, 437-39, 554-55, 668-69.
 "Remarks on the Writings of Lord Byron, Particularly on the
   Poem of Don Juan," (Gold's) London Magazine, 1 (Mar.
   1820), 269-70.
 "Lines in Reply to Lord Bryon's 'Lines to Jessy'," (Gold's)
   London Magazine, 1 (June 1820), 670.
 "On the Living Novelists," (Gold's) London Magazine, 2
   (Aug. 1820), 149.
 "Newstead Abbey," Man of Kent, 2 (May 8, 1819), 533-34.
 "[Appreciative Letter to the Editor]," Mentor, 1 (Aug. 16-
   23, 1817), 149-53, 161-64.
 "[Letter to the Editor on Byron's Gloomy Characters]," Men-
   tor, 2 (Apr. 25, 1818), 279-84.
 "[Observations on the Poetry of Lord Byron," 2 (May 16,
   1818), 309-11.
 "Byroniana. No. 1," Meteor, or General Censor, 2 (Mar.
   1814), 350-53.
 "Line, Occasioned by Lord Byron's...'Weep, Daughter of a
   Royal Line'," Meteor, or Monthly Censor, 2 (May 1814),
   61-62.

Byron, George Gordon, Baron (continued).
  "Biographical Memoir of the Right Honourable Lord Byron,"
    Miniature Magazine, 3 (Aug. 1819), 109-15.
  "Line to Lord Byron. On Reading Don Juan," Miniature Maga-
    zine, 3 (Nov. 1819), 321.
  "Lord Byron [an anecdote]," Miniature Magazine, 3 (Jan.
    1820), 391-92.
  "Lord Byron's Don Juan," Miniature Magazine, ns,vl (July
    1820), 25-28.
  "An Essay on Self-Assumed Poets, by John Hatt," Miniature
    Magazine, ns,vl (Aug. 1820), 83-84.
  "[A Letter to the Editor censuring the dramatizing of The
    Bride of Abydos]," Modern Spectator, 1 (Jan. 23, 1819),
    65-66.
  "[Letter to the Editor concerning Lord Byron and Dr. Reid],"
    Monthly Magazine, 37 (May 1814), 298-300.
  "[Letter to the Editor on Passages Imitated by Byron],"
    Monthly Magazine, 37 (June 1814), 410-11.
  "[Letter to the Editor on Byron as a Mediocre Poet],"
    Monthly Magazine, 42 (Sept. 1816), 113-15.
  "[Letter to the Editor in Defense of Byron's Poems],"
    Monthly Magazine, 42 (Nov. 1816), 299-300.
  "[Letter to the Editor in Defense of Byron's Poems],"
    Monthly Magazine, 42 (Dec. 1816), 417-18.
  "[On Byron's Popularity]," Monthly Magazine, 45 (Feb. 1818),
    68.
  "[Byron Charged with Plagiarism]," Monthly Magazine, 46
    (Aug. 1818), 20-21.
  "Contemporary Authors. No. IX. Lord Byron," Monthly Maga-
    zine, 50 (Sept. 1820), 102-03.
  "Giovanni Sbogarro," Monthly Magazine, 50 (Oct. 1820), 267.
  "Memoirs of the Right Hon. George Gordon Byron...," Monthly
    Museum, 1 (Feb. 1814), 257-58.
  "[A Brief Announcement and Discussion of Byron]," New
    Annual Register, 37 (1816), [290].
  "Lord Byron and the Island of Mitylene," New Bon Ton Maga-
    zine, 1 (Sept. 1818), 305-09.
  "The Wandering Poet, or the Lord of the Lyre," New Bon Ton
    Magazine, 2 (Nov. 1818-Apr. 1819), 40-43, 75-78, 134-37,
    261-62, 348-51.
  "Lord Byron in Greece," New Bon Ton Magazine, 2 (Apr. 1819),
    365-66.
  "Lord Byron's Travels in Greece. By John Mitford," New Bon
    Ton Magazine, 3 (May, July 1819), 11-16, 158-63.
  "Lord Byron and His Supposed Letter," New Bon Ton Magazine,
    3 (July 1819), 185-87.
  "Don Juan and Lord Byron. To the Editor," New Bon Ton Maga-
    zine, 3 (Sept. 1819), 300-03.
  "[Concerning Lord Byron and R. C. Dallas]," New Monthly
    Magazine, 1 (Apr. 1814), 262-63.
  "[Byron regains Possession of Newstead Abbey]," New Monthly
    Magazine, 2 (Oct. 1814), 282.
  "Some Account of the Right Hon. George Gordon, Lord Byron,"

Byron, George Gordon, Baron (continued).
    New Monthly Magazine, 3 (July 1815), 527-30.
"Lord Byron's Imitation," New Monthly Magazine, 5 (Apr.
    1816), 199.
"[Letter to the Editor Defending The Siege of Corinth],"
    New Monthly Magazine, 9 (June 1818), 390-91.
"Observations on a Letter to Lord Byron," New Monthly Maga-
    zine, 9 (Aug. 1818), 31-33.
"Nugae Literariae. No. I. Coincidence between Lord Byron
    and Waller," New Monthly Magazine, 10 (Sept. 1818), 110.
"Observations on the Poetical Style of Lord Byron," New
    Monthly Magazine, 10 (Sept. 1818), 111-12.
"Nugae Literariae. No. 2. Coincidence between Lord Byron
    and Burton," New Monthly Magazine, 10 (Oct. 1818), 207.
"On Literary Imitation," New Monthly Magazine, 10 (Nov.
    1818), 298-99.
"Lord Byron's Residence on the Island of Mitylene," New
    Monthly Magazine, 10 (Nov. 1818), 309-11.
"Nugae Literariae. No. IV. Coincidence between Lord Byron
    and Other Writers," New Monthly Magazine, 10 (Dec. 1818),
    400-02.
"To Lord Byron. Written after Perusing His Epitaph on a
    Newfoundland Dog," New Monthly Magazine, 10 (Dec. 1818),
    426.
"Lines, Written in a Blank Leaf of Lord Byron's Bride of
    Abydos," New Monthly Magazine, 10 (Dec. 1818), 427.
"Modern Plagiarists," New Monthly Magazine, 10 (Jan. 1819),
    500-01.
Observations on Lord Byron's Juvenile Poems, with Speci-
    mens," New Monthly Magazine, 11 (Feb. 1819), 1-9.
"Extract of a Letter from Geneva, with Anecdotes of Lord
    Byron," New Monthly Magazine, 11 (Apr. 1819), 193-95.
"On the Character and Poetry of Lord Byron," New Monthly
    Magazine, 11 (May 1819), 330-32.
"Lord Byron's Travels in Greece," New Monthly Magazine, 11
    (June 1819), 388-92.
"Lines on Reading the Last Canto of Childe Harold," New
    Monthly Magazine, 11 (July 1819), 527-28.
"Mazeppa," New Monthly Magazine, 12 (Sept. 1819), 165-66.
"Critique on Modern Poets," New Monthly Magazine, 12 (Nov.
    1819), 377-84.
"Remarks Critical and Moral on the Talents of Lord Byron,
    and the Tendencies of Don Juan," New Monthly Magazine,
    13 (Apr. 1820), 486.
"Biographical Account of Lord Byron," Newry Magazine,
    1 (July-Aug. 1815), 242-48.
"Lord Byron's Residence in the Island of Mitylene," Newry
    Magazine, 5 (Nov.-Dec. 1815), 330-33.
"Hours after Tea. No. 5. [Byron's indebtedness to other
    writers]," Northern Star, 3 (Aug. 1819), 89-95.
"Fragments [Random Jottings]," Portfolio, Political and
    Literary, 1 (Dec. 14, 1816), 164-65.
"To the Editor [on The Giaour]," Reasoner, 1 (Nov. 1813), 313.

Byron, George Gordon, Baron (continued).
"Which Is the Best Poet, Lord Byron or Walter Scott, Esq.?"
  Reasoner, 1 (Apr. 1814), 509-28.
"Answer to Mr. Gifford [Letter to the Editor]," Reasoner,
  1 (Apr. 1814), 539-43.
"Second Reply to Mr. Gifford [Letter to the Editor],"
  Reasoner, 1 (June 1814), 687-93.
"Stanzas. Suggested by Some Lines of Lord Byron," Reposi-
  tory of Arts, ns,v3 (Mar. 1817), 185.
"John Gilpin and Mazeppa," Repository of Arts, ns,v8 (Oct.
  1819), 192-94.
"[Letter to the Editor, on Manfred]," Sale-Room, 1 (June 21,
  1817), 200.
"[Letter to the Editor, on Manfred]," Sale-Room, 1 (June 28,
  1817), 201-07.
"[Appreciative Article on Byron by the Editor]," Sale-Room,
  1 (July 5, 1817), 209-16.
"Lord Byron," Salopean Magazine, 2 (May 1816), 216-22.
"[A defense of Mazeppa]," Salt-Bearer, no27 (1820), 189-202.
"The Cantab. No. III. [Lord Byron to His Bear]," Satirist,
  4 (June 1808), 364-69.
"Lord Byron," Satirist, 8 (May 1811), 385-89.
"Lord Byron and the Edinburgh Reviewers," Satirist, 11
  (Nov. 1812), 447-48.
"Address to Lord Byron," Scots Magazine, 78 (June 1816),
  454.
"On the Poetry of Scott and Byron," Scots Magazine, 79
  (Jan. 1817), 26-27.
"Upon Reading Lord Byron's Hebrew Melodies," Scottish Epis-
  copal Review and Magazine, 1 (Aug. 1820), 329.
"Lord Byron," Scourge, 1 (Mar. 1811), 191-211.
"Poetical Epistle to Lord Byron," Scourge, 10 (Dec. 1815),
  409-11.
"The Wrongs of Lady Byron, Mrs. Mardyn's Letter, and Lord
  Byron's Farewell to England," Scourge and Satirist, 12
  (July 1, 1816), 9-18.
"To a Young and Unfortunate Exile, the Friend of Lord Byron,
  and His Present Companion," Scourge and Satirist, 12
  (Sept. 1816), 225.
"The Faustus of Goethe," Spirit of the Magazine, no5-6
  (1820), 243-46, 257-65.
"To Lord Byron [From the Morning Post, Feb. 7]," Spirit of
  the Public Journals, 18 (1814), 62.
"To Lord Byron [From the Morning Post, Feb. 16]," Spirit of
  the Public Journals, 18 (1814), 75.
"Lord Byron's Epic Poem [from the Morning Herald, June 7],"
  Spirit of the Public Journals, 18 (1814), 155-57.
"[Concerning Lord Byron and Lord Elgin. A Letter to the
  Editor]," Thanet Magazine, 1 (Sept. 1817), 139-44.
"Address to Lord Byron. On His Leaving England," Theatri-
  cal Inquisitor, 8 (June 1816), 457-58.
"Address to Lord Byron," Theatrical Inquisitor, 9 (Aug.
  1816), 135-36.

Byron, George Gordon, Baron (concluded).
"Address. Written for the Opening of the Drury-Lane
    Theatre. [Passing reference to Byron]," Town Talk, 3
    (Nov. 1812), 293-95.
"Lord Byron and Mr. Murray," Town Talk, 6 (Mar. 1814), 6-7.
"A Critique on the Address Written by Lord Byron, Spoken at
    Drury Lane Theatre," Universal Magazine, ns,v18 (Dec.
    1812), 490.
"Lord Byron," Universal Magazine, ns,v21 (Mar. 1814), 207.
"The Ballad on Which The Corsair Is Founded," The Wanderer,
    1 (Aug. 8, 1818), 118-20.
"Lord Byron's Travels in Greece," Weekly Entertainer,
    1 (June 7, 1819), 452-56.

Campbell, Thomas.
"Portraits of Authors. No. II. Mr. Campbell," Champion,
    Jan. 30, 1814, p. 39.
"On the Genius of Thomas Campbell," Edinburgh Magazine and
    Literary Miscellany (Scots Magazine), ns,v3 (Aug. 1818),
    143-46.
"Remarks on the Poetry of Mr. Campbell," The Honeycomb,
    1 (Aug. 19, 1820), 73-77.
"On the Modern Poets--Mr. Campbell," Literary Gazette, Apr.
    19, 1817, pp. 196-97.
"T. Campbell's Lectures on Poetry," Literary Gazette, Apr.
    22, 1819, p. 267.
"Contemporary Authors. No. IV. Estimate of the Literary
    Character of Thomas Campbell," Monthly Magazine, 44
    (Jan. 1818), 489-90.
"Memoirs of Thomas Campbell," Monthly Mirror, ns,v5 (May-
    June, 1809), 259-61, 350-57.
"Modern Poets. Mr. Campbell. No. II," Scourge, 10 (July
    1815), 46-53.

Claris, John Chalk.
"Arthur Brooke [pseud. for John Chalk Claris]," Man of
    Kent, 1 (Sept. 19, 1818), 6-8.

Coleridge, Samuel Taylor.
"Explanation of the Satirical Print," Antijacobin Review
    and Magazine, 1 (Aug. 1798), 115-16.
"The Anarchists: an Ode," Antijacobin Review and Magazine,
    1 (Sept. 1798), 365-67.
"To the Reviewer of Coleridge's Biographia Literaria, in
    Blackwood's Magazine for October," Blackwood's Edinburgh
    Magazine, 2 (Dec. 1817), 285-88.
"David Hume Charged by Mr. Coleridge with Plagiarism from
    St. Thomas Aquinas," Blackwood's Edinburgh Magazine, 3
    (Sept. 1818), 653-57.
"The Rime of the Auncient Waggonere," Blackwood's Edinburgh
    Magazine, 4 (Feb. 1819), 571-74.
"Letter from Mr. Odoherty, Enclosing the Third Part of
    Christabel," Blackwood's Edinburgh Magazine, 5 (June

Coleridge, Samuel Taylor (continued).
    1819), 286-91.
    "Essays on the Lake School of Poetry. III. Coleridge,"
        Blackwood's Edinburgh Magazine, 6 (Oct. 1819), 3-12.
    "Portraits of Authors. No. VI. Mr. Coleridge," Champion,
        Mar. 27, 1814, pp. 102-03.
    "Mr. Coleridge's Alternate Lectures on the History of
        Philosophy; and on Six Plays of Shakespeare," Champion,
        Dec. 20, 1818, pp. 808-10.
    "A Parody of Christabelle: The Baron Rich," Déjeuné, Nov. 6,
        1820, pp. 105-08.
    "Theatrical Examiner No. 126. Drury Lane," Examiner, Jan.
        31, 1813, pp. 73-74.
    "Mr. Coleridge and the Edinburgh Reviewers," Examiner, Nov.
        24, 1816, pp. 743-44.
    "Mr. Coleridge and Mr. Southey. To the Editor," Examiner,
        Apr. 6, 1817, pp. 211-12.
    "Memoir of S. T. Coleridge, Esq.," European Magazine, 76
        (July 1819), 4-8.
    "Intelligence--Literary [Coleridge's Lectures]," General
        Chronicle, 4 (Mar. 1812), 310-11.
    "The Hypocrite 'Reasons for Contentment' Examined," Hone's
        Reformists' Register, 1 (Apr. 19, 1817), 406-07.
    "A Tale for a Chimney Corner [Coleridge and Tales of Ter-
        ror]," Indicator, 1 (Dec. 15, 1819), 73-79.
    "Original Communications. Strictures on Messrs. Leigh
        Hunt, Coleridge, and Company," Literary Chronicle, 2
        (July 29, 1820), 489-91.
    "Modern Poets. Defence of Coleridge," Literary Gazette,
        May 3, 1817, p. 227.
    "Polite Literature [defense of Coleridge and Wordsworth],"
        Literary Gazette, May 17, 1817, pp. 257-58.
    "Mr. Coleridge's Lectures," Literary Gazette, Dec. 12,
        1818, p. 800.
    "Mr. Coleridge's Lectures," Literary Gazette, Dec. 19,
        1818, p. 808.
    "Table Talk No. III. On the Conversation of Authors,"
        (Baldwin's) London Magazine, 2 (Sept. 1820), 250-62.
    "On the Theatres [and Remorse]," Monitor, 1 (June 1817),
        129.
    "To the Editor of the Monthly Magazine," Monthly Magazine,
        5 (Jan. 1798), 8.
    "Cantabrigiana. No. CXLVIII. Mr. Coleridge," Monthly Mag-
        azine, 17 (Mar. 1, 1804), 125.
    "To the Editor [concerning The Fall of Robespierre]," Mon-
        thly Magazine, 44 (Sept. 1, 1817), 108-09.
    "Contemporary Authors. An Estimate of the Literary Charac-
        ter and Works of Mr. Coleridge," Monthly Magazine, 46
        (Dec. 1818), 407-09.
    "To the Editor," Monthly Magazine, 48 (Oct. 1, 1819), 203-
        05.
    "[Letter on the Three Graves]," Monthly Mirror, 8 (June-
        Sept. 1810), 26-31, 98-105, 186-96.

Coleridge, Samuel Taylor (concluded).
"To S. T. Coleridge, Esq. On the Attack on the Unitarians
    in His Second Lay Sermon," Monthly Repository, 12 (Apr.-
    May 1817), 213-16, 268-72.
"Memoir of S. T. Coleridge, Esq.," New Monthly Magazine,
    11 (Apr. 1, 1819), 240-43.
"The Early Life of a Poet," Repository of Arts, ns,v10
    (Sept.-Oct. 1820), 170-75, 241-43.
"To the Editor," Thanet Magazine, 1 (July 1817), 55-57.
"Poets of the Present Age. Mr. Coleridge," Ulster Regis-
    ter, 3 (Aug. 8, 1817), 35-38.
"Political Poets," Ulster Register, 3 (Oct. 10, 1817), 249-
    50.
"The Press. Coleridge, Southey, Wordsworth, and Bentham,"
    Yellow Dwarf, Jan. 3, 1818, pp. 1-5.
"Mr. Coleridge's Lectures," Yellow Dwarf, Feb. 21, 1818,
    pp. 60-61.

Cottle, Joseph.
"The Reflector. No. LIII-LVII. [Alfred, an Epic Poem],"
    Monthly Visitor, 13 (July-Aug. 1801), 223-27, 328-32;
    14 (Sept.-Dec. 1801), 23-27, 116-20, 223-27, 328-32.

Crabbe, George.
"Portraits of Authors, No. VII. Mr. Crabbe," Champion,
    Apr. 10, 1814, p. 118.

Darwin, Erasmus.
"Remarks on Darwin's Botanic Garden," Blackwood's Edinburgh
    Magazine, 5 (May 1819), 153-55.
"Memoirs on the Life of Dr. Darwin....By Anna Seward [a re-
    view]," Edinburgh Review, 4 (Apr. 1804), 230-41.
"Memoirs of the Life of Dr. Darwin....By Anna Seward [a re-
    view]," Literary Journal, a Review..., 3 (Mar. 1, 1804),
    193-98.
"Memoirs of the Life of Dr. Darwin....By Anna Seward [a re-
    view]," North British Magazine and Review, 1 (June 1804),
    369-74.

Dimond, William.
"Memoir of William Dimond," Monthly Mirror, ns,v2 (Dec.
    1807), 379-80.

D'Israeli, Isaac.
"Calamities of Authors...[a review]," Scourge, 4 (July 1,
    1812), 3-8.

Edgeworth, Maria.
"Miss Edgeworth and Female Intellect," Champion, Mar. 12,
    1815, p. 86.
"English Novelists. Miss Edgeworth," Champion, Feb. 19,
    1815, p. 63.
"Letter to the Editor in defense of Tales of Fashionable

Life," Gentleman's Magazine, 80[1] (Mar. 1810), 210-12.

Fawcett, Joseph.
  "The Reflector. Civilized War, a Poem," Monthly Visitor,
    ns,v2 (Nov.-Dec. 1802), 222-26, 330-34.

Finlay, John.
  "Some Account of the Late John Finlay, with Specimens of
    His Poetry," Blackwood's Edinburgh Magazine, 2 (Nov.
    1817), 186-92.

Gifford, William.
  "Portraits of Authors. No. XI. Mr. W. Gifford," Champion,
    July 9, 1814, p. 223.
  "Biographical Sketch of William Gifford, Esq.," Monthly
    Mirror, 14 (Sept. 1802), 147-51.

Gisborne, John.
  "Gleaner. No. XII [Strictures on The Vales of Wever],"
    Edinburgh Magazine, or Literary Miscellany, ns,v14 (Oct.
    1799), 243-48.

Godwin, William.
  "Remarks on Mandeville," Blackwood's Edinburgh Magazine,
    2 (Jan. 1818), 402-08.
  "Letter of Advice to a Young American, on the Course of
    Studies It Might Be Most Advantageous for Him to Pursue.
    [A review]," Champion, Apr. 19, 1818, pp. 250-51.
  "Of Population--An Enquiry concerning the Power of Increase
    in the Numbers of Mankind, Being an Answer to Mr. Mal-
    thus's Essay on the Same Subject [A review]," Champion,
    Dec. 16, 1820, p. 822.
  "Of Population--An Enquiry, &c. &c. [A review]," (Baldwin's)
    London Magazine, 2 (Dec. 1820), 654-60.

Hazlitt, William.
  "Notice of a Course of Lectures on English Poetry, Now De-
    livering at the Surrey Institution," Blackwood's Edin-
    burgh Magazine, 2 (Feb. 1818), 556-62.
  "Notice on Mr. Hazlitt's Lectures on English Poetry, Now in
    the Course of Delivery at the Surrey Institution," Black-
    wood's Edinburgh Magazine, 2 (Mar. 1818), 679-84.
  "Notice on Mr. Hazlitt's Lectures on English Poetry, Now in
    the Course of Delivery at the Surrey Institution...On
    Burns and the Old Ballads," Blackwood's Edinburgh Maga-
    zine, 3 (Apr. 1818), 71-75.
  "Jeffrey and Hazlitt," Blackwood's Edinburgh Magazine, 3
    (June 1818), 303-06.
  "Hazlitt Cross-Examined [Letter to the Editor]," Black-
    wood's Edinburgh Magazine, 3 (Aug. 1818), 550-52.
  "Mr. Hazlitt and The Times Correspondent," Examiner, Nov.
    15, 1818, p. 727.
  "Mr. Hazlitt (From the Morning Chronicle)," Examiner, Jan.

10, 1819, pp. 25-26.

"On the Regal Character," Examiner, Aug. 29, 1819, pp. 554-56.

"Mr. Hazlitt's Account of the Reformation, and the Effects of the Translation of the Bible on the Literature of Elizabeth's Age," Examiner, Nov. 21, 1819, pp. 747-48.

"Mr. Hazlitt's Lectures," Examiner, Jan. 16, 1820, p. 46.

"Characters of Living Poets [Hazlitt quoted]," Literary Panorama, ns,v8 (July 1818), 673-81.

"On the Cockney School of Prose Writers. No. I. Hazlitt's Lectures," New Monthly Magazine, 10 (Oct. 1818), 198-202.

"On the Cockney School of Prose. No. II. Hazlitt's Lectures," New Monthly Magazine, 10 (Nov. 1818), 299-304.

"On the Cockney School of Prose. No. III. Hazlitt's Lectures," New Monthly Magazine, 10 (Jan. 1819), 487-92.

"Remarks on Hazlitt's Lectures on the English Poets and the History and Present State of Poetry in This Country," Scots Magazine, 82 (July 1818), 3-12.

Hill, Mary.
"Comparative Criticism Extraordinary, No. VI," Satirist, 5 (July 1809), 99.

Hogg, James.
"Remarks on The Life and Writings of James Hogg," Letter-Box, 1 (Mar. 28, 1818), 81-92.

"Letters on Poetry, by the Ettrick Shepherd," Scots Magazine, 68 (Jan. 1806), 17-18.

Hunt, Leigh.
"Classic Tales, Serious and Lively; with Critical Essays on the Merits and Reputation of the Authors [A review]," Le Beau Monde, 1 (Jan. 1807), 150-52.

"Letter from Z. to Mr. Leigh Hunt," Blackwood's Edinburgh Magazine, 2 (Jan. 1818), 414-17.

"The Literary Assize Court [Ridicule of Keats and Hunt]," Déjeuné, Oct. 27, 1820, pp. 44-48.

"Portraits of the Metropolitan Poets. No. I. Mr. Leigh Hunt," Honeycomb, July 15, 1820, pp. 33-37.

"Original Communications. Strictures on Messrs. Leigh Hunt, Coleridge, and Company," Literary Chronicle, 2 (July 29, 1820), 489-91.

"Review of New Books. To the Editor," Literary Gazette, May 3, 17, June 7, 1817, pp. 228-30, 259-61, 308-10.

"Memoir of Mr. Leigh Hunt. Written by Himself. To the Editor of The Monthly Mirror," Monthly Mirror, ns,v7 (Apr. 1810), 243-48.

"The Feast of the Poets," Reflector, a Quarterly Magazine, 2 (1811), 313-23.

"The Bard of Horsemonger Lane," Satirist, 13 (Oct. 1813), 302-07.

"Bellman's Verses," Satirist, 14 (Feb. 1814), 161-63.

"An Address in the Quarterly Reviewer Who Touched on Mr.

Leigh Hunt's Story of Rimini," <u>Theatrical Inquisitor</u>, 9 (Aug. 1816), 119-22.

Irving, Washington.
"On the Writings of Washington Irving," <u>Blackwood's Edinburgh Magazine</u>, 6 (Feb. 1820), 554-61.

Jeffrey, Francis, and John Gordon.
"[A Letter to the Editor on <u>The Craniad</u>]," <u>Sale-Room</u>, May 17, 1817, 153-59.

Keats, John.
"Keats and the <u>Quarterly Review</u>," <u>Alfred, West of England Journal</u>, Oct. 6, 1818.
"The Literary Assize [Ridicule of Keats and Hunt]," <u>Déjeuné</u>, Oct. 27, 1820, pp. 44-48.
"Remarks on Keats's Poems," <u>Edinburgh Magazine and Literary Miscellany</u> (<u>Scots Magazine</u>), ns,v7 (Aug., Oct. 1820), 107, 313.
"To a Poetical Friend," <u>European Magazine</u>, 70 (Oct. 1816), 365.
"Literary Notices, No. 44. [Defense of Keats]," <u>Examiner</u>, Oct. 11, 1818, pp. 648-49.
"The <u>Quarterly Review</u>--Mr. Keats," <u>Examiner</u>, Oct. 12, 1818, pp. 648-49.
"Mr. Keats's <u>Endymion</u>," <u>Examiner</u>, Nov. 1, 1818, p. 696.
"Hunt's Farewell to Keats on His Departure for Italy," <u>Indicator</u>, Sept. 20, 1820, 399-400.
"The Lion's Head," (Baldwin's) <u>London Magazine</u>, 2 (Aug. 1820), 123.
"Dramatic Review," (Baldwin's) <u>London Magazine</u>, 2 (Dec. 1820), 686.
"[A Letter Protesting against the Attack on <u>Endymion</u> in the <u>Quarterly Review</u>]," <u>Morning Chronicle</u>, Oct. 3, 1818.
"Modern Periodical Literature," <u>New Monthly Magazine</u>, 12 (Sept. 1, 1820), 304-10.

Lamb, Charles.
"Horae Nicotianiae. No. I," <u>Blackwood's Edinburgh Magazine</u>, 5 (Apr. 1819), 47-51.
"On Christ's Hospital, and the Character of the Christ's Hospital Boys," <u>Gentleman's Magazine</u>, 83[1] (June 1813), 540-42; 83[2] (Suppl. 1813), 617-22.
"Getting Up on Cold Mornings," <u>Kaleidoscope</u>, 2 (Mar. 7, 1820), 138.
"On May Day," (Baldwin's) <u>London Magazine</u>, 1 (May 1820), 489-92.
"Christ's Hospital Five and Thirty Years Ago," (Baldwin's) <u>London Magazine</u>, 2 (Nov. 1820), 483-90.

Leyden, John.
"Remarks on the Poetry of the Late Dr. John Leyden," <u>Scots Magazine</u>, ns,v7 (Oct. 1820), 301-05.

Lloyd, Richard.
"Anecdotes of the Author of <u>Beaumaris Bay</u>," <u>Monthly Mirror</u>,
12 (Dec. 1801), 371-72.

Macneill, Hector.
"Some Account of the Life of Hector Macneill," <u>Blackwood's</u>
<u>Edinburgh Magazine</u>," 4 (Dec. 1818), 273-77.

Maturin, Charles Robert.
"[Letter to the Editor]," <u>Liverpool Magazine</u>, 1 (July 1816),
254-62.

Montgomery, James.
"Portraits of Authors. No. V. Mr. Montgomery," <u>Champion</u>,
Mar. 13, 1814, p. 87.

Moore, Thomas.
"Strictures on the Literary Character and Writings of Anac-
reon Moore," <u>La Belle Assemblée</u>, 1 (Aug.-Sept. 1806),
344-49, 397-400.
"Remarks on the Poetry of Thomas Moore," <u>Blackwood's Edin-
burgh Magazine</u>, 4 (Oct. 1818), 1-5.
"Portraits of Authors. No. IV. Mr. Moore," <u>Champion</u>,
Feb. 27, 1814, 70-71.
"[Letter to the Editor concerning Moore]," <u>Lonsdale Magazine</u>,
1 (Feb. 1820), 69-70.
"Character of Thomas Moore, Esq. as a Poet," <u>Talisman</u>, Dec.
20, 1820, pp. 1-2.

More, Hannah.
"The Reflector. No. 67. The Search after Happiness. A
Pastoral Drama," <u>Monthly Visitor</u>, ns,v2 (Oct. 1802),
117-21.

Opie, Mrs. Amelia.
"English Novelists. Mrs. Opie," <u>Champion</u>, Jan. 22, 1815,
pp. 30-31.

Owenson, Sydney.
"On the Wild Irish Girl, and Ida of Athens [Letter to the
Editor]," <u>Belfast Monthly Magazine</u>, 2 (May 1809), 334-35.

Polwhele, Richard.
"The Unsexed Females [Letter to the Editor]," <u>Antijacobin
Review</u>, 4 (Dec. 1799), 468-71.

Procter, Bryan Waller.
"Portraits of the Metropolitan Poets. No. II. Mr. Barry
Cornwall," <u>Honeycomb</u>, July 29, 1820, pp. 49-56.

Rogers, Samuel.
"Portraits of Authors. No. X. Mr. Rogers," <u>Champion</u>, June
19, 1814, p. 198.

Scott, Sir Walter.
"Tale of My Landlord," Blackwood's Edinburgh Magazine, 1
(June 1817), 298-99.
"Tale of My Landlord," Blackwood's Edinburgh Magazine, 1
(June 1817), 302.
"Memoirs of Rob Roy Macgregor, and Some Branches of His
Family," Blackwood's Edinburgh Magazine, 2 (Oct.-Dec.
1817), 74-80, 149-55, 288-95.
"Letter to the Author of Rob Roy," Blackwood's Edinburgh
Magazine, 2 (Mar. 1818), 662-64.
"Portraits of Authors. No. III. Mr. Walter Scott," Cham-
pion, Feb. 12, 1814, pp. 54-55.
"Walter Scott and the Greater and Minor Theatres," Champion,
June 24, 1820, pp. 413-14.
"To the Editor. The Real Author of Waverley, Rob Roy,
&c.," Champion, Aug. 12, 1820, p. 519.
"Remarks on the Poems of Walter Scott [by a Correspondent],"
Cosmopolite, June 11, 1812, pp. 116-20.
"The State Papers and Letters of Sir Ralph Sadler [a re-
view]," Critical Review, 21 (Oct.-Nov. 1810), 165-79,
267-83.
"Literary News. Sir Walter Scott and the Scotch Novels,"
Déjeuné, 1 (Oct. 21, 1820), 3.
"Parallel Passages from Walter Scott's Lady of the Lake,
and Tasso's Gerusalemme Liberata," Dublin Examiner, 1
(Aug. 1816), 254-58.
"On the Authorship of Waverley [Letter to the Editor],"
Dublin Magazine, 2 (Oct. 1820), 283-87.
"[Letter to the Editor on The Lady of the Lake]," Edinburgh
Christian Instructor, 1 (Aug. 1810), 26-31.
"[Letter to the Editor on The Lady of the Lake]," Edinburgh
Christian Instructor, 1 (Oct. 1810), 166-73.
"On the History of Fictitious Writing in Scotland; with Re-
marks on the Tale Entitled The Heart of Mid-lothian,"
Edinburgh Magazine and Literary Miscellany (Scots Maga-
zine), ns,v3 (Aug. 1818), 107-17.
"Stricture on Ivanhoe," Edinburgh Magazine and Literary Mis-
cellany (Scots Magazine), ns,v6 (Jan. 1820), 54-61.
"The State Papers and Letters of Sir Ralph Sadler [a re-
view]," Edinburgh Review, 16 (Aug. 1810), 447-64.
"Memoir of Sir Walter Scott," European Magazine, 78 (Dec.
1820), 483-86.
"Visit to Walter Scott," Fireside Magazine, 1 (Oct. 1819),
393-96.
"Remarks Philosophical and Literary (on the Poetry of Byron
and Scott)," Gentleman's Magazine, 89^2 (Oct.-Nov. 1819),
315-17, 397-400.
"Walter Scott, Esq.," Hibernian Magazine, 3 (Apr. 1811),
220-23.
"The Works under the Name of Walter Scott," Kaleidoscope,
1 (Nov. 24, 1818), 71.
"The Novels of the Author of the Tales of My Landlord,"
Kaleidoscope, 2 (Feb. 22, 1820), 129.

Scott, Sir Walter (continued).
"Scott, Byron, Herbert, and Moore," Kaleidoscope, 2 (Feb.
29, 1820), 135.
"Sir Walter Scott Pronounced Not To Be the Author of Tales
of My Landlord," Kaleidoscope, ns,vl (Aug. 8, 1820),
41-42.
"Tales of My Landlord. Sir Walter Scott Declared Not To Be
the Author of Waverley, &c. (From the Champion)," Kaleidoscope, ns,vl (Aug. 22, 1820), 57.
"[Scott Declared To Be the Author of Waverley]," Kaleidoscope, ns,vl (Sept. 5, 1820), 73.
"[Scott Declared to Be the Author of Waverley]," Kaleidoscope, ns,vl (Oct. 17, 1820), 121.
"[Is Walter Scott the Author of Waverley?]," Kaleidoscope,
ns,vl (Oct. 24, 1820), 133-34.
"[Is Walter Scott the Author of Waverley?]," Kaleidoscope,
ns,vl (Oct. 31, 1820), 140-41.
"Illustration of the Novel of The Antiquary," Lady's Magazine, s2,vl0 (Oct. 1820), 509-12.
"Remarks on Walter Scott's Poetry," Leeds Literary Observer, 1 (Apr. 1819), 147-50.
"The Heart of Midlothian," Literary Chronicle, 1 (May 22,
1819), 11-12.
"Of the Modern Poets--Walter Scott," Literary Gazette, Apr.
12, 1817, pp. 178-79.
"Lines, Descriptive of the Catastrophe of the Bride of Lam-
mermuir [a parody]," Literary Gazette, Aug. 28, 1819, pp.
555-56.
"Kenilworth [Castle]," Literary Gazette, Oct. 28, 1820,
pp. 689-91.
"Kenilworth in 1819," Literary Gazette, Dec. 30, 1820, pp.
840-41.
"Tales of My Landlord [said to be by Scott]," Literary
Journal and General Miscellany, 1 (Oct. 31, 1818), 499.
"Lord Somers' Collection of Tracts [a review]," Literary
Panorama, 6 (June 1809), 418-24.
"Memoir of Sir Walter Scott," (Gold's) London Magazine, 2
(Aug. 1820), 109-17.
"Biographical Memoir of Walter Scott," Miniature Magazine,
3 (June 1819), 1-7.
"[Letter to the Editor on Scott's Poetry]," Monthly Maga-
zine, 33 (Mar. 1812), 131-32.
"[Letter to the Editor on Scott's Poetry]," Monthly Maga-
zine, 33 (June 1812), 428-30.
"Query to Mr. Scott, Respecting a Passage in Marmion,"
Monthly Mirror, ns,v4 (Sept. 1808), 158.
"Walter Scott's Poems. To the Editor," Monthly Mirror,
ns,v5 (Apr. 1809), 205-07.
"Mr. Walter Scott's Poetry," Monthly Mirror, ns,v8 (Oct.
1810), 256-58.
"Observations in Reply to Strictures on Walter Scott's
Poetry," Monthly Museum, 1 (Jan. 1814), 224-26.
"A Letter to the Author of Waverley, Ivanhoe, &c., on the

Scott, Sir Walter (concluded).
Moral Tendency of Those Popular Works," <u>Monthly Review</u>,
ns,v93 (Oct. 1820), 169-74.
"Memoir of Walter Scott," <u>New Monthly Magazine</u>, 10 (Nov.
1818), 355-57.
"On the Poetry of Walter Scott," <u>New Monthly Magazine</u>, 11
(June 1819), 400-01.
"On the Living Novelists. No. II. The Author of <u>Waverley</u>,"
<u>New Monthly Magazine</u>, 13 (May 1820), 543-48.
"The Scotch Novels," <u>Newcastle Magazine</u>, 1 (Sept. 1820),
41-49.
"The State Papers and Letters of Sir Ralph Sadler [a re-
view]," <u>Quarterly Review</u>, 4 (Nov. 1810), 403-14.
"Which Is the Best Poet, Lord Byron or Walter Scott, Esq.?"
<u>Reasoner</u>, 1 (Apr. 1814), 509-28.
"Rokeby the Second. Canto the First [a parody]," <u>Satirist</u>,
12 (Mar. 1813), 207-17.
"Critical Sketches of Living Characters in Edinburgh,"
<u>Scots Magazine</u>, 75 (Jan. 1813), 9-10.
"French Criticism on <u>The Antiquary</u>," <u>Scots Magazine</u>, 79
(May 1817), 324.
"On the Political and Religious Tendency of the Work En-
titled <u>Tales of My Landlord</u>," <u>Scots Magazine</u>, 79 (June
1817), 431-38.
"Romances, and the Drama, on Public Taste and Manners; and
the History of the Knights Templars, in Reference to the
Romance of <u>Ivanhoe</u>," <u>Spirit of the Magazines</u>, 1 (1820),
57-60.
"Modern Novels [and Scott]," <u>Spirit of the Public Journals</u>,
8 (1804), 129-30.
"Parody on Walter Scott's Boat Song, from <u>Poetical Effu-
sions</u>," <u>Theatrical Inquisitor</u>, 2 (June 1813), 309-10.

Seward, Anna.
"Table Talk. No. VII. [Miss Seward]," <u>General Chronicle</u>,
6 (Nov. 1812), 305-06.

Shelley, Percy Bysshe.
"Salutary Attention to Morals in the University of Oxford
[including <u>St. Irvyne</u>]," <u>Antijacobin Review</u>, 41 (Feb.
1812), 221.
"Critical Remarks on Shelley's Poetry," <u>Dublin Magazine</u>,
2 (July-Dec. 1820), 393-400.
"[Quotes from <u>Morning Chronicle</u> a brief report on the West-
brook vs. Shelley proceedings]," <u>Examiner</u>, Jan. 26,
1817, p. 60.
"The Quarterly Review and <u>Revolt of Islam</u>," <u>Examiner</u>,
Sept. 26-Oct. 10, 1819, pp. 620-21, 635-36, 652-53.
"Portraits of the Metropolitan Poets. No. III. Mr. Percy
<u>Bysshe Shelley</u>," <u>Honeycomb</u>, Aug. 12, 1820, pp. 64-72.
"<u>A Proposal for Putting Reform to the Vote</u> [a Review],"
<u>Quarterly Review</u>, 16 (Jan. 1817), 511-12.
"[A Letter to the Editor answering A Refutation of Deism],"

Theological Inquirer, 1 (June 1815), 242-47.
"An Estimate of the Poetry of the Present Age," Weekly En-
    tertainer, ns,v2 (Aug. 21, 1820), 149-51.

Smith, Charlotte.
  "Memoir of Mrs. Charlotte Smith," Monthly Mirror, ns,v3
    (Mar. 1808), Supplementary Number.

Southey, Robert.
  "Parodies of Southey's Poetry," Antijacobin Review, or
    Weekly Examiner, 1 (1799), 35-36, 71-72, 168-69, 200-01.
  "Wat Tyler, a Dramatic Poem; and A Letter to William Smith,
    Esq.," Blackwood's Edinburgh Magazine, 1 (June 1817), 302.
  "Portraits of Authors. No. 1. Mr. Southey," Champion,
    Jan. 15, 1814, pp. 22-23.
  "The Courier and the Wat Tyler," Examiner, Mar. 30, 1017,
    pp. 194-97.
  "Mr. Coleridge and Mr. Southey. To the Editor," Examiner,
    Apr. 6, 1817, pp. 211-12.
  "Death and Funeral of the Late Mr. Southey [i.e., his mental
    death and decline]," Examiner, Apr. 13,1817, pp. 236-37.
  "Extraordinary Case of the Late Mr. Southey," Examiner,
    May 11, 1817, pp. 300-03.
  "Apostasy and Corruption," Hone's Reformists' Register, 1
    (Feb. 22, 1817), 157-58.
  "Of Modern Poets--Mr. Southey," Literary Gazette, Apr. 26,
    1817, pp. 210-11.
  "Defence of Southey," Literary Gazette, May 3, 1817, pp.
    227-28.
  "On Miss Seward's Opinion of Southey's Thalaba," Literary
    Journal, a Review..., 1 (Mar. 31, 1803), 406-07.
  "Contemporary Authors. No. V. Robert Southey," Monthly
    Magazine, 45 (Mar. 1818), 120-22.
  "Memoir of Robert Southey, Poet Laureat," Monthly Museum,
    2 (Nov. 1814), 337-40.
  "Philosophers!" Scourge, 7 (Apr. 1814), 288-89.
  "A New Vision, by Robert Southey, Esq.!! Poet Laureat [a
    parody]," A Slap at Slop, no1 (1821), 3.
  "The Press. Coleridge, Southey, Wordsworth, and Bentham,"
    Yellow Dwarf, Jan. 3, 1818, pp. 4-5.

Stockdale, Percival.
  "The Memoirs of the Life and Writings of Percival Stock-
    dale," Quarterly Review, 1 (May 1809), 371-86.

Struthers, John.
  "Observations on Struthers' Winter Day. To the Editor,"
    Glasgow Magazine, 2 (June 1811), 143-47.

White, Henry Kirke.
  "Sketch of Henry Kirke White," Christian's Pocket Magazine,
    3 (Oct. 1820), 173-80.
  "Critical Examination of the Poems and Genius of Henry

Kirke White," <u>Contemplatist</u>, Sept. 8-22, 1810, pp. 209-24, 225-40, 241-56.

"Outline of a Memoir of Mr. Henry Kirke White," <u>Monthly Mirror</u>, ns,v2 (Sept. 1807), 161-66; ns,v3 (Mar. 1808), 228-31; ns,v5 (Dec. 1809), 335-37.

"Henry Kirke White," <u>Monthly Mirror</u>, ns,v4 (Sept. 1808), 139.

Wolcot, John.
"Portraits of Authors. Dr. Wolcot, alias Peter Pindar," <u>Champion</u>, Aug. 14, 1814, pp. 262-63.

Wordsworth, William.
"Vindication of Mr. Wordsworth's Letter to Mr. Gray on a New Edition of Burns," <u>Blackwood's Edinburgh Magazine</u>, 2 (Oct. 1817), 65-73.

"Letters from the Lakes," <u>Blackwood's Edinburgh Magazine</u>, 4 (Jan. 1819), 397-404.

"Yarrow Unvisited [a parody]," <u>Blackwood's Edinburgh Magazine</u>, 6 (Nov. 1819), 194.

"Portraits of Authors. No. VII. Mr. Wordsworth," <u>Champion</u>, May 28, 1814, pp. 174-75.

"Heaven Made a Party to Earthly Disputes--Mr. Wordsworth's Sonnets on Waterloo," <u>Examiner</u>, Feb. 18, 1816, pp. 97-99.

"Mr. Wordsworth and the Westmoreland Election," <u>Examiner</u>, July 5, 1818, p. 427.

"Polite Literature [defense of Wordsworth and Coleridge]," <u>Literary Gazette</u>, May 17, 1817, pp. 257-58.

"Living Authors. No. II. Wordsworth," (Baldwin's) <u>London Magazine</u>, 1 (Mar. 1820), 275-85.

"Mr. Wordsworth," <u>Lonsdale Magazine</u>, 1 (July 1820), 321-22.

"[Letter to the Editor]'," <u>Lonsdale Magazine</u>, 1 (Nov. 1820), 484-87.

"[Letter to the Editor]," <u>Man of Kent</u>, 1 (Oct. 24, 1818), 93-94.

"Contemporary Authors. No. 9. Wordsworth and the Lake School of Poets," <u>Monthly Magazine</u>, 50 (Nov. 1820), 307-10.

"Memoir of William Wordsworth," <u>New Monthly Magazine</u>, 11 (Feb. 1819), 48-50.

"Lake School of Poetry. Mr. Wordsworth," <u>New Monthly Magazine</u>, 14 (Oct. 1820), 361-68.

"On the Genius and Writings of Wordsworth," <u>New Monthly Magazine</u>, 14 (Nov. 1820), 498-506.

"[Letter to the Editor]," <u>Salt-Bearer</u>, no25 (1820), 278-84.

"Cobbett and Wordsworth," <u>Satirist</u>, 8 (June 1811), 486-88.

"Modern Poets--Wordsworth. No. III," <u>Scourge</u>, 10 (Oct. 1815), 266-75.

"The Press--Coleridge, Southey, Wordsworth, and Bentham," <u>Yellow Dwarf</u>, Jan. 3, 1818, pp. 4-5.

APPENDIX B

GENERAL AND GENRE CRITICISM

B-1
Volumes of General and Genre Criticism Reviewed

The volumes listed below have already been recorded in the
foregoing pages, where reviews of them have been cited. They
are repeated here because each is logically related to the
general or genre criticism of which this appendix is composed.
For the attitude of the reviewers toward these volumes the
reader will need to turn to the appropriate author and title
in the pages above.

Aikin, John.
Letters to a Young Lady, on a Course of English Poetry.
1804.

Alison, Archibald.
Essays on the Nature and Principles of Taste. 1811. (1st
ed. 1790)

Anonymous.
Essays on the Sources of the Pleasures Received from Literary Compositions. 1809.

Barrett, Rev. B.
Pretensions to a Final Analysis of the Nature and Origin of
Sublimity, Style, Beauty, Genius, and Taste; with an Appendix Explaining the Cause of the Pleasure Which Is Derived
from Tragedy. 1812.

Barron, William.
Lectures on Belles Lettres and Logic. 1806.

Bowles, William Lisle.
The Invariable Principles of Poetry: In a Latter Addressed
to Thomas Campbell, Esq. Occasioned by Some Critical
Observations in his Specimens of British Poets, Particularly Relating to the Poetical Character of Pope. 1819.

Campbell, Thomas.
Specimens of the British Poets; with Biographical and

Critical Studies, and an Essay on English Poetry. 1819.

Carey, John.
A Key to Practical English Prosody and Versification. 1809.

Conder, Josiah.
Reviewers Reviewed: Including an Enquiry into the Moral and
Intellectual Effects of Habits of Criticism, and Their
Influence on the General Interests of Literature. To Which
Is Subjoined a Brief History of the Periodical Reviews Pub-
lished in England and Scotland. By John Charles O'Reid
(pseud. for Josiah Conder).

De Brusasque, Elizabeth Annabella.
Illustrations of the Theory and Principles of Taste, Con-
sidered as They Are Applicable to the Fine Arts in General,
and to Various Species of Literary Composition in Particu-
lar. 1806.

Duncan, John.
An Essay on Genius; or the Philosophy of Literature. 1814.

Dunlop, John.
History of Fiction. From the Earliest Greek Romances to
the Novels of the Present Age. 1814.

Edwards, Richard.
Specimens of English Accentuated Verse, Wherein the Inten-
sity of Pronunciation Is Measured, and the Length of the
Syllables Unnoticed. 1813.

Ellis, George.
Specimens of the Early English Poets; to Which Is Prefixed
an Historical Sketch of the English Poetry and Language.
1801. (1st ed. 1790; enlarged ed. 1801)

Fisgrave, Anthony.
Midas; or, a Serious Inquiry concerning Taste and Genius;
Including a Proposal for the Certain Advancement of the
Elegant Arts. 1808.

Foster, John.
Essays in a Series of Letters to a Friend. 1805.

Gilliland, Thomas.
A Domestic Synopsis; Containing an Essay on the Political
and Moral Use of a Theatre, Involving Remarks on the Dramatic Writers of the Present Day and Strictures on the Performers of the Two Theatres. 1804.

Green, Edward.
Observations on the Drama, with a View to Its More Beneficial Effects on the Morals and Manners of Society. 1803.

Gregory, George.
  Letters on Literature, Taste, and Composition, Addressed to
  His Son. 1808.

Harpur, Joseph.
  An Essay on the Principles of Philosophical Criticism, Applied to Poetry. 1810.

Jamieson, Alexander.
  A Grammar of Rhetoric and Polite Literature; Comprehending
  the Principles of Language of Style, the Elements of Criticism. 1818.

Kames, Henry Home, Lord.
  Elements of Criticism. 1805. (9th ed. With the Author's
  Last Corrections and Additions.)

Knight, Richard Payne.
  An Analytical Inquiry into the Principles of Taste. 1806.

Mackenzie, Sir George Stewart.
  An Essay on Some Subjects Connected with Taste. 1817.

Mangin, Rev. Edward.
  An Essay on Light Reading, as It May Be Supposed to Influence Conduct and Literary Taste. 1808.

Mitford, William.
  An Inquiry into the Principles of Harmony in Language, and
  of the Mechanics of Verse, Modern and Antient. 1804.

Murray, Lindley.
  Sequel to the English Reader; or, Elegant Selections in
  Prose and Poetry: Designed to Improve the Highest Class of
  Learners, in Reading; to Establish a Taste for Just and Ac-
  curate Composition; and to Promote the Interests of Piety
  and Virtue. 1805.

Plumptre, James.
  Four Discourses on Subjects Relating to the Amusement of
  the Stage. 1809.

Price, Uvedale.
  Essay on the Picturesque, as Compared with the Sublime and
  Beautiful; and on the Use of Studying Pictures for the Pur-
  pose of Improving Real Landscape. 1814. (1st ed. 1794-98)

Schlegel, A. W.
  Lectures on Dramatic Literature. Translated from the German by John Black. 1815.

Siddons, Henry.
  Practical Illustrations of Theatrical Gesture and Action,

Adapted to the Business of the English Stage, and the Characters of the English Drama. From the Original Work of M. Engel, Member of the Academy in Berlin. By Henry Siddons.

Smith, Eaglesfield.
On the Tragic Ballad, with Some Account of Legendary Tales.

Stockdale, Percival.
Lectures on the Truly Eminent English Poets. 1807.

Styles, John.
An Essay on the Character (and the) Immoral and Anti-Christian Influence of the Stage. 1806.

Thompson, William.
An Enquiry into the Elementary Principles of Beauty, in the Works of Nature and Art. To Which Is Prefixed an Introductory Discourse on Taste. 1798.

Turner, W. H.
Essays on Subjects of a Miscellaneous Nature. 1803.

Vigors, N. A.
An Inquiry into the Nature and Extent of Poetic License. 1813.

B-2
Articles of General Criticism

"Modern Literature," Aberdeen Magazine, 3 (July 1798), 338-40.

"On the Poetic of Aristotle," Le Beau Monde, 1 (July 1807), 473-76.

"General Observations on the Sublime," Le Beau Monde, 2 (Aug., Oct.-Nov. 1807), 16-18, 125-28, 171-74.

"On the Use of Translations; Applied to Preceptors and Pupils," Belfast Monthly Magazine, 6 (Feb. 1811), 95-101.

"On the Word Picturesque," Belfast Monthly Magazine, 6 (Feb. 1811), 116-21.

"Remarks on Stewart's Theory of the Sublime," Belfast Monthly Magazine, 6 (Apr. 1811), 284-86.

"On the Cultivation of Taste," Belfast Monthly Magazine," 9 (Nov. 1812), 345-47.

"On the Advantages Derived from Cultivating Taste," Belfast Monthly Magazine, 9 (Nov. 1812), 350-52.

"On Originality and Plagiarism," <u>Belfast Monthly Magazine</u>, 12 (Mar. 1814), 204-07.

"On Sensibility," <u>Belfast Monthly Magazine</u>, 12 (May 1814), 372-74.

"Fragment of an Essay on Taste," <u>Blackwood's Edinburgh Magazine</u>, 3 (Apr. 1818), 21-24.

"On the Revival of a Taste for Our Ancient Literature," <u>Blackwood's Edinburgh Magazine</u>, 4 (Dec. 1818), 264-66.

"On Critics and Criticism," <u>Blackwood's Edinburgh Magazine</u>, 8 (Nov. 1820), 138-41.

"On Taste," <u>The Casket</u>, 1 (June 1819), 163-64.

"On the Influences of the Scenery of Nature on the Intellectual and Moral Character, as Well as on the Taste and Imagination," <u>Champion</u>, Sept. 9, 1820, pp. 590-91.

"The New Project for Enslaving the Literary Genius of the Country, and Rendering It Subservient to the Purposes of Corruption," <u>Champion</u>, Dec. 30, 1820, pp. 849-51.

"On Taste," <u>Cosmopolite</u>, Oct. 1, 1812, pp. 294-98.

"[On Grandeur, Sublimity, &c.]," <u>Devonshire Adventurer</u>, 1 (Oct. 1814), 31-34.

"Hints to a Young Author, by a Gentleman," <u>Dublin Magazine</u>, 1 (Oct. 1798), 228-31.

"Select Literary Information [War and Literature]," <u>Eclectic</u> 1 (Feb. 1805), 156.

"On a Criterion of Perfection in Writing," <u>Edinburgh Magazine, or Literary Miscellany</u>, ns,v15 (Apr. 1800), 253-60.

"On Imagination," <u>Edinburgh Magazine, or Literary Miscellany</u>, ns,v22 (Nov. 1803), 348-52.

"Thoughts on Taste," <u>Edinburgh Magazine, and Literary Miscellany</u> (<u>Scots Magazine</u>), ns,v3 (Oct. 1818), 308-11; ns,v5 (July 1819), 13-16.

"[Letter to Mr. Urban on Epithets]," <u>Gentleman's Magazine</u>, 70[1] (Jan. 1800), 5.

"[Letter to Mr. Urban on Ornateness]," <u>Gentleman's Magazine</u>, 75[1] (May 1805), 405-07.

"[Letter to Mr. Urban on Morality in Literature],"

Gentleman's _Magazine_, 78[2] (Nov. 1808), 975-76.

"Reflections on the Study of Classical Literature," _Glasgow_
Repository _of_ _Literature_, no4 (Apr. 1805), 205-11.

"Is a Poetical Imagination the Gift of Nature or the Product
of Education?" _Gleaner's_ _Port-Folio_, 1 (Oct. 1819), 103-07.

"[On Enthusiasm]," _Gloucestershire_ _Repository_, 1 (Nov. 28,
1817), 468-70.

"[On Enthusiasm]," _Gloucestershire_ _Repository_, 1 (Dec. 12,
1817), 490-91.

"On Style," _Ipswich_ _Magazine_, 1 (Dec. 1799), 419-26.

"Practical Instructions on Taste, Literature, and the Art of
Composition," _Juvenile_ _Library_, 1 (1800), 34-36, 103-07,
182-85, 249-54, 328-32, 393-98; 2 (1801), 25-30, 101-06,
165-70, 239-44, 306-12, 369-74; 3 (1801), 90-99, 157-63,
213-17, 272-76, 333-39; 4 (1802), 34-38, 108-13, 184-88,
249-53, 323-28, 404-08; 5 (1802), 49-54, 102-08, 186-90,
256-60, 320-25, 398-403; 6 (1803), 50-55, 126-30, 206-13.

"Essay on the Fine Arts. On Taste," _Kaleidoscope_, 2 (Sept.
1, 1819), 22.

"[The Sublime and the Beautiful]," _Kaleidoscope_, 2 (Sept. 15,
1818), 29.

"Great Events Promotive of Genius and Literature," _Lady's_
Magazine, 43 (Nov. 1812), 518-19.

"Modern Criticism," _Literary_ _and_ _Statistical_ _Magazine_, 2
(Feb. 1818), 31-38.

"On the Decay of Romance and Romantic Feeling," _Literary_ _and_
Statistical _Magazine_, 2 (May 1818), 142-49.

"Augustan Writers and Edinburgh Reviewers," _Literary_ _Gazette_,
Feb. 15, 1817, pp. 49-50.

"General View of Literature for 1803," _Literary_ _Journal_, _a_
Review..., 3 (Jan. 16, 1804), 1-12.

"The New Schools," (Baldwin's) _London_ _Magazine_, 1 (May 1820),
543.

"Immortality in Embryo; or, Genius in Its Night-gown,"
(Gold's) _London_ _Magazine_, 2 (July-Aug., Oct. 1820), 39-43,
151-54, 365-66.

"For the Weekly Essayist. On Taste," _Mentor,_ _or_ _Edinburgh_

Weekly Essayist, 2 (Dec. 6, 1817), 25-32.

"[The Ancients, Genius, &c.]," _The Monitor_, 1 (Aug. 1817), 183-90.

"On Taste," _The Monitor_, 1 (Aug. 1817), 198-205.

"[On the Prevailing Prejudice against Modern Literature]," _Monthly Magazine_, 48 (Aug. 1819), 12.

"On Literary Resemblances," _Monthly Mirror_, 16 (Nov. 1803), 306-08.

"An Attempt to Point Out Some Leading Errors in Burke's Treatise on the Sublime and Beautiful," _Monthly Register_, 3 (June 1803), 65-67.

"Criticism on the Attempt to Point out Some Leading Errors in Burke's Treatise on the Sublime and Beautiful," _Monthly Register_, 3 (July 1803), 126-27.

"Three Discourses: On the Use of Books; On the Result and Effects of Study; On the Elements of Literary Taste," _Monthly Review_, ns,v42 (Oct. 1803), 220-21.

"The Reflector. No. XVII. On Taste," _Monthly Visitor_, 4 (July 1798), 227-33.

"The Reflector. No. XVIII. On Criticism," _Monthly Visitor_, 4 (Aug. 1798), 334-38.

"Comparative Estimate of Ancient and Modern Writers," _New Annual Register_, 28 (1807), 207-15.

"On Taste in Literature and the Fine Arts," _New Monthly Magazine_, 2 (Sept. 1814), 130-32.

"On Literary Criticism," _New Monthly Magazine_, 5 (May 1816), 305-07.

"What Is Beauty?" _New Monthly Magazine_, 13 (May 1820), 580-83.

"Remarks on the Influence of the Fine Arts and Works of Fiction on the Moral Character," _Northern Star_, 2 (Apr. 1818), 295-98.

"On Gracefulness in Composition," _Oxford Miscellany and Review_, no2 (1820), 33-40.

"Essay on Taste, Literature, and Philosophy," _Repository of Arts_, 2 (Dec. 1809), 362-64.

"On the Progress of Literature," _Retrospective Review_, 2 (1820), 204.

"On Taste," <u>Talisman</u>, <u>or</u> <u>Literary</u> <u>Observer</u>, 1 (July 15, 1820), 26-27.

"Directions concerning Style," <u>Weekly</u> <u>Entertainer</u>, 33 (July 28, 1799), 75-76.

B-3
Articles on Poetry

"Poetry," <u>Annual</u> <u>Review</u>, 4 (1805), 535.

"On the Independency of Painting on Poetry," <u>The</u> <u>Artist</u>, vl (May 9, 1807), noIX.

"[The Metaphysical in Poetic Criticism]," <u>The</u> <u>Artist</u>, 2 (1809), 109-33.

"On the Epic Poetry of the Ancients," <u>Le</u> <u>Beau</u> <u>Monde</u>, 2 (Dec. 1807), 230-33.

"On the Cockney School of Poetry. No. I," <u>Blackwood's</u> <u>Edinburgh</u> <u>Magazine</u>, 2 (Oct. 1817), 38-41.

"On the Cockney School of Poetry. No. II," <u>Blackwood's</u> <u>Edinburgh</u> <u>Magazine</u>, 2 (Nov. 1817), 194-201.

"Letter from Z. to Leigh Hunt, King of the Cockneys," <u>Blackwood's</u> <u>Edinburgh</u> <u>Magazine</u>, 3 (May 1818), 196-201.

"Essays on the Lake School of Poetry. No. I. Wordsworth's White Doe of Rylstone," <u>Blackwood's</u> <u>Edinburgh</u> <u>Magazine</u>, 3 (July 1818), 369-81.

"The Cockney School of Poetry. No. III," <u>Blackwood's</u> <u>Edinburgh</u> <u>Magazine</u>, 3 (July 1818), 453-56.

"Cockney School of Poetry. No. IV," <u>Blackwood's</u> <u>Edinburgh</u> <u>Magazine</u>, 3 (Aug. 1818), 519-24.

"Essays on the Lake School of Poetry. No. II. On the Habits of Thought Inculcated by Wordsworth," <u>Blackwood's</u> <u>Edinburgh</u> <u>Magazine</u>, 4 (Dec. 1818), 257-63.

"On the Cockney School of Poetry. No. V," <u>Blackwood's</u> <u>Edinburgh</u> <u>Magazine</u>, 5 (Apr. 1819), 97-100.

"Sanctandrews [Cockney Poetry and Cockney Politics]," <u>Blackwood's</u> <u>Edinburgh</u> <u>Magazine</u>, 5 (Aug. 1819), 634-42.

"On the Cockney School of Poetry. No. VI," <u>Blackwood's</u> <u>Edinburgh</u> <u>Magazine</u>, 6 (Oct. 1819), 70-76.

"On the Progressive Change of Poetical Style," Blackwood's
Edinburgh Magazine, 6 (Jan. 1820), 363-69.

"Extracts from Mr. Wastle's Diary [on the Cockneys]," Blackwood's Edinburgh Magazine, 7 (Sept. 1820), 663-67.

"The Building of the Palace of the Lamp [on the Cockneys],"
Blackwood's Edinburgh Magazine, 7 (Sept. 1820), 675-79.

"Sonnet-Writers. To the Editor," British Stage and Literary
Cabinet, 4 (Nov. 1819), 67-68.

"[Principally on the Sonnet]," Cabinet, 3 (Mar. 1808), 162-65.

"On the Sonnets of Thomas Warton...William Lisle Bowles...
and William Mason," Cabinet, 3 (Apr. 1808), 225-28.

"On the Poetry of the Present Times," Catholic Gentleman's
Magazine, 1 (Mar. 1819), 92-94.

"Modern Poetry," Champion, Nov. 12, 1815, pp. 366-67.

"Popular Poetry; Periodical Criticism; &c.," Champion, Oct.
13, 1816, pp. 326-27.

"The Arithmetic of Poetry," Champion, Feb. 16, 1817, p. 54.

"On the Influence of the Poets of the Present Day," Champion,
July 19, 1818, pp. 458-59.

"The Renovator. No. XII. On Pastoral Poetry," Champion,
Sept. 23-30, 1820, pp. 622-23, 639.

"On the Melancholy of Poets," Déjeuné, Dec. 1, 1820, pp. 281-
85.

"On the Sonnet," Déjeuné, Dec. 11, 1820, pp. 347-52.

"[Concerning Poetry]," Devonshire Adventurer, 1 (Nov. 1814),
76-81.

"[On Descriptive Poetry]," Devonshire Adventurer, 1 (Mar.
1815), 213-221.

"On the Sonnet," Dublin Magazine, 2 (Sept. 1820), 216-18.

"Fogarty Furioso. Erratics, No. 3 [On Modern Poets]," Dublin Magazine, 2 (Dec. 1820), 463-73.

"Of the Living Poets of Great Britain," Edinburgh Annual Register, 1^2 (1808), 417-43.

"On the Darwinian School of Poetry," Edinburgh Magazine and

Literary Miscellany (Scots Magazine), ns,v2 (Apr. 1818),
313-16.

"Cursory Remarks on Poets and Poetry," Edinburgh Magazine and
Literary Miscellany (Scots Magazine), ns,v4 (Mar. 1819),
228-31.

"On Poetry, and Our Relish for the Beauties of Nature," Edinburgh Magazine, or Literary Miscellany, ns,v11 (Apr.
1798), 266-70.

"The Gleaner, No. 2," Edinburgh Magazine, or Literary Miscellany, ns,v12 (Dec. 1798), 403-08.

"Observations on Pastoral Poetry," Edinburgh Magazine, or
Literary Miscellany, ns,v13 (Mar. 1799), 187-91.

"The Gleaner, No. IX [On Descriptive Poetry]," Edinburgh Magazine, or Literary Miscellany, ns,v14 (July 1799), 3-5.

"On English Verse," Edinburgh Magazine, or Literary Miscellany, ns,v15 (Feb. 1800), 94-96.

"On Lyric Poetry," Edinburgh Magazine, or Literary Miscellany, ns,v16 (Sept. 1800), 211-14.

"Observations on the Advantages Arising to Poetical Science
from the Study of the Various Manners of Composition in
Different Nations," Edinburgh Magazine, or Literary Miscellany, ns,v18 (Aug. 1801), 83-87.

"Observations on Sonnet Writing," Edinburgh Magazine, or Literary Miscellany, ns,v22 (Aug. 1803), 121-24.

"On the Difference between Epic Poetry and History," Edin-
burg Magazine, or Literary Miscellany, ns,v22 (Sept.
1803), 197-200.

"Loose Thoughts on Rural Poetry," European Magazine, 42 (Aug.
1802), 107-08.

"Leisure Amusement. No. XI. On the Sonnet," European Magazine, 45 (Jan. 1804), 24-26.

"Young Poets," Examiner, Dec. 1, 1816, pp. 761-62.

"The Projector. No. XXXII. [The 'New' Poetry]," Gentleman's
Magazine, 74[1] (June 1804), 500-03.

"Remarks Philosophical and Literary," Gentleman's Magazine,
89[2] (Oct.-Dec.-Suppl. 1819), 315-17, 397-400, 498-502,
582-87.

"On Poetical Genius, and Its Subjection to Rule," Gentleman's

Monthly Miscellany, no2 (Feb. 1803), 64-66.

"Poetry," Historical, Biographical, Literary, and Scientific Magazine, 1 (Apr. 1799), 60-69.

"The Pastoral Poets of Italy, and a Word on Mr. Leigh Hunt's Translation of the Amyntas," Honeycomb, no5 (1820), 37-40.

"On the Emotions Excited by Poetry," Inquirer, or Literary Miscellany, 1 (Jan. 1815), 329-31.

"On the English and Italian Sonnet," Kaleidoscope, 2 (Sept. 14, 1819), 40.

"Remarks on Modern English Poetry," Leeds Literary Observer, 1 (Feb. 1819), 48-50.

"Original Correspondence. Cockneyism Vindicated," Literary Chronicle, 1 (May 22, 1819), 10-11.

"Cockneyism Vindicated," Literary Chronicle, 1 (June 19, 1819), 74-76.

"Original Correspondence. Cockneyism Vindicated," Literary Chronicle, 1 (June 24, 1819), 153-54.

"On the Present State of English Poetry," Literary Gazette, July 19, 1817, pp. 40-41.

"Petrarca; a Selection of Sonnets from Various Authors, with an Introductory Dissertation on the Origin and Structure of the Sonnet," Literary Journal, a Review..., 3 (Mar. 16, 1804), 268-70.

"[On the Sonnet]," Literary Leisure, 2 (Dec. 4, 1800), 329-32.

"On English Sonnetteers," Literary Panorama, 7 (Dec. 1809), 502-07.

"On the Connexion between the Character and Poetry of Nations," (Baldwin's) London Magazine, 2 (Oct. 1820), 421-26.

"The Mohock Magazine," (Baldwin's) London Magazine, 2 (Dec. 1820), 666-85.

"Essay on Poetry with Observations on the Living Poets," (Gold's) London Magazine, 2 (Oct.-Dec. 1820), 370-74, 470-74, 557-62.

"On Poetry," The Mentor, 1 (June 21, 1817), 57-58.

"On Poetry," <u>Microscope</u>, 1 (June 1799), 61-62.

"On Poetry," <u>Miniature Magazine</u>, ns,v1 (Aug. 1820), 110-12.

"Lyceum of Ancient Literature. No. XX. Lyric Poetry," <u>Monthly Magazine</u>, 27 (Feb. 1, 1809), 19-22.

"On Pastoral Poetry," <u>Monthly Magazine</u>, 27 (May 1, 1809), 332-35.

"[On Heroic Poetry]," <u>Monthly Magazine</u>, 30 (Dec. 1810), 407-10.

"Remarks on the English Poets [including Descriptive Poetry]," <u>Monthly Mirror</u>, 12 (Oct. 1801), 230-32.

"Melancholy Hours. No. V. [The Sonnet]," <u>Monthly Mirror</u>, 16 (July 1803), 20-24.

"Modern Poetry," <u>Monthly Mirror</u>, 18 (Oct. 1804), 224.

"[Pastoral Poetry]," <u>Monthly Mirror</u>, 18 (Nov. 1804), 332-33.

"On the Utility of Composing Poetry," <u>Monthly Mirror</u>, ns,v4 (July 1808), 9.

"Ausonianus. On the Structure of the Sonnet," <u>Monthly Mirror</u>, ns,v7 (Jan.-Feb. 1810), 14-16, 96-98.

"Additional Remarks on the Structure of the Sonnet," <u>Monthly Mirror</u>, ns,v7 (Mar. 1810), 199-200.

"Illustrations of Rhythmus: Selections for the Illustration of a Course of Instructions in the Rhythmus and Utterance of the English Language," <u>Monthly Review</u>, ns,v64 (Mar. 1813), 293-305.

"Strictures on the False Taste of Modern Poetry," <u>Monthly Visitor</u>, 3 (Jan. 1798), 40-45.

"Strictures on the Language of Modern Poetry," <u>Monthly Visitor</u>, 3 (Feb. 1798), 153-59.

"Strictures on the Versification and Sentiment of Modern Poetry," <u>Monthly Visitor</u>, 4 (July 1798), 259-66.

"Remarks on Pastoral Poetry, and Its Appropriate Diction, Imagery, and Incidents," <u>New Annual Register</u>, 19 (1798), 100-07.

"[Comparison of Rhyme and Blank Verse]," <u>New Annual Register</u>, 36 (1817), [254-57].

"State and Character of the Present Age--Burns--Cowper--
Wordsworth--Scott--Moore--Byron--Campbell," New Annual
Register, 38 (1817), [43-50].

"Poetry," New Annual Register, 39 (1818), [170-71].

"On the Present State of Poetical Talent," New Bon Ton Magazine, 4 (Aug. 1820), 233-37.

"On the Study of English Poetry," New Monthly Magazine, 3
(Mar. 1815), 118-20.

"On Amatory Poetry," New Monthly Magazine, 10 (Dec. 1818),
391-94.

"A Cockney Pastoral, cum notis variorum," New Monthly Magazine, 11 (Mar. 1819), 133.

"What Is Poetry?" New Monthly Magazine, 13 (Mar. 1820), 276-
79.

"Defence of Young Writers of Poetry against the Denunciation
of the Edinburgh," New Review, 3 (Apr. 1814), 345-50.

"On Epic Poetry. To the Editor," New Universal Magazine,
3 (July 1815), 9-13.

"[On Elegiac Poetry]," Non-descript, 1 (Oct. 19, 1805), 85-92.

"On the Difference betwixt Epic Poetry and History," North
British Magazine and Review, 2 (Oct. 1804), 223-26.

"An Attempt to Estimate the Poetical Talent of the Present
Age, Including a Sketch of the History of Poetry, and
Characters of Southey, Crabbe, Scott, Moore, Lord Byron,
Campbell, Lamb, Coleridge, and Wordsworth," Pamphleteer,
5 (1815), 413-71.

"On the Lake School of Poetry," Portfolio, 1 (Nov. 26, 1818),
21-23.

"On the Connection and the Mutual Assistance of the Arts and
Sciences, and the Relation of Poetry to Them All," The Reflector, 1 (1811), 346-60.

"Why Are There So Few Excellent Poets?" The Reflector, 2
(1811), 249-74.

"Cursory Remarks on Poetry," Repository of Arts, 3 (Mar.
1810), 142-45.

"Classical Hours. No. IV. Cursory Remarks on the Origin,
the Effects, and the Ends of Poetry," Repository of Arts,

3 (Apr. 1810), 213-15.

"Miscellaneous Fragments and Anecdotes [including Blank Verse]," Repository of Arts, 9 (Feb. 1813), 84.

"Various Prospects of Mankind, Nature, and Providence [including a defense of Modern Poets]," Retrospective Review, v2,pt.1 (1820), 185-206.

"[Letter to the Editor concerning Verse]," Sale-Room, May 24, 1817, pp. 161-68.

"To a Young Poet," Salopean Magazine, 3 (Feb. 1817), 83-85.

"The Bards of the Lake," Satirist, 5 (Dec. 1809), 548-56.

"Literary Modesty," Satirist, 8 (Apr. 1811), 322-25.

"Applications for the Laureatship," Satirist, 13 (Sept. 1813), 241-56.

"On the Phraseology of the Highland Poetry," Scots Magazine, 64 (June 1802), 459-60.

"On Poetry," Scots Magazine, 66 (June 1804), 409-12.

"Observations on the Introduction of Moonlight Scenery into Poetry...," Scots Magazine, 70 (July 1808), 501-05.

"On Poetical Taste and Criticism," Scots Magazine, 71 (Jan. 1809), 17-20.

"Subjects for Poetry, or the Land of Promise," Scourge, 2 (Aug. 1811), 160-66.

"Modern Poets," Scourge, 6 (Nov. 1, 1813), 375-81.

"Modern Poets. No. 1," Scourge, 9 (June 1815), 441-47.

"Living Poets," Scourge, 10 (Nov. 1815), 341-52.

"Epic Poetry," Spirit of the Public Journals, 5 (1801), 333-35.

"On the Sonnet," Talisman, or Literary Observer, 1 (July 15, 1820), 30-31.

"On Poetic Originality and Imitation," Talisman, or Literary Observer, 1 (Aug. 12, 1820), 57-58.

"Of the Modern Antique in Poetry," Talisman, or Literary Observer, 1 (Aug. 12, 1820), 58-59.

"British Maecenases, and Fashionable Writers," Town Talk, 4
  (May 1813), 257-62.

"On the English Poets," Ulster Register, 2 (May 23, 1817),
  289-91.

"The Inspector. No. IV. Does the Study of the Fine Arts, and
  Especially of Poetry, Tend to the Improvement of Practical
  Morality," Universal Magazine, ns,v1 (Apr. 1804), 378-81.

"[Concerning the Pastoral]," Universal Magazine, ns,v10 (Oct.
  1808), 317-18.

"Essay on the Origin of Poetry, and the Different Species of
  Composition," Walker's Hibernian Magazine, 14 (Aug. 1799),
  73-76.

"Remarks on Pastoral Poetry, and Its Appropriate Diction,
  Image, and Incidents," Walker's Hibernian Magazine, 14
  (Oct. 1799), 263-69.

"Modern Poetry," Walker's Hibernian Magazine, 19 (Nov. 1804),
  666.

"[On Modern Literature]," The Wanderer, 1 (Aug. 22, 1818),
  128-30.

"Remarks on Descriptive Poetry," Weekly Entertainer, 33 (Jan.
  7, 1799), 15-16.

"On the Lake School of Poetry," Yellow Dwarf, May 7, 1818,
  pp. 79-80.

B-4
Articles on Fiction

"No. XIV. Novel Writing," The Artist, 1 (June 13, 1807),
  9-19.

"On Novels and Romances, with a Cursory Review of the Literary Ladies of Great Britain," La Belle Assemblée, 1 (Nov.
  1806), 531-33.

"Novels and Romances," La Belle Assemblée, ns,v2 (1810), 358-
  64.

"Some Remarks on the Use of the Preternatural in Works of
  Fiction," Blackwood's Edinburgh Magazine, 3 (Sept. 1818),
  648-50.

"Thoughts on Novel Writing," Blackwood's Edinburgh Magazine,

4 (Jan. 1819), 394-96.

"On the Absurdity of Modern Romances," Bradford Instructive and Entertaining Miscellany, 1 (May 1818), 7.

"On the Evil Consequences Resulting from the Descriptions of Horror in Various Modern Writings," British Lady's Magazine, s3,v2 (Feb. 1819), 63-65.

"On the Subserviency of Modern Romance to the Interest of Virtue," The Casket, 1 (Apr. 1819), 105-07.

"The Reader. No. XII," Champion, Aug. 11, 1816, p. 254.

"On Novel Reading," Christian's Pocket Magazine, 3 (Dec. 1820), 298-303.

"On the History of Fictitious Writing in Scotland...," Edinburgh Magazine and Literary Miscellany (Scots Magazine), ns,v3 (Aug. 1818), 107-17.

"[On the Ill Effects of Novel-Reading]," European Magazine, 48 (Nov. 1805), 326-27.

"An Essay on the Origin and Progress of Novel-Writing," European Magazine, 59 (Apr.-May 1811), 270-73, 365-71.

"[Concerning the Novel]," The Galvinist, no.11 (1804), 5-9.

"[The Repute of the Novel as a Literary Form]," Gentleman's Magazine, 70^1 (Jan. 1800), 6.

"The Projector. No. XLIX," Gentleman's Magazine, 75^2 (Oct. 1805), 911-14.

"The Projector. No. LXXXVIII. [The Influence of Novels]," Gentleman's Magazine, 78^2 (Oct. 1808), 882-85.

"[Concerning Novels]," Gleaner, or Cirencester Weekly Magazine, 1 (Dec. 23, 1816), 623-24.

"On Works of Fiction," Green Man, 3 (June 19, 1819), 37-39.

"Works of Fiction," Historical, Biographical, Literary...Magazine, 1 (Feb. 1799), 55-59.

"Novels," Historical, Biographical, Literary...Magazine, 1 (Apr. 1799), 69-87.

"Dramatic Fiction," Historical, Biographical, Literary...Magazine, 1 (Apr. 1799), 87-92.

"[On Fiction]," Historical, Biographical, Literary...Magazine,

1 (Aug. 1799), 292-306.

"On Novel Reading," _Imperial Magazine_, 1 (Nov. 1819), 977-78.

"Whether Such a Love of Novels as Excludes All Other Reading, or No Reading At All, Is Most to Be Condemned," _Juvenile Library_, 1 (1800), 121-23, 124-26, 127-28, 129.

"On Novel-Reading, and the Mischief Which Arises from Its Indiscriminate Practice," _Lady's Magazine_, 43 (May 1812), 222-24.

"[Brief discussions of Contemporary Novelists]," _Lady's Monthly Museum_, ns,v4 (Jan.-June 1808), 21 ff., 121 ff., 196 ff., 233 ff., 306 ff.

"_Manners._ The Influence of the Drama and Novel," _Literary Journal, a Review..._, 2 (Oct. 17, 1803), 427-31.

"Essay on Novel Writing," _Literary Leisure_, 2 (Nov. 20, 1800), 304-15.

"On Novel Reading; with Observations on the Living Novelists," (Gold's) _London Magazine_, 1 (May-June 1820), 493-98, 604-07.

"[Remarks on Novels and Romances]," _The Miniature_, Apr. 30, 1804, pp. 13-22.

"[On Novels]," _The Miniature_, June 25, 1804, pp. 110-20.

"An Essay on the Works of Fiction," _Miniature Magazine_, 2 (Apr. 1819), 217-21.

"The Blessed Advantages of Novel Reading," _Modern Spectator_, 1 (Mar. 20, 1819), 155.

"[Letter to the Editor on Modern Novels]," _Monthly Magazine_, 29 (Mar. 1810), 110-12.

"A Romance Writer," _Monthly Mirror_, 5 (Mar. 1798), 143-44.

"Novels and Romances [the Effects of Reading Them]," _Monthly Mirror_, 14 (Aug. 1802), 81-82.

"Endymion in Exile. Letter XIII," _Monthly Mirror_, ns,v5 (Feb. 1809), 70-72.

"Novels and Novel Reading," _Monthly Pantheon_, 1 (Apr. 1809), 289-91.

"Novels," _Monthly Visitor_, 4 (May 1798), 67-68.

"On the Reading of Novels," <u>Monthly Visitor</u>, 4 (July 1798),
   242-46.

"Novels," <u>Monthly Visitor</u>, 6 (Feb. 1799), 132-33.

"Novels," <u>Monthly Visitor</u>, 8 (Sept. 1799), 38-39.

"Novels," <u>Monthly Visitor</u>, 9 (Feb. 1800), 172.

"Character of the Fictitious Narratives of the Present Age,"
   <u>New Annual Register</u>, 38 (1817), [51-58].

"On British Novels and Romances...," <u>New Monthly Magazine</u>,
   13 (Feb. 1820), 205-09.

"[On Novels and Romances]," <u>The Non-descript</u>, 1 (Dec. 21,
   1805), 161-90.

"On the Influence of Novel-Reading on Public Morals," <u>Northern Star</u>, 2 (Feb. 1818), 116-17.

"To the Editor [On the Tendency of Novels]," <u>Northumberland
   and Newcastle Monthly Magazine</u>, 1 (Aug. 1818), 247-48.

"[On the Eminence of Fiction Writing]," <u>Oxford Miscellany and
   Review</u>, no2 (1820), 21-30.

"[A Discussion of Novels, Tales, &c.]," <u>Salt-Bearer</u>, no 28
   (1820), 324-32.

"On Novels and Romances," <u>Scots Magazine</u>, 64 (June-July 1802),
   470-74, 545-48.

"Humourous Stricture on Modern Fashionable Novels," <u>Scots
   Magazine</u>, 69 (Oct. 1807), 738-41.

"On Modern Tales or Novels," <u>Scots Magazine</u>, 72 (June 1810),
   418-19.

"Terrorist Novel Writing," <u>Spirit of the Public Journals</u>, 1
   (1797), 223-25.

"Novel-Writing," <u>Spirit of the Public Journals</u>, 2 (1798),
   255-58.

"Modern Novels," <u>Spirit of the Public Journals</u>, 4 (1800),
   257-62.

"On the Cause of the Popularity of Novels," <u>Universal Magazine</u>, 103 (Dec. 1798), 413-15.

"Critical Rules of Novel Writing," <u>Universal Magazine</u>, 110
   (June 1802), 431-32.

"Hints toward a Just Taste in Novel Reading," _Universal Magazine_, ns,v5 (Apr. 1806), 316-21.

"Novels and Novel Writing," _Walker's Hibernian Magazine_, Feb. 1809, pp. 89-92.

B-5
Articles on Drama and Theatre

"Observations on the Drama, with a View to Its More Beneficial Effects on the Morals and Manners of Society," _Annual Review_, 2 (1803), 635-38.

"No. V. On Dramatic Style," _The Artist_, 1 (Apr. 11, 1807), no.5.

"On the Imitation of the Stage in Painting," _The Artist_, 1 (July 11, 1807), 1-12.

"Theatrical Representations," _The Artist_, 2 (1809), 308-28.

"No. XX. Reform of Our Stage," _The Artist_, 2 (1809), 392-422.

"Thoughts on the Dramatic Unities," _Athenaeum_, 3 (May 1808), 409-12.

"Remarks on the British Drama," _Augustan Review_, 1 (Aug.-Sept. 1815), 409-20, 522-23.

"The Drama," _Augustan Review_, 1 (Oct. 1815), 637-38.

"An Essay on the Present State of British Comedy," _Le Beau Monde_, 2 (Oct. 1807), 130-33.

"On Tragedy among the Ancients," _Le Beau Monde_, 4 (Sept. 1808), 110-13.

"National Varieties of the Drama," _Le Beau Monde_, 4 (Dec. 1808), 275-79.

"Remarks on Greek Drama," _Blackwood's Edinburgh Magazine_, 1 (Apr.-May, July, Sept. 1817), 39-42, 147-52, 352-58, 593-96.

"Notices on the Acted Drama in London," _Blackwood's Edinburgh Magazine_, 2 (Jan.-Mar. 1818), 426-31, 567-70, 664-69.

"On Jeremy Collier and the Opponents of the Drama," _Blackwood's Edinburgh Magazine_, 7 (July 1820), 387-92.

"On the Drama," _British Magazine_, 1 (Mar. 1800), 215-16.

"On German Drama," British Magazine, 2 (July 1800), 26-27.

"An Essay on Dramatic Simplicity of Sentiment and Diction," British Magazine, 2 (Sept. 1800), 193-95.

"On the Early Dramatic Poets," Champion, Jan. 7, 1816, 6-7.

"On the Early English Dramatists. II," Champion, Mar. 3, 1816, p. 70.

"Essay on the Buffoonery of Pantomine and Farce," Champion, Jan. 3, 1819, pp. 10-11.

"A Defence of Edmund Kean, Esq.," Champion, Apr. 4, 1819, pp. 219-20.

"The Examiner and the Theatres," Champion, Dec. 12, 1819, pp. 794-95.

"Sadler's Wells...with an Essay on the Probable Influence of the Minor Theatres on Dramatic Taste and Morality," Champion, Sept. 23, 1820, pp. 621-22.

"The Drama. No. 1," The Charles James Fox, no2 (Oct. 10, 1814), 11.

"Thoughts on the Stage," Christian Mirror, no6 (1805), 51-63.

"On the Stage," Christian Mirror, no.11 (1805), 102-14.

"A Defence of the Theatre," Christian's Pocket Magazine, 1 (Oct. 1819), 351-56.

"A Brief View of the Stage, Drama, &c.," The Corrector, 1 (1816), 9-20.

"On the Present State of Drama in England," Correspondent, Consisting of Letters, &c., 1 (1817), 206-31.

"Why Do You Not Go to the Play?" Cottager's Magazine, 5 (Sept. 1816), 313-15.

"An Impartial Review of the Stage from the Days of Garrick and Rich to the Present Period: Of the Causes of Its Degenerated and Declining State, and Shewing the Necessity of a Reform in the System...," Critical Review, s5, v5 (Jan. 1817), 73-79.

"An Impartial Review of the Stage from the Days of Garrick and Rich to the Present Period...," Critical Review, s5,v5 (Feb. 1817), 190-93.

"The Structure of Our Theatres," <u>The</u> <u>Director</u>, <u>a</u> <u>Weekly</u> <u>Lit-</u>
<u>erary</u> <u>Journal</u>, 1 (Feb. 28, 1807), 171-76.

"[Report of Mr. Crowe's Lectures on Dramatic Poetry]," <u>The</u>
<u>Director</u>, <u>a</u> <u>Weekly</u> <u>Literary</u> <u>Journal</u>, 1 (Mar. 21-Apr. 11,
1807), 282-87, 311-14, 375-78; 2 (Apr. 18-May 9, 1807),
25-26, 54-55, 93-96, 123-24.

"On the Drama," <u>The</u> <u>Director</u>, <u>a</u> <u>Weekly</u> <u>Literary</u> <u>Journal</u>, 1
(Apr. 11, 1807), 349-64; 2 (May 2, June 6, 1807), 65-82,
225-43.

"[Miscellaneous Articles on Drama]," <u>Dramatic</u> <u>Censor</u>, 1
(1811), 1 ff.

"Modern Dramatists," <u>Dramatic</u> <u>Miscellany</u>, no1 (Apr. 8, 1820),
3-4.

"Essay on the Moral Nature and Properties of Comedy," <u>Drury</u>
<u>Lane</u> <u>Theatrical</u> <u>Gazette</u>, Nov. 5, 1816.

"Observations on Pantomime," <u>Drury</u> <u>Lane</u> <u>Theatrical</u> <u>Gazette</u>,
Dec. 26, 1816.

"Historical Remarks Respecting the Introduction of Operas in
England," <u>Drury</u> <u>Lane</u> <u>Theatrical</u> <u>Gazette</u>, Mar. 8, 1817.

"The Drama," <u>Edinburgh</u> <u>Annual</u> <u>Register</u>, 1^2 (1808), 253-325.

"The Drama," <u>Edinburgh</u> <u>Annual</u> <u>Register</u>, 2^2 (1809), 350-401.

"The Drama," <u>Edinburgh</u> <u>Annual</u> <u>Register</u>, 3^2 (1810), 382-406.

"Thoughts on Tragedy," <u>Edinburgh</u> <u>Magazine</u>, <u>or</u> <u>Literary</u> <u>Mis-</u>
<u>cellany</u>, 12 (Dec. 1798), 427-32.

"Thoughts on Comedy," <u>Edinburgh</u> <u>Magazine</u>, <u>or</u> <u>Literary</u> <u>Miscel-</u>
<u>lany</u>, 13 (Jan. 1799), 20-25.

"Reflections on the Peculiarities of Style and Manner in the
Late German Writers, Whose Works Have Appeared in English;
and on the Tendency of Their Productions," <u>Edinburgh</u> <u>Maga-</u>
<u>zine</u>, <u>or</u> <u>Literary</u> <u>Miscellany</u>, ns,v20 (Nov.-Dec. 1802),
353-61, 406-08; ns,v21 (Jan.-Feb. 1803), 9-18, 89-96.

"Letters on Dramatic Poetry, and More Particularly on the
Comparison of the Ancient and Modern Drama," <u>Edinburgh</u>
<u>Magazine</u> <u>and</u> <u>Literary</u> <u>Miscellany</u> (<u>Scots</u> <u>Magazine</u>), ns,v7
(Dec. 1820), 516-21.

"On the Influence and Character of the Stage," <u>Edinburgh</u> <u>Re-</u>
<u>flector</u>, 1 (July 29, 1818), 36-39.

"Essay on Private Theatrical Exhibitions," Entertaining Magazine, no1 (1803), 25-28.

"Humorous Essay on Theatrical Hearers," Entertaining Magazine, no5 (1803), 211-14.

"Ancient and Modern Drama Contrasted," Flowers of Literature, 6 (1807), 170-78.

"Theology of the Theatres," Flowers of Literature, 7 (1808-09), 146-48.

"On Theatrical Amusements," General Chronicle, 4 (Jan. 1, 1812), 5-7.

"[Letter to Mr. Urban on Profaneness on the Stage]," Gentleman's Magazine, 70[1] (Jan. 1800), 6-7.

"[Letter to Mr. Urban on the Quality of Theatrical Productions]," Gentleman's Magazine, 71[1] (Jan. 1801), 38-39.

"Observations on the Effect of Theatrical Representations with Respect to Religion and Morals," Gentleman's Magazine, 76[2] (July 1806), 639-42.

"The Laputian. The Depravity of Theatrical Taste," Historical, Biographical, Literary, and Scientific Magazine, 1 (1799), 255-59.

"A Sketch of the Rise and Progress of Dramatic Literature in This Country," Inquirer, or Literary Miscellany, May, 1814, pp. 82-93.

"The Drama," Inquirer, or Literary Miscellany, Sept. 1814, pp. 228-35.

"The Drama," Inquirer, or Literary Miscellany, Jan. 1815, pp. 352-58.

"On the Ancient Drama," Inspector, a Weekly Dramatic Paper, Jan. 9, 1819, p. 1.

"On Pantomime," Inspector, a Weekly Dramatic Paper, Jan. 16, 1819, p. 1.

"On the Decay of Dramatic Genius in This Country," Inspector, a Weekly Dramatic Paper, Jan. 23, 1819, pp. 1-2.

"The Drama," Knight Errant, 1 (June 5, 1817), 9-10.

"Literary Hours. No. 1-4. On the Rise and Progress of Dramatic Poetry and Representation in England," Lady's Monthly Museum, s3,v1 (Jan.-June 1815), 18-20, 77-81, 130-33, 318-22.

"The Virtuous Tendency of Ancient Tragedy," Leeds Literary
Observer, 1 (July 1819), 241-43.

"English Drama," Literary Journal, and General Miscellany,
1 (Sept. 19, 1818), 409-10.

"On the Dramatic Art, as Influenced by the Present Practice
of the Theatre," (Baldwin's) London Magazine, 1 (Feb.
1820), 146-49.

"General Reporter. The Drama. No. IV," (Baldwin's) London
Magazine, 1 (Apr. 1820), 432-40.

"The Drama. No. XI," (Baldwin's) London Magazine, 2 (Dec.
1820), 685-90.

"Comparison between Ancient and Modern Dramatists," (Gold's)
London Magazine, 1 (Jan. 1820), 86-89.

"On the Origin of the Greek Tragedy," (Gold's) London Magazine, 1 (Apr.-May 1820), 379-81, 483-87.

"Sentiments of Primitive Christians, Respecting Theatrical
Amusements," Missionary Magazine, 4 (Aug. 19, 1799).

"[An Essay on the Stage]," Modern Spectator, 1 (Mar. 20,
1819), 145-47.

"Excuse for an Appalling Name...Opinion of the Unities...,"
Monitor, 1 (Apr. 1817), 20-25.

"On Mr. Kean. Probable Effect of His Style on the Perform-
ance and the Poetry of the Stage," Monitor, 1 (Apr. 1817),
44-48.

"On the Theatres. The Drama Not Kept at a Proper Elevation,"
Monitor, 1 (June 1817), 124-31.

"On the Prevalence of Musical Quackery in the Theatres of
London," Monthly Mirror, 10 (July 1800), 39-40.

"Summary of Arguments against the Amusements of the Stage,"
Monthly Mirror, 10 (July 1800), 42-43.

"[Concerning the Immorality of the Stage]," Monthly Mirror,
10 (Aug. 1800), 103-06.

"Thoughts in Vindication of the Stage. To Which Are Subjoined a Few Proofs of Its Moral Purpose," Monthly Mirror,
10 (Aug.-Oct. 1800), 100-03, 178-80, 240-43.

"On the Absurdities of the Modern Stage," Monthly Mirror,
10 (Sept. 1800), 180-82.

"Essay on the Drama, as Contra-distinguished from Tragedy and Comedy," Monthly Mirror, 10 (Dec. 1810), 387-89.

"Defence of the Stage," Monthly Mirror, 10 (Dec. 1800), 389-90; 11 (Jan. 1801), 43-45.

"A Few Words in Behalf of the Professor of the Stage," Monthly Mirror, 11 (Feb. 1801), 122-24.

"Sketches of the History of the Scottish Stage," Monthly Mirror, 11 (Apr.-June 1801), 276-80, 415-17; 12 (July 1801), 62-65.

"The British Stage. Cursory Remarks on Tragedy," Monthly Mirror, 13 (Apr. 1802), 262-65.

"The British Stage. Strictures on the Effect of Tragedy," Monthly Mirror, 13 (May 1802), 337-39.

"The British Stage. The Dramatic Essayist. No. 1. On Tragedy," Monthly Mirror, 15 (June 1803), 405-09.

"Observations on the English Theatre," Monthly Mirror, 16 (Nov. 1803), 336-40.

"The Modern Drama," Monthly Mirror, 17 (Mar. 1804), 189-90.

"The Dramatic Essayist. On Comedy," Monthly Mirror, 17 (June 1804), 409-12; 18 (Aug.-Oct. 1804), 118-20, 183-85, 264-69.

"The British Stage. On the Advantages of Theatrical Entertainments," Monthly Mirror, 18 (Aug. 1804), 114-17.

"The British Stage. Aristotle Refuted," Monthly Mirror, ns,v1 (Feb. 1807), 127-29.

"Play-Writing," Monthly Mirror, ns,v5 (Jan. 1809), 40-42.

"Drama," Monthly Visitor, 4 (May 1798), 67.

"Drama," Monthly Visitor, 6 (Feb. 1799), 133-34.

"Drama," Monthly Visitor, 8 (Sept. 1799), 40.

"Drama," Monthly Visitor, 9 (Feb. 1800), 172-73.

"State and Character of the Dramatic Works--the Drama and the Fine Arts--Painting and Sculpture--of the Present Age," New Annual Register, 38 (1817), 59-65.

"Progress of the Drama [in the Age of Elizabeth]," New Annual Register, 39 (1818), [147-52].

"Cursory Thoughts on Public Taste in Regard to the Drama,"
New Monthly Magazine, 1 (June 1814), 436-37.

"On the Present State of the English Stage," _New Monthly
Magazine_, 13 (Mar.-Apr. 1820), 265-71, 435-43.

"Remarks on Virginius, and on Modern Tragedy," _New Monthly
Magazine_, 14 (July 1820), 68-72.

"The Effect of Tragedy," _Newcastle Magazine_, 1 (Sept. 1820),
58-61.

"State of the Drama," _Newcastle Magazine_, 1 (Sept. 1820),
87-91.

"State of the Drama," _Newcastle Magazine_, 1 (Nov. 1820), 216-
19.

"State of the Drama," _Newcastle Magazine_, 1(Jan. 1821), 323-24.

"On Drama," _Newry Magazine_, 1 (Mar./Apr., Sept./Oct. 1815),
78-80, 349-55.

"On Tragedy," _North British Magazine and Review_, 2 (Sept.
1804), 143-46.

"Dramatic Emancipation; or Strictures on the State of the
Theatres, and on the Consequent Degeneration of the Drama,"
Pamphleteer, 2 (1813), 369-95.

"French Drama; or, a Discussion on...Which Are the Best Means
of Making Theatres Vie with Each Other in Promoting the
Perfection of Taste and the Improvement of Morals," _Pam-
phleteer_, 11 (1818), 49-77.

"Biographica Dramatica; or a Companion to the Play-House,
Containing Historical and Critical Memoirs, and Original
Anecdotes...," _Quarterly Review_, 7 (June 1812), 282-92.

"Greek and English Tragedy," _Reflector, a Quarterly Magazine_,
1 (Oct. 1810), 62-72.

"Retrospect of the Theatre," _Reflector, a Quarterly Magazine_,
1 (Oct. 1810), 232-36.

"Retrospect of the Theatre," _Reflector, a Quarterly Magazine_,
1 (Jan. 1811), 467-73.

"On the Custom of Hissing at the Theatres, with Some Account
of a Club of Damned Authors," _Reflector, a Quarterly Maga-
zine_, 2 (1811), 122-27.

"Retrospect of the Theatre," _Reflector, a Quarterly Magazine_,
2 (1811), 428-32.

"Defence of the Stage," <u>Satirist</u>, 2 (June 1808), 352-58.

"To the Editor. On the Comparative Merit of Philosophers and Poets," <u>Scots Magazine</u>, 60 (June 1798), 390-91.

"Thoughts on Comedy," <u>Scots Magazine</u>, 61 (Apr. 1799), 238-43.

"Degeneracy of the Stage," <u>Scots Magazine</u>, 61 (June 1799), 378-80.

"Remarks on Some Modern Tragedies," <u>Scots Magazine</u>, 61 (Dec. 1799), 807-09.

"On the Dramatic Taste of the Eighteenth Century," <u>Scots Magazine</u>, 61 (Appendix 1799), 862-72.

"On the State of the Drama in This Country," <u>Scourge</u>, 7 (Mar. 1814), 185-94.

"State of the English Stage," <u>Shadgett's Weekly Review</u>, 2 (Feb. 13, 1819), 55-56.

"Some Account of a Dreadful Disease, Called the Kotzebue-Mania, Which Was Epidemical in London at the Close of the Eighteenth Century," <u>Spirit of the Public Journals</u>, 6 (1802), 93-96.

"An Essay on the Art of Acting," <u>Theatrical Inquisitor</u>, ns,vl (Sept. 1820), 220-24.

"The Modern Drama," <u>Union Magazine</u>, 1 (May 1801), 329.

"Thoughts on Tragedy," <u>Universal Magazine</u>, 103 (Nov. 1798), 319-24.

"Remarks on the Various Effects of Comedy and Farce," <u>Weekly Entertainer</u>, 32 (July 23, 1798), 77.

"The Italian Opera," <u>Weekly Magazine</u>, 1 (Jan. 6-20, 1816), 17-18, 42-43, 66-67.

"Nature and State of British Drama," <u>Weekly Register and Political Magazine</u>, 1 (Dec. 9, 1809), 11-20.

"On Drama," <u>Weekly Register and Political Magazine</u>, 2 (Jan. 6, 1810), 206-10.

"On Drama," <u>Weekly Register and Political Magazine</u>, 2 (Nov. 3, 1810), 625-26.

"On the Present State of the Drama," <u>Weekly Review of Henry Redhead Yorke</u>, Aug. 17, 1811, pp. 165-71.

"Remarks on the [bad example of the] Stage," <u>Youth's Instructor and Guardian</u>, 2 (Apr. 1818), 139-41.

"Theatrical Amusements," <u>Youth's Instructor and Guardian</u>, 3 (Feb.-Mar. 1819), 46-51, 87-89.

REVIEWS OF OPERAS

Anonymous.
The Libertine, an Opera.
Theatrical Inquisitor, 11 (July 1817), 59-60.

The Promissory Note, an Operetta.
Theatrical Inquisitor, ns,v1 (July 1820), 48-49.

The Quadrille; or, a Quarrel, for What? An Operetta.
Theatrical Inquisitor, 15 (Aug. 1819), 94.

Reformed in Time. A Comic Opera. 1798.
British Critic, 12 (Oct. 1798), 425.
Critical Review, ns,v27 (Oct. 1799), 238.
Monthly Review, ns,v28 (Jan. 1799), 105-06.

Thirty Thousand. A Comic Opera.
Literary Journal, a Review..., 5 (Feb. 1805), 206.

Virginia, an Opera. 1800.
Antijacobin Review, 7 (Dec. 1800), 414-15.

Arnold, Samuel James.
The Shipwreck. A Comic Opera. 1797.
British Critic, 11 (May 1798), 561.

Bishop, H. R.
The Slave. An Opera.
British Stage and Literary Cabinet, 1 (Mar. 1817), 59-60.

Brandon, Isaac.
Kais, or Love in the Deserts. An Opera.
Monthly Mirror, ns,v3 (Mar. 1808), 248-49.
Poetical Register, 7 (1808), 581-82.
Satirist, 2 (Apr. 1808), 193-99.

Cherry, A.
The Travellers; or, Music's Fascination. An Operatic
Drama. 1805.
Antijacobin Review, 23 (Feb. 1806), 208.
Critical Review, s3,v8 (May 1806), 99.

Monthly Magazine, Suppl. v21 (July 25, 1806), 609.
Poetical Register, 6 (1806), 529-30.

Spanish Dollars; or, the Priest of the Parish. An Operatic
Sketch. 1806.
Annual Review, 5 (1806), 538.
British Critic, 29 (Feb. 1807), 201.
New Annual Register, 27 (1806), [371].

Peter the Great; or, Wooden Walls. An Opera.
Monthly Magazine, Suppl. v23 (July 20, 1807), 644.
Oxford Review, 2 (July 1807), 92.
Poetical Register, 6 (1807), 565-66.

Cobb, James.
Ramah Droog. A Comic Opera. 1800.
Antijacobin Review, 7 (Sept. 1800), 61.
British Critic, 17 (Apr. 1801), 433.
Critical Review, ns,v30 (Oct. 1800), 229.
Monthly Mirror, 9 (June 1800), 353.
Monthly Review, ns,v33 (Sept. 1800), 107-08.
New London Review, 3 (Mar. 1800), 282.

A House To Be Sold. A Musical Piece. 1802.
Annual Review, 1 (1802), 717-20.
British Critic, 21 (Apr. 1803), 434.
Critical Review, ns,v38 (May 1803), 115.
Poetical Register, 2 (1802), 455.

Cumberland, Richard.
The Jew of Mogadore. A Comic Opera. 1808.
British Critic, 34 (Oct. 1809), 407-08.
Monthly Magazine, Suppl. v25 (July 30, 1808), 597.
Poetical Register, 7 (1808), 582.

Dibdin, Thomas.
Il Bondocani, or the Caliph Robber. A Comic Opera. 1801.
British Critic, 20 (Sept. 1802), 321.
Critical Review, ns,v37 (Feb. 1803), 236-37.
Poetical Register, 1 (1801), 463.

Family Quarrels. A Comic Opera. 1804.
British Critic, 26 (Nov. 1805), 569.
Poetical Register, 5 (1805), 507.

Thirty Thousand; or, Who's the Richest? A Comic Opera.
Annual Review, 5 (1806), 538.
New Annual Register, 27 (1806), [371].
Poetical Register, 4 (1804), 508-09.

The Cabinet. A Comic Opera. 1805.
Annual Review, 4 (1805), 643.
British Critic, 26 (Sept. 1805), 320.

Critical Review, s3,v5 (July 1805), 333.
Monthly Mirror, 21 (May 1806), 333.
Monthly Review, ns,v47 (May 1805), 100.
Poetical Register, 5 (1805), 506.

The English Fleet in 1342. An Historical Comic Opera. 1805.
Critical Review, s3,v5 (May 1805), 104-05.
Monthly Review, ns,v47 (May 1805), 100.
Poetical Register, 5 (1805), 507.

Two Faces under a Hood. A Comic Opera.
Monthly Review, ns,v57 (Sept. 1808), 100.
Poetical Register, 7 (1808), 582-83.

Zuma; or the Tree of Heath. An Opera.
Monthly Review, ns,v85 (Mar. 1818), 322.

Dimond, William.
Youth, Love, and Folly. A Comic Opera. 1805.
Annual Review, 4 (1805), 643.
British Critic, 27 (Jan. 1806), 80.
Poetical Register, 5 (1805), 507.

The Young Hussar; or Love and Mercy. An Operatic Piece.
Annual Review, 6 (1807), 599.
Monthly Magazine, Suppl. v23 (July 30, 1807), 644.
Poetical Register, 6 (1807), 566-67.

The Peasant Boy. An Opera.
Poetical Register, 8 (1811), 641.

Fitzsimmons, Edward.
Anziko and Coanza. An Opera. 1819.
British Stage and Literary Cabinet, 4 (Nov. 1819), 53.

Franklin, Andrew.
The Egyptian Festival. An Opera. 1800.
British Critic, 16 (Oct. 1800), 437.
Monthly Mirror, 9 (May 1800), 290-91.
Monthly Review, ns,v33 (Nov. 1800), 317-18.
New London Review, 3 (Apr. 1800), 378.

Hamilton, Colonel Ralph.
David Rizzio. A Serious Opera.
Theatrical Inquisitor, ns,v1 (July 1820), 49-53.

Hoare, Prince.
The Three and the Deuce. A Comic Opera.
Annual Review, 5 (1806), 538.
New Annual Register, 27 (1806), [371-72].

Holman, Joseph George.
What a Blunder! A Comic Opera. 1800.

Critical Review, ns,v31 (Feb. 1801), 233-34.
Monthly Magazine, Suppl. v11 (July 20, 1801), 607.
Monthly Review, ns,v34 (Apr. 1801), 441.

Hook, Theodore Edward.
  The Soldier's Return; or, What Can Beauty Do? A Comic Opera.
  British Critic, 26 (Sept. 1805), 320.
  Literary Journal, a Review..., 5 (June 1805), 643.

  Safe and Sound. An Opera.
  Poetical Register, 7 (1809), 617-18.

Houlton, Robert.
  Wilmore Castle. A Comic Opera. 1800.
    British Critic, 17 (Mar. 1801), 314-15.
    British Critic, 17 (Apr. 1801), 433.
    Critical Review, ns,v32 (July 1801), 351.
    Monthly Magazine, Suppl. v11 (July 20, 1801), 607.
    Monthly Mirror, 11 (Apr. 1801), 260.
    Monthly Review, ns,v35 (July 1801), 323-25.

Hull, Thomas.
  Elisha; or, the Woman of Shunem. A Sacred Oratorio. 1801.
    Critical Review, ns,v34 (Jan. 1802), 116.

Irwin, Eyles.
  The Bedouins, or the Arabs of the Desert. A Comic Opera.
  1802.
    Annual Review, 1 (1802), 692.
    British Critic, 20 (Oct. 1802), 433.
    Poetical Register, 2 (1802), 454.

Kenney, James.
  Matrimony. A Petit Opera. 1804.
    Critical Review, s3,v4 (Jan. 1805), 107.
    Poetical Register, 4 (1804), 510-11.

  False Alarms; or, My Cousin. A Comic Opera. 1806.
    British Critic, 32 (July 1808), 74.
    Critical Review, s3,v10 (Feb. 1807), 205-08.
    Flowers of Literature, 5 (1806), 502-03.
    Oxford Review, 1 (Mar. 1807), 314.
    Poetical Register, 6 (1807), 565.

Lambe, George.
  Whistle for It. A Comic Opera. 1807.
    British Critic, 32 (July 1808), 74-75.
    Poetical Register, 6 (1807), 566.

Lee, Henry.
  Caleb Quotem and His Wife! Paint, Poetry, and Putty. An
  Opera.
    Critical Review, s3,v20 (Aug. 1810), 445.

632

Monthly Mirror, ns,v8 (Sept. 1810), 210.
Monthly Review, ns,v64 (Mar. 1811), 318.
Poetical Register, 8 (1810), 595.

Moore, Thomas.
M. P. or the Blue Stocking. A Comic Opera.
Poetical Register, 8 (1811), 640.
Town Talk, Sept. 21, 1811, pp. 161-63.

Noble, Thomas.
The Persian Hunters; or, the Rose of Gurgistan. An Opera.
1817.
Theatrical Inquisitor, 11 (Oct. 1817), 285-86.

Plowden, Mrs. Frances.
Virginia. An Opera. 1800.
British Critic, 18 (Sept. 1801), 314.
Critical Review, ns,v32 (July 1801), 350-51.
Monthly Mirror, 11 (Apr. 1801), 259-60.
Monthly Review, ns,v36 (Sept. 1801), 97.

Plumptre, James.
The Lakers. A Comic Opera.
British Critic, 17 (June 1801), 650-51.
European Magazine, 34 (Nov. 1798), 328.
Gentleman's Magazine, 70[1] (Apr. 1800), 337-38.

Shepherd, Henry.
The Orphans; or, Generous Lovers. An Opera. 1800.
British Critic, 16 (Oct. 1800), 439.
Critical Review, ns,v31 (Jan. 1801), 114.
Monthly Magazine, Suppl. v10 (Jan. 20, 1801), 611.
Monthly Magazine, Suppl. v11 (July 20, 1801), 607.
Monthly Mirror, 10 (Dec. 1800), 386.
Monthly Review, ns,v32 (July 1800), 325-26.

WITHDRAWAL